FOR THE HOMELAND

The Stackpole Military History Series

FOR THE HOMELAND

The 31st Waffen-SS Volunteer
Grenadier Division in World War II

Rudolf Pencz

Translated by C. F. Colton, MA

STACKPOLE
BOOKS

English edition © 2002 by Helion & Company Limited

Published in paperback in 2010 by
STACKPOLE BOOKS
5067 Ritter Road
Mechanicsburg, PA 17055
www.stackpolebooks.com

Cover design by Tracy Patterson

Printed in the United States of America

10 9 8 7 6 5 4 3 2 1

Library of Congress Cataloging-in-Publication Data

Pencz, Rudolf, 1967–
  [Vor Haus und Hof und Kind und Weib. English]
  For the homeland : the 31st Waffen-SS Volunteer Grenadier Division in World War II / Rudolf Pencz.
      p. cm. — (Stackpole military history series)
  Originally published: Solihull, West Midlands : Helion, 2001.
  Includes bibliographical references and index.
  ISBN 978-0-8117-3582-7
  1. Waffen-SS. SS-Freiwilligen-Grenadier-Division, 31. 2. World War, 1939–1945—Regimental histories—Germany. 3. World War, 1939–1945—Personal narratives, German. I. Title.
  D757.85.P4613 2010
  940.54'1343''089310439—dc22
                                                    2009027631

Dedication

To our dead, whose honour was loyalty, and to our living comrades, whose honour still is loyalty.

'To Those Born After' (Walter Meyer):

'They went their way, true to their oath,
In the grey, the simple soldier's kit,
They were exactly like you and I,
They secretly asked: why, and for what?
They knew fear and did not succumb,
They fought and suffered, true to their duty.
They fell and died – flying like sand,
The burning waves, the icy border,
The gloomy forest, the steppe so wide,
These cover them – for all eternity.
You who are born after, revile them not,
They knew one word, they called it duty.
And should you some time seek it, you will find no more
The grey – but the great, the glorious army.'

Contents

List of Maps and Map Key

All maps in this edition drawn by Katy Rodda

Key:

⊢——⊥——⌐	Frontline
→	German forward/retrograde movement
⇒	Soviet forward/retrograde movement
⇥⇒	Soviet attack repulsed
↩	Forward movement turning into a retreat
⚑	Army
⚑	Corps
⚐	Infantry/Grenadier Division HQ
⚑	Grenadier Regiment HQ

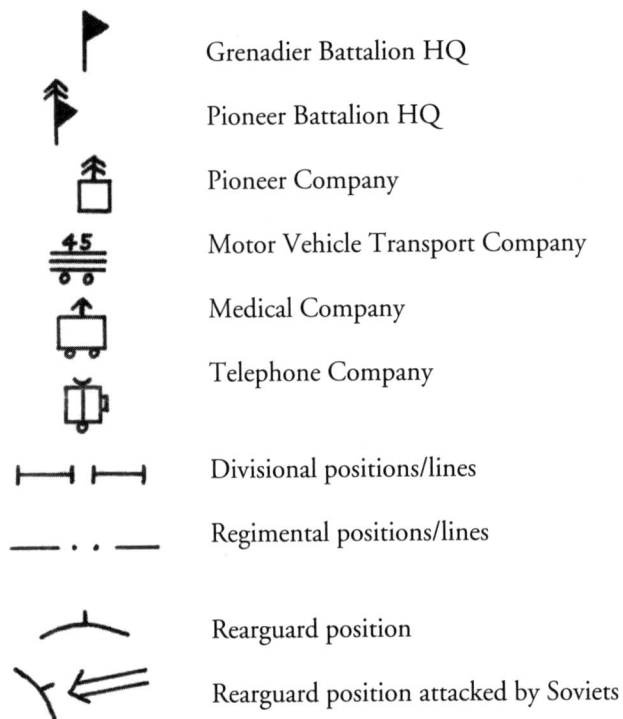

Grenadier Battalion HQ

Pioneer Battalion HQ

Pioneer Company

Motor Vehicle Transport Company

Medical Company

Telephone Company

Divisional positions/lines

Regimental positions/lines

Rearguard position

Rearguard position attacked by Soviets

Foreword

This is the history of the 31st SS Volunteer Grenadier Division, in which Rudolf Pencz has attempted to record a permanent memorial to the soldiers of this division.

In the near future, it may no longer be possible to present a clear picture of the insurmountable difficulties faced during this small division's formation and its eventual commitment into battle. It is a case study of the conditions that Germany and its armed forces faced in 1944 as they conducted a hopeless struggle against nearly the entire world.

The men of this division, mostly ethnic Germans from the Batschka, some of them mere boys, were not volunteers in so far as the name is concerned, but were willing to perform their duty to their Fatherland, which stood in mortal danger.

Thus the story of the 31st SS Volunteer Grenadier-Division will now enter into history and only to the judgement of history must we submit, even if the struggle was in vain. So, just as Leonidas led his outnumbered Spartans at Thermopylae against the mighty Persian army, history will also remember General Lombard and his 31st SS Volunteer Grenadier Division. I wish the book much success!

Offenburg, 11 August 1996

Otto Kumm
SS-Brigadeführer und Generalmajor der Waffen-SS
(Last commander of the 1st SS *Panzer* Division 'Leibstandarte Adolf Hitler' and recipient of the Knight's Cross of the Iron Cross with Oak Leaves and Swords.)

Introduction

The 31st SS Volunteer Grenadier Division can certainly be said to be the least well known SS Division, not only because it was one of the latest divisions to be formed, and the last to be formed on Hungarian soil under the terms of the 1944 agreement between the German and Hungarian governments. In other respects too it rarely came into the foreground at the time and has remained largely unknown. While, for example, the 22nd SS Cav. Div. perished after a glorious struggle in *Festung* Budapest, the 'Stalingrad on the Danube', or the 18th SS-Pz.Gren.Div. – formed from the remnants of the tried and tested 1st SS-Inf.Brig. – came to prominence and distinguished itself in northern Hungary, Slovakia, and at least partly also in Galicia, the 31st SS-Div. quietly did its duty on secondary fronts.

It had not borne a name laden with historical associations and had not even inherited a coherent framework from one of the old Waffen-SS units. Its recruits were elderly or very young, primarily ethnic German farmers, craftsmen and workers from Hungary, mostly from the Batschka, the country that their ethnic group, called Swabians or Danube Swabians, had settled and brought under cultivation in the 18th century. It is true that many of them had already received military training in the Hungarian or Yugoslavian armies, but for the majority it was only within the Division that they learned to be soldiers. To achieve this, however, not only were the most basic requirements in terms of personnel and material lacking, but there was also a lack of the most elementary of these requirements – time. To all intents and purposes the Division had to be formed at the front or directly behind the front, on the march and in retreat. It was only granted a few, short pauses to draw breath, but these too were not enough for the process of formation and a programme of training really to be completed, or for it to be able to reach its full complement in personnel and material.

Understandably, in the last eight depressing months of the war, it was only for the most part with tenacious and dogged effort that the ethnic Germans, already robbed of their homeland, were able to summon up at least a degree of enthusiasm, but always willingness. Despite all hardships, wherever and whenever the brave Danube Swabian lads acquired the most necessary elements of military ability and knowledge they were a reliable support, and when they rallied round the few officers, NCOs and other ranks of the core personnel, or even one of these, who were time-served soldiers with experience of the front, they achieved remarkable results. This was shown often enough even when they were still on the Danube, but to its fullest extent in Silesia, where the Division was at the end of the war. The end of the war, but not the end of hardship, only now broke over the men, who were now defenceless. A tragedy of unimaginable proportions now began in the witches' cauldron of Czechoslovakia, so that being taken prisoner by the Soviets really meant salvation for many, because in Soviet captivity they could, at first, at least be sure that they would stay alive. At first, that is, because for most of them their captivity lasted a long, long time, even up to eight years, and many more were snatched away by death in the inhuman conditions of the Soviet camps.

We, the younger generation, their sons and grandsons, stand deeply moved before their sacrifice and suffering and bow our heads in reverence before the human greatness with which they bore and overcame their heavy fate, without a lot of fine words, but always in quiet love for their people and their homeland. We stand deeply moved before their heavy lot, and in truth there is nothing we would wish for less than the hellish times in which they had to prove themselves. But even so if there were to come a time of trial we would emulate them to the best of our power, not wishing to fall short of their example and to become worthy of them, for their honour and our honour is, and remains, loyalty. May it be granted to us not to be any worse than our fathers.

CHAPTER 1

Beginnings of the 31st SS Volunteer Grenadier Division

The beginnings of the 31st SS Volunteer Grenadier Division stretch back far further than the September 1944 order that was issued announcing its formation. They actually begin in July of that year, when, in accordance with an agreement signed by the German and Hungarian governments during the previous April, the first large contingents of Germans living in Hungary were inducted into German military service in the Batschka region.

The idea of forming a new SS division composed of these men was raised for the first time on 24 September 1944, when the SS Operations Office ordered (a) the disbanding of the 23rd Waffen-Gebirgs-Division der SS 'Kama' (Croatian Nr 2) in Batschka, (b) the retention of its German cadre in the area, and (c) their mobilisation for the formation of a new SS infantry division. This day can thus be viewed as that on which the seeds of the 31st SS Volunteer Grenadier Division were sown.

Ten days later, on 4 October, a second order was issued authorising the formation of the 31st SS Volunteer Grenadier Division within the 'Kama' Division's former garrisons in Batschka. Charged with the formation was *SS-Oberführer* Gustav Lombard, who was also selected to be the eventual division commander. In these respects the appointment mirrored the order of 24 September.

It was decided that the division was to be formed as a type 1944 infantry division. During its formative period, it was operationally subordinated to the SS-FHA (SS Operations Office) and tactically subordinated to the Commander of Waffen-SS Forces in Hungary (*Befehlshaber der Waffen-SS Ungarn*), *SS-Obergruppenführer* Karl von PfeiferWildenbruch. On 1 November, he was replaced by *SS-Obergruppenführer* Georg Keppler.

The German officers, NCOs, and men of the former 'Kama' Division stood at Lombard's disposal as cadre for the new division. They were to be supplemented with those ethnic Germans from the Batschka region who had been inducted into service during mid-summer. In addition, 1,000 rifles from the 'Kama' Division were provided.

The Division's Title and Insignia

The 31st SS Volunteer Grenadier Division was unique among the divisions of the Waffen-SS in that Hitler never afforded it an honorific title, such as those borne by the 'Wiking' or 'Das Reich' divisions, etc. Similarly, it did not possess any subtitle in its name indicating its ethnic origin, as was the case with the Estonian 20th Waffen-Grenadier Division der SS (Estonian Nr 1) and a number of other formations.

1

Post-war literature has often ascribed the name 'Böhmen und Mähren' ('Bohemia and Moravia') to the division, but this is incorrect. There were indeed two Waffen-SS brigades named 'Böhmen' and 'Mähren' formed near the war's end; it was intended that they were to be amalgamated into a division and, presumably, would bear the honorific title 'Böhmen und Mähren' but this formation, which never possessed any numerical designation, was no relation to the 31st SS Volunteer Grenadier Division. In fact, it was not until the first gathering of Waffen-SS veterans after the war that someone researching individual SS field formations mistakenly afforded the 'title-less' division the name of the 'numberless' division. This error continues to be made in modern literature, in which some authors - most of whom did not serve in the Waffen-SS - simply cannot believe that there was actually a SS division that was not awarded an honorific title.

It should be noted, however, that the division did bear several unofficial designations. Owing to its close ties with the Batschka region, the Germans occasionally referred to it as the 'Division Batschka' (Hungarian: 'Bácska-hadoszály'). Some German military sources seem to prefer 'Division Lombard', after its popular commander. A nickname was also coined: the 'Kukuruz Division', a reference to the many farmers from the Batschka's rich cornfields who served within its ranks.

A number of humorous suggestions were received when the question was raised of what the young division's insignia should be. Soldiers from the medical battalion proposed a corncob; a signal company even produced a sketch of a paprika husk. Although both of these submissions were certainly appropriate, the insignia that was chosen was a stag's head, a twelve-pointer to be exact. Research reveals that it was used as early as November 1944 and employed until the end of the war. The design was chosen by none other than the division commander himself, who was known as a passionate hunter (Lombard in fact used a similar seal on his personal letterhead until his death in 1992). The symbol was also fitting because, as legend had it, the largest twelve-pointer ever hunted down was a product of the Batschka's Karapancsa Forest, where a statue was erected in honour of this majestic beast. And not only that: on the shores of the Hungarian Danube, not far from where the division was to see action, stands the Gemencer Forest, a renowned hunting reserve in its own right. Here, too, lie the sprawling estates once owned by Archduke Friedrich, where Kaiser Wilhelm II once hunted. When the division was transferred to Silesia, this 'deer' did not abandon it, for as we will see, its bloodiest battle was fought in the city of Hirschberg.

Before we begin the division's history, we must first study both the fundamental elements from which it was built, i.e. the 23rd Waffen-Gebirgs-Division der SS 'Kama' (Croatian Nr 2), and the recruitment of ethnic Germans from Hungary into German military service, and the general military situation in 1944.

CHAPTER 2

23rd Waffen-Gebirgs-Division der SS 'Kama' (Croatian Nr 2)

By the middle of 1944, the German military situation was critical on all fronts. To counter the increasingly serious Balkan insurgency, the Germans had already raised one SS division composed of Bosnian Muslim volunteers (the 'Handschar' Division), and they now sought to form a second. On 17 June 1944, the SS-FHA announced Hitler's order to form this division, and its award of the name 'Kama'. The *kama*, a small edged weapon used by Balkan shepherds, was particularly appropriate for the new division, as Bosnian SS men preferred to carry large combats knives into battle in place of standard bayonets. Sporting 20cm long blades, these daggers were the weapon of choice in hand-to-hand fighting.

The formation of the division was to begin on 10 June 1944. Responsible for its completion was *SS-Brigadeführer* Sauberzweig, who was also ordered to form a corps headquarters element to lead both the 'Handschar' and 'Kama' divisions. The new division was to be raised in north-eastern Bosnia, i.e. in the territory bordered by the Sava, Bosna, Spreèa, and Drina Rivers, but the SS-FHA issued a second order a week later decreeing that both the 'Kama' and the corps headquarters were to be formed in Hungary's Batschka region, where the 18th SS *Panzergrenadier* Division 'Horst Wessel' was stationed. Its garrisons lay along the Franzen Canal; its two mountain infantry regiments north and south of the line Zombor-Verbász, the artillery in the Kúla area, and the reconnaissance battalion in Szenttamás. The SS-FAH specified that the formation of the division and the training of its soldiers was to be completed by year's end.

The 'Kama' Division was to be built around a cadre provided by its sister 'Handschar', consisting of 54 officers, 187 NCOs, and 1,137 enlisted men. Specifically, 'Handschar' was to hand over an entire cavalry squadron, one artillery battery from each of its artillery battalions, as well as signalmen, doctors, veterinarians, and other specialists. In addition, German officers and NCOs were transferred to the 'Kama' from various SS replacement units. Most of the enlisted men were Bosnian Muslims who had recently volunteered for service. On 10 September, a division report listed its strength as 126 officers, 374 NCOs, and 3,293 enlisted men. This was of course far lower than its prescribed strength, which stood at around 19,000.

The 'Kama' Division's commander was *SS-Standartenführer* Hellmuth Raithel (1906-1990), who had led a regiment in the 'Handschar' Division. The division's order-of-battle was as follows:

Division Commander: *Staf.* Raithel
Ia (Operations Officer): *Hstuf.* Reuter
IIb (Logistics Officer): *Ostuf.* Fritscher

Waffen-Gebirgsjäger-Regiment der SS 55 (Croatian Nr 3):
Ostubaf. Holzinger
    I/55: *Stubaf.* Praefke
    II/55: *Ostubaf.* Domes
    III/55: *Ostubaf.* Schneider
Waffen-Gebirgsjäger-Regiment der SS 56 (Croatian Nr 4):
Stubaf. Syr
    I/56: *Stubaf.* Albrecht
    II/56: *Hstuf.* Schumacher
    III/56: ?
Waffen-Gebirgs-Artillerie-Regiment der SS 23: *Stubaf.* Dehnen,
later *Stubaf.* Zeysing
    I/AR 23: *Hstuf.* Mailhammer
    II/AR 23: *Stubaf.* Dehnen
    III/AR 23: ?
    IV/AR 23: ?
SS Aufklärungs Abteilung 23: *Stubaf.* Syr (later *Hstuf.* Zeitz)
SS-Panzerjäger Abteilung 23: *Stubaf.* Landwehr
SS-Gebirgs-Pionier-Bataillon 23: *Stubaf.* Otto
    HQ with HQ Company
    3 *Gebirgs-Pionier* Companies
SS-Gebirgs-Nachrichten-Abteilung 23: *Stubaf.* Reimann
SS-Feldersatz Btn 23: ?
Divisions-Nachschub-Truppe 23: *Hstuf.* Morisse
Workshop Company ?
Administrative Section ?
SS Medical *Abteilung* 23: *SS-Stubaf.* Dr Matz
Veterinary Company: ?

The design adapted as the division's insignia was a sun from which sixteen rays burst, the ancient symbol of the Macedonian king Alexander the Great. The insignia was also to be reproduced on a special collar badge, but it is unlikely that it ever reached the troops in the field. The division's official headgear was the Muslim fez, in field-grey colour for wear with the service uniform, and in red for wear with the dress uniform. Khaki-coloured tropical uniforms with short trousers were often worn during the blazing Batschka summer. Most of those who had served previously in the 'Handschar' division continued to wear the special collar badge afforded to that division. These peculiarities also found their way into the 31st Division when it was formed in October.

The 'Kama' Division conducted intense training under the leadership of young, energetic officers. Known to their superiors as 'Mujos', the Muslims were proficient soldiers and for the most part simple, good-natured men. Their religious customs were strongly observed; pork was not served in the rations and Fridays were devoted to worship. Under the direction of *imams*, or Muslim clerics, the men conducted the *Ju'mah*, the Islamic prayer rite. Some of the German instructors found it difficult to relate to the Muslims and some of their unfamiliar customs. Hans Villier, a platoon leader in the division's signals battalion, was a veteran of the

SS Cavalry Brigade and the bloody winter battle at Rzhev in Russia. Shortly after his arrival in the 'Kama,' he observed the following incidents:

> On one occasion, my Muslims entered a village and shot all the pigs! The Hungarian farmers were furious. I too was angry and raised hell with them about it. Ali, my interpreter, told me that this was normal, and that pigs were dirty animals anyway.
>
> There was a Muslim festival that was celebrated by firing shots into the air. I wanted to obtain blank ammunition and prohibited the use of live rounds for this purpose. The Muslims ignored my order and used live rounds anyway, whereupon I too became 'live' and nearly came to blows with them.
>
> Late that night, I awoke to find Ali seated near me with his dagger drawn. At first I was startled and thought that he was going to kill me, until he told me that he was there for my protection, as many of the comrades were quite angry at me.

Heinz Hummel, a platoon leader in the pioneer battalion, offered a similar account:

> There were a number of shady characters among the Muslims. Several of the ethnic Germans believed that these individuals were actually partisans who had volunteered for the division simply to receive military training, and would desert back to the partisan ranks after the return (to Bosnia). An example:
>
> (1/Pi. Btl. 23) was quartered in a Stiechowice school. I bunked with two NCOs, Werner Rauner from Thuringia, and a Muslim. We knew that this Muslim had contacts with local Czechs. One day he took leave of us; he had received a furlough. His last words were that he would not be returning. We took this as a joke. In fact, never saw him again.

There were also many ethnic Germans from Croatia in the division. Their primary function was to serve as interpreters between the Germans from the Reich and the Bosnians, but they also performed a secondary role, that of 'stiffeners' within the ranks. In September 1944, a handful of ethnic Germans from Hungary volunteered or were conscripted into the division. These young men were certainly intimidated by the fierce-looking Bosnians, who projected a proficient, almost exotic soldierly bearing while parading under the strains of their marching songs. 'Moj schetzi dilo, moj schetzi dalo', and 'Marschirala, marschirala Hitlerowa garda' ('March, March, Hitler's guards').

The flow of Bosnian volunteers into the division also continued, these being inducted at SS recruiting depots in Zombor and Bosnjaci. There they were mustered and received rudimentary military drill before being seconded to the division. After the dissolution of the 'Kama' Division in October, many of the German personnel manning the Zombor depot were transferred to the 13th Company of the 31st Division's 80th Regiment. Men from the Bosnjaci depot were also slated for the division, but it is believed that they were sent elsewhere. This assumption is based on the field post numbers that were assigned to the depot.

During the summer of 1944, the Eastern Front lay so far away from the Hungarian border that those in the Batschka region might have assumed that it was peacetime. But the events of 23 August dramatically changed this. It was on this day that King Carol of Romania suddenly pulled his country out of the war, paving the way for a quick Soviet occupation and the virtual destruction of an entire German army group. Individual German units mounted fierce resistance, but they were unable to secure the vital mountain passes of the southern Carpathians. By the middle of September, Soviet spearheads reached the Hungarian border.

The front line now stretched from the Temeschwar area through Arad to Grosswardein, where it swung eastwards along the Romanian-Hungarian border. It passed through Klausenburg and Neumarkt, snaked around the Szekler-Zipfel, and continued along the crests of the Carapthians towards the Polish frontier. The Temeschwar-Arad-Grosswardin region lay in particular danger, as its sole defence consisted of Hungarian border guards. These were eventually reinforced by replacement units and General Vitéz József Heszlényi's 3rd Hungarian Army.

Bitter fighting erupted in the passes of the eastern Carpathians. On 5 September, Soviet forces reached the Iron Gate and Turnu-Severin. They took Kronstadt two days later. Seeking to encircle Axis forces in the Szekler-Zipfel, the Soviets planned the main thrust of their next offensive at an overextended sector of the German line in Transylvania. Before they could begin their assault, however, the Germans mounted a surprise counter-attack that achieved some initial success before grinding to a halt near Torda. On 7 September, the Germans evacuated the Szekler-Zipfel and after hard mountain fighting in the eastern Carpathians, were able to stabilise their defence line. Again and again the Soviets attempted to break into Transylvania but were met by stubborn German resistance. By 25 September, they abandoned their attempts. For the Germans, this was clearly a significant defensive victory, although the strategic initiative remained firmly in Soviet hands.

With the Soviets marching on Hungary and Serbia, the 'Kama' Division's situation became critical. So many Bosnian soldiers were deserting from the 'Handschar' Division in Bosnia that the Germans decided to reorganise both of their Croatian SS Divisions. An order dated 24 September outlined their plans:

> Under command of the staff of the IX SS Corps, all available men and material from the 'Handschar' Division and the Bosnians from existing elements of the 'Kama' will be reorganised and formed into two new divisions:
>   13th Waffen-Gebirgs-Division der SS 'Handschar' (Croatian Nr 1) (*Staf.* Hampel)
>   23rd Waffen-Gebirgs-Division der SS 'Kama' (Croatian Nr 2) (*Staf.* Raithel)
>   The formation of the 'Kama' Division in Hungary is hereby cancelled. All [Bosnian] officers, NCOs, and men are to be transferred to [Bosnia]... All other personnel [i.e. the German officers, NCOs, and men] as well as material are to remain in their present sector to form a SS infantry division.... *SS-Oberführer* Lombard ... is charged with this task.

This order practically brought the 31st SS Division to life. It. was to be formed from the German personnel and equipment from the dissolved 'Kama' elements. The unit garrisons would remain the same; the departing Bosnians would simply be replaced with the ethnic Germans from Hungary who had been inducted since mid-summer.

The Bosnians, who were to be transferred by rail to the Gradište-Zupanja-Bosnjaci area to form a new 'Kama' Division, did not leave the Batschka area overnight. In fact, the 'Kama' and new 31st SS Division actually existed side by side for a short period. Sometime in early October, the men were engaged on the Tisza River under the command of German officers in the so-called *Kampfgruppe* Syr, in a vain attempt to stem the Soviet advance. After about a week or so in the front lines, they were disengaged and sent on their way towards the Croatian frontier.

The success of the new Soviet offensive had a profound effect upon the Bosnians, who were well aware of the impending threat to their homeland. When the movement towards Croatia began, a number of them deserted their units and struck out on their own in efforts to reach their families. One group actually mutinied before reaching the Croatian border. A German serving in the 31st Division recalled:

> Some of the Bosnians attempted to desert. *Untersturmführer* Fiedler tried to stop them and stood in their way. They just shot him and threw his body in the water! *Sturmbannführer* Syr believed himself forced to let them go. They took a large number of weapons, including machine guns and a considerable amount of ammunition with them.

Upon reaching Croatia, the Bosnians were inducted into the 'Handschar' Division. Realising that their plan to re-form the 'Kama' could not be completed, the SS officially dissolved the 'Kama' Division on 31 October.

CHAPTER 3

Waffen-SS Recruiting in Hungary 1944

Himmler's lieutenants had long seen Hungary's ethnic German minority as a source of potential manpower for the Waffen-SS. After obtaining the agreement of the Hungarian government, recruiting drives were conducted in 1942 and 1943. Both campaigns yielded significant successes, even if the recruiting methods employed by the German community leaders led some to believe that not all of the inductions were 'voluntary.' A total of about 40,000 men were mustered, about half of these in the Batschka. The Waffen-SS also received many ethnic German volunteers from within the Hungarian army (*Honvéd*) who sought the higher pay and benefits offered by the SS. However, the volunteers feared that they would forfeit their Hungarian citizenship. They had believed that the Hungarians would use them as cannon fodder on the Russian Front. Moreover, many of the Batschka Germans could not speak Hungarian, as the region had only passed on to Hungarian sovereignty in 1941. A significant agreement reached during the first negotiations was that the volunteers would lose their citizenship. The second agreement altered this somewhat, in that the forfeiture would only take place after the war.

During the third drive of 1944, all of this changed dramatically. This agreement, which was reached on 14 April, saw the Hungarians withdraw their control over its German minority's military obligation and transfer it *en-masse* to its German ally. The agreement defined a 'German' as "one who through his habits and ethnic characteristics shows himself to be (German) or who readily identifies with the German nationality". To put it simply, as Hungarian Minister-President Sztójay did to the Germans, "If you want to recruit in the ethnic German regions, go ahead." The Waffen-SS, which for years had enjoyed the exclusive right to recruit Germans living outside the Reich, was now entrusted with access to this considerable source of manpower.

An important new clause in the agreement was the stipulation that those who entered into German service would retain their Hungarian citizenship. In addition, those Germans who had been mustered during the first two recruiting drives were afforded this right. During this third effort, ethnic Germans serving in the Hungarian army were handed over to the SS, although the Hungarians retained the right to recall them if desired. During the first two drives, the Germans sought men born between the years of 1908 and 1925; in light of the total mobilisation, they now wanted all males born between the years 1894 and 1927.

Although the inductions were to begin as soon as the agreement was ratified, i.e. that April, the effort did not begin in earnest until summer; thus most of the recruits were not mustered until September. The primary reason for this delay was the all-important harvest. Another problem was the internal squabbling within the German minority between the 'Browns', who professed national socialist beliefs, the Christian Conservative 'Blacks', and the so-called 'Magyars', who favoured assimilation with the Hungarian majority. The men were being legally conscripted

8

and those who did not comply were forwarded to the Hungarian authorities. A number of Germans attempted to enlist in the Hungarian army so as to avoid service in the SS, but Hungarian authorities were prohibited from accepting them. The trend of the previous two years had undergone a fundamental change, and no wonder, as much had changed since the first recruiting drive. All of this earned this latest recruiting drive the accusation of being a 'forced' effort. Without desiring to dispute this undoubtedly prescient fact, it should be pointed out that within every combatant nation there were those who, in spite of legal obligation, do not report for military service and must be made to do so.

The precise number of ethnic Germans inducted during the third recruiting drive is not known; estimates range between 80,000 and 100,000. As of 25 August 1944, 42,000 men, about half of this total, had been mustered. Most of these were used to form the SS Divisions 'Horst Wessel' and 'Maria Theresia', while the older men were sent to police units. In September, the recruiting further increased; more time had passed and after the fall of Romania, the military situation had changed so drastically that Hungary was no longer an island of tranquillity and stood in great peril. In the Batschka region, the majority of its recruits entered service in September and October. The first towns to see their men drafted were those in the northern Batschka, among them Vaskút, Gara, Csátalja, Bácsbokod, Bácsalmás, Csávoly, Hajos, and Nemesnádudvar. In Váskut, a town of about 4,000 inhabitants, 400 men were conscripted on 15 September. Two days later, 300 more draftees, mostly older men, were mustered for service. A report from Neu-verbass (Verbász) describes the inductions there:

> In the beginning of September, it was announced that all men born before 1927 were to appear for induction. Nearly all of those eligible appeared, the younger men with enthusiasm, the older ones less so. These were the last available men, but they all wanted to do their duty to their people. There were individuals who did not appear for induction; these were later forced to appear, and those who absolutely refused their 'voluntary' inductions were sent home by the Muster Committee. In mid-September, the new recruits were sent to various duty stations to which they had been assigned. It should be noted that even in mid-September there was no shortage of willingness to volunteer.

As the masses of ethnic Germans were mustered in mid-September, there was no 31st SS Division. It was because of this large influx of new recruits that the division was ordered into being on 24 September. Thus there were soldiers before there was a division.

Generally speaking, most of the ethnic Germans inducted in September were from the Batschka, and among these the majority hailed from the 'Swabian Turkey' region. They were sent to their assigned garrisons throughout northern and western Batschka, these consisting of temporary barracks and private quarters at the Zombor recruiting depot and, later, in the former garrisons of the 'Kama' Division units that were stationed in the area. For a look at how these localities turned from sleepy little towns into army garrisons housing SS units, Muslims, Luftwaffe, and Hungarian troops, Cservenka, the site of an artillery battalion, will be used here as an example:

In the large royal estates along the main thoroughfare, a small drill field was established for basic training. In the Lelbach house, a kind of barracks area was constructed, while the clothing depot was set up in one of two shops in the Fuchs home on the lower main road.

As far as the actual inductions are concerned, A. G. recalled:

I volunteered for service in the Hungarian army on 1 September to a field artillery unit in Szeged. A few days later, however, we ethnic Germans were singled out and sent home, where we were drafted into the Waffen-SS on the 15th. We were moved by train to Zombor, and from there to Bajmok, where we joined our new unit. We were issued uniforms, were tattooed, sworn in, and assigned to the individual companies. I was sent to Kompakossuthfalva, where training began.

Some of the newly conscripted Germans were immediately inducted into the 'Kama' Division, where they were posted to duty positions they retained when the 'Kama' evolved into the 31st Division in October. Two men from 'Swabian Turkey' recount their experiences, first A. Frei:

I volunteered for service in Pécs! We were inducted in Baja and quartered in the agricultural school. We were then taken by train to Ujvidek, and from there to Bajmok, where we were uniformed and equipped. Then we moved through Szabadka to Bácsalmás, where the staff of *Sturmbannführer* Albrecht's battalion (I/55, later I/79) was quartered. We were also sworn in here. The companies were garrisoned in local towns. I remained with the staff and was appointed as *Obersturmführer* Michael Ambrozy's 'Adju' [adjutant].

Josef Gratwohl:

On 14 September, I was inducted in Baja. After short stays in Zombor and Apatin, we were outfitted in Bajmok and assigned to individual units. I was transferred to the small town of Kunbaja, to an infantry company in I/56 (Albrecht). The battalion sergeant major in Bácsalmás was Otto Kohler, a former *Volksbund* functionary. I was assigned as adjutant to the company commander, with whom I quickly became quite friendly. *Obersturmführer* Alfred Berger was only about five years older than me. He was a Sudeten-German and a very fine fellow! He had seen action in Finland, where he served with the 6th SS-Gebirgs- Division 'Nord.' In Kunbaja, he wore the fez and 'Handschar' Division collar insignia, even after the Muslims were transferred.

During training, we always marched to the strains of military songs like 'Erika,' 'We Wear the Silver Eagle on our Tunics' etc. Our NCOs, who were actually only NCO candidates, were ethnic Germans from Croatia. They spoke only Croatian among themselves and were really rough follows. I still remember *Sturmmann* Woche, whose regimen always made us sweat. Well, the saying was 'Sweat Saves Blood.'

Rottenführer Bennert recalled an unexpected problem that arose during clothing issue:

There was a great shortage of uniform tunics and belts in the required sizes, particularly for men of larger girth. So from two belts, one was made. Because of the tunic shortage the men wore overcoats, which was not particularly pleasant in the August heat. The train that was bringing the new uniforms from the Dachau Clothing Depot was attacked by enemy aircraft and the car carrying the caps received a direct hit. Consequently, the men had to wear their steel helmets everywhere, even off duty.

Boots were also in short supply, in a few cases, the recruits were reduced to shuffling around in slippers, the preferred footwear of local civilians. This spectacle led some to dub the new formation 'The Sleeping Cap Division'.

Within the improvised training areas, the new recruits began their basic military training. This was administered by personnel from the 'Kama' Division, whose division was nearing the end of its existence, although the recruits themselves were not formally inducted into the 'Kama.' It was not until 24 September that the order was issued welding the recruits with their German instructors from the dissolved 'Kama' into the new 31st Division. Under the prevailing circumstances, the training itself was rushed and incomplete at best. Nevertheless, it was still physically demanding; few of the former recruits look back on these days with any kind of nostalgia. St. R.:

> [I was] inducted in Bajmok on 15 September and sent to Bácskossuthfalva, where we remained for about a month and received some training. The training officer, *Untersturmführer* Schwenk, was a harsh man who was exceptionally hard on us. Once, as I repeatedly missed a target, he grabbed me by the rump, picked me up, and slammed me to the ground.

Although the enthusiasm observed during induction quickly disappeared during the training period, the exacting drill was ultimately responsible for saving more than a few lives. The instructors, who were primarily Germans from the Reich, were unfamiliar with the rural ethnic Germans from Hungary. Unlike boys in Germany, who received pre-military training in the Hitler Youth, those ethnic Germans in Hungary did not; only those who had partaken in the seemingly insignificant activities of the 'Levente' Organization were spared by their superiors. The older men, who for the most part were reservists in either the Hungarian or former Yugoslavian armies, and in which some had served for many years, were often annoyed by the new basic training they were receiving from the Waffen-SS instructors. 'Down! Up! Down! Up!' There were even instances in which the older men simply refused to drill. As they saw it, they already possessed the basic skills of soldiering, and although their abilities in this regard may not have been to Prussian standard, in light of the military situation Germany faced in September 1944, it hardly mattered.

CHAPTER 4

Order of Battle of the 31st SS Division

In the previous two chapters, we have examined both the 'Kama' SS Division and the conscription of the German minority in Hungary in 1944. These two entities were eventually combined to form the 31st SS Division.

The formation order issued on 4 September decreed that the division was to be organised as follows[1]:

> Division Staff (19970)
>> Motorised Mapping Office (19970)
>> SS Field Police Troop 31 (part-motorised) (19970B)
>> (no band)
>
> SS Volunteer Grenadier Regiment 78
>> Regimental Staff (45334A)
>> Staff Company (45334B)
>> I Btn with 1st-4th Grenadier Companies (36293)
>> II Btn with 5th-8th Grenadier Companies (20797)
>> III Btn with 9th-12th Grenadier Companies (44219)
>> 13th Infantry Gun Company[2] (21356)
>> 14th *Panzerzerstörer* Company[3] (21356)
>
> SS Volunteer Grenadier Regiment 79
>> Regimental Staff (48865A)
>> Staff Company (48865B)
>> I Btn with 1st-4th Grenadier Companies (21714)
>> II Btn with 5th-8th Grenadier Companies (37565)
>> III Btn with 9th-12th Grenadier Companies (31579)
>> 13th Infantry Gun Company[4] (46452)
>> 14th *Panzerzerstörer* Company[5] (46452)
>
> SS Volunteer Grenadier Regiment 80
>> Regimental Staff (26445A)
>> Staff Company (26445B)
>> I Btn with 1st-4th Grenadier Companies (24378)

1 The number in brackets represents that unit's field post number. These were taken over from the 'Kama' Division.
2 2 heavy and 6 light mortars.
3 1 motorised *Panzerjäger* platoon with 3 x 7.5cm anti-tank guns, and 2 *Panzerzerstörer* platoons.
4 See note 2.
5 See note 3.

II Btn with 5th-8th Grenadier Companies (33535)
III Btn with 9th-12th Grenadier Companies (40166)
13th Infantry Gun Company[6] (40166)
14th *Panzerzerstörer* Company[7] (40166)

SS Volunteer Fusilier Btn 31 (22397)
Staff
1st Motorcycle Company
2nd-3rd Fusilier Companies (bicycles)
4th (Heavy Weapons) Company

SS Volunteer *Panzerjäger Abteilung* 31 (48064)
Staff
Mixed Staff Company
1st motorised *Panzerjäger* Company[8]
2nd *Sturmgeschütz* Company[9]
3rd Flak Company[10]

SS Volunteer Artillery Regiment 31
Regimental Staff (38377A)
Staff Battery (38377B)
I *Abteilung* with Staff Battery and 1st-3rd Batteries[11](34775)
II *Abteilung* with Staff Battery and 4th-6th Batteries[12] (23497)
III *Abteilung* with Staff Battery and 7th-9th Batteries[13] (47259)
IV *Abteilung* with Staff Battery and 10th-12th Batteries[14] (32713)

SS Volunteer Pioneer Btn 31 (43199)
Staff
1st-3rd Pioneer Companies (partly equipped with bicycles)
(no pontoon train)

SS Volunteer *Nachrichten* Btn 31 (39839)
Staff (part-motorised) with message dog section
1st Telephone Company (part-motorised)
2nd Radio Company (motorised)
Supplies section (part-motorised)[15]

6   See note 2.
7   See note 3.
8   9-12 guns.
9   10-14 guns, also known as a *Sturmgeschütz Abteilung*.
10 12 x 2cm self-propelled guns.
11 Each with 4 x 10.5cm light field howitzers.
12 As note 11.
13 As note 11.
14 Each with 4 x 15cm heavy field howitzers.
15 Also known as a Light Signals Column.

SS Volunteer *Feldersatz* Btn 31 (41036)
   Staff
   1st-5th Companies
   Supplies Company

SS Volunteer Supply *Abteilung* 31
   Staff, Commander Divisional Supply Troops (part-motorised)
(40349)
      1st and 2nd Supply Columns (motorised)[16] (40349)
      3rd and 4th Supply Columns (horse-drawn)[17] (29101)
      SS Volunteer Supply Company (30967)

SS Volunteer Motor Vehicle Workshop Company 31 (motorised)
(25211)

SS Volunteer *Verwaltungstruppen Abteilung* 31
   Staff (motorised) (48519A)
   SS Bakery Company 31 (motorised) (48519B)
   SS Butchery Company 31 (motorised) (48519C)
   SS Administrative Company 31 (motorised) (48519D)
   SS Field Post Office 31 (motorised) (27578)

SS Volunteer Medical *Abteilung* 31 (42169)
   Staff
   1st SS Volunteer Medical Company 31
   2nd SS Volunteer Medical Company 31 (motorised)
   SS Volunteer Motor Ambulance Company 31 (motorised)

SS Volunteer Veterinary Company 31 28248

This order of battle is typical of a German horse-drawn division. In fact, it assumed the form of what the Germans designated a '1944 Infantry Division'; partially motorised, but mostly horse-drawn; possessing three infantry regiments, each comprised of three battalions; and about 100 artillery pieces, making it a formidable battlefield opponent.

Because it was a mountain division, the 'Kama' division's order of battle had been somewhat different that that of the new 31st. The most significant difference was that it possessed only two infantry regiments, this owing to the fact that the battalion is the primary manoeuvre element in mountain warfare. Thus some of the units had to be altered upon their induction into the 31st. Other elements remained in large part unaffected by the transition; in fact, the conversion from the 'Kama' into the 31st SS occurred so smoothly that some hardly noticed change. In fact, a number of veterans continued (and continue to this day) to believe that they

---

16 Also known as Motor Vehicle Companies (90 t).
17 Also known as Supply Squadrons (60 t).

were still serving in a mountain division, this in part because some men continued to wear the elite 'Edelweiss' mountain insignia on their uniforms.

After the approximately 1,400-strong German cadre from the 'Kama' was reorganised, it was merged with the newly-inducted ethnic German recruits. The latter, who now formed the majority of the division's enlisted men, were primarily those mustered in September.

October saw even further conscription among the German minority, and again the number of new men inducted was considerable. The city of Cservenka even reported that the SS City Commander conducted an *ad-hoc* induction of fifteen and sixteen year old boys on 4 October in which the youths were simply grabbed off the streets. It has also been alleged that able-bodied men were seized from the masses of German refugees fleeing westward towards the Reich; confirmation of this has yet to come to light. These actions were in any case spontaneous in nature and instigated by local commanders; whether or not they were in accordance with the bilateral German-Hungarian recruiting agreement is highly questionable. Nevertheless, similar episodes continued to take place: in the division's future garrisons west of the Danube (after 7 October), for example, it is known that fifteen boys born in 1927 and 1928 were mustered in the village of Bán on 30 October.

In addition, several units of the *Deutsche Mannschaft Standarte* 'Michl Reiser,' which belonged to the German *Heimatschutz* in Banat and had provided security to the columns of German civilians fleeing the south-east, were forcibly inducted into the division *en-masse*. It cannot be ruled out that this also occurred with elements of the German *Ungarische Heimatschutz* militia. These actions posed obvious legal dilemmas to the division's commanders, as the men of the *Heimatschutz* were not subordinated to the German military but to the leadership of the German minority. There was, however, an even stricter law in effect: that of survival. With the desperate situation in the area, all available forces had to be engaged on the Tisza River to at least slow the Russian advance.[18]

Divisional Command

The Divisional Command was located in Neu-Werbass where there were still many usable school buildings. The Divisional Commander of the 'Kama' Division, *SS-Standartenführer* Hellmut Raithel, was not taken over into the 31st SS Volunteer Grenadier Division. By an order of 24 September 1944 he had to proceed with forming a new 'Kama' Division. He had also to hand over the remaining parts of the old 'Kama' to *SS-Oberführer* Gustav Lombard, who had arrived at the end of September. The order of 4 October 1944, for the formation of the 31st SS

18 Dr Sepp Janko, leader of the German minority group in Banat, reported that a German army unit (Division 'Brandenburg'?) detained a company of 100 men from the *Deutsche Mannschaft Standarte* 'Michl Reiser' in Alther and sought to engage them in the frontline along the Tisza River. The company commander, Hans Berdon, escaped through a window and was able to report the incident to the minority group leadership, which was able to win the men's release. In the case of units from the German *Heimatschutz* from the Banat absorbed into the 31st SS Division, Janko made no effort to effect their release. They remained with the division until the end of the war.

Volunteer Grenadier Division, had appointed Lombard as divisional commander. Lombard was a cavalryman of the old school and a holder of the Knight's Cross of the Iron Cross. In fact, he remained the only holder of the Knight's Cross in the 31st SS Volunteer Grenadier Division. He had proved his worth as a soldier and troop commander on the Eastern Front. He came out of the *Führer* Reserve to go to the 31st SS Volunteer Grenadier Division while it was being formed. Shortly before this Lombard had passed the Divisional Commander Course at the War Academy in Hirschberg. Now he was faced with the great challenge of bringing up the new division to the high standards required of an SS division.

First General Staff Officer (Ia) was *SS-Sturmbannführer* Otto Reuter who had held this post in the 'Kama'. Born in 1913, this educated businessman joined the SS as early as 1933. He too was a cavalryman, and wore the cavalry insignia. He served in the SS reserve troops and then, for a short time, in the 2nd SS *Panzer* Division 'Das Reich'. Later he became commandant of the Hirschberg War Academy, arriving there via the 'Handschar', in the 'Kama'. He held the Iron Cross, classes II and I, and the 'Fried Egg', the German Cross in Gold, from 1942.

Second General Staff Officer (Ib) was, at first, *SS-Obersturmführer* Ernst-Friedrich Fritscher, but at the beginning of November he was relieved by *SS-Obersturmführer* Anton Burgen.

Third General Staff Officer (Ic) was *SS-Obersturmführer* Gerhard Kraushaar, but probably only from 1 November 1944.

Divisional Armourer (Weapons and Equipment) was *SS-Hauptsturmführer* Neubert from Halle an der Saale. The TFK (Technical Commander, Motor Vehicles) was *SS-Obersturmführer* Sebastian Vital.

Divisional Adjutant (IIa) was *SS-Obersturmführer* Georg Kuhnert. The Orderly Officer (OO, IIb), until October, was *SS-Obersturmführer* Robert Meyer, and from October to December was *SS-Untersturmführer* Friedrich Kox. All three commanders had been together in the 'Kama'.

The post of Divisional Intendant (IVa) was held by an 'old war-horse', *SS-Obersturmbannführer* Karl von Turck. Like Lombard, he too was the personification of an old school cavalryman. Born in 1888, he received his lieutenant's commission in the K.u.K. uhlans on 18 August 1910, and fought during the First World War as a uhlan officer. He also came to prominence in defeating the Red 'terror' regime of Béla Kun in 1919. As 'Cap'n Török' he successfully led rebellious farmers, in the Nagycenk area, against the Reds. Then he served as an officer of hussars, eventually colonel, in the Royal Hungarian *Honvéd*, until in 1944 he transferred to the Waffen-SS.

The Divisional Medical Officer (IVb) was *SS-Sturmbannführer* Dr Karl Matz who had held this post in the 'Kama'. The post of Divisional Pharmacist (IVe), that had been additionally approved, was held by *SS-Obersturmführer* Franz Geiger from Homolitz in the Banat.

The Divisional Veterinary Officer (IVd) was *SS-Untersturmführer* Dr Besselberg.

The post of a Divisional Chaplain for the 31st SS Volunteer Grenadier Division was dropped, in accordance with the formation order. With regard to the posts of Sections III (Divisional Judiciary) and V (Technical Officer) there are few available details. Unfortunately, there is little known of the additional post of Divisional Dental Officer (IVc) that had been approved, in the formation order, nor of the 4 officers, 5 NCOs and 2 other ranks posts in Section VI (NSFO, National Socialist Leadership Officer).

SS-Untersturmführer Eduard Franz Bakos was either Officer Interpreter in the Divisional Command (Hungarian and probably also Croatian) or Commander of the Field Police. He too came from the Royal Hungarian *Honvéd*. Born in 1918, he had served as a professional soldier since 1933, until, at the end of 1940, he transferred to the Waffen-SS. At first he acted as an interpreter. Then, from April 1942, he was *Oberscharführer* in the Field Police unit of the 7th SS Volunteer *Gebirgs*-Division 'Prinz Eugen'. From November 1943 he was in the 13th Waffen-SS *Gebirgs*-Division. On 20 April 1945 he was again promoted to *Obersturmführer*. However, at the end of the war, he was posted as missing.

To the Divisional Staff belonged SS Field Police Unit 31. This unit was formed by using the Field Police unit of the dissolved Division 'Kama', itself originally put together from the SS Field Police Training and *Ersatz* Company, in the SS Motor Vehicle Training and *Ersatz Abteilung* Weimar-Buchenwald.

SS Volunteer Grenadier Regiment 78

The formation of Regiment 78 was begun in the Batschka. The area it covered lay to the south of the Franzen Canal. The units were based on the Reich German and ethnic German personnel of the Waffen-SS *Gebirgsjäger* Regiment 55 (Croatian Nr 3) of the dissolved Division 'Kama'. To the ethnic groups available were added newly recruited ethnic Germans who originated from the communities of the southern Batschka (Lower Batschka).

The Regimental Staff was located in Miletitsch/Rácmilitics, where the regimental commander was also the local commandant. In this village there were 1,000 Waffen-SS men. One battalion of the regiment (probably II/78) also had its base there. Another battalion (probably I/78) was in Hodschag. Units of the regiment were quartered, among other places, in Brestowatz, Palanka, Paratbusch, as well as in Despot-St Iwan, Bulkes, Gajdobra, Schowe, etc.

Of the planned organisation, at first only the I and II Battalions were formed. The III was not then formed. But the formation of the 13th (Infantry Gun) and the 14th (*Panzerjäger*) companies was under way. The core personnel of the IV Battalion of *Gebirgsjäger* Regiment 55 were used as a basis.

The Regimental Commander was *SS-Sturmbannführer* Robert Schneider, who replaced *SS-Obersturmbannführer* Holzinger. The Battalion Commander of the I/78 was, firstly, *SS-Sturmbannführer* Kurt Praefke who had commanded the regiment's predecessor, i.e. the I/55 of the 'Kama'. Praefke had also been transferred into the 31st SS Volunteer Grenadier Division, but had soon handed over the battalion to *SS-Sturmbannführer* Kurt Pachur, who had recently joined the Division. Before this command, Pachur had been commander of the Field *Ersatz* Battalion of the 4th SS *Panzergrenadier* Brigade 'Nederland'. When exactly he came to the 31st SS Volunteer Grenadier Division from this Dutch unit can no longer be determined with any certainty. However, he was still at Riga on 20 September 1944. Therefore his move must have been in October or November 1944. Kurt Pachur had been a member of the SS from its very beginning. In 1935 he was already an *Untersturmführer* in the 'Leibstandarte-SS Adolf Hitler'.

The II/78 was at this time commanded by *SS-Hauptsturmführer* Theodor Clausen, who probably took over this post from *SS-Sturmbannführer* Walter Domes, Battalion Commander of the II/55 Battalion of the 'Kama'. Clausen had earlier served with the 'Totenkopf' Division.

The Company commander of the 14th (*Panzerjäger*) Company was *SS-Obersturmführer* Franz Stibich, a German from Slovakia, born in 1919. Shortly before this he had been transferred, as a Slovakian First Lieutenant, into the Waffen-SS. As a former participant in the fighting of the Slovakian Rapid Division (*richla divisia*) on the Eastern Front in 1941 and 1942, he was an 'old hand' of the front line.

The formation of the regiment could only be mentioned briefly before it was transferred to Transdanubia, where the process of formation was continued in the new bases in Swabian Turkey.

SS Volunteer Grenadier Regiment 79

The formation of Regiment 79 was begun in the Batschka, in the bases of the 56th Waffen-SS *Gebirgsjäger* Regiment (Croatian Nr 4) to the north of the Franzen Canal, using the Reich German and ethnic German personnel of this regiment.

The Regimental Staff were most probably located in the barracks in Topola/Topolya. Battalion Staff were in Bácsalmás and Bajmok. Companies were quartered in Bácsalmás, Kunbaja (*SS-Untersturmführer* Berger), Bajmok, Pacsér (probably the I/79), Bácskossuthfalva (probably the 4/79) etc. After taking over the unit cadres located there, they immediately began to assign the newly recruited Batschka German recruits who had enlisted shortly before in the above-mentioned villages. At first the I and II battalions were formed, but a certain amount of progress also seems to have been made with the formation of the III Battalion. The 13th (IG) Company was apparently formed, at the latest, in Swabian Turkey. There are no indications as to when and where the 14th (*Panzerjäger*) was formed. In the Regimental Staff (probably in the Staff Company), a cycle unit was formed.

About half of the ethnic German recruits assigned to this regiment came from the communities of the northern Batschka (Upper Batschka). These included Vaskút, Gara, Csátalja, Katymár, Kunbaja, Bácsalmás, Bácsbokod, Csávoly, Nemesnáduvar, Hajós and Czászártöltés, as well as from Swabian Turkey. These origins were particularly evident in the I Battalion and the II Battalion. Almost two-thirds of their recruits came from these districts, while the II Battalion mainly recruited from ethnic Germans of the southern Batschka.

The Regimental Commander was *SS-Sturmbannführer* (later *SS-Obersturmbannführer*) Joseph Syr, often called simply Sepp Syr, a commander very popular with his ethnic German soldiers. Syr, born in 1903 in Vohenstrauss, was a horseman through and through. (Even after the war he was president and later, up to his death in Augsburg in 1977, honorary president of the riding and motoring club in Swabia, in which capacity he was awarded the Federal Cross of Merit). From 1921, in the *Reichswehr*, he served in Cavalry Regiment 17. In 1937 he was a trainer in the main riding school in Munich, at this time still as a sergeant-major in the Army. On 1 August 1941, however, the well-qualified Syr was already a *Hauptsturmführer*. On 21 June 1942 he was a *Sturmbannführer* in the Waffen-SS. From 1942 to February 1943 he was commander of the SS Cycle *Aufklärungs*

Abteilung of the SS Cavalry Division. From May 1943 to January 1944 he was commander of SS Cavalry Regiment 3. Shortly afterwards, he became commander of the Ukrainian *Aufklärungs Abteilung* 14 of the 14th Waffen-SS Grenadier Division (Galician Nr 1). On 16 June 1944 he was transferred to Division 'Handschar', and on 11 August 1944 Syr went to the Division 'Kama', where he commanded *Gebirgs Aufklärungs Abteilung* 23, as it was being formed. Afterwards he took over command of Waffen-SS *Gebirgsjäger* Regiment 56.

Commander of I/79 was *SS-Sturmbannführer* Heinrich Albrecht, a professional officer, who was a 1935 graduate of the Braunschweig *Junkerschule*. He had been transferred from the Heidelager troop training ground to Division 'Kama' as commander of the I/56. Albrecht was a soldier through and through and, like Sepp Syr, a striking figure who made a great impression on his Hungarian German soldiers.

Commander of the II/79 was *SS-Hauptsturmführer* Ewald Schuhmacher, who was transferred on 1 July 1944 from the 10th SS *Panzer* Division Frundsberg to be Battalion Commander of II/56 of the Division 'Kama'.

Commanding III/79 was probably *SS-Sturmbannführer* Egon Zill, one of the first men in the *Schutzstaffel* (SS). He had the impressively early SS membership number 535 and the Golden Party Badge. For a time he had been commandant of the Natzweiler concentration camp in Alsace, which brought him a long stretch in prison after the war. As a result of this, and of similar employment, he was lacking in basic military training. Therefore, with the best will in the world, when he came to lead the frontline troops in 1943 he was unable to completely fulfil the responsibilities of a battalion commander in the 'Handschar' Division. In the 'Kama', therefore, he was given only one company in Waffen-SS *Gebirgsjäger* Regiment 55, to allow his experience as a company commander to 'ripen' him into a battalion commander. Then, in October and November, he seems to have been given command of the III Battalion of Regiment 79, which at first only existed as a framework. (It is true that other sources mention a *SS-Hauptsturmführer* Werner Zimmermann or a *SS-Hauptsturmführer* Georg Petrus in this post).

There were six company commanders in SS Volunteer Grenadier Regiment 79. *SS-Untersturmführer* Alfred Berger, a Sudeten German, had served in the 6th SS *Gebirgs* Division 'Nord' in Karelia, before he was transferred to the 'Handschar' Division. *SS-Untersturmführer* Fritz Holderer, company commander of the 4/I, was born in Pressburg. By profession he was proprietor of a paper business in that town. He was moved over, on 21 August 1944, from the Slovakian Army into the Waffen-SS. He went first to the SS *Panzergrenadier* School, then into Division 'Kama'. At twenty-five years of age he was killed, (at the end of November in the fighting on the Danube), as was his fellow-countryman and NCO, *SS-Unterscharführer* Julius Lázár from Gross-Lomnitz/Zips. *SS-Untersturmführer* Karl-Heinz Consilius appears to have been commander of the 3/I. The Sudeten German *Obersturmführer* Michael Ambrosi served in Regimental Staff 79, and was posted missing at the end of the war. *SS-Untersturmführer* August Arnold from the southern Batschka probably commanded the Staff Company of Regiment 79. *SS-Hauptscharführer* Hans Zick came from the northern Batschka, the community of Vaskút, as did most of his soldiers. He served until Autumn 1944 in the Royal Hungarian *Honvéd* with the rank of junior officer, when he was taken into the

Waffen-SS as *Hauptscharführer* and served as a platoon leader. He was killed in December 1944 in western Hungary.

SS Volunteer Grenadier Regiment 80

According to the formation orders, a third regiment for the 31st SS Volunteer Grenadier Division was also to be formed. But since the 23rd Waffen-SS *Gebirgs* Division 'Kama' only had two regiments, no unit cadre could be provided for the SS Volunteer Grenadier Regiment 80. For this reason there was no complement, up to the end of October, only its I Battalion could be formed, for which the core personnel of *Nachschub-Trupp* 23 and the supply columns of Division 'Kama' were used. Complements were also lacking for the other units. The men came mainly from the southern Batschka.

It would appear that SS Volunteer Grenadier Regiment 80 was the regiment commanded by *SS-Sturmbannführer* Friedrich-Karl Scanzony von Lichtenfels. He was an officer ordered from the Army into the Waffen-SS. The commander of I Battalion was probably *SS-Obersturmbannführer* Walter Domes, born in German Moravia, who on 21 August 1944 was taken over from the Slovakian armed forces. There, he was a regimental commander in Leutschau and also participated in the Slovakian actions on the Eastern Front. When *SS-Sturmbannführer* Scanzony von Lichtenfels was killed on 25 November 1944, Domes took over command of Regiment 80.

SS Volunteer Artillery Regiment 31

The reorganisation of Waffen *Gebirgs* Artillery Regiment 23 of the dissolved Division 'Kama' was already begun in the Batschka. The individual batteries were around Kula, and the Regimental Staff was probably in the village itself. The Staff of I *Abteilung* had its base in Tscherwenka, II *Abteilung* probably in Kutura or Torschau, and III *Abteilung* in Brestowatz. It was virtually impossible to provide artillery training on the improvised training grounds, so that the artillery training was to take place in special courses at SS Artillery School II Beneschau. But this happened later, probably only in December were troops allowed to be sent there.

Little progress was made in Hungary in forming the Artillery Regiment. When the retreat to the western bank of the Danube had to be begun, for the most part only the cadres for the regiment were available. The new recruits had had hardly any infantry training, and they had not been equipped with any weapons at all. At the beginning of October the 10th Company and the Signals *Abteilung* of *DM-Standarte* 'Michl Reiser' of the Banater *Heimatschutz*, retreating with the columns of refugees, were taken over *en bloc* into Artillery Regiment 31. From then on they formed the Staff Battery and its signals section (*SS-Oberscharführer* Josef Ohl).

SS-Sturmbannführer Karl-Friedrich Dehnen, who formerly served on the teaching staff of SS Artillery School II, was given command of the artillery regiment of the 'Kama'. At the end of September *SS-Obersturmbannführer* Hans Zeysing, previously commander of SS Flak *Ersatz* Regiment, then SS Artillery *Ersatz* Regiment, took over from him the regimental command, which he held until about the end of the year. Dehnen was then used to command II *Abteilung*.

Commander of the I *Abteilung* was *SS-Hauptsturmführer* Josef Mailhammer, a battle-tested, 'old hand' from the Eastern front. He was also a veteran of Volkov in the artillery *Abteilung* of the *Polizei* Division, and was transferred from the Mountain Artillery School Dachstein into the flat Batschka. The command posts in the III and IV *Abteilung*s were at first not filled. The commander of III *Abteilung* is said to have been an *Obersturmführer*.

The *Abteilung* Medical Officers were ethnic Germans from the Serbian Banat or the Batschka, in II *Abteilung SS-Hauptsturmführer* Dr Franz Gettmann, in III *Abteilung* Dr Weber.

SS Volunteer Fusilier Battalion 31

The framework of forces for this battalion was formed by combining the Reich German, and the ethnic German personnel of the Waffen-SS *Gebirgs Aufklärungs Abteilung* 23 from the dissolved Division 'Kama'. The Battalion was in the area of Szenttamás/Srbobran and Alt-Betsche/óbecse, with the Battalion Staff probably in Szenttamás. One unit of the Fusilier Battalion might have been in Jarek. It was topped up with Batschka Germans, mostly born in 1926 and 1927.

The first *Abteilung* commander of *Aufklärungs Abteilung* 23 of the 'Kama' Division was *SS-Sturmbannführer* Sepp Syr, who took over Waffen *Gebirgsjäger* Regiment 56, and later SS Volunteer Grenadier Regiment 79. His successor was *SS-Hauptsturmführer* Ludwig Zeitz.

Parts of the battalion that were ready for combat took part in the fighting within the framework of SS *Kampfgruppe* Syr. They were also twice involved in fighting with communist units that caused heavy casualties. On 19 October 1944 they were the last unit of the 31st SS Volunteer Grenadier Division to cross the Danube at Bezdán and continued with the formation process in the Mohács area. The battalion's state of armament and equipment was completely insufficient, especially as regards the motorcycle and heavy units that were planned for in the order of battle.

SS Volunteer *Nachrichten Abteilung* 31

The formation of *Nachrichten Abteilung* 31 was probably already begun in the Batschka, probably in the village of Topolya. The Reich German and ethnic German personnel of the dissolved Waffen-SS *Gebirgs Nachrichten-Abteilung* 23 'Kama', were taken over. The formation of this *Abteilung* was already fairly far advanced during the course of September when it was broken off. The *Gebirgs Nachrichten Abteilung* was changed into the *Nachrichten Abteilung* of the 31st SS Volunteer Grenadier Division that was to be reformed. *SS-Untersturmführer* Hans Villier (Telephone Company) gave this account:

> Suddenly we were able to change the fez again for the peaked or field cap. The emblems of the 'Kama' were put away. The formation of the 23rd SS-Division was abandoned. The Muslims came into the 13th SS *Gebirgs* Division 'Handschar'. We, most of the Germans, were transferred into the 31st SS *Gebirgs* Division. The official name, 31st SS Volunteer Grenadier Division, was not used amongst us. We said *Gebirgs* Division. It's true that for some time the Muslims were still with us in the Telephone Company, until one day they had

all moved off west of the Danube, leaving not one behind. Looking back, I am astonished how quickly this Division was formed, under such very adverse circumstances. The Divisional Commander, *SS-Oberführer* Lombard, I had known from earlier, when he was regimental commander of the 'Florian Geyer'.

To the core personnel who had been taken over were added newly enlisted Batschka German recruits. H. Villier continued:

Our ethnic German men had such typical German names as Müller, Meier, Schulze, Mosbacher or even Coutaillon, who was a good laugh. As an experienced valet, he had been valet to a Hungarian nobleman, he was the orderly to our sarge, *Stabsscharführer* Albert Vollenbroich. He was also our chief interpreter in negotiating with Hungarians and Hungarian authorities. Many ethnic Germans had also earlier served in the *Honvéd.*

Ethnic Germans, from the SS *Nachrichten Ersatz Abteilung* 'Nuremberg', were also brought in as wireless operators. Men also came from SS *Nachrichten* Training *Abteilung* 3 'Goslar'. Among them were some former members of the aviation *Nachrichten* unit. In accordance with an SS *Führungshauptamt* order of 23 September 1944, the five officers, Jost, Keller, Villier, Meitzel and Graf from the SS *Nachrichten Ersatz Abteilung* 'Eichstädt', were transferred to the *Gebirgs Nachrichten Abteilung* of the 'Kama' to fill command posts.

The planned organisation was achieved, in essence, even if the dog section never materialised. The Staff was fully motorised, the 1st Telephone Company and the 2nd Wireless Company were both partly motorised, and the 2 third platoons were horse-drawn. But there were never enough motor vehicles. Thus the planned light *Nachrichten* column could only be formed much later, in Silesia.

Taking his place as *Abteilung* Commander was *SS-Hauptsturmführer* R. Albert Reimann. He had already commanded the *Nachrichten Abteilung* of the 'Kama' and remained in this post until December 1944, when *SS-Hauptsturmführer* Alois Kindshofer became the new *Nachrichten Abteilung* commander. *Abteilung* Adjutant was the Sudeten German *SS-Obersturmführer* Hentschel. The *Nachrichten Abteilung* wireless officer was *SS-Oberscharführer* Alfred Schulz, from Kiel. The TFN (Technical Officer, *Nachrichten* Equipment) was *SS-Untersturmführer* Karl Stecker from Olmütz, who had been an officer in the Slovakian Army. The supply unit was led by *SS-Oberscharführer* Hugo Krallmann.

Commanding the Telephone Company was the Silesian *SS-Obersturmführer* Karl Heinz Dreiucker. His platoon commanders were, in I Platoon *SS-Untersturmführer* Siegfried Koller (from Klagenfurt), in II Platoon *SS-Untersturmführer* Georg Bantelmann (from Soest), in III Platoon *SS-Untersturmführer* Hans Villier (from Westphalia). The officer for special duties was *SS-Untersturmführer* Jürgen Joost (from Hamburg). All these officers had, in the same capacities, served in the 'Kama'. To the Telephone Company's corps of NCOs belonged the 'sarge' Albert Vollenbroich from Mönchengladbach. Transferred from the Luftwaffe, were Richard Knorrn from Strehlen, Rudi Kurzweg from Berlin, and Jupp Vossen from Düsseldorf. In III Platoon were Willi Pagel from Pomerania, Hein Flor from Lüdenscheid, Heinz Frank from Frankfurt, Schulert from Leipzig, Tyll from Karlsbad, Paul Kuhn from Iserlohn, Fritz Schuster from Transylvania, and *SS-Oberscharführer* Schmidt from Berlin. Added to all these were Kurt Matthes from Neuruppin and Franz Vogtle from Oranienburg (both half-platoon leaders).

Commanding the Wireless Company was *SS-Obersturmführer* Ottfried Schwalbe, a Vogtlander, who, in May 1945, took his own life when in Czech territory. His platoon commanders were *SS-Untersturmführer* Kurt Meitzel from Kassel and *SS-Untersturmführer* Waldemar Graf. *Sturmmann* Fritz Mock from Berlin was the wireless unit leader, *SS-Oberscharführer* Josef Vossen from Silesia the storekeeper.

Other officers in the *Nachrichten Abteilung*, whose duties we do not know, were *SS-Untersturmführer* Günther Voss, *SS-Untersturmführer* Otto Eichhorn from Eisenach, *SS-Untersturmführer* Hans Reich from Munich, *SS-Untersturmführer* Werner Fleishhauer and the Slovakian German *SS-Untersturmführer* Wladi Sopko. Shortly before the end of the war, *SS-Untersturmführer* Gerd Lingner, from Transylvania, also joined the *Nachrichten Abteilung*.

Abteilung Medical Officer was the Batschka German Dr Peter Reidl who, at first, served without a post as a SS wireless operator, but also worked as *Abteilung* medical officer. Later he was assigned the appropriate rank of a *SS-Oberjunker*. After the war ended he, too, fell victim to the terror of the Czech partisans.

The process of forming the *Abteilung* could only be begun in the Batschka. Later it was continued, after the withdrawal to the western bank of the Danube in the area Nemetbóly–Szederkeny.

SS Volunteer Pioneer Battalion 31

The Pioneer Battalion was formed using the Reich German and ethnic German personnel of the Waffen-SS *Gebirgs* Pioneer Battalion 23 'Kama'. It was not formed in the Batschka, as were the other units, but in Stiechowitz, near Prague, on SS Troop Training Ground Bohemia. Responsible for the formation was Inspectorate 5 (Pioneers) of the *SS Führungshauptamt*.

Waffen-SS *Gebirgs* Pioneer Battalion 23 'Kama' was at the troop training ground from about the middle of June. Its core personnel were partly taken over from the 13th Waffen-SS *Gebirgs* Division SS 'Handschar' and partly, including the battalion commander, from SS Pioneer School Hradischko. In mid-June, another four newly-minted *SS-Oberjunker*, including Hummel, Pabel, and Kiebauch, who had just completed the 12th Reserve Officers' course, were transferred to the Battalion. They were all soldiers with frontline experience who had proved their worth. Hummel, for instance, joined up in September 1939, served in the reserves and, for over two years, in the SS Pioneer Battalion 6 'Nord' in Finland. The Weapons Technology Education Institute at Dachau provided armourers and assistants. The posts held in the battalion were as follows:

Battalion Commander: *SS-Sturmbannführer* Hermann Otto
Battalion Adjutant: *SS-Hauptscharführer* Hoffmeister
Battalion MO: *SS-Hauptsturmführer* Dr Albrecht Hermann
Battalion SDG: *SS-Oberscharführer* Kurt Simang
Battalion Stores: *SS-Oberscharführer* Fritz Ziege
Commander 1 Company: *SS-Obersturmführer* Gerhard Hillmann

Commander I Platoon: *SS-Oberjunker* Heinz Hummel
  1 Group: *SS-Unterscharführer* Fritz Dielschneider
  2 Group: *SS-Unterscharführer* Hans Zink
  3 Group: *SS-Unterscharführer* Rumpf
Commander II Platoon: *SS-Oberjunker* Bernd Pabel
Commander III Platoon: *SS-Oberscharführer* Werner Rauer
Commander 2 Company: *SS-Obersturmführer* Hans Bahr
  Commander I Platoon: *SS-Untersturmführer* Kurt Schmidt
  Commander II Platoon: *SS-Oberjunker* Kiebauch
  Commander III Platoon: *SS-Untersturmführer* Jahn
Commander 3 Company: *SS-Obersturmführer* Werner Schroder
Group leaders: *SS-Oberscharführer* Josef Schilz, *SS-Oberscharführer* Jakob Sagmeister

The men were mostly Muslims, with some ethnic Germans who were responsible for interpreting. By September the whole Battalion had received complete pioneer training. They were ready for transport to arrive to take them into action, as a complete unit, in the Yugoslavian area. But a few days before, Division 'Kama' was dissolved and a new order reached the battalion. The Muslims were to set off by rail transport for the Balkans. This actually happened, under the command of a *SS-Untersturmführer* from the 3rd Company, of whom there has since been no trace. Also, there are no traces to tell what became of the Muslims who left on the rail transport. The entire complement of officers and NCOs, and the majority of the German core personnel, had to remain in Stiechowitz.

This unit cadre was then used for the formation of SS Volunteer Pioneer Battalion 31. The allocation of posts remained in force and the Battalion was now to be topped up with ethnic German recruits. Probably many Hungarian Germans of the 31st SS Volunteer Grenadier Division had at this time, i.e. the beginning of October, already set off from Transylvania to go to Prague, because the Battalion always included men who needed to be trained. Most of the later pioneers, however, were only transferred to the Pioneer Battalion in December 1944, after the Division had to a certain extent recovered from its shattering experience in the maelstrom of the defensive fighting on the Danube. They had sent off a strong contingent of men, mostly on a voluntary basis, to Stiechowitz. Among these men there was a particularly large number from Swabian Turkey and the northern Batschka.

In addition to the ethnic Germans, Hungary was also strongly represented in Pioneer Battalion 31. According to *SS-Untersturmführer* Hummel, a third of the battalion consisted of Magyars, in that every platoon had two groups of ethnic Germans and one group of Hungarians.

"It was only possible", wrote Hummel, "to converse with them through interpreters, and that was often difficult. For all that, though, the Hungarians were first-class lads".

The organisation, set out in the formation order, was achieved with some exceptions. The Battalion Staff was only partly motorised, 2nd Company probably relied on bicycles, but 1st and 3rd Companies had not even that mobility.

Remaining as Battalion commander, until the end of the war, was *SS-Sturmbannführer* Hermann Otto, who was born in 1911. From September 1939 to summer 1941 he was in the SS 'Totenkopf' Division. From then, until Spring 1942, he was commander of the pioneer company in SS Infantry Regiment 6 in the 6th SS *Gebirgs* Division 'Nord'. In 1942 he joined the SS Pioneer Training and *Ersatz* Battalion in Dresden. He then went to SS Pioneer School Hradischko, where, finally, he was the training group commander. In June 1944 he took over command of Waffen-SS *Gebirgs* Pioneer Battalion 23 'Kama', then, after giving up the Muslims, formed SS Pioneer Battalion 31. He eventually entered the field again at its head.

SS Volunteer *Panzerjäger Abteilung* 31

The formation of the *Panzerjäger Abteilung*, planned in accordance with the formation order, took place, as did the Pioneer Battalion, at Troop Training Ground Bohemia, in the SS *Panzerjäger* School Janowitz (near Prague). Because of this, the *Abteilung* was spared all the hardships suffered by the other divisional units in Hungary. The personnel of the dissolved Division 'Kama' were taken over. Reich German complements were brought up. At the beginning of December, at the latest, ethnic German recruits, from the greater part of the 31st SS Volunteer Grenadier Division in Hungary, were marched off to the *Abteilung*. SS Volunteer *Panzerjäger Abteilung* 31 certainly remained a unit in which, as the exception to the rule, Reich Germans, not Hungarian Germans were predominant.

Abteilung commander was *SS-Sturmbannführer* Richard Landwehr. He had come from the post of *Abteilung* commander in the SS Flak *Ersatz* Regiment, via the *Panzerjäger Abteilungen* of the divisions 'Das Reich' and 'Prinz Eugen', to command the *Panzerjäger* of the 'Kama'. He retained his command right up to 'the bitter end', as did his *Abteilung* Adjutant, *SS-Obersturmführer* Heinz Sebastian. *SS-Obersturmführer* Günther Gottwald, a regular soldier, was company commander of 1st *Panzerjäger* Company, in the *Panzerjäger Abteilung*, and was posted as missing after Silesia.

SS Volunteer Supply *Abteilung* 31

The cadre for the supply services was formed by the core personnel of the divisional supply troops from the dissolved Division 'Kama'. These units were mainly in the Bajmok area. At first, there was no question of completing the organisation originally planned in the formation order. The equipment was totally insufficient and was limited to farm horses and agricultural vehicles from the Batschka. There was also a shortage of specialist personnel. Only later, in November, were driving instructors and storekeepers transferred to the *Abteilung* as NCOs. However, it was only in December that they were able to have an effect. This was because, in November, the Division was involved in heavy fighting whilst withdrawing.

It appears that the battalion commander was *SS-Hauptsturmführer* Wilhelm Morisse, who had held this post in the 'Kama'. He was one of the first men in the SS, as can be seen by his SS membership number, 3874. At the end of the war he fell into Soviet captivity, from which he never returned home. Company commander of the Supply Company was *SS-Hauptsturmführer* Alois Kindshofer from

Munich. Other sources say he was the *Abteilung* commander of the Supply *Abteilung*, and that Morisse must have held the post of Divisional Supply Officer. *SS-Obersturmführer* Rudolf Herzog was the company commander of Motor Vehicle Company 31, which was formed from the motorised columns of the Division. At first, however, there were neither sufficient numbers of motor vehicles, nor trained drivers but, most importantly, they did not have enough petrol.

SS Volunteer Workshop Company 31

The personnel and materiel of the Motor Vehicle Workshop Company of the dissolved 'Kama' Division, formed originally in the SS *Panzer* Repair Training and *Ersatz Abteilung* 'Oranienburg', were transferred to the 31ˢᵗ SS Volunteer Grenadier Division. The Company, at first only a single section, was topped up, in the Funfkirchen area, by bringing up more personnel from the SS Motor Vehicle Training and *Ersatz Abteilung*.

SS *Verwaltungstruppen Abteilung* 31

The administrative troops' *Abteilung* of the dissolved 'Kama' Division, originally formed in the Training and *Ersatz Abteilung* of the SS Administrative Services Dachau, was transferred, with the exception of its Muslim personnel, to the 31st SS Volunteer Grenadier Division with effect from 1 October 1944. It was topped up with newly-enlisted, mostly older, ethnic Germans. The *Abteilung* was organised, in the Fünfkirchen area, in accordance with the formation order, into Staff, Bakery Company, Butchery Company and Administration Company, together with SS Field Post Office 31. The plans to motorise the *Abteilung* were at first only sketchily implemented.

The *Abteilung* was under the command of the Division's IVa, at this time *SS-Sturmbannführer* von Türck. A Sudeten German, who was also a senior postal inspector, *SS-Hauptsturmführer* Heinrich Planer took command of SS Field Post Office 31. He was posted missing at the end of the war.

SS Volunteer Veterinary Company 31

The 'Kama' Division had two veterinary companies (1 and 2), the core personnel of which were, after the Division was dissolved, at the disposal of SS Volunteer Veterinary Company 31. The Company was topped up with Batschka Germans. The Company Commander was *SS-Untersturmführer* Dr Peter Pertschy, who held this post until the end of the war. Another officer, *SS-Untersturmführer* Fritz Bittner, also served in the Veterinary Company.

SS Volunteer Medical *Abteilung* 31

The formation of Medical *Abteilung* 31 was begun in the Batschka as early as mid-September. The Reich German, and ethnic German, personnel of the medical services of the dissolved 'Kama' Division formed the establishment core of the new *Abteilung* 1st and 2nd Medical Companies and Motor Ambulance Company. This basic framework was topped up by newly recruited, mostly older, ethnic Germans.

Ethnic German medics were also drafted in and trained in the Medical *Abteilung*, to serve later as battalion or *Abteilung* medical officers.

At first the medical services were located in Neu-Werbass, then the formation of the 2nd Medical Company was begun in Zombor, while the 1st Medical Company remained in Werbass. Commander of the Medical Company, and at the same time Divisional Medical Officer, was *SS-Sturmbannführer* Dr Karl Matz from Stralsund. He had held this post in the 'Kama' Division and earlier in the 'Handschar' Division. The Company commander of the 1st Medical Company was *SS-Hauptsturmführer* Dr Siegfried Klaus Bock. A Schleswig-Holsteiner, he had served earlier in the 12th SS *Panzer* Division 'Hitlerjugend'. The commander of the 2nd Medical Company was *SS-Hauptsturmführer* Dr Erich Scherer, an ethnic German from the Banat. The SS Volunteer Motor Ambulance Company was led by *SS-Obersturmführer* Hans Keller. The pharmacist was *SS-Untersturmführer* Geiger from the Banat. The internist *SS-Untersturmführer* Krummel was from Transylvania. The important posts of the 1st and 2nd Surgeons at first remained unfilled because there was a shortage of appropriate specialists.

In addition, too, the formation process proceeded sluggishly as there was also a shortage of equipment. At this time the 2nd Medical Company, for instance, only had one single lorry and two air-cooled ambulances that broke down all too often. The only other vehicles they had were farm vehicles. All of this was a long way from the 'motorised' condition specified in the formation order.

It should be emphasised that, as early as the last week in September, the Medical *Abteilung* did take up its medical duties. This can be seen as the very first time that a unit of the $31^{st\,SS}$ Volunteer Grenadier Division saw action. It involved receiving, treating and nursing wounded from the combat areas in Serbia and in the Banat. This service was carried out in the hospital in Zombor and probably also in Neu-Werbass.

The experiences of an *SDG-Reichsrottenführer*, Ernst Bennert, should serve to recall the Medical *Abteilung*'s time in the Batschka:

> As a stout Hitler Youth from Stettin, born in 1924, I volunteered for the Waffen-SS at the beginning of 1942. After various kinds of service at the front I came to the SS Main Medical Store Berlin, where, at the beginning of August 1944, I was transferred to the 'Kama' Division with *Rottenführer* Peter Glitzar from Danzig, and a third *Rottenführer*, who also came from northern Germany. Each of us was sent off alone, so that we only met each other at India, changing trains for Peterwardein. We came to Neu-Werbass, to the Medical *Abteilung* of the 'Kama' that was just being formed. There it was intended that we should be trainers for the Muslims. Immediately after we arrived in Werbass, where the Divisional Staff also was located, we reported to the sarge. In civilian life he was a customs official in Hamburg. He said to us, 'What's the point of struggling with the Mujos. You've got a good posting, where things aren't at all bad'. No sooner said than done. We were transferred to the medical stores, two miles away from the company, where we really had very little to do. The equipment was intended for the mountain medical services, and designed to be carried on pack animals, but only arrived in dribs and drabs. However, the jungle telegraph worked well. If an officer was on his way to us, we were immediately tipped off by field telephone, so that we could pretend to be working feverishly. That August it was red hot. Thank God, we were kitted out in tropical uniform.

Soon we got eight Batschka Germans on transfer from the *Honvéd*, where they were reserve officers or NCOs. They were all academics, whom we had to instruct in German commands and to whom we had to give a lightning course in basic training, so that later they could be used in the Division as *Oberscharführer* or officers, according to the rank they had brought with them. In age, some of them were old enough to have been our fathers, so of course we didn't knock around with them all that much. As far as the medical service was concerned, at this time we didn't appear especially well equipped. We still had no motor vehicles, nor any HVPs (Main Dressing Stations), and no field hospitals. The officer with whom we had most contact at this time was *SS-Untersturmführer* Geige, a pharmacist from Homolitz in the Banat. At the beginning of September the Batschka Germans were drafted in and already the Number 31 was in the air, but we didn't really know what it meant.

There was at this time hardly any activity by partisans, but one time we got to know a good deal about them. Oh yes, a good deal! One day I had to travel on service business from Werbass to Szabadka. I travelled by train, accompanied by three Mujos. In one place the tracks had been blown up and we could go no further. We were really late. Luckily for us! On the very morning we should have arrived in Szabadka, the town suffered an American terror attack and it is very probable that we would have been killed at the station in the hail of bombs.

Another time, too, we were lucky. One day, *SS-Oberscharführer* Biel was driving through the countryside to get fodder for our horses, and ran over and killed a pig. He loaded up the animal and handed it over to our field kitchen to prepare it for eating. Shortly afterwards the farmer who owned the pig appeared at the divisional field police post and was raising hell. After some palaver we had said that we were prepared to pay for the pig, and did so. In spite of this, the field police confiscated it, and prepared it for eating themselves. Luckily for us! Because as it later turned out, the pig was infested by trichina, and according to rumours, but also by credible accounts, fourteen comrades of the field police we said to have died of trichina poisoning. In any event, several of them had to have treatment by calcium injections for months on end. Bad luck for some – good luck for others.

Some days previously, before the Soviets advanced into the Banat, I was given the task, by *SS-Untersturmführer* Geiger, or rather, he asked me, to bring his wife and his son from the Banat to Werbass. I drove as co-driver of a lorry to Betschkerek, spent the night in the SS hospital and next morning travelled by train to Pantschowa. From there we went by horse-drawn cab to Homolitz. Frau Geiger got ready for the journey with her child and a few possessions, we went back the same way and arrived back in Werbass safe and sound. On the way it never occurred to me to make some provision to defend ourselves, even though the Soviets were already quite close.

In the last days of September the Muslims were discharged, but I, together with a part of the medical equipment, was sent off to Zombor, where I had to report to the 2nd Medical Company at the municipal hospital. I was received with the words: 'You're very welcome to the 2nd Medical Company – we've now got one more man, you're number 12!' The man who welcomed me was *SS-Untersturmführer* Krummel from Transylvania, no militarist, for all that he had the Iron Cross Second Class, but a first-class doctor and a very nice chap.

He always did most of the work at the HVPs and was always very caring of the wounded.

Then we had to set ourselves up in the hospital and the first sick and disabled men arrived. In the whole Division we had no surgeons, so that no larger operations were possible. Nevertheless, we 'borrowed' a civilian surgeon. However, personnel did arrive, nurses, plasterers, and also 40 to 50 older Batschka Germans for whom at first we couldn't find a use. I was also able to persuade six German Red Cross Sisters, who were wandering about fairly aimlessly in Zombor, to join us. Then they stayed with us in the company for about three months, until our time in Styria. Between one of the sisters, a German girl from the Banat, and our driver from Berlin, Kriehe, there developed a romance, and soon, at our next base, Mohács, they were celebrating their engagement.

Soon, too, there followed our first action as a medical unit. At the station a provisional hospital train with wounded from the Army, the Luftwaffe, and SS Division 'Prinz Eugen' coming from Rumania or Serbia, was left stranded because there was no locomotive. We had to fetch the poor lads into the hospital to give them further treatment. Motor vehicles were at a premium. Our lorries from captured Italian stocks broke down with damaged transmission. But for the two that were operative, however, we had no petrol. So the wounded were brought in on a horse-drawn cab. Those slightly wounded were then, after they had been treated, sent by horse-drawn cab to the ferry station at Bezdán. The serious cases stayed with us. The Hungarian doctors gave us quite excellent help in treating them.

The evacuation of the Batschka was imminent, the Medical *Abteilung* was one of the first units of the 31st SS Volunteer Grenadier Division to have to retreat to the western bank of the Danube. Now we had to mobilise. Our Batschka Germans swung into action and got hold of horse-drawn vehicles. That they got them from their best friends I can have no doubt. So we loaded up our equipment, and the wounded, and moved to Bezdán, to the ferry. It was overcast, rainy, misty, so we were spared low-flying aircraft. We crossed to Kisköszeg where we waited for two days for stragglers, to move then to Németbóly and finally, about the 10 to 12 October, to Mohács, where we set up a collection point in the municipal hospital.

A SS Division of a regional character

In summary, it can be said that the 31st SS Division came into being surprisingly quickly. Although it was only a little later, on the other side of the Danube in the Fünfkirchen area, that the whole grouping assumed a more definite form. In the Batschka it could only receive basic formation, basic equipment and hardly any training. Important divisional units such as Pioneers and *Panzerjäger* were formed at distant troop training grounds, while for many units only the core personnel were available. These only to be topped up in the Fünfkirchen area or even later on. The new Division showed distinct signs of being formed in haste, as did many 'peculiar' organisations that were, in this sixth year of war, no longer unusual. At the same time it had a unique south-east German, even Hungarian, character.

The officer corps of the Division that was already in the Batschka in Summer 1944, for the formation of the 'Kama' Division, was fairly heterogeneous, as regards frontline experience and age. As well as real old veterans who had proved themselves time and time again on the Eastern Front, from Finland to the gorges of the Balkans, there were also many other officers. They came from posts on the home front, or in *Ersatz* units, but without sufficient experience of the front line, or of the command of troops, who were also, on average, older men. At the other extreme were officers who were very young, but who had already been tested and had proved their worth in combat. Holding the rank of *SS-Untersturmführer* or *SS-Obersturmführer*, they were already commanding companies and batteries. They were later to pay a high price in casualties. Alongside men who had been among the first members of the SS, stood many who had been transferred to the SS from the Wehrmacht. As well as police officers, there were cavalrymen and *Gebirgsjäger*. Next to Reich Germans from all regions were also south-east Germans, especially from the Banat. Many officers of the Royal Hungarian *Honvéd*, now released to join the Waffen-SS, were also there.

A significantly strong contingent, in itself, was represented by the many Carpathian Germans, i.e. Pressburgers, Zipsers, and Hauerlanders, who were officers and NCOs from Slovakia. Up to the summer of 1944 some of these had already become combat-experienced officers and NCOs in the Slovakian Army. Many had been released and taken over into the German Wehrmacht.

As a representative of them all, a few more details should here be given of *SS-Oberscharführer* Hans Sator. Sator was born in 1918 in Pressburg and did his military service from 1939, in the Leutschau/Löcse/Levoca Regiment under *Kommandeur Major* Domes, with whom he took the field in 1941, fighting as a sergeant, in Russia. In 1943 he was discharged. In April 1944 he got married. Called up again by the Slovakian Army on 10 August 1944, he was immediately transferred to the Waffen-SS. He was killed in action on the Danube front in November 1944. He never knew of the birth of his baby daughter.

It was the same for the NCOs as it was for the officers. They were mostly Reich Germans from all regions, even including a Bürgenland Hungarian, *SS-Oberscharführer* Béla Meszaros (I/80). Among them, regular soldiers were underrepresented. On the other hand they were mostly of younger ages and were almost all volunteers, some already with combat experience that was very useful to the young Division. However, there were not enough of them and a shortage of good NCOs always had an adverse effect. To even out this shortage, the participants in the whole NCO course in the Division 'Kama', a course which consisted of young Croatian German volunteers from Syrmia and Slavonia, were all assigned as NCOs. This was despite the fact that they had not yet completed the course and thus had not been promoted, but were just NCO candidates.

Another component of the corps of NCOs was made up of those Hungarian Germans who were NCOs of the Royal Hungarian *Honvéd*. In accordance with the agreement between the two states, they had been released from the *Honvéd* and made available for transfer into the Waffen-SS. For the most part these were very valuable personnel, since many of them had for a long time wanted to join the Waffen-SS. But as specialists and reserve NCOs of the *Honvéd* they had, understandably, not been released. In addition to the former *Honvéd* platoon commanders, there were *SS-Unterscharführer*, Jakob Beck and Franz Peter (I/79). To represent all of them, mention should be made here of wireless sergeant Josef Holzinger.

The complement was made up as follows: Reich Germans made up about 10% to 15% of the total complement, but they also formed the greater part of the complement of NCOs. They were the 'backbone of the army'. Not a few of the *Rottenführer*, as well as the NCOs, were transferred to the Waffen-SS from the Luftwaffe. When ground crews were no longer needed, they were released within the framework of the so-called 'Hermann Göring Donation'. Representatives of many of these should be mentioned here, including *SS-Oberscharführer* Josef Hinze (II/78), Heinrich Gustav (*Panzerjäger*), Martin Mustroph (Signals), *SS-Unterscharführer* Rolf Kruse (IV/A.R.), Josef Schwarzwald (*Panzerjäger*), and *SS-Rottenführer* Paul Wengler (III/A.R.), Andreas Schmidt (Fusilier Battalion) and Otto Lipacz (II/80).

A small indication of the Pan-European character of the Waffen-SS was shown in one volunteer from Western Europe, the twenty year old Dutch student, *SS-Mann* Nijhof Dante Bern (Divisional Staff). Some Bosnian Muslims also, who were the last of those in the 'Kama', still remained, here and there, in auxiliary services in various units, right up to January 1945.

The greater part of the other ranks, however, was made up of newly recruited ethnic Germans from Hungary. About 75% of them came from the Batschka. 25% came from Swabian Turkey (Komitate Baranya, Tolna and Somogy), and from other areas of German settlements in Hungary, for instance from the Elek district at the tip of the Banat, which still remained in Hungary. They were joined by smaller numbers of ethnic Germans from Croatia, and from the Serbian or Rumanian Banat. Some of these had been assigned to the 'Kama' Division in the summer. They were now taken over into the new 31st SS Volunteer Grenadier Division. Some had been taken, at the beginning of October, from the Banat German refugee columns.

The fact that the majority of personnel came from a certain narrow district, and that the complements of entire units often came from the same village, and hence some of them were even related to each other, lent the 31st SS Volunteer Grenadier Division a regional, territorial character unusual among the SS Divisions. This character came, too, with all its disadvantages. Among the Germans there were even a few Bunjewatzen (Croatians) from the Batschka, representing the ethnic composition of this country. For them, let mention be made of *SS-Mann* Marin IV Kovic (Supply Troops), a twenty years old agricultural worker.

As regards the age mix of these ethnic Germans, the picture was not as good. A third of them were older than forty years of age, and a third younger than nineteen years of age! Only a bare 15% fell into the 'capable' age ranges of between twenty and thirty. Among the Reich German core personnel the picture was the exact opposite. It should be noted that the SS recruiting campaigns of 1942 and 1943, in the Batschka, provided contingents of volunteers at a rate very much above the average. Another special recruiting campaign, restricted only to some districts of the Batschka (the so-called 'Streckenbach-Aktion' in March 1944), had already very much exhausted the manpower of the Batschka. These now had to form the 31st SS Volunteer Grenadier Division. So it becomes clear that, together with the continuing relaxation of the once very strict requirements and fitness criteria, it was really a matter of the last draft from the country of the Batschka! Again, this lent the 31st SS Volunteer Grenadier Division a character, which was unusual for an SS Division, which was that of a *Volkssturm* or *Landwehr* unit in which fathers and sons stood together. It is true that in this way, one advantage was that a considerable number of already trained reservists were available who could all be sent into action at the same time.

As to their occupations these ethnic Germans were about 80% farmers or village craftsmen. Among them there were fewer industrial workers. On the other hand, school-leavers, students, and also school pupils, were represented in considerable numbers. As for the concerns about their basic attitudes, these were, as might be expected from the situation, fairly diverse. The Batschka itself was, indeed, fairly conscious of its German heritage, but in the course of the volunteers presenting themselves in earlier years, it was mainly these very people, i.e. those with National Socialist sympathies, who left their villages. Since recruitment from 1942 was no longer carried out on a voluntary basis, the majority then, i.e. those with Christian-conservative leanings, were drafted in, along with the smaller numbers of *Magyaronen*. Even members of the movement 'Dem Vaterland die Treue' (Loyalty to the Fatherland (Hüségmozgalom)) of the former Apatin clergyman Adam Berenz, with their policy of assimilation, were now in the ranks of the 31st SS Volunteer Grenadier Division. Later, they too 'held their own,' in the field. There were also many there, from mixed marriages, who had already assimilated to such an extent that they could no longer understand German (*Volksliste* C).

But there were also the last officials of the *Volksbund*, who had not been released in earlier recruiting campaigns, but were now following the last draft. Among many others, there were also in the 31st SS Volunteer Grenadier Division, the youth leaders Hans Schmidt, who was killed in action in the fighting on the Danube, and Otto Kohler, the black-bearded, slim sportsman who brought with him his bride, Josefa. Robert Kohler, too, the provincial youth leader of the *Deutsche Jugend* (German Youth), joined the 31st SS Volunteer Grenadier Division after he had worked, in October 1944, in the *Deutsche Volksgruppe* Central Office for Refugee Questions.

All these background factors, together with the general war situation and the political events at home, left their mark on the spirit and the morale of the young Division. The view that the Soviets should not be allowed to invade the homeland, was one with which all the members of the Division were certainly in agreement. In many places there was no lack of enthusiasm among the new recruits, just as there were many who flocked voluntarily to the colours. As representative of many brave volunteers, mention here should be made of Anton Frei from Swabian Turkey (SS Regiment 79), who had already served for many years in the *Honvéd*. In the Yugoslavian campaign, in 1941, he had taken part in the forward thrust of the Hungarian Rapid Corps as far as Valievo, under General Béla Miklós von Dálnoki, who later became a holder of the Knight's Cross. In the 31st SS Volunteer Grenadier Division, Frei was, in 1945, awarded the Iron Cross, Second Class, in Silesia.

Nevertheless, other not inconsiderable numbers of recruits were decidedly unwilling. People were in general simply tired of war. This attitude became increasingly strong in the following weeks of October. This was as a result of the withdrawal from the Batschka, and the occupation by the enemy of the home villages of many members of the Division. This unwillingness was given a powerful boost, on 15 October 1944, by the appeal of Regent von Horthy, in which he announced that Hungary was withdrawing from the war.

The ending of the war was also the dearest wish of many new recruits, with the result that many simply ran away and went home. The poor equipment and clothing meant that many men had to eat out of rusty jam tins and had no change of underclothes. The almost non-existent rations lead to seriously depressed morale. Added to this was the very short period of training, and a serious shortage of weapons, all of which gave rise, in the young soldiers, to a feeling of being powerless in the face of the approaching enemy.

One thing is certain, despite everything, these Danubian Swabians, whether old or young, farmer, 'townie', or workman, by virtue of their innate discipline, physical and mental capabilities, as well as by their decency, were absolutely destined to be soldiers. This would only happen if the young Division was granted enough time and opportunity to educate, train, and equip them. But this was denied to them through force of circumstances.

Finally, something more should be said concerning the relationship between the ethnic German other ranks and the Reich German officers. Some of the Reich Germans could never properly understand, or deal with, the character and singular mentality of the ethnic German farmers. They were never able to get really close to them as human beings. They even drew wrong conclusions from their manner, and certainly from their dialect, which were of course very different from High German. So that when the ethnic Germans were not approached with sympathy and interest, they actually did not respond, and there remained an invisible wall between superiors and inferiors, between *Deutschländern* and *Batschkanesen*. It was originally the breaking down of this wall, and the rapprochement of the Reich German and ethnic German parts of the *Volk,* which were seen as the revolutionary tasks faced by the Waffen-SS. But it was 1944, there was total war, and everything was already being dictated by the harsh necessities of repelling the 'Red menace' that was approaching from the East.

On the other hand, there were many Reich German officers and NCOs, and it should be noted that they were in the majority, who found a way to the hearts of their ethnic German subordinates. These were above all the young *Unter-* and *Obersturmführer* who had grown up in the spirit of the Waffen-SS. They were not much older than their young subordinates, but were already experienced frontline soldiers, tested in combat. There were also many higher ranks who were at the front for years on end and to whom comradeship meant more than just a word. However, experience at the front, and successfully mastering the art of handling weapons would always seriously impress the ethnic German recruits. Thus, if they were dealt with humanely and well, they would follow their commanders through thick and thin.

At the time, points of view like this, some of an emotional nature, also determined the psychological relationship of the Hungarian German soldiers with their Divisional Commander. Lombard was heart and soul a cavalryman of the old school, even in his appearance. As a man of the world, he gave the impression of a 'lord of the manor', and represented the very epitome of the Prussian officer. The contrast between him and his new ethnic German soldiers could scarcely have been greater. The somewhat awkward farmers from the 'Sallaschen', and the village craftsmen, who were also either elderly or very young, were not to be turned into Prussian 'show horses' overnight. Not even the junior officers who had already served in the *Honvéd*, and who otherwise were soldiers to the marrow, could be quickly changed. Of the various German types, they had especial respect in particular for the Prussian officers, but in their own manner were far closer to the Austrian mould. Moreover, Lombard placed great value on smartness, even in moments when his ethnic Germans might have expected this smartness to be relaxed. This gave the impression that he was lacking in warmth. Certainly, he never meant it that way. But he was not a leader close to his men, as were 'Papa' Phleps, or Sepp Dietrich.

This 'young' Division had come into being very quickly, in the way already described in detail, but now they had to continue the process of formation and training in very difficult, adverse circumstances. Equipment was only available in very moderate quantities and the same could also be said of armaments. At first there were no heavy weapons at all. Naturally this also caused training to suffer. These difficulties were more especially compounded because of the accelerated Soviet advance on Hungary, where the Soviets were already approaching the Theiss. On the one hand this resulted in a greater intensification of the danger from Titoist groups in the Batschka, and on the other in the need to evacuate the Batschka Germans. The question of a military defence of the Batschka had also arisen. These three events left their mark, on what was going on, in the 31st SS Volunteer Grenadier Division, in the first half of October. In the event, despite efforts to participate, the Division was not directly called upon to fight against the partisans, but it did contribute, with one *Kampfgruppe* (*Kampfgruppe* Syr), towards the defence of the Batschka. In fact the evacuation of the Germans cannot be imagined without the part the Division played. In the following three chapters these events will be described in detail. But firstly, a glance at developments at the Front.

CHAPTER 5

Developments at the Front and the Situation with Partisan Units in the Batschka

End of September – beginning of October

At the end of September, after many unsuccessful frontal attacks to the north on the Transylvanian front, the Soviets finally discontinued their attacks. They moved their weight westwards and sought to break through in that direction. Two focus points became apparent, one directed at Szeged in the Temeschburg–Arad–Gyula area, the other directed against Debrecen in the Nagyszalonta area. This was a highly dangerous situation! If the Soviets succeeded in breaking through and swinging northwards along the Theiss, they could cut off the entire front in northern Transylvania. Also, because heavy fighting had been raging for weeks in the Beskiden, there was the danger of a gigantic *Kessel* (encirclement). The German counter-strategy planned to hit the advancing enemy in their far flank with armoured forces, to drive them away, and cut them off from the mountains. Then they would press on to the Eiserne Tor and the Rotturm Pass and block these off (Operation 'Zigeunerbaron' ('Gypsy Baron').

To the south of Grosswardein–Arad–Temeschburg, the IV and VII Hungarian Army Corps were facing the Soviet offensive grouping. In mid-September they pushed across the Hungarian Trianon frontier into Transylvania. They gained some territory, together with the town of Arad. The 4th SS *Polizei Panzergrenadier* Division, in the process of being brought up from Greece, received orders to take Temeschburg. Then, with the IV Hungarian Corps, they had to advance into the Mieresch, Temesch, and Bega Valleys in order to block off the enemy advance. This came from the direction of the river valleys of the Karánsebe and Déva/Dimrich, at the passes where they emerge into the Banat plain.

But for various reasons the Division arrived too late and found a changed situation. At Birda, Gátalja and St. Andreas they were already encountering Soviets, and became involved in heavy defensive fighting. They were forced to move on to the defensive, west of Temeschburg. No link was established with the Hungarian troops which had advanced to Arad, apart from one Hungarian voluntary patrol that had pushed forward as far as Billéd.

On 19 September 1944, while the greater part of the 4th SS *Polizei* Division was still being brought up, a Soviet attack threw back the Hungarian troops at Arad. On 21 September 1944 the town fell, the *Honvéd* retreated towards Battonya, and the Soviets followed them. Once again a very dangerous situation was developing. If the enemy had pushed forward further westwards or northwestwards, they would have met only very weak resistance and the way to Budapest would have lain open! But the Soviets were deceived by misinformation. This suggested that the Wehrmacht had prepared an enormous grouping of forces, with 18 *Panzer* divisions, in western Hungary, to hit the advancing Red Army with all its strength. (In 1944, of course, these forces still only existed 'on the moon'.) For this reason the Soviets did not exploit their initial successes at Arad on 19 September 1944. Instead, they shifted their large-scale offensive to the Hungarian Plain and first tried a feint, swinging suddenly southwards in the direction of Belgrade.

In parallel with these events, further to the south, along both banks of the Danube in the Army Group F sector, the Soviets had also slowly but stubbornly advanced. On 22 September 1944 they began an attack across the Danube to the south of Turnu-Severin. That marked the beginning of the battle for Serbia. Soon the Soviets had the entire arc of the Danube in their hands. A serious crisis was imminent, since there were scarcely any German troops in the area. Therefore reinforcements had to be brought up.[1] It is true that parts of Police *Gebirgsjäger* Regiment 18, that had arrived from Greece on 25 September 1944, had advanced 30km into the Rumanian Banat along the Nera. However, after a few days, they too had to give way to the superior forces of the enemy and withdraw into the Lagerdorf/Straza/Temesör area (north-west of Weisskirchen). Similarly, a *Kampfgruppe* of the Division 'Brandenburg', advancing from the Werschetz area, had temporarily taken Deta, Jampal, Mare and Klopadia. On 29 September 1944 the Soviets broke through at Negotin and pushed on, in the direction of Bor, into Serbia.

The situation in the Banat was critical. Only in the north and south of the wide area of the Banat were there any German forces worth mentioning. At Temeschburg, the 4th SS *Polizei* Division, and in the Werschetz-Weisskirchen area a *Kampfgruppe* from Division 'Brandenburg' and Police *Gebirgsjäger* Regiment 18, in *Kampfgruppe* Hillebrandt, were all tied to their own front. By contrast, between the two groupings, i.e. between the southern wing of Army Group South and the northern wing of Army Group F, there was an enormous gap in the central Banat, with virtually no German troops. After they had at first held back from breaking through to the Hungarian Plain, and swinging southwards, Malinowski's troops then pushed into the gap from the Temeschburg area. They moved against Betschkerek, while two regiments advanced, through Steiersdorf/Anina, on Werschetz and Weisskirchen.

In the area of the main enemy thrust the Banat Deutsche *Volksgruppe* was, to all intents and purposes, thrown back on to its own resources and on to its *Deutsche Mannschaft* and its *Verfügungstruppe*.[2] The particular tragedy of the following combat actions it is necessary to describe in detail, not only to honour their involvement, but also because the combat actions that later followed in the Batschka were an exact continuation of the battle for the Banat.

---

1   These events at the front at Arad, Temeschburg and on the Danube were what caused the process of formation of the 'Kama' Division in the Batschka to be broken off.

2   In addition to the existing units of the *Deutsche Mannschaft* (DM), the *Volksgruppe* leadership of the Banat also formed from the end of August a so-called *Verfügungstruppe* (Home Defence) under the name *DM-Standarte* 'Michl Reiser'. This comprised 10 companies and a signals section and for the most part consisted of young men (18 and younger).

Battle for the Banat

30 September 1944

On the night of 28 September 1944 a strong Soviet breakthrough succeeded in the Modosch area. The enemy moved towards Setschan and Stefansfeld, which they reached on 30 September 1944. There, a company of *DM-Standarte* 'Michl Reiser' battled against the enemy vanguards and retook the village, capturing 15 Soviets. But the village could not be persuaded to evacuate and soon the company had to give way to the superior enemy force. In the afternoon Soviets also appeared in Lazarfeld.

1 October 1944

The Soviets continued to march on westwards. After the villages of Lazarfeld, Sigmundsfeld and Klek were occupied, a defensive ring crystallised around Betschkerek. It was already clear that a broad-based Soviet attack was imminent, directed at the one firm bridge over the Theiss at Rudolfsgnad-Titel. Even Army Group F at last realised that the attackers were not partisans, as had previously been thought, but regular Soviet troops. In response to the desperate and urgent telephone calls of the *Volksgruppe* leader, Dr Janko despatched Colonel Dünsing to Betschkerek to organise the defence. But even he at first had no troops at his disposal, apart from the *DM* and *Heimatschutz* units in the immediate vicinity, who now withdrew to Betschkerek. At last, just in the nick of time, Wehrmacht troops arrived by air. *Kampfgruppe* Walter of Division 'Brandenburg' (II/1st Regiment 'Brandenburg') came from Werschetz. 200 men from Assault Regiment 'Rhodes', Luftwaffe flak and ground staff, parts of *Sturmgeschütz Abteilung* 191 and one armoured train arrived. But during the afternoon it was no longer possible to land at the airfield. All these troops, on arrival, were placed under the command of the Division 'Brandenburg' Commander, *Generalleutnant* Kühlwein, and were given the name *Kampfgruppe* Kühlwein.

With the first forces that arrived, the armoured train, plus *Kampfgruppe* 'Brandenburg', plus two companies of *DM-Standarte* 'Michl Reiser', under Company Commander Krifka, an attack on Lazarfeld was launched as early as first light on 1 October 1944. Klek was fought free. Positions were established in and around Alexandrowo and at Klek. Artillery shells struck the enemy, who was dug in at Lazarfeld, and the attack went forward under the cover of the tank unit. But the enemy in Lazarfeld was already too strong. The armoured train received a direct hit and had to retreat. Nevertheless, half of the village was fought free.

In the community of Deutsch-Etschka, flak artillery from the airfield held up the Soviets until the afternoon, to keep the airfield open for flying in reinforcements. Under the increasing enemy pressure they gradually had to withdraw. The ring around Betschkerek closed tighter and tighter.

2 October 1944

During the morning the Soviets gained reinforcements, and three enemy divisions moved against Betschkerek. At 10am fighting was already going on at the edge of the town. Towards midday the sugar factory was lost and the bombardment of the town increased in strength. The evacuation of the German population of the town, to the extent that they were willing to go, was completed. At about 2pm the *Volksgruppe* leadership, the *DM*, the *Verfügungstruppe* and the Wehrmacht troops withdrew and crossed the Theiss over the pontoon bridge at Aradatz. At 4pm Betschkerek was in enemy hands.

The defenders of the hotly contested village of Bega-St.Georgen, the four companies of *DM-Standarte* 'Michl Reiser', units of the *DM*, of Division 'Brandenburg' and Wehrmacht Company 'Otto', also withdrew, through Deutsch-Elemer, avoiding Betschkerek, towards Aradatz.

On this day Werschetz, heroically defended under *SS-Sturmbannführer* Bachmann, also fell. 200 soldiers of the Wehrmacht, of *DM-Standarte* 'Michl Reiser' and of the *DM* were killed. Some 100 men were taken prisoner.

On 1 and 2 October 1944, parts of the Police *Gebirgsjäger* Regiment 18 were encircled in the area of Lagerdorf-Straza-Temesör. But they were able to break out and withdraw, fighting towards Pantschowa, which they held until 6 October 1944. However, the remaining villages of the southern Banat fell into enemy hands on 23 October 1944.

The northern Banat was still free of Soviets until 8 October 1944! The tragedy of the local German population was that they were not willing to be evacuated, although for some days they could still have fled in the direction of Szeged. But, because of their unwillingness, almost the entire German population fell into the power of Tito's partisans and the Soviets. The central and southern Banat, under much more difficult circumstances, could still reasonably have been evacuated safely. Unfortunately, there also, despite the constant urging of the *Volksgruppe* leadership, evacuation was not set under way in time. This failure to evacuate then led to the shattering tragedy of the German *Volksgruppe* in the Serbian Banat.

3 October 1944

The battalion of *DM-Standarte* 'Michl Reiser', including four companies under *Bannführer* Adam Paul, withdrew from Bega-St.Georgen. On 3 October 1944 they were still holding the Dt. Elemer railway station and only on that day withdrew to Aradatz. But the pontoon bridge had already been blown and once again the battalion suffered severe casualties from the enemy who were pushing up behind.

On 3 October 1944 the main fighting line in the Banat area ran approximately as follows. At Rudolfsgnad, a small bridgehead was being held on the eastern bank of the Theiss. From there the Theiss formed the main fighting line almost as far as Zenta, where it joined the broad land front of the 4th SS *Polizei* Division. This Division was located south of the Maros, in defensive positions, without support to left or right. On the western bank of the Theiss were Hungarian troops, mostly frontier *Jäger* units, and also at Zenta a section of hussars. Facing the Alt-Betsche bridgehead stood *Kampfgruppe* Kuhlwein with some Hungarian troops. At Titel, and at the Rudolfsgnad bridgehead, were parts of Assault Regiment 'Rhodes' with more Hungarian troops. On 1 October 1944, Hungarian artillery had taken up positions at Rudolfsgnad. That was a very important place. The refugees from the Banat travelled uninterruptedly across the Theiss bridge, and then into the free

Batschka. From there the main fighting line continued along the Danube as far as Pantschowa, where Police *Gebirgsjäger* Regiment 18 was holding a bridgehead.

Those were the events at the front that so aggravated the situation in the Batschka. The situation with partisan units was also becoming more and more ominous. The pressure to evacuate was constantly increasing. Conditions were becoming more and more chaotic, and the opportunities for forming troop units more and more impossible. On 6 October 1944, Pantschowa and with it practically the whole Banat, apart from a small bridgehead at Borcsa opposite Belgrade, was held by Police *Gebirgsjäger* Regiment 18. But on 10 October 1944, the whole area fell into Soviet hands. Thus, the situation in the Batschka became completely untenable.

The 31st SS Volunteer Grenadier Division, still in the process of formation, and the Muslims from the 23rd Waffen-SS *Gebirgs* Division 'Kama' (Croatian Nr 2), still in the Batschka, were moved away from the Batschka after 7 October 1944. The 31st SS Division was moved across the Danube into the Baranya. The leadership did not want to send the unprepared Division to be uselessly slaughtered. At the same time the evacuation of the Batschka Germans was under way, to which the 31st SS Division and the other German services in the Batschka lent assistance. The columns of Batschka German refugees crossed the Danube under the protection of the 31st SS. This evacuation lasted until about 15 October 1944, but it was only fully completed on 20 October 1944.

The situation with partisan units in the Batschka

In 1941 the Yugoslavian army had evacuated the Batschka after a few days. The Royal Hungarian *Honvéd* moved in without a shot being fired. But soon a Serbian underground movement developed, to which more and more partisans, some coming over from the Banat and Syrmia, attached themselves. A restricting effect on their activity was the fact that the Dobrowoljatzen, i.e. Serbian colonists, who had settled there after the First World War, had been expelled from the Batschka immediately after the Hungarian occupation. The result was that the partisans were deprived of their most important support. Vigorous and successful action by the Hungarian security services (on 5 October 1941 they even raided a meeting of communist spies), and the imposition of martial law, delivered severe setbacks time and time again to the terrorist band movement.

When finally, despite this action, the surprise attacks and acts of sabotage increased, after a particularly grim bloodbath in the Tscurug and Schabali area, the most vigorous action was taken. This was the notorious Razzia of January 1942 in the Tschaikist district and in Ujvidek-Neusatz, which finally broke the back of the prevailing partisan activity. It will not be gone into in any great detail here. In fact there were most regrettable incursions. But one thing is certain, the partisan movement which was growing up was not able to recover fully until well into 1944.[3]

3   This was also recognised by the leadership of the communist groups (report of Svetozar Markovic to Tito dated 10.9.1942). Should this not be ranked as a success? In Croatian areas and Italian areas of occupation soon a terrible hell was unleashed. But where Hungarians and Germans determined policy, such as in the Batschka, the Banat, and even in Serbia, under the National Serbian General Nedic, the flood of partisan was

Then, when an essentially peaceful policy superseded, the Batschka in the following two years, in stark contrast to the other former Yugoslavian districts, became an island of calm and peace. However, there were some isolated incidents of murder, and of arson, mostly on hemp factories and wheat stacks, which it was possible to contain. The ethnic German community guards carried out sentry duty in the village and in the fields. On one occasion at Paratbusch, together with the Hungarian police, they raided a terrorist hideout, and thus made their own 'contribution' to keeping the peace.

Only from the spring of 1944 did Tito consider that the time had again come, to be able to carry out larger scale acts of aggression. Three groups from Velickovic, Stojakovic and Alimpic were smuggled from Syrmia into the Batschka. Soon after that a goods train was blown up at Obrowatz. There was a surprise attack on the weapons depot in Dunagálos and Glozan. Railway bridges were blown up, people were ambushed and murdered, there were abductions and cases of arson. It is true that at the beginning of August 1944 these groups were again suffering very heavy reverses. But after 23 August 1944, when Romania suddenly pulled out of the war, they were reorganised so that they were stronger than ever. Surprise attacks became more frequent, when even military objects and community houses were attacked. The situation was becoming more and more ominous.

As well as the Hungarian gendarmerie, police, and *Honvéd*, the German security police and the Wehrmacht and Waffen-SS units located nearby were brought up to combat the partisans. But with the slow approach of the front it was less and less possible to bring under control a situation that was becoming more and more threatening. At the end of September, when the Soviets were already quite near to the Theiss, an open Serbian insurrection was feared! Voices were raised, urging that the German population be evacuated in time.

Even the recruits of the 31st SS Volunteer Grenadier Division could feel the growing menace that 'was in the air', so to speak. The situation deteriorated to such an extent that in many places the partisans quite openly rampaged through the streets. At first there were no attacks on members of the Division, but light clashes were reported in Bajmok, Topolya, Apatin and Zombor.

Anton Frei (I/79) reported:

> We were travelling with *SS-Unterscharführer* Wetzell, from Bácsalmás to Palanka, to fetch his parents. To travel about alone in the Batschka was at this time no longer particularly advisable for a German soldier. In Zombor we, too, became involved in a skirmish with snipers.

Over time, which here meant only days, such incidents multiplied. Attacks on men of the Division became more and more frequent, and more and more severe.

soon stemmed. The result was that in these districts until summer 1944 there was in essence scarcely any partisan activity. Without the Razzia, so often demonised, partisan activity in the Batschka, too, would have grown to the extent and assumed the forms that it did in the Balkans, which would have plunged the entire population of the Batschka into tremendous suffering. In any event, nothing is more indicative of the character of the partisan movement than that the name Tito was made up of the initial letters of the *Tajna Internacionalna Terroristicka Organizacia* (Secret International Terror Organisation).

On 10 October 1944, the seven SS men from Bulkes, Karl Klein, Peter Kurschner, Ludwig Weber, Jakob Lauterer, Philipp Walter, Anton Plein and Jakob Weissenbach, were ambushed and murdered by partisans in the vicinity of their home village!

Consideration was given to the possibility of bringing up the 31st SS Volunteer Grenadier Division to combat the partisans on a large scale. On 3 and 4 October 1944, there took place in Zombor, a meeting of the leaders of the Hungarian civilian and military authorities. The town commandant of Neusatz, *Oberstleutnant* Béla Rosza, mentioned that "to combat the partisans alongside the Hungarian forces, the Batschka SS Division that was being formed would be sufficient".

But two days later the Hungarian authorities gave up the Batschka, nor was the Division used for larger-scale actions. This was all the more the case since from 7 October 1944 it had begun to withdraw into Swabian Turkey, providing escort to the columns of evacuated ethnic German refugees who were also beginning their journey. It was thanks to this escort that the partisans did not dare to attack the departing refugee columns, as their 'respect' for the SS was still too healthy for that.

It is only known of Fusilier Battalion 31 that on 6 and 7 October 1944 in the Alt-Betsche area, which was more severely plagued by the Communist partisan movement than the western Batschka, it was involved in fighting with communist groups. Ten days later, the delaying fighting of *Kampfgruppe* Syr in the Alt-Betsche–Szenttamás area was over, and SS Fusilier Battalion 31 was the last unit of the Division to cross over to the western bank of the Danube north of Apatin. There they again clashed with Titoist groups, on 16 to 19 October 1944, suffering further considerable casualties.

CHAPTER 6

Evacuation of the Batschka Germans and the Withdrawal of the 31st SS Division

7-20 October 1944

The plans for evacuating the ethnic Germans in Hungary, especially in northern Transylvania and the Batschka, had already been thoroughly prepared during September. As early as the beginning of September the evacuation orders came from the *Volksdeutsche Mittelstelle* to Hungary. These ordered that preparations were to be made in time for evacuation. Of course, this did not happen without the approval, even the orders, of *Reichsführer-SS* Heinrich Himmler and Adolf Hitler himself.

In the first days of October, the Soviets were pushing forward, in places, as far as the Theiss. The activity of partisan groups was becoming more and more of a threat, leading to the expectation that soon much worse was in store. Thus the question of evacuating the ethnic Germans in the Batschka became precarious. So that, at first, the implementation of the well-prepared evacuation plans was forbidden. There were many reasons for this.

Above all, there was an economic reason, in that time was needed to secure the large stocks of agricultural products of the rich Batschka agricultural land, to complete the harvest and import it to Germany. The agricultural contribution of the Batschka was still considered to be highly important to the war economy.

The other reasons were of a political, or rather military-political character. The political situation in Hungary was so tense that with a premature evacuation of the Batschka an outbreak of panic had to be feared. This would threaten to have an effect on the attitude of the government and the morale of the *Honvéd*. Then, at the same time as the representative of the German Reich was declaring to the Hungarian government that the Reich would protect Hungary's borders as if they were its own, came the question, 'could not this declaration be counteracted', if there were an early evacuation of the ethnic Germans?

As well as the political considerations, a strategic consideration also played a part. The highest leadership wanted to hold the Balkans at all costs because it was hoped that, in their victorious progress, the Soviets would also attack the Bosphorus and thus come into conflict with the British. In such a case of conflict, Britain would be able to make good use of German assistance, which would bring about a strategic change of direction. This was their vain hope.

At the highest level there was a fourth reason for the dislike of the prospect of evacuation. It had been observed, when the Soviets were marching in to the German settlements in the Rumanian Banat and Transylvania that, in their plundering, raping, and other acts of violence they did not ask about their victims' nationality. It was observed that there were no worse attacks made on Germans, simply because they were German, than were made upon people of other nationalities. It was therefore thought that the assumption could be made that things would be no different in the former Yugoslavian districts of the Serbian Banat and in the Batschka. This was not only irresponsible and morally unjustifiable, but it was also fundamentally wrong. In spite of this, some Reich authorities fantasised that the German ethnic group, when it had been passed over by the Soviets, would ignite a partisan war behind the Soviets' backs.

This was a stupid supposition to make, of a people who had always had a great reverence for order. What made it even worse was that it had been completely overlooked that fact that the Titoist groups would, with Soviet help, seize power. The mission of these groups had often been declared. As early as 1943, in Jajca, they had anchored in the constitution for the new republic. They planned nothing less than the total extermination of the German ethnic group, irrespective as to whether, as the ethnic German historian Johann Wüscht put it, "the individual Germans had been angels or saints, whether they had had a *Kulturbund* and a 'Prinz Eugen' Division or they had not".

It was these considerations, outlined in detail above, which even at the beginning of October, when the Soviets were already feeling their way forward across the Theiss, stayed German hands and resulted in a strict ban on evacuation. For all that, there was no shortage of opposing voices. The German Embassy (Ambassador and Reich Plenipotentiary Dr Edmund Veesenmayer), and particularly the ethnic culture expert, Dr Rudolf Meckel, placed a higher priority on the evacuation of the German population than on securing agricultural stocks, and pressed for evacuation to be made in time, in fact, 'the sooner the better'. Similarly, the *Volksgruppe* leadership pressed for evacuation. The *Volksgruppe* leadership directed attention above all to the events in the Banat. During the first days of October the refugee columns from the Serbian Banat were travelling through the villages of the Batschka and were spreading the most awful horror stories.

While the German refugees from the Banat, whose faces showed their horror, were causing unrest among the local population, the *Volksgruppenführer* Banat, Dr Sepp Janko, hurried to Dr Basch and raised panic there. He said that, in the Banat, a disaster for the German population had resulted from the ban on evacuation. The ban had been maintained for too long, and even worse, was the fact that the evacuation was carried out too late. Janko begged Basch not to listen to anyone any more and to order the evacuation immediately. In this way he believed that Basch would not be in the same position as himself, Janko, who was being held responsible for everything. But, from all sides at once, his hands were being tied. Janko's accusations against the Reich German authorities were so strong that his statements were even labelled as deserving of a court-martial. In reality the situation was dramatic, as well as extremely confused.

Meanwhile, preparations were also beginning for the withdrawal of the 31st SS Volunteer Grenadier Division from the Batschka to Transdanubia. Understandably, this gave even more cause for concern to the families of Division members who were to remain at home. Also seriously concerned was the Divisional Commander, *SS-Oberführer* Lombard. In the eyes of the people, the 31st SS Division and its commander were responsible for their fate. On the other hand, Lombard feared adverse effects on his soldiers if their families were left behind.

This viewpoint of the military man was mixed with that of the purely human being and, although Lombard had nothing to do with the ban on evacuation, he set himself unflinchingly against it.

In describing this sequence of events we shall be following the text of the periodical *Der Freiwillige* of 1975, which refers back to Lombard's actual words. According to this source, things developed as follows:

> On 5 October 1944 *SS-Obergruppenführer* Lorenz, Head of the *Volksdeutsche Mittelstelle*, responsible for resettlement and migration, arrived at the headquarters of the district leadership in Zombor. He passed on a Führer order that specified that the Batschka Germans were not to be allowed to be moved to the West. *SS-Oberführer* Lombard had spent the night of 5 October 1944 with *Kampfgruppe* Syr on the Theiss. When he returned next morning to Neu-Werbass, the Ia, *SS-Sturmbannführer* Reuter, reported as a 'significant event', the fact that *SS-Obergruppenführer* Lorenz had arrived in Zombor with an order from the Führer concerning a ban on the movement of the Batschka Germans. During the night, Dr Krämer and Sepp Spreitzer from the Batschka district leadership hurried to the Division to ask for help. Lombard asked Lorenz to come to see him immediately, and Lorenz agreed to do so without delay. The outcome of the conversation, between him and the Divisional *Kommandeur*, was that both drove to the German Embassy in Budapest, because only a personal conversation with Himmler promised any hope of the Führer's order being lifted. By means of the Division's 100-watt transmitter, a radio bridge between Budapest and the Ia in Neu-Werbass was set up mid-way. Lorenz and Lombard arrived in Budapest at about 10pm. The Ambassador fully understood. The call was booked. Good fortune smiled. Himmler was contacted immediately.

This conversation is described in a situation of high drama. At the same time it is a model of how, with the necessary courage, a man can refuse to comply with orders, even from the highest authorities. It is truly an example of 'men's courage before the thrones of kings'. There follow the words of *Brigadeführer* Lombard himself, a conversation which he described, in his own inimitable way, to his circle of comrades:

> The Ambassador: '*Herr Reichsführer*, with me are *SS-Obergruppenführer* Lorenz and *SS-Oberführer* Lombard, who must speak to you on an urgent matter. Before I hand you over to the *Obergruppenführer*, may I stress that I fully subscribe to their suggestions. I am handing you over.'
>
> Lorenz: '*Reichsführer*, it concerns the implementation of the Führer order known to you concerning the non-resettlement of the Batschka Germans. I am handing you over to *SS-Oberführer* Lombard.'
>
> Lombard: '*Reichsführer*, I respectfully beg that arrangements be made this very night for the Führer order to be lifted. It concerns the families, parents, wives and children of the men of my Division.'
>
> Himmler interrupted. Until then he had only said at the beginning, '*Heil* Hitler, Lombard, what's the matter?' He then said, 'Lombard, you know that an order from the Führer is sacred to me'.
>
> Now I could interrupt him, and shouted, pushing my luck as far as it would go: 'I know that, *Reichsführer*, and that is why I am having this conversa-

tion. Because only the *Reichsführer* can prove to the Führer that it is impossible to carry out this order. Most of the Division will desert, and whether the Batschka Germans will really accept it as the order implies, should also not be taken for granted.'

Himmler said something, but I went on speaking and ended with the concluding sentence that I had been working out throughout the entire journey: '*Reichsführer*, what it is, is that the Führer has been wrongly advised, so wrongly I must insist, that whoever advised him can only have been, at best, an ignoramus who hasn't got a clue. *Reichsführer*, you must go to the Führer, now, immediately. The only thing at stake is the fate of a 100,000 Batschka Germans.'

There was a pause for the fraction of a second that seemed like an eternity. I heard him ask his adjutant something, then he said to me: 'I'll call you back. Remain available, Lombard, where you are now'.

Long after midnight there came a call from Führer Headquarters. Lorenz was asked for. 'Führer order rescinded. Tell Lombard that the Führer is making him responsible for the smooth implementation of the Batschka evacuation, including taking it across the Danube.

When I arrived back in Neu-Werbass next morning, Reuter reported to me as a significant development that the evacuation of the Batschka had begun! There's a great deal of difference between refusing to obey an order and insisting that it is rescinded!

Here ends the description of events according to Lombard's recollections. What effect did his courageous personal intervention actually have on the course of events? Today, more is known about the background and the circumstances that, at the time, must have been to a certain extent hidden from *SS-Oberführer* Lombard. Above all, one thing must be set straight. No single document is known, concerning the ban on evacuation of the Batschka Germans which could be regarded as a 'Führer order', or even anything similar. So Lombard is mistaken when he says that the evacuation had been prevented by a Führer order that had been passed on to him by Lorenz. There was no Führer order, but nevertheless the ban actually existed by reason of the considerations outlined earlier. There is also no doubt that to maintain this ban, during the first days of October, was being seen as very dangerous.

The explanation for these contradictions is simple. The reference to a supposed 'Führer order' in ordering the ban, was the result of a practice that was, unfortunately, all too often followed at that time. It was thought that orders could be better carried out, by referring back to the authority of a 'Führer order'. Thus an attempt could be falsely made to lend weight to a 'real' Führer order. So this was not an isolated case.

With the precise object of investigating the situation for himself, and of assessing the need to maintain the ban, or of allowing the possibility of the planned resettlement to go ahead, *Obergruppenführer* Lorenz, Head of the *Volksdeutsche Mittelstelle*, personally stayed in the Batschka from 2 October 1944. During that time he consulted with various bodies. He met, among others, the *Volksgruppe* leadership, and *SS-Oberführer* Lombard. Lombard was commander of the Batschka Division that was in the process of formation. During their conversation *SS-Oberführer* Lombard expressed his point of view very forcefully to *SS-Obergruppenführer* Lorenz, and a little later also to the *Reichsführer-SS*, Heinrich

Himmler. His reports had great weight. He pointed out that because of the fact that very little progress had been made in the formation of the 31st SS Volunteer Grenadier Division, it was impossible to count on remaining for any length of time in the Batschka. He also reported that the new soldiers could not be held in check, if their families were not removed in time from the Soviet danger.

That point of view was supported by other considerations requiring that the resettlement should be allowed to go ahead. The considerations raised by the situation had changed in the meantime. The process of securing agricultural products had partly been completed, and had partly become pointless anyway, on account of the precarious situation. Even the consideration that the Hungarian allies would accept an evacuation of the German population had become redundant. This was because, at about the same time that Lombard was telephoning Himmler, the southern Hungarian authorities also had 'shouted from the rooftops' their order. They ordered that the Hungarian population (meaning, in the first instance, the Hungarian so-called Csángós who had resettled from Bukovina into the Batscka after 1941) should take itself into safety.

It was only *Obergruppenführer* Lorenz's fact-finding trip that invalidated the earlier considerations of 'holding back' the evacuation, and allowed new considerations to arise concerning 'letting it go ahead'. The Führer had ordered that no German woman and no German child should fall into the hands of the Soviets. In this connection, *SS-Oberführer* Lombard's personal intervention, and his arguments, added a great deal of weight, and probably provided the immediate impetus towards allowing the resettlement to go ahead. But these were not the only deciding factors. That of course, did not by one jot diminish the high moral value of his actions.

From this point onwards, the officers of the *Volksdeutsche Mittelstelle*, *SS-Obergruppenführer* Lorenz, the Senior SS and Police Commander Hungary, *SS-Obergruppenführer* Otto Winckelmann, the Ambassador, Dr Veesenmayer, the *Volksgruppe* leadership, and Dr Basch, were able to set the evacuation of the Batschka Germans under way.

It was to proceed in two stages. The evacuation of the communities south of the Franz Joseph Canal was ordered for 7 October 1944. The provincial youth leader Kohler announced this in Werbass on the night of 7 October 1944. Soon the refugee columns set off. On 10 October 1944, total evacuation of the communities north of the Franzen Canal was ordered. Soon, an uninterrupted column 120km in length was formed, moving on the Zombor-Dunaföldvár highway towards the bridge at Dunaföldvár. (The bridge over the Danube, at Baja, was destroyed by American bombers on 21 September 1944). A smaller number of refugees crossed the Danube by ferry at Bezdán, Mohács and Baja.

From 7 October 1944, the 31st SS Volunteer Grenadier Division, still in the process of formation, moved across the Danube. At first the rearward services and the Medical *Abteilung* were withdrawn, as early as 7 October to 9 October 1944. At about the same time, the Artillery Regiment also moved. I *Abteilung* Artillery Regiment marched out of Tscherwenka on 8 October 1944, spent the night in Zombor, and on 9 October 1944 crossed the Danube by ferry at Bezdán.

SS Volunteer Grenadier Regiment 78 followed the Artillery Regiment, also via Bezdán. The ferry crossing at Bezdán was very important because it was the most southerly crossing point over the Danube in Hungary. Along the sector of the Danube's western bank, further to the south of this, there are no villages, only extended wooded floodplains. The next crossing point at Vukovar goes in to Croatia. For this reason all the Divisional units south of the Franzen Canal crossed the Danube at Bezdán.

SS Volunteer Grenadier Regiment 79, located north of the Franzen Canal did not set off until the evacuation for the communities in that part of the Batschka was also ordered, i.e. not before 10 October 1944. The crossing point for this regiment, and the other parts of the Division in the same area, was the ferry crossing near the town of Baja. Probably the ferries at Mohács and at Dunaszekcsö were also used to a lesser extent. However, strong contingents of this regiment remained behind and secured the withdrawal. Thus on 15 October 1944 some units, when other Divisional units had already set themselves up west of the Danube, were still in positions before Bacsalmas and only on 18 October 1944 did they leave the Batschka at Baja. They were the last unit of the regiment to do so.

The last section of the 31st SS Volunteer Grenadier Division to cross the Danube was the combat echelon of the Division, *Kampfgruppe* Syr, i.e. the reinforced SS Fusilier Battalion 31, which held out until the last on the Theiss. The badly weakened battalion, which had also been involved in fighting with partisan groups, arrived in Kisköszeg via Bezdán on 20 October 1944.

Since the movement of the 31st SS Division ran in parallel, in terms both of time and of route, with the evacuation of the Batschka Germans, the Division formed to a certain extent an armed protection for the departing refugees. Without this protection there would certainly have been partisan attacks on the refugees, but such instances did not occur (only a single instance is known[1]). There was still a healthy 'respect' for the SS.

Although the arrangement, organisation and implementation of the movement of the refugees was not the Division's responsibility, often the Division provided welcome help to the refugees. Some known instances are drawn from various local chronicles:

In Sekitsch, the evacuation was arranged by *SS-Sturmbannführer* Sepp Syr himself (Commander, SS Volunteer Grenadier Regiment 79). On 9 October 1944, in his command post in Topolya, he learned from the Sekitsch teacher Franz Glöckner that there was no evacuation order in Sekitsch. This order for the communities north of the Franzen Canal was indeed only issued on 10 October 1944. He sent a motorcycle despatch rider, as a courier to the mayor and local group leader of Sekitsch, with instructions to begin the evacuation immediately. This order was announced at 8pm and, as early as the night of 9 October 1944, eighty to eighty-five horse-drawn vehicles were moving northwards. The Fekitsch refugee column joined them.

In Kula the officers of SS Artillery Regiment 31 based there, arranged the evacuation, organised and set the first column on its way on 8 October 1944.

In Gajdobra the ethnic Germans were only able to decide on 12 October 1944 to leave their home village, and only after being urged by the unit of the 31st SS

---

1 In Katsch, a group tried to fire on the refugee column as it was leaving, but the local police immediately eliminated the nest, together with its secret transmitter and weapons, and set the house on fire.

Volunteer Grenadier Division stationed there, and after the evacuation had been repeatedly announced.

From this unit of the Division stationed in Gajdobra, an *Untersturmführer* with thirteen men went into the neighbouring village of Bulkes to implement the evacuation there, too. At first his attempt met with little success! Only when seven SS men had been ambushed and murdered by partisans did the development of opinion among the population change, so that some of them in fact set off on 11 and 12 October 1944.

The company of the 31st SS Division quartered in Despot-Sankt-Iwan saw to it that the villagers were provided with vehicles and began to flee in time. Their flight then proceeded in an orderly fashion.

Out of the Divisional units, Batschka German men were often released and given leave to help out with the evacuation of their fellow-countrymen. So, for instance, on 10 October 1944, Hans Klenz, given leave from his unit that was already in Swabian Turkey, prompted the evacuation of his home parish of Obrowatz. Until then it had not taken place, despite instructions to leave.

It is true that instances are also known when the 31st SS Division was reproached for having, in some cases, disrupted the evacuation of the population through measures which were militarily necessary, e.g. requisitioning horse-drawn vehicles for its own withdrawal. Certainly there were such instances. But it is also certain that no-one who desired to flee was left behind, on account of vehicles being requisitioned by the military. It must be taken into consideration that vehicles of Germans who did not wish to evacuate, and who stayed at home, and vehicles of other nationalities too, were requisitioned and claimed. Thus, both for the military and for civilian refugees, enough vehicles were finally available. In the village chronicle of Miletitsch it is recognised that, in spite of the lack of 66 horse-drawn vehicles requisitioned by *SS-Sturmbannführer* Schneider on 6 October 1944, those of the population who wished to flee were still able to evacuate in time. In the end it all happened fairly smoothly.

Of course, not only the 31st SS Volunteer Grenadier Division but also all the officers and units of the Army, the Luftwaffe and even the Navy stationed in the Batschka did their best to provide valuable help in the hasty evacuation. In several places (in Kutura, Altker, Hodschag etc) the Luftwaffe put lorries at the disposal of the refugees. In Jarek, the commander of the Luftwaffe Command based there, *Oberst* Böhme, systematically prepared the evacuation so that it happened in time, as early as 7 and 8 October 1944, and too in an exemplary manner. That was also the case in Titel where another Luftwaffe *Oberst* arranged the evacuation, as early as 3 October 1944, i.e. on his own responsibility, because at that time not even the Hungarian evacuation order had been issued.

Thus as early as 3 October 1944, many inhabitants of Titel departed by train, and the first refugee column set off on 4 October 1944. The very last refugees from the village were transported away on 11 October 1944 on Wehrmacht vehicles. For the inhabitants of Schajkatsch-Sankt-Iwan, who had no vehicles, the Neusatz Wehrmacht HQ made a goods-train available. Some communities fled on the Danube, such as some of those from Neusatz and Futok who evacuated on barges under escort from the German Danube Flotilla. Some left from Apatin where a Luftwaffe Command organised barges, motor boats and small boats. The

Heimatschutz units of the Deutsche *Volksgruppe* also made their own contribution to the evacuation.

From the above instances that are actually known to us, it is clear that, even if what is usually said, "The 31st SS Volunteer Grenadier Division brought 80,000 to 100,000 Batschka Germans back with them", is not exactly true, the 31st SS Division did play a distinctive and essential part in events that could not have happened without them.

In the above account, the question of 'willingness to evacuate' often occurred. In fact the Batschka Germans were divided on this question! Therefore the southern and the northern Batschka must be treated separately, because the latter were to go back to Yugoslavia, the former remained in Hungary. Those facts are by no means immaterial in judging the question.

The questions applied to both parts of the country. The panic caused by the passing columns of Banat German refugees had created a willingness to flee in many, but by no means all, sections of the population. When at the end of September this panic was over, the greater part of the Batschka Germans once again nurtured false hopes. Many believed that the coup would play itself out no differently than in 1918-1920 and that nothing would happen to them, since they represented no threat to anyone. Even the representatives of the Church, especially the Catholic Church, who were already against the *Volksbund*, SS, and National Socialism, often declared that the Germans had nothing to fear from the Soviets and that the claimed atrocities were only 'National Socialist propaganda'.[2]

The strong bond of Danubian Swabians with their land also contributed to the fact that a considerable number, despite urging, and attempts at compulsory evacuation, could not bring themselves to flee, but stayed at home. In the southern Batschka many Germans gave credence to well-intentioned recommendations from many decent Serbian neighbours. In 1941 they themselves had often intervened to help, in the certainty that the Serbians would vouch for them. However, in the northern Batschka, that was to remain in Hungary, the Germans believed that they were safe from the clutches of Tito's partisans.

So it happened, in the southern Batschka, that there were indeed settlements from where almost all Germans had fled. But there were also many settlements from where only a few families fled. In general, it can be said that in the average village in the southern Batschka, about a third of the German population stayed at home and fell into the hands of the new Yugoslavian rulers. The claims that estimate the number of those evacuated at 80,000 to 100,000 are therefore rather overestimated. In actual fact, 65,200 persons were evacuated from the southern Batschka, to which were added only a few thousands from the northern Batschka. There were still over 30,000 soldiers in the field. But in the homeland of the southern Batschka 80,300 persons stayed behind, a number that exceeds the number of those evacuated! It was a terrible fate that soon came to those who had stayed at home. Unimaginable atrocities happened, mass murders and individual murders,

2 What had the Church expected from the Bolsheviks? It is a fact, that while in the church that formed the property of the *SS Ordensburg* in Wewelsburg in Westphalia, divine services ran on, undisturbed, until the end of the war. Of the churches that had come under Red domination in the Batschka – together with their villages and populations - in a few years virtually all that was left were ruins!

deportation and total expropriation of property. Never had Germans to suffer more than under Tito's murderers.

In the villages of the northern Batschka that were to remain in Hungary, the rate of evacuation was very low. Only a few families set out to flee, with the result that very nearly the entire German population remained at home. In these villages, too, Titoist groups coming over the Trianon frontier set up a short-lived reign of terror. For a time it even seemed as if this area, too, would be snatched away from Hungary. In the end, that did not happen. So the Batschka Germans did not come to feel the full force of the Tito terror. They were 'only' exposed to the deportations to enforced labour in the Soviet Union, expropriation, being driven out and various kinds of harassment at the hands of the new Hungarian 'People's Democracy'.

After the refugee columns had crossed the Danube, they were given temporary quarters in western Hungary. The 280 SS men and 10 SS officers of the evacuation command, under *SS-Standartenführer* Weibgen, organised and directed the refugees. They found possibilities for accommodation and supplies in a western Hungary crammed to bursting with refugees. The Batschka Germans had to remain there until 14 November 1944. Only when it was declared that accommodation for them was available in the Reich could they move on, sometimes loaded on trains. By the 6 December 1944 the last Batschka German refugee had left Hungary.

In the Reich, the region of Silesia was determined as the main area for receiving the Batschka German refugees. It was there that most of them were accommodated, even before Christmas. People from Brestowatz went to Frankenstein. Those from Karawukowa went to Fellhammer near Waldenburg. The people from Gajdobra went to Ohls and Strehlen. Those from Obrowatz went to Glatz, Ols, Liegnitz and Landeshut. People from Despot-St-Iwan went to Militsch. Those from Schajkasch-St-Iwan went to Malsch. The people from Waldneudorf went to Hirschberg. Those from Josefsdorf went to Friedrichsgrund near Habelschwerdt. Some of those from Torschau went to Reichenstein in the county of Glatz. Some of those from Palanka went to Grünberg, the most northerly German, Silesian winegrowing district. People from Batsch-Neudorf went to Landeshut. Those from Altker went to Oberlauterbach in *Kreis* Jauer. Those from Tschonopol went to Göllschau, Liegnitz, Goldberg, Hirschberg, Jauer and Löwenberg. People from Batsch-Monoschtor went into *Kreis* Trebnitz. Those from Sekitsch went to Reichenbach. The people from Siwatz went into *Kreis* Goldberg. Those from Gakow went to Habelschwerdt, and people from Dorosslo and Filipowa went into the area round Breslau.

Even those from Batsch, Paratbusch, Weprowatz and some of those from Wekerledorf went to Silesia. A smaller number of the Batschka Germans were accommodated in other regions of the Reich. Thus the people from Teletschka were accommodated in the district of Grieskirchen in Upper Austria, some of those from Torschau in Wals near Salzburg, some of those from Palanka in East Saxony, some of those from Wekerledorf in the Sudetenland and in Lower Bavaria. Of course, too long a stay in Silesia was not granted to the Batschka Germans who were accommodated there. Soon they had to flee again, together with their Silesian hosts, from many places as early as in January and February 1945, from others in April and May 1945.

The remarkable thing in this connection is that a large number of the evacuated Batschka Germans went, in December 1944, into those Silesian districts which two months later had become the area in which the 31st SS Volunteer Grenadier Division was fighting. The possibility that a refugee family would meet again their husband, father or son serving in the 31st SS Division was by no means unlikely. It is not known whether such reunions actually took place, but the fact that the Batschka German men of the 31st SS Division were, in their fight, directly protecting their families, no doubt gave them moral strength.

CHAPTER 7

Battles in the Batschka and
Kampfgruppe Syr

While the majority of the Division was in the early stages of its formation, it began its withdrawal to the western bank of the Danube. The combat actions thus encroached upon the Batschka.

Malinowski's 2nd Ukrainian Front, which had recently, in a manoeuvre planned as a feint, swung in the direction of Belgrade as far as Pantschowa. They did not cross the Danube here, but, 'arriving at the threshold of Belgrade, took the historical route that the Turks had used in earlier centuries'. On 6 October 1944 they turned north-westwards, crossed the Theiss and pushed into Hungary. The large-scale offensive was begun from the general area between Arad and Grosswardein with three attacking wedges. They went from the Arad–Gyula area north-westwards, to the south of Arad and westwards over the Theiss, and north-westwards between Nagyszalonta and Grosswardein. (Incidentally, the shift of the large-scale Soviet attack, planned as a feint, only benefited the Axis forces, in that their defensive forces could roll on into eastern Hungary to prepare a reception for the Soviets who were now finally beginning their move).

South of Arad the enemy prepared for a push westwards on Szeged. The positions of the 4th SS *Polizei Panzergrenadier* Division became untenable on 6 October 1944. On 7 October 1944 the push from the south, in the Coka area, against Zenta, also met them. On this day Zenta was reported by Hungarian troops to be still free of the enemy. During the evening other parts of the Division were attacked by an enemy armoured thrust in the Törökkanizsa area. The units in the Coka area crossed the Theiss at Zenta and began the march along the Zenta–Magyarkanizsa–Horgos road to Szeged, which they reached on 8 October 1944. Zenta was evacuated without a fight on the night of 7 October 1944. On 8 October 1944 the Soviets also crossed at Törökkanizsa and slowly felt their way forwards.

These local attacks, however, were only 'side-shows' of the main thrust of the southern attacking wedge which ran along the Maros, where the enemy on 9 October 1944 pressed on the south-eastern edge of the town with several divisions. There, Hungarian troops held them back, while the enemy forces advancing northwards through Horgos and Röszke were brought to a halt by counter-attacks of the 4th SS *Polizei* Division.

Because enemy groups, which had advanced further north on 10 October 1944 had already penetrated into Kecskemét, the situation looked very serious. On 11 October 1944 Szeged was given up. The Hungarian troops were pushed back to the line Kiskundorozsma Lake area–Algyö.

In the area to the north-east there began the great tank battle on the Puszta at Debrecen. The 4th SS *Polizei* Division was then also brought up into that sector. It resulted in a great gap to the Danube appearing approximately between Horgos and Alt-Betsche. From Csongrád, to around Szeged in the north-west, there were three Hungarian divisions: the 1st Hussar Division, and the 8th and the 23rd Reserve Divisions, to which *Brigadeführer* Lombard testified. North of Szabadka was the 3rd River Blockade Section. At the same time the Soviets already had several bridgeheads on the western bank of the Theiss (Mindszent, Csongrád, etc.).

On the lower Theiss, at Alt-Betsche and Titel, things only then began to 'hot up', when Szeged had already fallen. At best, the Batschka simply remained a third-rank theatre of war, in which, from the point of view of the overall picture, both on the Soviet and on the German sides only insignificant forces were in action.

To these battles combat-ready parts of the withdrawing 31st SS Volunteer Grenadier Division, together with the Muslims of the 'Kama' who had remained behind, were also brought up. That was testified by a telegram of 9 October 1944 from the *Befehlshaber der Waffen-SS* Hungary, according to which "the combat-ready parts of *SS-Oberführer* Lombard's new Division, together with the Bosnians of the 'Kama' are to be thrown into the battle".

These parts of the 31st SS Division, mostly from Fusilier Battalion 31 and also from SS Volunteer Grenadier Regiment 79, were placed under the command of *SS-Sturmbannführer* Sepp Syr and called after him, *Kampfgruppe* Syr. As early as 5 October 1944 it was taking up positions on the Theiss, on both sides of Alt-Betsche, a move at which the Divisional Commander, *SS-Oberführer* Lombard, was present far into the night. It was, least tactically, placed under the command of *Kampfgruppe* Kühlwein from the Division 'Brandenburg' (*Generalleutnant* Kühlwein).

Little is known about the details of *Kampfgruppe* Syr. Even its strength can no longer be determined with any certainty. But a telegram dated 7 October 1944, from the *Befehlshaber der Waffen-SS* Hungary, speaks of "combat-ready parts of Division Lombard, including the Muslims of the 'Kama' Division (2,600 men) deployed on the Theiss to protect the Batschka". According to this, *Kampfgruppe* Syr also comprised Muslims, which cannot be completely excluded, but nevertheless is not very probable.

The deployment in action of *Kampfgruppe* Syr was the first deployment of a unit of the 31st SS Division. *SS-Oberführer* Lombard, too, recalled this *Kampfgruppe* in his memoirs, when he wrote:

> When I became Divisional Commander, during the first days of October, the process of formation was still under way. But we were able (thanks to the large numbers of former reservists from the Hungarian and Yugoslavian Armies joining us) to send into action a *Kampfgruppe* which played its part in ensuring that after the conquest of Romania the Soviets stopped short before central and southern Hungary. Before the formation area of my Division, the 'Brandenburg' was the only single German unit, but that, too, was only more or less a *Kampfgruppe*. In addition, there were there another three Hungarian divisions, certainly far to the left of us, but really reliable, not least thanks to their commanding generals.

12 October 1944

On 12 October 1944 the Soviets began, with two to three divisions, to push into the Batschka over the Theiss at Alt-Betsche. Hungarian Frontier *Jäger* from the

16th Frontier *Jäger* Battalion, *Kampfgruppe* Kühlwein, about 400 men strong (parts of Division 'Brandenburg' and StuG Brigade 191, command post at first in Josefsdorf), together with *Kampfgruppe* Syr held them up. The fighting lasted until 15 October 1944, when the front in the area of Szenttamás-Srbobran stiffened and a pause in the fighting ensued.

13 October 1944

Since the enemy had broken through at Alt-Betsche, the forces in the extreme south-east of the Batschka were threatened with being cut off. Therefore, during the morning of 13 October 1944, the Rudolfsgnad bridgehead was evacuated, after the church tower, which could have served the enemy as an artillery observation post, and the big bridge over the Theiss were blown sky-high. Among the forces making their withdrawal here was also the III Battalion/1 Regiment 'Brandenburg' which up to 12 October 1944 had to undergo hard fighting, with many casualties, against 9 large enemy groups on the curve of the Danube north of Belgrade. There was also the Hungarian *Kampfgruppe* Deák, whose 2 companies were also in action in the Banat.

15 October 1944

The situation at the front at Szenttamás on the Franzen Canal, however, was any-thing but clear. A corporal of the Division 'Brandenburg', J.A., born in Kula, to whom we owe this account, was sent off to reconnoitre the situation to the rear of the *Kampfgruppe*.

> No-one had any idea how far the Soviets had already advanced and whether it was still possible to get through to Kula. In Werbass there were still men of the 23rd Waffen-SS *Gebirgs* Division 'Kama' (Croatian Nr 2), but these too knew nothing about the Soviets' progress. Just as in enemy territory, one had to reckon with coming into contact with the enemy at any moment. But Kula was also still free of the enemy as a Hungarian unit was there. (Nevertheless, some Soviets had filtered through. On 15 October 1944 a reconnaissance unit arrived in Kleinker, i.e. far to the west of Kula, but no contact was established with it).
>
> Meanwhile, the news of Horthy's proclamation was being passed along, so that people were really uncertain. The Hungarian commanders here, however, gave assurances that they would fight on.
>
> On the day when the main line of resistance at Szenttamás was still firmly in our hands, Soviet reconnaissance units that had set out from the Szeged area appeared far to the north-west, in Orszállás. The southern Batschka was thus practically cut off!

16 October 1944

On 16 October 1944 the III/1st Regiment 'Brandenburg' (Wandrey, then John, later Friedrichsmeier) having been released as the Rudolfsgnad bridgehead was evacuated, arrived as a welcome reinforcement in Szenttamás. They joined up with *Kampfgruppe* Kühlwein and the II/1st Regiment 'Brandenburg' that had been in position there since 2 October 1944. As early as 16 October 1944 the newly arrived battalion was given the task of counter-attacking.

18 October 1944

On 18 October 1944, the Soviets mounted a tank attack on Szenttamás, on a broad front from the north and from the east. Here the Hungarian infantry evacuated their positions after the first shots were fired. The 16th Frontier *Jäger* Battalion marched away via Neusatz. Groups that had lodged in the town opened fire in their rear. But the gunners of the Neusatz Frontier *Jäger*, almost all of whom were from Kula, gave further support to *Kampfgruppe* Kühlwein.

There were many casualties in the fighting. Even the commander of the III/1st Regiment 'Brandenburg', *Hauptmann* John, was shot in the stomach and taken to the main dressing station in Carlowatz (opposite Neusatz). There was little of a coherent main line of resistance. Indicative was the fact that, even as early as this date, when the defensive fighting at Szenttamás was at its height, an advance force of Soviets appeared 30 kilometres north-west of Tscherwenka. As darkness fell the 'Brandenburg' forces also had to withdraw. The withdrawal took place after those who were killed in the fighting had been buried in the Orthodox cemetery of Szenttamás. Fighting was also taking place at Sekitsch. Some 30 to 40 men, who were in all probability from *Kampfgruppe* Syr made a brief attempt to defend the village. A Soviet officer was killed, a German officer wounded. The group moved off in the evening and probably joined the larger part of *Kampfgruppe* Kühlwein.

19 October

The Hungarian artillery unit moved off to the west. On 19 October 1944 they marched through Werbass. At first they were disciplined and orderly, but then increasingly in haste. They were fired on by Soviets who had moved up behind them. Thus, for a short time Werbass was under artillery fire. The Hungarian artillery took up positions and returned fire, which brought the enemy up short. Then the canal bridges and the ammunition store in the Annabring school were blown sky high and they moved out. During the afternoon Werbass fell into enemy hands.

Kampfgruppe Kühlwein moved back to the south in the direction of Neusatz. *Kampfgruppe* Syr moved off to the West and crossed the Danube by ferry at Bezdán. In this process, on 19 October 1944, they again became involved in fighting with Communist groups that gave rise to heavy casualties. Anton Heipl (4/79) wrote this account:

> Apart from this it was time to move off. When Széged fell on 11 October there was a short break in the fighting there while the enemy brought up a new Army. But then a strong attack began from the west of Széged. For that reason the preparations for the 16th Frontier *Jäger* Battalion at Bajmok to re-take Szabadka only remained a plan. To the north of the town, on 19 October, the 3rd River Blockade Detachment carried out another counter-attack, but with little success. On 18 October the Soviets broke through. The 3rd River Blockade Detachment once again took up position in Melykut and then on 19 October marched off via Baja. During the same few days, units of SS Volunteer Grenadier Regiment 79 (Syr) were covering in that area. One part (*Untersturmführer* Arnold) with the Regimental Staff was at Kiskunhalas. Other parts of the I/79, including the 4th Company (Holderer), with Hungarians from the 1st and 2nd River Blockade Detachments, provided cover at Bacsalmas.

On 15 October our company was in Bácsalmás, where the Battalion Staff Albrecht was also located. I was in the group of *Unterscharführer* Franz Peter, a fellow countryman from the Waschkut. Even if our armament was already somewhat better than in the very first days, when we had to stand guard with truncheons, we had no great fighting strength. Without making contact with the enemy, on 18 or 19 October we moved off and at Baja crossed the Danube by ferry.

At the latest, on 19 October 1944, the 1st and 2nd River Blockade Detachments withdrew. The Soviets moved carefully after them and on into the town of Baja during the evening of 19 October 1944. This was at the same time as the resistance began in Szenttamás. However, this meant that the entire Batschka was finally cut off.

20 October 1944

On 20 October 1944 *Kampfgruppe* Kühlwein crossed the Danube at Neusatz. As the small fighting force, marched into the town, the snipers fell silent. Only when it was over in Syrmia did they have the confidence to emerge, in order to blow up a bridge over the Danube behind the departing Germans. That seemed completely senseless. On 22 October 1944 there were no more German forces in the Batschka. The way into the southern, northern, and western Batschka was now open to the Soviets and they could join up with their comrades who had been feeling their way out of the Baja area since 20 October 1944. Into enemy hands fell the villages of the Zombor district on 20 to 21 October 1944. Those in the Apatin district fell by 25 October 1944, those in the Kula district on 18 to 20 October 1944. Finally, those in the Neusatz district fell, all for the most part without any fighting at all.

On 20 October 1944, Belgrade also fell. Eastern Syrmia was evacuated, and a new front was formed which defended western Syrmia, with iron determination, right up to February 1945. To the north, a main line of resistance, which was to secure the link to Army Group South, joined the Danube in the Danube-Drau triangle. Parts of the 'Brandenburg' Division were transferred there with the task of conducting mobile combat operations, of maintaining contact with Army Group South, and of holding up the Soviet advance. The *Kampfgruppe* went into its new area south of the Danube via Esseg.

CHAPTER 8

The Unprepared Division Is Brought Up to Secure the Danube

Continuation of the formation in Swabian Turkey, mid-October to the beginning of November 1944

From 7 October 1944, and for the most part between 10 and 15 October 1944, after the individual units of the Division had been brought back out of the Batschka on to the Western bank of the Danube, they were quartered in the general area between Fünfkirchen and the Danube. This was in the mainly German villages in so-called Swabian Turkey (Komitat Baranya, administrative centre: Fünfkirchen).

The units of Regiment 79 were quartered in the villages between the towns of Mohács and Batsek. Those of Regiment 78 to the south of this area were in the Villány area and in the Danube-Drau triangle. The *Nachrichten Abteilung* was at first quartered in Villany, then in Szederkeny. The supply services worked in the Villany area. The Medical *Abteilung* was temporarily in Kisköszeg, then in Nemetbóly. Finally, the 2nd Medical Company moved to Mohács, while the 1st Medical Company probably remained in Nemetbóly. But since the villages were soon hopelessly overcrowded, the units only slowly settled down. A.Gl. (I/79) gave this account:

> From Kossuthfalva we went through Bajmok and Bácsalmás to Baja, crossing the Danube here. We went to Alsónána, where we were supposed to have our quarters, but the village was already full. So, we turned back and went to Bar, where we finally found some quarters. Two days later we also moved on from here. We marched to Somberek.

In these places, there continued the formation of the Division. In the Batschka, progress had been greater with some units, and less or hardly at all with others. It was only here in the Udvar-Mohács area that a beginning had been made with the formation of the SS Volunteer Field *Ersatz* Battalion 31 comprising five companies. To form the basic complement of the Field *Ersatz* Battalion of the 'Kama' Division, young Batschka-German recruits arrived with dates of birth between 1926 and 1927. At that time they had to manage without any training. The *Nachrichten Abteilung*, too, was actually set up in this area. *SS-Untersturmführer* Villier wrote:

> With the *Nachrichten Abteilung* we crossed the Danube by ferry at Mohács and landed in Villány. Here I lived for about three weeks in the Deanery with a Dean and his chaplain, together with *SS-Untersturmführer* Siegfried Koller and our *Stabsscharführer* Albert Vollenbroich. When we were moving on, the Dean

pressed a cross on each of our foreheads and said: ' May God's blessing be with you and may you have it no worse than we have in Villany'. I often thought of that later. From there we went to Szederkeny and here the whole *Nachrichten Abteilung* stayed for some weeks. In setting up our quarters, *SS-Untersturmführer* Karl Stecker, who could speak Hungarian as well as Slovakian, was a great help to me.

It was in Szederkény that significant progress continued with our formation and it was here that many ethnic German volunteers joined us. Here there were no more Muslims, they had been taken out earlier. Certainly those still west of the Danube. Since it was only here in Szederkény that we finally managed to get some rest on our long march, the process of formation could make good progress. The recruits were trained with us in the Telephone Company, and none of them were sent to schools in the Reich. Some ethnic Germans 'skedaddled', among them three men from my platoon. No wonder, since, on our march we were passing through places where these chaps had their homes.

It was also in Szederkény that we received most of our uniforms, weapons, and equipment. But we never had all the equipment that we were entitled to. For example, there were not enough motorised vehicles. Accordingly many units had to share vehicles. Even horses and carts had to be requisitioned, to be able to carry everything. In doing so our men had to carry and drag along their own personal equipment.

As *Nachrichten Abteilung* we were, from the beginning, a self-contained unit, but we did not go into action on the Danube. But some of us who volunteered were assigned to the parts of the Division who did see action, and this even involved some casualties.

During these weeks the *Nachrichten Abteilung* was joined by *SS-Rottenführer* Fritz Schuster, who wrote:

As a Transylvanian Saxon from Bistritz, in May 1941 I went East with the first 1,000 volunteers in a Transylvanian Battalion in the 1st (motorised) SS Brigade as far as the front before Moscow. After twice being wounded, and frost-bitten during 1941, I was signed off as medically unfit and joined a training regiment in Prague-Dewitz. I was not a good lines of communication soldier and the fact that even being a former grammar-school boy, and after five years of war service, I never made it further than *Rottenführer* is due to this. That's a brief outline of my previous career as a soldier.

About the end of September, I joined the 31st SS Volunteer Grenadier Division in Baja. Immediately I had to help drag lorries up on to the western bank of the Danube through muck and slime. Soon, both I and the organisers who were present (officers), had to realise that I had little aptitude for this kind of work. So on the formation of the Telephone Company I was assigned as unit leader and brought along for a while with them in Szederkény, Villány and Fünfkirchen.

The morale of the newly enlisted ethnic Germans was, in general, fairly poor. Most of them had only just left their homeland and had seen it overrun by the enemy. They were worried about their nearest and dearest. Some had not been evacuated, others were even now heading for a distant unknown destination, and all faced an uncertain, but extremely disturbing future for their homeland. The local political uncertainty and the general war-weariness also had their effect.

When, on 15 October 1944, Horthy's proclamation was issued, according to which the war for the Hungarians had ended, many new recruits, especially those from the nearby villages of the Northern Batschka, felt that they were free to simply make off and go home. In the confusion of the retreat, this did not involve any particular difficulties. Many simply remained behind even before they came to the Danube. Others came back from Transdanubia and went back to their nearby home villages. Even then there were no Soviets to be seen anywhere. Elsewhere the Soviets had already penetrated deep into the southern and eastern Batschka. Just how the chaotic events were viewed at that time by the bewildered young Hungarian-Germans, was vividly recounted in a personal account (S.R.):

> The retreat began, we left Kossuthfalva and marched away on foot in the direction of Bajmok, the old, grey-haired *SS-Untersturmführer* Pradl accompanied us on his little Sachs motorbike. In the evening we arrived at the edge of the town of Baja from the direction of Wikitsch (Bokod), here we were given a rest. Then we crossed the Danube. We remained for three days in Bátaszék, from there our unit came into the village of Bar. Here we heard Horthy's armistice proclamation. Having heard this, many men made off. Finally two of us good mates, also decided to make off. Soon our number had grown to 10 men! We found a boat and an old man who took us over on to the eastern bank of the Danube for 10 *Pengö*. Then we went back on foot to our home parishes. Many shouted out that this one or someone else was home. A mother, weeping, begged us to go back, otherwise we would be caught, and because they were looking for us. Some were actually arrested by Hungarian policemen and handed over, but even the police no longer wanted to co-operate, and let the lads go, with the proviso that they would lay low as civilians. There were also still many German soldiers to be seen.
>
> Then came Szálasi's appeal that Hungary ought to and must fight on. This disturbed us. What now? Should we go back to our units? We decided to do that. Soldiers of the Hungarian river guard took us across the Danube. For the journey westwards we now didn't have to pay, it was free. We went back to Bár, but our unit was no longer there. It had in the meantime marched to Babarc, where we found it. When we arrived we got a terrible cursing and dressing down!

It is worthy of particular note, for it was not an isolated case, even if it was also probably not the general rule. Men went back to their units, once the confusion stirred up by Horthy's proclamation was clarified by Szálasi's appeal to fight on. This says a lot for the innate decency, and the voluntary intention to do their duty, on the part of the young Hungarian Germans! Not one case is known of one of them, if he returned voluntarily, being court-martialled for desertion, instead, the incident was treated as being absent without leave.

But Horthy's appeal of the 15 October 1944 caused much confusion and consternation in the Divisional staffs. How would the Hungarian *Honvéd* units behave now? Even a catastrophe of Romanian proportions could not be excluded from the realm of possibility. There were no instructions from higher command authorities for this eventuality, and so the individual parts of Divisions reacted decisively in the only way they could. They instantly 'crippled' the *Honvéd* troop units in their immediate vicinity in order to prevent the latter eventually disarming. *SS-Rottenführer* Ernst Bennert of the 2nd Medical Company recalled such an action:

> *SS-Untersturmführer* Krummel, who spoke perfect Hungarian, came into our quarters in the early morning of 15 October in a state of excitement and said that Hungary had capitulated, that the Hungarian soldiers have been required to turn their arms against the Germans and to prevent them from reaching their homeland.
>
> In Mohács a *Honvéd* battalion was stationed in the middle of the town, in a large building which had been converted into a barracks and in front of which was a small park. Some of us from the Medical Company and some men from the squadron of the Division that was also in Mohács now took up position in this little park. *SS-Untersturmführer* Krummel called over the Hungarian duty officer and said to him that they should not use their weapons and that none of them should show themselves at the windows for we would immediately open fire. In this practical way we locked up the Hungarian battalion in their own barracks.
>
> After some toing and froing, towards midday we were able to locate the battalion commander, a *Honvéd* major, who now declared himself ready to fight on the German side. Thus our state of alert no longer applied.
>
> It was an exciting day and in the evening we began to wonder what had happened to our two *Unterscharführer* who had stayed in the village 20 kilometres to the west of Mohács (Nagynyárád?). Immediately five men were sent out to look for them. They were found, too, in an inn, already quite tipsy. They were celebrating the end of the war with the Hungarians.

Elsewhere, too, the events that had at first seemed ominous took a similarly peaceful course and soon the whole business was over. Skorzeny occupied the castle, Ferenc Szálasi, leader of the Arrow Cross, came to power and appealed for the fighting to go on. The overwhelming majority of the *Honvéd* units obeyed this appeal. In the units of the 31st SS Volunteer Grenadier Division training continued, it is true, under conditions which were little better than they had been in the Batschka, except that the danger, from partisans which was always threatening there, was no longer present. Once again, SS man S.R. (I/79) painted a graphic picture of this period:

> In Babarc we had to dig trenches, we didn't even have weapons, there was only one weapon for the whole group of thirteen men. Then we got three more, so that the whole group had four of them.
>
> In the neighbouring village of Szajk, old men were digging trenches, they also belonged to our unit. In charge of them was *SS-Hauptscharführer* Hans Zick, a fellow countryman from our home village. One old man suggested to Zick that every day at noon he would bring him two buckets of wine if he only didn't have to dig. 'Done, it's a bargain'. And the old man actually went away, then came back, on his shoulders a pole with hooks, from the hooks hung the two buckets full of wine.
>
> One day the *Sturmbannführer*, Albrecht, came past on his motorbike not sitting but standing up. He chose a number of men. We were among them and we went to Mohács. We were quartered in the cellar of the leather factory in

Mohács. Here we also received a bit of training on the machine gun and the *Panzerfaust*. We were shown in the Mohács silk factory how to use the *Panzerfaust*. The holes we shot in the wall can still be seen today. It is true that there were not enough *Panzerfäuste* available for us to be able to fire them ourselves. It only went so far as a demonstration.

This was an unsatisfactory state of training. There was a complete insufficiency of equipment such as small-arms, and a complete lack of any heavy weapons. The process of formation of the Division had to be suddenly interrupted on 26 October 1944. As a result of the developing situation, the Division was brought forward to secure the Danube. How did the situation appear, what had happened in the meantime?

Situation at the front up to the end of October 1944

The Soviets began their large-scale offensive on 6 October 1944, between Arad and Grosswardein, with three offensive thrusts. The first was north-westwards from the area Arad–Gyula. The second was south of Arad, over the Theiss westwards. The third was north-westwards between Nagyszalonta and Grosswardein. They set up several bridgeheads on the Western bank of the Theiss, and took Szeged on 11 October 1944. They threatened to encircle Army Group Wöhler on the eastern wing of Army Group South, as a result of which the withdrawal of this army became unavoidable.

On 10 October 1944 the Soviet point units attacking north-north-westwards were actually cut off. At Debrecen, on the Puszta, a bitter tank battle unfolded between the enemy forces that were encircled. The German forces encircled them, and the enemy forces sought to break open the encirclement from the outside. As reinforcements, the Soviets brought up all their forces into the Debrecen area, including those already standing on the Western bank of the Theiss. The tank battle raged until 14 October. It ended with a clear victory for the German defenders. The line of retreat of the Transylvanian front, which had begun in the meantime, could be secured. But first Grosswardein fell, then Debrecen too, on 17 October 1944.

In the south, to the west and to the north-west of Szeged, and in the Batschka, the fighting took the course which has been described already in chapter 7. The weak forces of the 3rd Hungarian Army were thrown back. The VII and VIII Hungarian Army Corps, together with LVII *Panzerkorps*, had to withdraw to the line Kiskunhalas-Kiskunmajsa-Pálmonostora-Ujfalu. All this made the situation, even on the western bank of the Danube, increasingly precarious.

On 17 October 1944 the order was given to defend the Danube line. It was divided into three defensive sectors. The first stretched from the Drau estuary as far as Paks (148 km long). It was held by the 1st Hungarian River Brigade (*Generalkapitän* Ödön Trunkwalter, command post Szekszárd). The troops under its command were three river guard battalions, one Frontier *Jäger* battalion, one guard and one police battalion, four batteries and four guard boats of the Guard Boat Squadron. The second sector stretched from Paks as far as Rácalmás (55km). It was held by *Kampfgruppe* Matolcsy (later Kesseö, one battalion and one flak *Abteilung*) and also included the bridgehead at Solt with two battalions and two flak *Abteilungen.* The third sector stretched from Rácalmás as far as Waitzen (Vac) and was held by the VI Hungarian Army Corps. The 31st SS Volunteer Grenadier Division was at first not included in the forces securing the Danube. That would not have been possible due to the state of the Division.

On 19 October 1944 the Soviets took Baja and there reached the Danube. On 20 October 1944 the 31st Guard Rifle Corps pushed into the Mohács islands and similarly reached the eastern bank of the Great Danube, opposite the town of Mohács. On that day SS Fusilier Battalion 31 was the last unit of the 31st SS Division to leave the Batschka. Already the Soviets were face to face with the Division!

During that time the 3rd Hungarian Army carried out a counter-attack in the direction of Szeged, which eventually failed. On 22 October 1944 the Soviets broke through north of Debrecen and took Nyiregyháza. The withdrawing Army Group Wöhler was thus cut off. But Wöhler took a firm grip on his *Strassenbelagerer,* who were also being attacked in the rear. They soon had to realise, in some consternation, that they were trapped. The Soviets were wiped out in heavy fighting and the situation was restored. Nyiregyháza was liberated again on 26 October 1944.

At the same time the entire Batschka fell into the hands of the Soviets. From then on they were standing on the eastern bank of the Danube, facing, along its entire length, the area in which the 31st SS Volunteer Grenadier Division was being formed.

On 24 October 1944 the defence of the Danube line was reorganised. The 2nd Hungarian Army was relieved from supporting Army Group Wöhler in northern Hungary and moved on to the western bank of the Danube. The Danube line, until then defended as a single unit, was split in two. The sector from Csepel Island to Kisköszeg was assigned to the 2nd Hungarian Army. They were entrusted with the task of preventing the enemy from attempting to cross. Their particular task was to hold the Solt bridgehead, and to hold down enemy forces by making limited attacks. At first, the sector from Kisköszeg to the Drau estuary came within the command area of Army Group F. The Division into two parts, of a sector that by its very nature was one command area, was later to give rise to a series of difficulties between Army Groups South and F, regarding command and areas of responsibility.

The 2nd Hungarian Army had two Hungarian Army Corps. VI Hungarian Corps was in the Rácalmás–Waitzen sector. II Hungarian Corps (FML István Kudriczky, command post Högyesz) with the River Brigade and the 23rd Hungarian Infantry Division was in the Kisköszeg–Rácalmás sector.

Army Group F was charged with responsibility for the sector Kisköszeg–Drau estuary under the 'Brandenburg' Division. From 23 October 1944 their *Kampfgruppe* Kühlwein, newly relieved from the Szenttamás front, was just arriving, via Vukovar and Esseg, at its new defensive line Keskend–Vörösmart–Kisköszeg. In addition, other parts of the 'Brandenburg' Division (I/2nd *Jäger* Regiment under *Hauptmann* Steidl, and parts of 1st *Jäger* Regiment 'Brandenburg' from Belgrade) were now brought up to the *Kampfgruppe* in this area. They were attached as far south as the Drau estuary. Thus, considerably reinforced, the *Kampfgruppe* was now, once again, designated as *Kampfgruppe* Division 'Brandenburg'. The divisional command post was in Dárda. *Generalmajor*

Kühlwein was relieved and *Oberst* Schulte-Heuthaus became the new divisional commander. In this sector there was also the 54th Frontier *Jäger* Battalion, River Blockade Detachment Bezdán, together with some other small Hungarian units and 2 batteries.

On 26 October 1944 the dividing line between Army Group South and Army Group F was established, from then on, along the line Monostorszeg (Batsch-Monoschtor) North–Keskend South–Szentistván South. The line of Army Group South was by this means somewhat extended and it thus had to take over part of the sector of the Division 'Brandenburg'.

Toward the end of October the remaining front of Army Group South ran as follows: Baja–Kiskunhalas–Kiskunfélegyháza-Kreisch (Körös) estuary and from there along the Theiss as far as Csap–Erjala. On the western bank of the Theiss there were some smaller enemy bridgeheads. Army Group (AG) Wöhler (8th Army and 1st Hungarian Army) was defending the line from the extreme left flank to Polgárdi. From Polgárdi down the Theiss was Army Group Fretter-Pico. On the land front from the Kreisch estuary to Baja was the 3rd Hungarian Army (*Generaloberst* Jozsef Heszlényi) with the LVII *Panzerkorps* (General Kirchner).

The Soviet plan envisaged an advance through the weak front of the 3rd Hungarian Army in the direction of Budapest. To cover the advance they concentrated their forces and brought up the 57th Army from the Belgrade area to the line Sremska-Mitrowitza–Zombor. This army was brought up between 25 and 30 October 1944. Between Homorúd and Bezdán two divisions (one Soviet, one of Tito's) marched up, similarly, two from Bezdán to the Drau estuary. These large-scale Soviet troop movements, together with some others, did not remain unnoticed by the German Wehrmacht command. A large-scale enemy offensive was suspected on both sides of the Drau, in the general direction of Agram. That would have been ominous because such a breakthrough would have cut off almost all the German forces in the south east. The really weak forces of the 2nd Hungarian Army securing the line here invited just such an attempt. The point at which both Army Groups South and F joined, represented a particularly high risk.

Incorporation of the 31st SS Volunteer Grenadier Division into the Danube defence

From this situation it resulted that Army Group South finally felt itself compelled, from 26 October 1944, to bring up the 31st SS Volunteer Grenadier Division straight from training. This was to help secure the Danube, despite the Division being equipped with insufficient weapons. Despite, too, its total lack of heavy weapons and low level of training.

The battalions of the 31st SS Division, which were at best only half-ready for action, were now moved to the junction point between the two army groups. This was to the line Dunaszekcsö–Mohács–Udvar–Kiskoszeg–Vorosmart,[1] and dispersed along the defensive line as follows:

I/80 occupied positions south of Kiskoszeg, as far as Vörösmart and Hercegszölös, which it took over from the 'Brandenburg' Division

II/78 with 14/78 attached themselves to the left, from Kisköszeg to Udvar, with focus in the village of Kisköszeg

I/78 stood between Udvar and Mohács, the Fusilier Battalion and the Field *Ersatz* Battalion were in the same area

I/79 provided security in and around Mohács

II/79 attached itself to the left, to about as far as Dunaszekcsö

The Regimental Staff had its quarters in Mohács, Regimental Staff 78 in Iszép.

The available core personnel of the Artillery Regiment were, because of the shortage of weapons, partly deployed as infantry. The Regimental Staff may have been in Magyarbóly. The *Nachrichten Abteilung*, although it was not fully equipped either in personnel or material, provided wireless units to the Grenadier units. The supply services had been placed further to the rear, into the area to the south-east of Fünfkirchen. The 2nd Medical Company maintained a main dressing station (HVP) in this town, while the 1st Medical Company was based further west of Fünfkirchen. The Divisional headquarters were in Nemetbóly.

On 2 November 1944 reinforcements in the form of flak units, and some Hungarian support units, together with the Waffen-SS *Gebirgs* Brigade der SS (Tartar No 1)[2], were placed under the command of the Division. From out of them all it formed Group 'Lombard'. For a time the Hungarian SS *Kampfgruppe* Deák, which was in the area south of Szekszárd, was probably also under the command of the Division. It was, however, not incorporated in the Danube defence, but withdrawn from the front because of the heavy casualties it had suffered earlier on 28 October 1944. A few days later, on 4 November 1944, Grenadier Training Regiment 44 (also called Infantry *Ersatz* Regiment 44), with four battalions at full complement, but insufficiently trained, and with three heavy anti-tank guns and two heavy mortars, was also placed under the command of Group 'Lombard'. This regiment occupied the line between Dunaszekcsö and Bátaszék.

Seen purely from the point of view of personnel, the 31st SS Volunteer Grenadier Division had at this time indeed reached its full complement (a total strength

1   This sector is an historic one. In 2nd century AD the *limes*, the frontier of the Roman Empire, ran along the Danube here and in this very area was liberally provided with forts. Ad Novas stood where present-day Vörösmart is, Ad Miliare was the same as Kisköszeg, Altinum as Kolked, Lugio controlled the Danube in what later became Dunaszekcsö. Small remains of this Roman fort were still to be seen in 1944 – and at that time the village of Várdomb was called Ad Statuas. In the same places in which Roman legionaries had stood in their forts almost 2000 years before, in 1944 the grenadiers of the 31st SS Division stood guard to defend the freedom of Europe against the enemy from the East.

2   The Waffen *Gebirgs* Brigade consisted of Crimean Tartars and from June 1944 was in training in Hungary under *SS-Standartenführer* Willy Fortenbacher. On 20 September it had an overall strength of 2,421 men, including 1,097 ethnic Germans, together with 11 officers and NCOs of police as core personnel. In spite of being placed under the command of Group 'Lombard', probably no single unit of the brigade saw action on the Danube: on the situation map of 3.11 it is true that it is shown in the Németbóly–Udvar area, but over and above this there are only negative indications concerning the brigade. There are, however, some names shown in the war cemetery in Budapest which are definitely Crimean Tartar in origin, and thus it may be assumed that some Crimean Tartars did fight and fall in the fortress of Budapest. The brigade was dissolved at the end of December 1944.

of circa 14,800 men), but the greater part of these received completely insufficient training. A good 8,000 men still had no weapons! The minutes of a meeting at the end of October between General Staff *Oberstleutnant* Schäfer (Army Group South) and the Plenipotentiary General of the Wehrmacht in Hungary, indicated that the entire 31st SS Division could only provide 1,370 men fully equipped with weapons and ready for action! By way of other weapons ready for action there were 54 light machine guns available. A note of 4 November 1944 refers to another 8 anti-tank guns and 2 light batteries. The mobility of the Division left quite a lot to be desired, and was principally achieved by the use of horse-drawn country vehicles. Also, the organisation of the individual divisional units had not been completed.

For just this reason, one thing should be made quite clear for the following accounts concerning the period up to December 1944. The 31st SS Division was not a unit that was ready for action. Its units were still practically all training units. So they were not coherent units which went into action, since there were none of these. Only *Kampfgruppen*, consisting of groups or individuals, often from various units, were ready for action (core personnel) or, at least, not completely unfit for action. When, in the following accounts, mention is made of the battalions and companies of the 31st SS Division, this meant that the combat unit in question consisted mostly of members of the unit, or that they were commanded by the staff of that unit. The more the battle escalated with the course of time, day after day, the more this was the case. While, at the beginning of November 1944, there was some justification for talking about precisely designated units e.g. I/79, from the middle of November this became less and less the case. It came to a point from the last week in November onwards, that it was at best, only possible to talk about 'parts of the 31st SS Volunteer Grenadier Division'.

The boundary of Group 'Lombard' on the right flank (with Division 'Brandenburg'), which coincided exactly with the boundary of the Army Group, ran somewhat to the south of Vörösmart–Hercegszölös. That on the left flank (with the Hungarian 1st River Brigade) was hard to the north of Bátaszék. Thus the area for which the Group was responsible comprised over 60km of river, held by twelve battalions (eight from the 31st SS Division and four from Grenadier Training Regiment 44).

According to the handbook of tactics, the task of securing a 3km-wide river sector ought to be the responsibility of a fully trained infantry battalion with its full complement of armament. Therefore it becomes clear that the front of the eight Grenadier battalions of the 31st SS Division, which was 40 miles in length from Hercegszölös even just as far as Mohács, was already somewhat over-extended, even for fully-trained and equipped battalions. If account was taken of the fact that these battalions, some only half-ready, some still only just a cadre, were insufficiently trained and armed, the picture darkened. It soon became quite clear that the greatly over-extended area of divisional responsibility did not allow a proper operation of securing the river, but only of keeping it under observation. This fact applied with equal truth to the sector under Grenadier Training Regiment 44 and to the entire sector under Group 'Lombard'.

Even in the adjoining sectors to right and left things looked little better. On the right, in the southern Baranya, from Hercegszölös to about as far as Esseg, was *Kampfgruppe* Division 'Brandenburg'. It was a 'torso' of a Division, since the pro-

cess of its formation had never been able to be completed because of the ever present need for action. Moreover, parts of it, while it was still taking up position, had
already been withdrawn and set off on the march to Baden near Vienna, for the re-
formation and reorganisation of the Division 'Brandenburg' had long been necessary.

In the command area of the *Kampfgruppe* Division 'Brandenburg' there were
still Police Regiment 6 (1,320 men, 17 light machine guns, 11 heavy machine
guns, 5 mortars), as well as the Hungarian 54th Frontier *Jäger* Battalion
(*Oberstleutnant* Arpad Szabó) at Darda. A little later, Police Regiment 6 was withdrawn into the area to the south-east of Fünfkirchen.

On the left, to the north of Bátaszék, the Hungarian 1st River Brigade (General Captain Trunkwalter) was attached to Group 'Lombard'. The River Brigade
consisted at that time of three river patrol battalions, the 16th Frontier *Jäger* Battalion, a police company, a rocket battery, a mortar company, together with six 8cm
field guns, and was defending the line as far as Paks. Adjoining to the north, as far
as Rácalmás, was Group 'Kesseö' ('Matolcsy').

In addition to this, there were available (according to the minutes of Staff
Oberstleutnant Schäfer quoted above) two further police regiments (SS Police Regiments 1 and 38) with a total of 1,591 men, 77 LMGs, 15 HMGs, 44 mortars and 8
anti-tank guns). In anti-aircraft forces there were three German flak *Abteilungen*, as
well as 37 Hungarian 8cm anti-aircraft guns at the Solt bridgehead. Finally, the
troops defending the city of Budapest consisted of alarm battalions, flak units and
the 22nd SS Cavalry Division.[3]

Group 'Lombard' was on 2 November 1944 put under the command of the
IV Hungarian Army Corps of the 2nd Hungarian Army, as were all the other units
on this sector of the Danube. Immediately afterwards the command arrangements
were changed. The II Hungarian Army Corps (FML Kudriczky) was given responsibility for defending the Danube from Kisköszeg as far as Paks, while General
Command IV Hungarian Corps was withdrawn to the area to the rear. So, on 5
November 1944 the 31st SS Volunteer Grenadier Division came under the command of II Hungarian Corps.

Immediately after the three companies of I/80 and II/78 had taken up positions around Kisköszeg, they experienced some small-scale skirmishes with Soviet
reconnaissance forces on 26 and 27 October. This clash was, in itself, insignificant,
but it was the first contact with the enemy that the Division had had on the Danube front.

At first, however, the Soviets did not try to cross the Danube. The sector of the
front remained quiet. The combat activity in the sector of the 31st SS Division was
limited to harassing artillery fire carried out by both sides, as a war diary entry of 4
November 1944 noted. The continuing reinforcement of the assembled enemy
forces was at first intended for the frontal offensive under way on Budapest. The

3   The 22nd SS Cavalry Division 'Maria Theresia' could, in the light of the places from
     where its men came and the hurried nature of its formation, be regarded as the sister
     Division of the 31st SS Division. It was almost immobile and had a total strength of
     13,911 men, completely insufficiently trained and equipped, lacking 24 heavy anti-
     tank guns, 57 artillery guns, 486 LMGs and 11,386 rifles, carbines and pistols, but,
     even so, somewhat better armed than the 31st SS Division.

Soviet plan envisaged breaking through the main line of resistance on a broad front against Budapest, then a group of forces was to swing northwards in order to cut off the German forces on the upper Theiss by closing off the area of the Mátra mountains. To carry out this plan, the enemy, as well as covering the Danube line as already outlined, had to fight to gain a strong base on the western bank of the Theiss. But their attempts to cross the river on a broad front were repeatedly repulsed by the 3rd Hungarian Army. In this fighting the Hungarian 1st Armoured Division, the Hungarian 1st Hussar Division, the 4th SS *Polizei Panzergrenadier* Division and Flak Regiment 133 particularly distinguished themselves.

Then, on 29 October 1944, concentrating on the area Rém–Borota–Jánoshalma–Kiskunhalas–Kiskunfélegyháza, the Soviets advanced on a broad front. The units of the 3rd Hungarian Army in positions here withdrew to the line Törtel–Solt. In this place, which had been shown to be a weak spot, the Soviets wanted to effect a penetration of the front. The concentration of their forces was shifted to the Kecskemét area, where a fierce tank battle unfolded between the advancing hordes of enemy tanks and vehicles that were distributed in depth, and the 24th *Panzer* Division. In order to effectively counter this large-scale offensive, Army Group Fretter-Pico was formed, under the command of which were placed the 6th Army released from the Theiss, the 3rd Hungarian Army and Group 'Budapest'.

Heavy fighting raged at Nagykörös, at Abony and at Kunszentmiklós. Here the enemy advanced and could only be held, on 2 November 1944, by the 13th *Panzer* Division at Bugyi, Alsónémedi and Ocsa. Here, the Soviets were on the approaches to Budapest and some were already able to break into the first defensive line. However, the situation was soon cleared up.

The Solt bridgehead, too, had to fend off strong enemy attacks between 2 and 5 November 1944. The 5 November 1944 was a day of crisis. The situation on the southern flank of the bridgehead was only cleared up by the successful counter attack of the IV/8 SS *Polizei* Regiment.

After a series of further enemy attempts to break open the gates of the capital of Hungary were vigorously repulsed, the fighting abated temporarily. On 6 November 1944 the enemy withdrew the points of their offensive back to the line Monor–Taksony. The tension on the approaches to Budapest relaxed. The 8th and the 22nd SS cavalry divisions immediately followed up and occupied the earlier defensive ring.

The Soviet desire to lay the heart of Hungary at the feet of their Stalin as a present for 7 November 1944, the anniversary of the Red revolution, had proved to be vain. Once again the latter-day Tartar assault could be halted at the city gates. For them to take it would take them another three months.

In the light of their failed attempt to occupy Budapest as they advanced, the Soviet high command worked out a new strategy. Instead of a frontal offensive, the advance was, from then on, to be made via the flanks. On the Soviet right flank, in the Tokaj–Szolnok sector north and north-westwards over the Theiss, and on the left flank, in the general direction Stuhlweissenburg–Raab over the Danube, they would try to encircle Budapest from the west. These giant pincers were to encircle and annihilate the 6th, 2nd Hungarian and 3rd Hungarian Armies.

The strike to the south was to be carried out by the 4th Guard Army and the 57th Army. The 4th Guard Army, after crossing the Danube, had to swing north-westwards to form the western jaw of the pincers, while General Sarochin's 57th Army had to advance further westwards to cover the whole operation from the south.

With this Soviet decision the die was cast. The crucial test of the Danube defence, and thus that of the 31st SS Volunteer Grenadier Division, was imminent. The Soviets scheduled the beginning of their large-scale offensive for 7 November 1944.

During those days, between 29 October and 6 November 1944, the situation of the Danube defence changed little. During the first days of November the Hungarian 23rd Reserve Division took over the sector Paks–Dunaföldvár and the Hungarian 10th Infantry Division took over the sector Dunaföldvár–Rácalmás. No significant reinforcements were brought up to the front of the 1st River Brigade and the 31st SS Division.

The 2nd Hungarian Army was supplied with provisions for its men, and fodder for its horses, from the 4th Provisions Store in Fünfkirchen, or its depots in Bátaszék, Nagynyárád, Siklós, Barcs and Dombóvár, as well as from the Dunaföldvár depot of the 2nd Provisions Store in Stuhlweissenburg. The Corps Field Hospital of II Hungarian Army Corps was in Vsezprém, its medical column in Szentgál. In addition, the field hospitals in Fünfkirchen, Kaposvár, Dombovár, Enying and Sarbogárd were at the disposal of the 2nd Hungarian Army.

The morale of the Hungarian troops of the 2nd Hungarian Army was often quite poor. Hungarian police reports even spoke in some cases of signs of disintegration. In the 31st SS Division there was no place for such absurd behaviour. During these days, the strongly increasing instances of young recruits taking off were discounted, because of the loss of the Batschka. This fact has been mentioned above.

At the end of October the Division complained of its shortage of weapons, especially heavy weapons. On 31 October 1944, the *SS Führungshauptamt* thereupon sent a telegram to Army Group South and asked for heavy weapons to be brought up. At the same time they lodged a complaint that the 31st SS Division had been snatched from its proper process of formation. Army Group South responded on 2 November 1944 by telegram as follows:

To: *SS-Führungshauptamt*

Signal: OKH/General Staff Army/ Operations Section 2 Hungarian Army via *Deutsches Verbindungskommando Stab 2*

Re: Telegram *Führungshauptamt* /Ia No 3767/44 General Command of 31 October 1944

The fact that the 31st SS Volunteer Grenadier Division has a low level of equipment with weapons and limited training is well known to the Army Group. The situation at the moment between Theiss and Danube requires the assembly of all available forces including assault guns, artillery, etc., to repulse the planned advance of the Soviets on Budapest and by counter-attack to throw the enemy back to the south.

The Army Group is therefore, at the moment, not in a position to agree to the understandable wishes of the 31st SS Volunteer Grenadier Division for heavy weapons to be brought up, particularly since the current intelligence picture of the enemy facing this Division gives us no reason to expect strong enemy attacks westwards over the Danube.

2 November 1944

2100 hrs

Army Group South

The Chief of the General Staff

Ia No 4284/44. General Command

Perhaps not at the moment, but this amounted to a false estimation of the enemy situation, because the storm clouds were already gathering and in a few days the storm would break.

By 4 November 1944, at the latest, the enemy's intentions had been quite clearly realised by the high command. The Supreme Commander of Army Group South, *Generaloberst* Johannes Friessner, on 5 November 1944 drew to the attention of the Hungarian National Leader and Prime Minister, Szálasi, the danger that was looming. He ordered the head of *Luftflotte* 4, *Generaloberst* Hans Dessloch, to increase aerial reconnaissance in the area of the Drau estuary.

In the *Wolfsschanze*, too, the Führer's headquarters in Rastenburg/East Prussia, they were aware of the danger. *Generalleutnant* Walther Wenck, the Chief of the OKH Operations Section, outlined to Hitler the situation on the Danube at the situation meeting on 6 November 1944 around noon. He suggested at the same time bringing up, as reinforcements, the 44th *Reichsgrenadier* Division 'Hoch und Deutschmeister' to cover the point at which Army Group South adjoined Army Group F. Hitler agreed and the order to transfer the Division from Istria to the Danube was issued by the evening.

At this situation meeting the 31st SS Volunteer Grenadier Division also came under discussion and it is instructive to find out that even at this highest command level they had a clear picture of the state of the Division. *SS-Gruppenführer* Fegelein was, it is true, unclear about the origin and designation of the Division, but he hit the nail squarely on the head as regards its combat readiness, when he explained, verbatim:

> The 31st SS Division, *mein Führer,* consists for the most part of Hungarians [in actual fact: Hungarian Germans – author's note], volunteers. There are scarcely any of the Soviet personnel left [actually: Muslim–author's note]. Only the German core personnel of Division Kammerer [actually: 'Kama' –author's note] have been put in. But it (i.e. formation) will take another two months. It has no force as a combat unit because they are all completely untrained.

There were no false illusions, but nevertheless the Division had to hold and stand where it was. But the Soviet offensive began exactly on time on 7 November 1944. The young SS Volunteer Grenadier Division was facing a hard test!

CHAPTER 9

The Battle for the Enemy Bridgeheads, 7–25 November 1944

7 November 1944

On the night of 6 November 1944 the enemy undertook combat reconnaissance of the west bank of the Danube. Two companies of the Soviet 74th Rifle Division of the 57th Army (according to other sources, one Soviet company and a partisan battalion) crossed the Danube. This was accomplished during the night, 4km north-west of Apatin, in the area of the *Kampfgruppe* Division 'Brandenburg'. They occupied a small bridgehead in the Kutska area. The Soviet Apatin bridgehead came into being. The territory in this sector was confused and difficult. A dense canal network, with a dam system, some 15 to 20km deep, existed between marshy wooded flood plains. This was the reason that Division 'Brandenburg' only sighted the newly formed bridgehead during the morning of 7 November 1944. It immediately attacked the bridgehead and during the course of the day brought to bear against the enemy several counter-attacks that certainly blocked the breakthrough but could make no further impression.Further north, too, at Mohács, the enemy felt their way forward on that day and occupied the little island in the Danube, 2km to the north of Mohács, in which process they became involved in fighting with the I/79.

8 November 1944

The heavy fighting at the Apatin bridgehead continued. Despite vigorous counteraction by the Division 'Brandenburg' and successful air attacks on the German side (for example, an entire enemy ferry with its load was sunk), the Soviets succeeded in extending the bridgehead to a breadth of 3km and reinforcing it with two further battalions of the 74th Rifle Division.

In the Batina-Kisköszeg area the enemy 233rd Rifle Division, in company strength, tried to carry out reconnaissance over the Danube during the early hours of the morning.

9 November 1944

Against Apatin there was further loss of ground, despite repeated German counterattacks. The enemy extended their bridgehead to a width of 12km and to a depth of 18km. The battalions of Division 'Brandenburg' under I/1st 'Brandenburg' *Rittmeister* von Mertens, II/1st 'Brandenburg' *Hauptmann* Heine, III/1st 'Brandenburg' *Hauptmann* Wandrey, I/2nd 'Brandenburg' *Hauptmann* Steidl, together with the Hungarian units under their command, i.e. parts of Infantry Regiment 9, 54th Frontier *Jäger* Battalion, 1st River Patrol Battalion, withdrew 6 to 8km. Then they were behind the old dams of the Vörösmart – Hercegszölös –

Map 1 Battle for the bridgeheads. Course of the fighting between 7 and 26 November 1944 (to 27 November 1944 in the south).

Laskó – Daróc – Bellye road and left the difficult low ground behind them. In the new positions their resistance stiffened and this new main line of resistance would remain firmly in German hands until 26 November 1944.

In the 'upper gardens' of Dunaszekcsö on the Danube island (today: Dunafalva) the units of the III/79, after two days of fighting, withdrew and crossed the Danube into the village of Dunaszekcsö, where they took up new positions. During the course of these events a tragic incident occurred. A young *Oberscharführer* left his position on his own initiative too soon and was there and then put before a firing squad and shot. He was laid out in the beer garden of the ferry station. It seems that they wanted to make an example of him in order to reinforce the morale of the troops. As a result of poor armament and training, morale was not solid.

In another place, too, the Soviets began to feel their way forward on that day. Two companies of the 233rd Rifle Division crossed the Danube between 5 and 6am, in the Bezdán area, to carry out combat reconnaissance of the western bank, on both sides of the village of Kisköszeg or Batina.[1] Here the Danube was some 400 to 500m wide, but its marshy flats extended, as they do opposite Apatin, far into the hinterland, and with their quagmires, backwaters and flooded woodlands they formed very difficult ground for combat. From the marshy flats vineyards rise up, on which is the village of Kisköszeg, a Hungarian-Croatian-German community that did well from wine growing. Anyone sitting up there on the heights and in the village would have a very good defensive position against an enemy struggling forward with difficulty on the uneven ground below. It was not by chance that the Romans built their fort Ad Miliare there.

On 9 November 1944 parts of II/78 of the 31st SS Volunteer Grenadier Division were in Kisköszeg, with units of the Hungarian 16th Frontier *Jäger* and 117th Police Battalions under their command, and immediately sighted the two enemy companies crossing. One group was about 1km to the north of the village, the other about 500m south of the position. Even before the enemy could reach the village or begin to set up somehow on the bank, they were attacked and shattered, or rather driven back over the Danube. This was the first fighting at this place. In a few days it would be fiercely fought over and go down in the history of the war as 'bridgehead Kisköszeg or Batina'.

10 November 1944

Since, in the previous days, the units of the 31st SS Division had their first contact with the enemy and engagements, on the Danube island and at Kisköszeg, it became unavoidable that some consideration should at last be given to equipping the Division with weapons, if it was to hold on. The liaison officer of the *SS-Reichsführer* with the Supreme Commander South-East, *SS-Standartenführer* Constantin Canaris, was charged with obtaining a clear picture of the actual situation.

Opposite Apatin nothing new was happening. The Division 'Brandenburg' was holding its positions against the enemy who was struggling up from the river

---

1   In the language spoken at that time were used both the then official Hungarian place name of Kisköszeg and the Croatian name of Batina which had been used before 1941 and was to be used after 1945.

flats. Finally reinforcements arrived. The fully motorised SS *Aufklärungs Abteilung* 13 of the 13th Waffen-SS *Gebirgs* Division 'Handschar' (Croatian Nr 1), which set off on 9 November 1944, occupied its newly assigned positions at Darda. As early as that evening they became involved in fighting against a Soviet battalion crossing to the west of Kutska. Fierce fighting raged during the night, in which *SS Aufklärungs-Abteilung* 13 took some part. Then, on 11 November 1944, the I/27 from Division 'Handschar' arrived and a main line of resistance was formed on the dam on the western edge of the Danube flats.

From mid-day on that day new command arrangements came into force: 2nd *Panzer* Army (*General der Artillerie* de Angelis) took over command in the Danube sector from the Drau estuary as far as Baja. With this, the boundary between Army Group South and Army Group F was shifted further northwards and established along the Baja–Bátaszék–Dombóvár railway line and on the line Dombóvár–Kaposvár–eastern edge of Lake Balaton, under which arrangement those positions belonged to the 2nd *Panzer* Army. The forces deployed between the Drau and this dividing line, i.e. mainly Group 'Lombard' with 31st SS Volunteer Grenadier Division and Grenadier Training Regiment 44, were at the same time placed under the command of 2nd *Panzer* Army–Army Group F–Supreme Commander South-East. It is true that Army Group F placed no value on the Hungarian command authorities of the II Hungarian Corps or the 2nd Hungarian Army and later wished to remove the Hungarian troops from the frontline and use them in the areas to the rear. In spite of the change in tactical command, the supply of the troops affected by the changes would also henceforth be the responsibility of Army Group South, as would the extension of the positions to the rear.

Army Group F was also to receive a *Panzerjäger Abteilung* from Army Group South, but this was not possible, no matter how beneficial it would be for the bridgehead battles. In an OKH telegram of that date, however, the 44th *Reichsgrenadier* Division 'Hoch und Deutschmeister' was promised to the 2nd *Panzer* Army. The instruction was that the task of the 2nd *Panzer* Army should be the construction of a defensive front on the western bank of the Danube, with its focus at Mohács and Baja. They were also given the task of the prevention of further enemy attempts to cross the river, and the destruction of the enemy forces that had already crossed the river at Apatin and Kisköszeg.

During the course of the day, another Soviet attempt to cross the river was made at Kisköszeg. The units of the 31st SS Division (II/78) beat them off in a counter-attack. On the night of 10 November 1944, however, the enemy, in the strength of one-and-a-half battalions (one battalion of the 703rd Regiment of the 233rd Rifle Division and one partisan company), crossed the Danube and stormed the village. It was no longer possible to throw these forces straight back.

11 November 1944

The battle for Kisköszeg developed on this day. Despite their good defensive position, the parts of the II/78 and I/80, totalling 3 companies of the 31st SS Volunteer Grenadier Division, the Hungarian 16th Frontier *Jäger*, and the 117th Police Battalions in position in front of and in the village, had to give way under the strengthened enemy pressure. They withdrew, some into the village, some behind the Karasica Canal to the north of the village.

Heavy fighting flared up around the railway station (I/78) where the Soviets were able to consolidate their position. The main line of resistance ran approximately round the railway station, the southern and south-western edge of the village and through the vineyards hard to the north of the village. During the course of the day, the fighting increased in intensity. The three companies of the II/78 and I/80 put up several counter-attacks against the enemy who were steadily increasing in strength, but were not able to throw them out of the village again.

Apart from the railway station, the important Hill 169 in the vineyards was the other most hotly contested spot. Under heavy enemy artillery fire from the eastern bank of the Danube, the fighting took on an unexpectedly bitter character. During this the enemy river crossing operation continued. During the course of the day, two entire partisan brigades, and all three battalions of the 703rd Regiment of the 233rd Rifle Division were brought across with considerable firepower.

The situation had become very critical and even in Army Group F, they began to realise that the three companies of the 31st SS Volunteer Grenadier Division and the Hungarian units, despite stubborn resistance, were not able to hold out for long against the strong enemy pressure. Reinforcements had to be brought up without delay! During the previous days, it was still expected that the Soviets would also attack to the south of the Drau estuary in the direction of Agram. Reserves were held in readiness for this eventuality. It had been thought that the enemy's troop movements, at Apatin and Kisköszeg, were feints to divert attention from the main advance on the Syrmian front. This turned out now to be wrong. *General der Artillerie* de Angelis, commander of the 2nd *Panzer* Army, wanted to ask for paratroops. This request could be granted, but Army Group F at last received agreement from RF-SS (*Reichsführer SS*) 'temporarily' to bring up and deploy, in the threatened Danube sector, the 13th Waffen-SS *Gebirgs* Division 'Handschar' (Croatian Nr 1) which was withdrawing from the former pacification area of eastern Bosnia. As a result, the I/27 was immediately sent to Darda. From the other elements, the Division 'Handschar' had to form a *Kampfgruppe* of regimental strength (principally out of SS *Gebirgsjäger* Regiment 28) in the Vinkovici-Brcko area and thereby to support principally the front of the 31st SS Division. The 2nd *Panzer* Army also intended to bring up some of the Army coastal artillery from the Adriatic. The 44th *Reichsgrenadier* Division 'Hoch und Deutschmeister' was also on the march to the Danube and arrived on that date in Fünfkirchen.

In the afternoon, *Generaloberst* Jodl, Chief of the Wehrmacht Staff, asked for intelligence from Army Group F on the situation and pointed out that "there is some concern about SS Division 'Lombard'". This proved that even in the highest command authority they were fully aware of the problems of the Division. Army Group F sketched out briefly to Jodl the state of the 31st SS Division, that "it had good men" (!), but that it only had "had a shortened period of training and has no heavy weapons". *Generaloberst* Jodl suggested incorporating parts of the Division 'Handschar' within the 31st SS Division, but there was no question of that.

In the hours of the late evening the heavily struggling front of the units of the 31st SS Division was finally reinforced to some extent. The Hungarian *Kampfgruppe* Balkay, parts of Frontier *Jäger* and police units, with three flak batteries, were brought up. The Soviets also increased their efforts, and during the night also brought across the river the 572nd Regiment of the 233rd Rifle Division.

12 November 1944

At the Kisköszeg bridgehead the defensive fighting raged on with undiminished intensity. The Soviets already had 77 guns in the bridgehead, which was some 3.5 by 3km in size. Because of the reinforcement of the whole sector by *Kampfgruppe* Balkay, parts of the motorised Grenadier Brigade 92 and the I/27 'Handschar', using 12 assault guns and 2 heavy batteries, undertook a counter-attack. It was effectively supported by the Luftwaffe, and was able to throw back the enemy to the eastern and northern edge of Kisköszeg.

During the course of the day, *Oberst* Bürker of Army Group F personally obtained a clear picture of the state of the 31st SS Volunteer Grenadier Division.

Opposite Apatin, a combat outpost which on the night of 11 November 1944 had been pushed back during the course of the day fought its way back into its old positions, breaking the enemy's resistance and taking 10 prisoners.

On the night of 12 November 1944, the Soviets were relieved by the 19th Rifle Division. Their 233rd Rifle Division had been fighting at the Kisköszeg bridgehead and had left behind many a 'feather' lost to the stubborn German-Hungarian resistance.

13 November 1944

On the eastern bank of the Danube more lively enemy movements with tanks, artillery, bridge-building equipment and motor vehicles were observed.

Out of the bridgehead facing Apatin, the Soviets tried three times, in battalion strength, to break through to the west and to the north-east of Tikves. Local breakthroughs were cleared up with greater casualties to the enemy. An attack supported by the Luftwaffe, gained only a little ground against tough enemy resistance. To continue the attack, the arrival was expected on 14 November 1944, of parts of the 44th *Reichsgr*enadier Division 'Hoch und Deutschmeister'. Of these, only eight detachments of the intelligence section and the 1st Regiment had arrived in the Pélmonostor area.

The counter-attack in Kisköszeg, aimed at clearing the Danube bank, continued during the morning, but then it fell and could not prevent all three regiments of the enemy 19th Rifle Division gaining a foothold at Kisköszeg during the course of the day.

Up to the waist in water, the enemy waded around some key points on high ground and stormed them by surprise from behind, with the result that these key points had to be evacuated. In the process, the men of the 31st SS Division and *Kampfgruppe* Balkay inflicted heavy casualties on the enemy. Nonetheless, the Soviets were still able to increase the size of their bridgehead to 3.5 by 2.5km.

Further to the north, in the Mohács area, there was during these days only a little combat activity. It was limited to reconnaissance operations. Artillery and mortar duels were carried out by both sides, over the Danube. Thus on 13 November 1944 fairly weak enemy forces attempted to gain a foothold on the Danube island to the south-east of Mohács, but they were thrown back with casualties by units of the 31st SS Volunteer Grenadier Division (certainly I/78 or 14/78). St. R. (I/79) gave this account of repelling an enemy attempt to cross the river:

They were trying to cross at Mohács, we spotted them and attacked with the light machine-gun. Huber from Bácsalmás was wounded straight away, I leapt to take his place as machine-gunner 2. But we had had virtually no practice on this type of weapon, there was only a small chance of any accuracy. Then *Sturmbannführer* Albrecht gave us a good dressing-down for that. Nevertheless, we still succeeded in forcing the 'Ivans' to retreat.

P.D. (Regiment 79) gave this account of divisional reconnaissance operations:

I was assigned as a dispatch rider to Regimental Staff Syr; I rode a motorbike, my cousin, Hauser, also a dispatch rider, was on horseback. We were based in Mohács and one day a reconnaissance detachment of three men with a boat was sent across onto the eastern bank of the Danube. As it was just about to reach the opposite bank, the Soviets spotted it, opened fire and destroyed it. Then I was sent to look for survivors and I was actually able to rescue one comrade called Ill.

The bursts of Soviet fire across the Danube also claimed sacrifices in dead and wounded, as many eyewitness accounts testified. The command arrangements, which had become somewhat confused as a result of shifting the Army Groups' command areas, were rearranged on this date. The 31st SS Division, as well as *Kampfgruppe* Balkay, on 11 November 1944, temporarily passed from under the command of the II Hungarian Corps into that of Divisional Command 'Brandenburg'. They were then placed under the command of the LXVIII Corps (Luftwaffe General Helmuth Felmy, Corps command post in Rácpetre, present-day Ujpetre). From the Danube sector that had remained with Army Group South (from Baja up the Danube), the Army High Command 2nd Hungarian Army was withdrawn and dissolved. Its place was taken by the 3rd Hungarian Army (*Generaloberst* Heszlényi, Army HQ in Balatonalmádi), whose units still included the Hungarian 10th and 20th Infantry Division and 5th Reserve Division.

In terms of the broader situation, a trouble spot developed on the upper Theiss and a breakthrough was threatening on the line Hatvan–Gyöngyös. On the Cegléd–Szolnok front the Soviets began a large-scale offensive on 11 November 1944. At Jászpáti and Jásberény a desperate tank battle developed, but then the 4th *Polizei Panzergrenadier* Division and parts of the 18th SS Volunteer *Panzergrenadier* Division 'Horst Wessel' bore the brunt of the attack. On 12 November 1944 the Soviets began an attempt to break through to Miskolc between the Theiss and the Bükk Mountains and also in the Ungvár area on the extreme left flank of Army Group South they mounted an attack westwards. All fronts were under fire but were held, unshaken.

However, it was on 13 November 1944 that the most lasting loss was suffered. The Solt bridgehead, maintained for so long, was lost. The Hungarian *Kampfgruppe* Kesseö was wiped out in the heavy fighting, but one part surrendered. The remnants of the group crossed to the western bank of the Danube to Dunaföldvár, while the Police Battalion 'Edelweiss' (which counted among its ranks many men from the South Tyrol) at first only withdrew to the Danube island, the so-called 'Upper Island'. The bridge between the eastern bank of the Danube and the island were certainly blown up, but this did little to prevent the enemy following up across the arm of the Danube, which was narrow there, on to the island. There too Police Battalion 'Edelweiss' put up a fierce fight against them but finally, in the early hours of 14 November 1944, had to give way to enemy pressure and cross to the western bank, blowing the western bridge sky-high behind them. The battalion left behind 7 dead, 57 missing and brought out 68 wounded.

Especially dangerous was the fact that among the Hungarians surrendering to the Soviets was also Colonel Otto Hátszegi-Hatz, the Chief of Staff of the VII Hungarian Army Corps, and that with him all the plans for the Danube and Margarethe positions fell into enemy hands!

14 November 1944

At the bridgehead facing Apatin nothing new was happening. On the night of 13 November 1944 the three enemy regiments, after trying repeatedly but unsuccessfully to push forward on both sides of Tikves, remained firmly blocked and were sitting among the river flats. But the Germans did not have enough forces to push back the enemy bridgehead completely. An account of the fighting in this area was given by *Hauptmann* Steidl (I/2nd 'Brandenburg'). His description of the nature of the fighting was also generally applicable to other sections along the Danube front as far as Mohács:

> In front of us is the woodland thicket with its many backwaters. The dam on which we are forming the main line of resistance is built to hold the Danube at high water. At its foot is a pumping station with a high chimney, where I set up my command post. *Leutnant* Simdes certainly does not agree with building the battalion command post directly into the main line of resistance, but I want to be with my men right at the front. All the advantage is on our side: the dam with its raised position, field of fire, if only for a few metres, while the 'Ivans' are crouching in the swamp and have wet feet, and also the river, after the rain we have had, is running at high water. But every night they try to break open a gap somewhere, and by day their snipers fire on us from the trees, which costs us casualties. They really are past masters at positioning snipers. By day we can scarcely lift our heads up out of our holes. We can't bear these sustained losses for long, every day six to ten casualties shot in the head. I manage to get some ammunition for my assault guns and fire as planned at the treetops. In this way we finally get some peace.
>
> My mortar chaps shoot two royal deer, we stalk through the woods to the dead animals. My neighbours to the left are an SS unit, to the right *Rittmeister* von Merten's battalion, he is an old south-westerner. From northern support points there are constant reports of river crossings. In the night you can hear loud swearing, the rolling of horse-drawn vehicles, the noise of piles being driven in. This all points to the fact that we must expect a large-scale attack.

The following was mentioned in the Army Group F war diary for this date as "a trivial incident". At Kiskoszeg, in the early morning, a fresh counter-attack was launched against the enemy, in the northern part of the village. 500 to 600 men occupied the village. Parts of a Grenadier regiment of the 44th *Reichsgrenadier* Division 'Hoch und Deutschmeister' had been brought up. However, as on the previous day, this attack did not break through. But the Soviets too could not push forward any further, although two more regiments, this time from the 3rd Rifle Division, had been sent across. The decisive high ground still remained firmly in German hands. Reinforcements, too, were rolling up. Newly arrived units of the 44th *Reichsgrenadier* Division 'Hoch und Deutschmeister' (I/Artillery Regiment 96) were sent off to Kisköszeg. In the evening the enemy began to feel their way forward with reconnaissance forces, from the bridgehead to the north-westward.

To the north of Mohács, an enemy attempt to cross over from the large Danube island was repulsed by parts of SS Volunteer Grenadier Regiment 79 located there. Colonel Bürker, who inspected the 31st SS Volunteer Grenadier Division during the previous days, reported the state of the Division thus: "full complement of personnel, but without weapons – 8,000 men out of 14,000 not armed, 1 machine-gun per company".

While the fighting at both enemy Danube bridgeheads was in full swing, the evacuation of the German villages of the southern Baranva took place. The mistakes that were made in the Banat and, subsequently, almost repeated in the Batschka were not repeated there. The German population was evacuated in time. Many communities had already been evacuated by 10 November 1944, according to plan, and within a framework well organised by the Volksbund. The Wehrmacht also helped out there. Many members of the 31st SS Division also had leave to bring the members of their families to safety. But the columns of refugees could not be protected from low-flying aircraft. Thus the column from Jagodnjak was on 20 November 1944 attacked by Soviet, then by British aircraft. An important factor is also the fact that part of the German population was even here unwilling to take flight before the approaching Soviets and Tito's partisans.

15 November 1944

At the bridgehead facing Apatin there were only fairly feeble enemy pushes against the blocking position in the west, and these were repulsed with heavy enemy casualties.

The *Kampfgruppe* which the 13th Waffen SS Mountain Division 'Handschar' (Croatian Nr 1) had assembled to support the front of the 31st SS Division, and which bore the name of its commander, *SS-Sturmbannführer* Hanke, had at last, on 14 November 1944, arrived in Pélmonostor. After a night march, they were moving in the early hours of the morning into the blocking position at Vörösmart at the Kisköszeg bridgehead. The *Kampfgruppe* Command Post was in Hercegszölös. The *Kampfgruppe* consisted of a *Gebirgsjäger* Battalion (*Obersturmführer* Hans König) with four companies (*Untersturmführer* Massanek, Cord-Henning, Knospe) an artillery *Abteilung*, a mixed signals unit and a pioneer detachment.

During the course of the day the situation in the Kisköszeg bridgehead grew more acute. The Soviets were continually reinforcing their strength (by means of a crossing traffic consisting of five ferries, spotted by German aerial reconnaissance), bringing up more anti-tank guns, artillery and mortars, all of which pointed to the formation of a focus in the Kisköszeg area. On this date enemy tanks appeared for the first time on the western bank. At first there were only two of them. One was immediately fired on and destroyed. The enemy attempted to break out and feel their way forward, with reconnaissance forces against the defences 4km to the north-west of Kisköszeg. They had already been begun on the evening of 14 November 1944, and gave reason, in short, to expect an enemy attack to break open the front and a further advance westwards.

The regiments of the Soviet 19th and 3rd Rifle Divisions were actually stubbornly trying throughout the whole day to break down the defence. Contested with particular ferocity was the decisive Hill 205 (Trojnas Mountain). Elsewhere, units had to give way to the strengthened enemy pressure. In the area of the village of Darazs, the defensive line on the southern edge of the village had to be withdrawn about 600m. The units of the II/78, I/80, *SS Feld-Ersatz Bataillon* 31, Group Balkay and SS *Kampfgruppe* Hanke, undertook during the course of the day no less than twelve counter-attacks!

These counter-attacks were supported by the few assault guns of *SS-Obersturmführer* Harry Paletta's *StuG* Battery 1007. To those fighting in Kisköszeg, Paletta was an invaluable help. Often enough he only had at his disposal a few assault guns ready for action. Since things had become 'very hot' in the Balkans, Paletta with his *StuG Abteilung* 105 everywhere acted as fire brigade. At the gates of Belgrade he had destroyed an entire enemy armoured point unit of 30 T-34s and 1,000 motor vehicles. At the end of October, the unit was no stronger than battery strength. Even at the time it had been formed within the 7th SS *Gebirgs* Division 'Prinz Eugen', i.e. the V SS *Gebirgskorps*, henceforth renamed as *StuG* Battery 1007, was placed under the command of the 2nd *Panzer* Army. From the last week of October it had been everywhere that things were 'hottest', such as at Kisköszeg.

The counter-attacks were covered by the three Hungarian flak batteries under the command of the 31st SS Volunteer Grenadier Division and by the artillery *Abteilung* of SS *Kampfgruppe* Hanke, from their firing positions around Hill 205 and the villages of Izsép, Podolje, Vörösmart and Czusa. Several times, these positions and others were fired on by a squadron of enemy fighter-bombers. The Luftwaffe was nowhere to be seen, however, the Ivans' air force was also not too successful.

Despite initial successes, the counter-attacks could get no further. The enemy could not be thrown out of the village and the lines they had reached had to be blocked. Army Group F wanted to await the arrival of the 44th *Reichsgrenadier* Division 'Hoch und Deutschmeister' that was being brought up, and only when it had all arrived did they repeat the counter-attack. From that Division, on 15 November 1944 the greater part of Grenadier Regiment 132, with parts of the II/A.R. 96, arrived in Pélmonostor.

As to the equipment of the 31st SS Division with weapons, things looked as bad as they ever did. That gave cause for grave concern to Army Group F. The Army Group had intervened at the OKH and requested that weapons be brought up to the Division. But as early as 13 November 1944 they received the information that re-equipping the Division with weapons, which would probably consist of captured Slovakian material, could not be counted on before December! Although the situation in the other sectors of the Division was at first still quiet, this news was not exactly reassuring. On top of this was the fact that Army Group F, now that the 31st SS Division had left its command, wanted to have back the three Hungarian flak batteries. With Group Balkay they had joined the units of the 31st SS Division fighting in Kisköszeg. At the same time, Army Group F had several times expressed the opinion that no value could be placed on Hungarian troops. This was of course not the case with individual heavy weapons used by the 31st SS Division, for which no replacements could be procured. For this reason, Army Group F decidedly declined the request of Army Group South.

The Soviet command was not at all pleased with the progress of the large-scale offensive launched on 7 November 1944, despite the local successes at Apatin, Kisköszeg and Solt. The main thrusts on both flanks had not been as successful as the Soviets had imagined they would be. On the upper Theiss they had been bogged down by the tough German resistance. On the Danube they had become involved in costly battles for the bridgeheads. Their only success worth mentioning was grinding down the German-Hungarian Solt bridgehead. On 15 November 1944, Marshal Malinowski, the commander of the 3rd Ukrainian Front, was reprimanded and fresh deadlines were given him. By 20 November 1944 he had to join up the two Danube bridgeheads at Apatin and Kisköszeg and advance as far as the line Hercegszölös–Magyarbóly–Töttös–Véménd–Bátaszék. Then he had to throw in more forces across the Danube and by 27 November 1944 to have reached the line Bátaszék–Pécsvárad–Fünfkirchen–Keszü–Harkány.

16 November 1944

However the situation had not got to that point. In fact much had changed. The 44th *Reichsgrenadier* Division 'Hoch und Deutschmeister' (*Generalleutnant* von Rost) arrived in full strength and was unloaded in Pélmonostor. Its units were essentially to support the front of the 31st SS Volunteer Grenadier Division and principally to play a decisive role at the bridgeheads.

The Divisional Staff set up their command post in Knezevo. The greater part of the Division was sent to the blocking positions at the Kisköszeg bridgehead: the I/131 (*Major* Tolkmitt) on the western edge of Kisköszeg, the II/131 (*Hauptmann* Zielke) on the dam at Lakanij. In the Koblice area were the Regimental Staff 131 (*Oberstleutnant* Fels) and II/ Regiment 'Hoch und Deutschmeister'. Regimental Staff 132 (Col. Hoffmann) was at Slatina. Regimental Staff 'Hoch und Deutschmeister' (*Major* Leitner) to the south-west of Darázs. I/32 took up positions to the north of Darázs. The II/132 (*Major* Freiherr von Rintelen) was on the dam at Sárkány with their right flank against the Danube. The II/Artillery Regiment 96 (*Hauptmann* Jandl) took up firing positions to the west of Izsép, in the Slatina meadows, to support the I/131, I/132 and II/132. Immediately after they had taken up their positions, they were destroyed by direct fire from a heavy enemy concentration, including units of women, opposite the sector of *Reichsgrenadier* Regiment 'Hoch und Deutschmeister'. The I/A.R.96 gave effective supporting fire to the II/'Hoch und Deutschmeister', *Kampfgruppe* Fels and the four battalions of the 92nd (motorised) Brigade (so-called 'Balkan Fire Brigade'). Later *StuG* Brigade Rudno assembled in the Sepse and Hercegszölös area between the two bridgeheads. *Aufklärungs Abteilung* 44 (*Rittmeister* Figlhuber) remained in the Pélmonostor area. Field *Ersatz* Battalion 135 was directed to Mohács to secure the river.

But even this élite Division, so deeply longed-for by two Army Groups, bearing a name that would go down in history was, at the end of 1944, only a shadow of its former self! Shattered three times in Italy, it had only recently been transferred to the Udine area to be refreshed and fully motorised. From here it was torn away after only a short time to be moved with the greatest haste to the Danube, where it was immediately to intervene in the fighting. They were in a state designated as "fit for limited defensive duties"! It was in effect completely without infantry! Firstly, it asked Army Group F for march battalions. Since it had a good cadre, the idea was to assign to it men from the 31st SS Division. At first 500 men were requested from *Reichsführer-SS* Himmler, whose approval was required to do this. But in the event it was not necessary to take this measure.

Scarcely had the newly arrived units of the 44th Infantry Division 'Hoch und Deutschmeister' taken up their positions at Kisköszeg than the counter-attack was resumed. It had stuck the previous day, and continued when these reinforcements arrived. It then progressed more smoothly. The few assault guns of *SS-Obersturmführer* Harry Paletta's *StuG* Battery 1007 carried out a dashing counter-attack and destroyed ten enemy heavy anti-tank guns and countless vehicles. Under the weight of the attack the Soviet defence collapsed and they were thrown out of the entire village of Kisköszeg and chased off. But then the counter-attack became stuck in the river flats that were not favourable to the offense. It did not succeed in completely pushing back and annihilating the enemy bridgehead. A considerable amount of territory remained in enemy hands, even though all the decisive heights had fallen into German hands with the re-liberation of Kisköszeg.

17 November 1944

The efforts to remove the enemy bridgehead continued. But the Soviets brought up reinforcements. Ten T-34 tanks and twenty assault guns were moved over the Danube. These were to halt the German attack and then to move over to counter-attack. The earth-brown Soviet infantry advanced under the cover of the tanks and of the artillery firing from the eastern bank of the Danube. Kisköszeg was lost once more.

Due to a shortage of sufficient tank defences on the German side, the enemy tanks were able to progress. The few assault guns of *SS-Obersturmführer* Paletta were plainly numerically inferior to this enemy superiority. Nonetheless, they attacked bravely, undertook numerous counter-attacks and once again inflicted heavy casualties on the enemy. *SS-Obersturmführer* Harry Paletta personally shot up 2 T-34s. But then it happened. The shell of an enemy heavy mortar hit the rear of his assault gun that itself remained undamaged. But because *SS-Obersturmführer* Paletta was looking out of the turret, in the open from his waist upwards, his back was riddled with splinters. Since the days of Belgrade, *SS-Obersturmführer* Harry Paletta had become a byword to his commanders, and to the units attacking under the cover of his assault guns, like the units fighting at the enemy Kisköszeg/Batina bridgehead, among them the 31st SS Division. His death was a heavy blow to the men at Kisköszeg! In his memory the LXVIII Corps Order of the Day Nr. 2, for 18 November 1944, should be cited here verbatim:[2]

> In a successfully-executed counter-attack there fell on 17 November 1944 the commander of the *StuG Abteilung* of the 7th SS *Gebirgs* Division 'Prinz Eugen',

2 Quoted from Otto Kumm, *Vorwärts, Prinz Eugen! Geschichte der 7 SS Freiwillige Div. 'Prinz Eugen'.* Munin Verlag, Osnabrück, 1978.

Obersturmführer Paletta, after he had personally fired on and destroyed two T-34s.

In the critical situation of recent days he again and again urged the infantry forwards by his daring and thus brought to a halt to the Soviet assault at Batina. Since the fierce fighting for Belgrade, the *StuG Abteilung* has enjoyed a special image. For the proven bravery and fighting spirit of both him and his section, *SS-Obersturmführer* Paletta was recommended for the Knight's Cross of the Iron Cross.

In proud mourning we honour the memory of this exemplary soldier and his great merits in the defensive fighting of recent weeks.

Men of the *StuG Abteilung*! You have the legacy of your commander to preserve, forwards, on to victory!

Long live the Führer!

Signed. Felmy.

SS-Obersturmführer Paletta was buried in Vinkovki and as the hero of Batina was posthumously awarded the Knight's Cross of the Iron Cross on 26 November 1944.

In the evening the Soviet assault was halted. It was blocked in positions in the vineyards. In order to reinforce the units of the 31st SS Volunteer Grenadier Division in the securing positions along the Danube, on this date the order was issued to remove 10% of the ration strength from all non-rifle companies and to incorporate them into the Grenadier units. Mostly, parts of the trained core personnel of the supply units were seconded and also parts of the artillery regiment were deployed as infantry.

18 November 1944

The fighting around the Kisköszeg bridgehead continued with undiminished intensity. Around midday the Army Group was still confident, but then severe setbacks had to be accepted. In heavy enemy artillery fire the units of the II/78 and I/80 of the 31st SS Volunteer Grenadier Division, as well as Infantry Regiments 131 and 132 of the 44th Infantry Division 'Hoch und Deutschmeister', had to give way to Soviet superiority. The villages of Darázs, Izsép, Kisfalud and Bán in the northern sector were lost, Group Balkay was driven from the important Hill 243 (Steinberg), and also in the sector of the II/ Regiment 'Hoch und Deutschmeister' ground was lost. At first, the enemy was able to considerably enlarge their bridgehead (to some 10km deep by 15km wide), but once again there was some success in partly restoring the situation. Darázs and Izsép, it was true, remained in enemy hands. Around Kisfalud bitter street fighting flared up, but the villages of Bán and the Steinberg were retaken. The fighting also claimed heavy casualties on the German side. During the following days, the Steinberg (Hill 243) was to be hotly contested and changed hands several times.

Further to the south and south-west of these places the Soviet attack faltered against the hard defence of the freshly-brought-up parts of *Gebirgsjäger* Regiment 98 of the 1st *Volks-Gebirgs* Division (*Generalleutnant* Wittmann). It was halted in the area Hercegszölös, Frigyesföld, Jesszeföld and Albertsdorf (the villages remained in German hands). The Bavarian *Gebirgsjäger* of the 1st *Volks-Gebirgs* Division only gradually arrived in stages. Thus they were not deployed as a whole unit. The similarly combat-trained soldiers of the 92nd (motorised) Brigade (the 'Balkan Fire Brigade') stood firmly wedged between the two enemy bridgeheads and prevented the Soviets from joining them up. Their tough resistance was given effective support by the artillery fire of I and II/Artillery Regiment 96.

This kind of support was necessary along the whole front. It was thus all the more inappropriate that, during the course of the day, Army Group South undertook an advance on account of the three Hungarian flak batteries recently put with the 31st SS Volunteer Grenadier Division. Army Group F insisted that the 31st SS Division had no artillery, the 44th Infantry Division 'Hoch und Deutschmeister' needed their own artillery themselves, and that everything that could be laid hold of must be taken to Batina.

The Soviets of the 75th Rifle Corps during the uninterrupted cold autumn rain were crouching on rafts in their bridgehead facing Apatin. On that day they tried several times to push through the blocking positions of the Division 'Brandenburg' to the east of the Albertsdorf–Laskó–Bellye road, in order to link up with their comrades coming from the north. Because of the tough resistance of the Brandenburgers, however, they escaped out of the wet flats of the Lesser Danube. It had been impossible for the previous ten days.

19 November 1944

The Soviets, still firmly contained within their two bridgeheads, tried on this date to break out and join up the two bridgeheads. But they ran up against the positions of *Gebirgsjäger* Regiment 98 of the 92nd (motorised) Brigade and Division 'Brandenburg'. They were unable to achieve a breakthrough either southwards or northwards. Round Kisfalud/Branijna to the north of the Karasica Canal the bitter fighting also continued. To prevent reserves being brought up into the area of the bridgeheads, the Il-2s of the Soviet 189th Fighter-Bomber Squadron constantly flew low-level attacks against the traffic routes in the depths of the LXVIII Corps.

20 November 1944

The struggle on the Danube was entering a decisive phase. The enemy deployed two divisions at Apatin and three at Kisköszeg, and over the newly built pontoon bridges brought after them more divisions and armoured forces. A total of 12 enemy divisions had to be reckoned with. On the Axis side, the shortage of ammunition, especially artillery ammunition, and the numberless casualties, weighed heavily. Even the last reserves from Syrmia were being brought up, remnants of the 117th *Jäger* Division from the forces securing the Drina. Further reinforcements that might have come from the area of Army Group E, in Croatia, could not be brought up in time. This was on account of the good weather, during which Anglo-American aircraft activity against the railway lines was increased.

Nevertheless, the decisive breakthrough was on this date once again denied the enemy, the main line of resistance only changing a little. In Kisfalud the street fighting continued. Round the village of Karancs, which could now be reached from the front, bitter fighting flared up, house by house, under artillery duels. During the defensive fighting on 20 and 21 November 1944 in the LXVIII Corps area a total of seven enemy tanks was destroyed.

The Soviet command was not satisfied with the advance. According to their order of 7 November 1944 their troops were supposed to have been already standing by that date along the line Bátaszék – Véménd – Töttös – Magyarbóly – Beremend – Torjanc, and they were far away from there. But also in the wider strategy, i.e. also on the other fronts in Hungary, things were not proceeding according to plan. It is true that Gyöngyös by the Matra Mountains fell, followed by Hatvan and Ecsed, and that the town of Miskolc threatened to be encircled. Even in the Ungvár sector in the extreme north-east, deep enemy penetration was developing. Nevertheless the front still remained unbroken. The decisive breakthrough was again and again denied to the Soviets. This was in spite of all setbacks and withdrawals in some sectors, in spite of rain and snowfall, and in spite of heavy casualties. An average battalion numbered 100 to 200 men. 100 metres of the main line of resistance were, on average, manned by four men. There were no towing vehicles for the anti-tank guns. The 8th *Panzer* Division, the strongest of all the *Panzer* Divisions, had only four to five tanks ready for action.

The tough German resistance caused the Soviets to take steps to look for a breakthrough elsewhere. They re-grouped, moved their motorised forces to the south-western flank and marched up on a broad front against the Danube line. The new focus now lay immediately facing the front of the 31st SS Volunteer Grenadier Division along its entire length. This did not remain hidden to the German command. There only remained the question of where the first blow would fall. Of course, the Soviet command already knew. According to the orders of the 3rd Ukrainian Front, it was to fall at Mohács, on 24 November 1944. The 4th Guards Army arrived in the Hercegszántó–Baia sector on the eastern bank of the Danube and bided its time. But at first another push would be made at Kisköszeg and Apatin, to relieve the pressure on those two bridgeheads and above all to bring about the strategic breakthrough to Stuhlweissenburg.

21 November 1944

In view of the approaching large-scale enemy attack orders were given to clear personnel and material out of the 5km wide combat area, and also to clear material from the 20km wide operational area on the Danube. Army Group South issued an order that was intended to stem the frequently appearing instances of disillusion, mainly in the Hungarian units. Cowardice in the face of the enemy would be punished by immediate death by firing squad. Germans were to be executed by Germans, Hungarians by Hungarians.

The situation in the enemy bridgehead at Kisköszeg remained unchanged until the evening, but on the night of 21 November 1944 a turn for the worse appeared to be looming. The fresh 113th Rifle Division was brought into the bridgehead.

At first, however, the worst happened for another, distant sector. At 11pm the Soviets, by surprise, without preparatory artillery fire, crossed the Soroksár arm of the Danube between Taksony and Dömsöd and occupied the southern half of the Csepel island. Counter-attacks instituted immediately by the Division 'Feldherrnhalle' remained unsuccessful. The enemy was beginning to prepare their Danube crossing.

22 November 1944

After the fresh 113th Rifle Division was brought up during the night, around noon on 22 November 1944, the enemy in the Kisköszeg bridgehead, with forces tightly packed from Darázs and to the south of it, lined up for attack. They succeeded in overrunning the combat-weary troops who were manning the defensive positions. By breaking into the positions, pushing them aside in a 2km-wide swathe and pushing forward as far as the Ari positions to the east of Podolje, the last reserve company of Pioneer Battalion 44 'Hoch und Deutschmeister' had to be brought up. Bitter fighting continued until darkness fell.

It was above all the units of the 44th Infantry Division 'Hoch und Deutschmeister' and parts of the 92nd (motorised) Brigade that were hardest hit by the attack. The enemy also overran SS *Kampfgruppe* Hanke in Vörösmart and threw them out of the village. The *Kampfgruppe* retreated to Hercegszölös. In this fighting many Bosnians, brave but completely inexperienced in this kind of warfare, ran headlong into the enemy attack and *SS-Obersturmführer* Hans König, commander of the *Gebirgsjäger* Battalion was wounded.In the bridgehead to the west of Apatin the enemy also began to attack. They broke through the thin security line between Kazuk and Monioros. The two supporting pillars of this defence, at first, held. By evening they were able to get as far as the area to the north of Mirkovác, as well as 7km south of Vörösmart, defended by alarm units. Here the Soviets were evidently making efforts to get to Suza, to the rear of the dam positions, to join up both their bridgeheads. But at first they could be pinned down with artillery. The ammunition for the light field howitzers, however, was in such short supply, that it would not last.

The local reserves were soon used up on both the places where the Soviets had broken through. In great haste *Kampfgruppen* and remnants of battalions were taken from quiet sectors and brought into position to counter-attack urgently in the sectors under threat. One such was the II Battalion/1st Regiment 'Brandenburg' under *Hauptmann* Heine, which in a heroic struggle fought literally to the last man to hold their positions against the Soviets rushing in from all sides. Only *Hauptmann* Heine and a dispatch rider emerged from the battle. The battalion was completely shattered. A weak battalion of the 117th *Jäger* Division, taken from the Syrmian front, was being brought up to the northern breakthrough area. However, due to the railway line being blown up to the north of Esseg, it was not able to get to the combat area before the afternoon of 23 November 1944. The battalion was nowhere near ready for a counter-attack. The 118th *Jäger* Division in Syrmia would also release forces. More parts of the 1st *Volks-Gebirgs* Division were marching up, but only on 24 November 1944 could they cross the Save. They reached the battlefield in two to three days. The most significant reinforcements promised were the 71st Infantry Division. But they only began to roll out from the Udine area on 24 November 1944.

The troops gave their utmost, but in spite of this, with the high losses of officers and NCOs, they were not able to stand up to the numerically superior enemy in the terrain cut into terraces and covered with vineyards. The strength of the battalions was on average 130 men, the recruits of the units of the 31st SS Volunteer Grenadier Division and also of Grenadier Training Regiment 44 were not yet reliable under fire.

The changing fighting, heavy in casualties for both sides lasted until nightfall. Eventually, a hold was established on the previous main line of resistance in the sectors of the less hard-hit Division 'Brandenburg' and the 31st SS Volunteer Grenadier Division, the units of both these divisions remaining at first in their own positions. The 44th Infantry Division 'Hoch und Deutschmeister', on the other hand, built a new defensive front along the approximate line Suza–Podolje–Dubosevica.In the judgement of the Army Group there was still a hope that it would be possible if not to stop the enemy, to tire them out. For the intelligence picture indicated that behind the two attacking enemy corps there were no reserve forces worth mentioning, since these had been shifted further to the north to the line Hercegszántó–Baja, where the Soviets also appeared to want to cross the Danube.

23 November 1944

During the morning the enemy began their attack afresh with strong forces under rolling fighter-bomber support, and broke through the new defensive line. An enemy group in regiment strength, with cavalry, advanced from the area to the north of Mitrovác, and gained the area to the south of Hercegszölös.

At the same time the enemy were also attacking, with the support of some 35 to 40 tanks, from the area Podolje–Gajic north-westwards. The units of the 44th Infantry Division 'Hoch und Deutschmeister' and of the 31st SS Volunteer Grenadier Division (II/78, I/80) were hit hard here. The focus of the fighting was at Kisfalud/Branijna and south of Dálvok/Dubosevica. Two enemy tanks were knocked out.

In the southern sector the Division 'Brandenburg' was building a new security line to the south of Kazuk and Jasenovac. In the centre II/'Hoch und Deutschmeister', parts of the 92nd (motorised) Brigade and of the III/2nd Regiment 'Brandenburg', had to give way before the enemy, the Soviets pushing forward as far as Karancs. In doing so they had formed a single, coherent, 50km-wide and 14 to 17km deep bridgehead on the line Dálvok–Laskó, and thus finally overcame the obstacle of the Danube!

At Karancs the breakthrough could only be foiled by deploying *Gebirgsjäger* Regiments 98 and 99 from the 1st *Volks-Gebirgs* Division. In addition, two battalions of *Jäger* Regiment 750 were brought to this trouble spot and deployed at Pélmonostor. That was exactly where a *Gruppenführer*, whose name is no longer known, of *Aufklärungs Abteilung* 44 'Hoch und Deutschmeister', with five men carried out a dashing counter-attack which captured many prisoners and ten MGs, and earned him the 'Fried Egg', the German Cross in Gold. The situation was certainly critical. Several times during the day, the enemy carried out infantry attacks supported by armoured thrusts.

A successful enemy breakthrough posed a double danger. If the Soviets thrust westwards to Agram, Army Group F would be cut off from its supply links, if they turned northwards, the southern flank of Army Group South would be encircled. In this situation of double danger it was even worse that the defence of the Danube line was divided. It was the responsibility of two army groups. On the one hand they had opposing views concerning the enemy's intentions (further enemy progress westwards versus progress northwards). On the other hand they were also under the command of different higher command authorities. The Army Group South on the actual 'Eastern Front' was under the command of the Army High Command (OKH), whereas for the 'Balkan Theatre of War', and hence for Army Group F, the Wehrmacht High Command (OKW) was responsible. That was a truly senseless arrangement, because the two theatres of war overlapped and merged, but when it was arranged in this way they were still far apart.

On that day, as happened several times before, Army Group South complained to the OKH because of this intolerable situation. It so exacerbated a coherent system of command because of difficulties with areas of responsibility, but once again the attempt was fruitless. *Generaloberst* Friessner, commander of Army Group South, wanted to see the entire Danube line as far as the Drau under his command. The OKH was proposing the opposite. He wanted to place the Danube sector up to below Budapest within the area of responsibility of Army Group F.

During this quarrel with the OKH, General Felmy, commander of LXVIII Corps, felt himself compelled, in view of the ominous situation, to call the military and civilian leaders of the Komitat Baranya to his command post in Ujpetre for a meeting. He requested Hungarian military assistance (upon which Army Group F had, only a few days before, placed so little value). FML Kálmán, Deputy Commanding General of IV Hungarian Army Corps and commander in the Fünfkirchen defensive area, promised 500 men from the battalion 'Mecsek'. *Obergespan* Péter Ivándy and Defence Commissioner Imre Mogvoróssy promised 1,000 Arrow Cross Party servicemen, of whom 500 reported the very next day to the command post of the Division 'Brandenburg' in Beremend. During the evening an attack of superior enemy forces hit the northern wing of the Division 'Brandenburg', and this necessitated a withdrawal of the parts deployed on the dam positions on both sides of Tikves. These were then brought up to clear up the situation to the south of Hercegszölös. After varying fighting even as darkness was falling, the line Kopacevo–Lug–Grabovac–Hercegszölös remained in German hands.

Further to the north, the units of the 31st SS Volunteer Grenadier Division, from II/78, I/80 and SS *Feld-Ersatz Bataillon* 31 stood in the crumbling front, hard-hit and separated from each other, shoulder to shoulder with their comrades of the 44th Infantry Division 'Hoch und Deutschmeister'. They put up a remarkable defence at the line Hercegszölös-Knezevi-Vinogradi. They were involved in fierce defensive fighting to the east of Sepse-Kotlin. That continued, from 18 November 1944. There was, for some time bitter street fighting in the south-western part of Kisfalud-Branijna. They also defended at its eastern edge the village of Dalyok-Dubosevica, against the enemy charging up under rolling fighter-bomber support. At Hercegszölös and Sepse it was mainly the men of the I/80, in Kisfalud the men of the II/78, and at Dálvok those of the SS *Feld-Ersatz Bataillon* 31 and the I/78 who defied the Soviets. The changing fighting, with heavy casualties for both sides, continued on even as night fell.

24 November 1944

The enemy fire from the Altwasser area faced Apatin against the Brandenburgers' positions. The enemy preparations to the east of Lug and Grabovac were effectively combated by artillery. The enemy, who attacked several times, with armoured support against Hercegszölös/Knezvi Vinogradi were repulsed with the loss of two tanks.

The enemy was also storming the front of the 31st SS Volunteer Grenadier Division and the 44th Infantry Division 'Hoch und Deutschmeister'. Throughout the whole day, the strong attacks, supported by artillery, against the positions of the 44th Infantry Division 'Hoch und Deutschmeister' continued, with their main weight to the south of Brajina-Kisfalud. While fighting was still continuing on the evening of 24 November 1944 around local breaks in the line south of Brajina-Kisfalud, the defence between Kamenec and the commanding Hill 243 was able to be built up.

At the junction point between 44th Infantry Division 'Hoch und Deutschmeister' and 31st SS Division the enemy, after several failed attacks, pushed into Dubosevica-Dálvok. In Dubosevica, too, the enemy were cleaned out, with another 2 enemy tanks being knocked out. In total, on 24 November 1944 in the area of LXVIII Corps, eight tanks had been destroyed.

While in the villages mentioned above the fighting raged on with undiminished intensity, the Soviets were also feeling their way forward in the area of their 4th Guards Army, facing the town of Mohács. On the night of 23 November 1944 the Soviets carried out combat reconnaissance across the Danube, in the sector secured by the 31st SS Division (I/78). In the early morning an enemy battalion was already on the western bank, to the south east of Zsidószállás, east of Kolked. During the afternoon the small bridgehead was already being reinforced by a further company and by anti-tank guns. The enemy bridgehead was only spotted during the evening, when six enemy companies were already in the 1km wide 200m deep bridgehead at Kölked. The enemy was attacked, but to completely destroy them was no longer possible.

Also, in other sectors of the 31st SS Division, enemy reconnaissance units tried during the night of 23 November 1944 to gain a foothold on the western bank of the Danube on both sides of Mohács. However they were shot to pieces on the river by the units of the I/78 and SS Volunteer Grenadier Regiment 79.

The Soviets were gathering their forces. They were planning, in view of their finally succeeding in setting up a strategic bridgehead, a double thrust, to the right towards Stuhlweissenburg and to the left towards Fünfkirchen–Kaposvár–Nagykanisza. The push to the north-west on Stuhlweissenburg was the responsibility of the 4th Guards Army, crossing at Mohács, the push west-north-westwards on Fünfkirchen the responsibility of the 57th Army. Seven large units were to line up for the forthcoming large-scale offensive, supported by a fleet of aircraft and the Red Danube Flotilla. On the 16th, a pontoon bridge laid at Kisköszeg allowed these units (consisting of 10th Guards Airborne Division, 20th and 61st Guards Rifle Divisions and 32nd Guards Mechanised Brigade) to roll uninterruptedly into their assembly area round Izsép-Topolje.

To meet this challenge on the German side on 24 November 1944, the following reinforcements brought into the Kisköszeg combat area: I/749 deployed on the heights to the south of Kisfalud and III/750 under the command of the Division 'Brandenburg'. A further *Jäger* battalion with a mountain battery set off this day on the march from Brcko. So, it was battalions against divisions! The weight of enemy superiority showed itself to be extremely serious! It was true that the removal of the entire 1st *Volks-Gebirgs* Division from the Drina front to be deployed north of the Drau was under way. However, it should be borne in mind that even the transport movements of the 44th Infantry Division 'Hoch und Deutschmeister' had only just been completed on this date, while their units, until now deployed in stages, were already knocked about a bit!

The fact that Army Group F was not in a position to bring up any significant reinforcements to destroy the extended enemy bridgehead disturbed Army Group South a great deal. Army Group South would wish the endangered sector to have been in their own area, so as to be able to tackle it with LXVIII Corps. But this, because of the difficulties of regrouping the *Panzerkorps,* remained only a plan.

During the course of the day the 3rd Hungarian Army ordered the evacuation of the Komitate of Tolna and Feiér, which had been declared operational areas. The battle for the bridgeheads could from this point on be considered as concluded, there was no longer any thought of pushing them back. For almost three weeks, from 7 November to 25 November 1944, the defensive fighting had raged at the enemy bridgeheads at Kisköszeg and facing Apatin, much longer than the Soviets had originally intended and than they would have liked. The Soviets' idea to try to cross the Danube in these really difficult sectors did indeed at first appear to be very sensible; they could have assumed that there they would be least expected. But then, that idea became their undoing: in the terrain of the Danube river flats, which was unfavourable for the attacker but advantageous to the defender, a few first-rate German soldiers prepared them a reception which blatantly thwarted the plans of the Soviet command. With small German forces a considerable enemy attacking force was tied up, an attacking force which stormed against the defenders with more and more fury.

The most hotly contested village of Kisköszegor, or Batina, was reduced in this fighting to rubble and ashes and has never risen from them. After the war the statue of the 'Heroic Woman Partisan' was erected there by the followers of Tito. An inscription on this memorial notes no fewer than 28,000 Soviets and partisans killed in the bridgeheads. That was an enormous number and, if one compares them with the total number of defenders, then one could simply call Kisköszeg a blood-pump that was pumping away the enemy's life blood.

A concomitant of this fighting should not go without mention. The Soviet *soldateska,* increasingly enraged by the lack of success at Kisköszeg, took out their revenge on the defenceless German population of the German villages opposite. Especially in Apatin and Batsch-Sentiwan, the Germans who had stayed behind suffered terrible excesses. They were brought up *en masse,* under fire, to build trenches. But, not only that, ethnic Germans were also forced into auxiliary service in the Soviet and partisan units. So that in the Soviet field hospitals, for instance, Batschka German doctors operated, without exception under compulsion. But they did it from a humanitarian point of view. But Germans were even forced into partisan units (so-called 'Petöfi Brigades') and compelled at gunpoint to go along with them as cannon fodder. If the often-used term 'compulsory draft' is used, it was that and not being called up into the Waffen-SS!

25 November 1944

Facing the sector of the Division 'Brandenburg' the enemy was reinforcing further from the Altwasser territory of the Danube and following up with heavy weapons. Apart from some enemy assault unit operations, which were repulsed, this front remained quiet.

At the front of the 44th Infantry Division 'Hoch und Deutschmeister' the heavy fighting continued. Enemy forces moving up against Kamenec with tanks were beaten back. In the high ground to the north of Kamenec and to the south of Branijna-Kisfalud the Soviets were able to gain ground locally.

The newly-brought-up I/ *Gebirgsjäger* Regiment 99 was set against fairly weak enemy forces which had trickled through to the south of Popovac/Bán.

In the 7km long sector between Udvar and Föherceglak-Knezevo, the enemy attack divisions occupied their assembly area facing the 31st SS Division. It remained relatively quiet there, as it did in the sector from Föherceglak to Bellye. During the night the batteries of Artillery Regiment 96 of the 44th Infantry Division 'Hoch und Deutschmeister' were withdrawn behind the Karasica and took up high ground positions on the ridge of the Villánver Mountains.

Things became hot that day in the 31st SS Division's sector in the area to the south of Mohács. Dubosevica-Dálvok, an area that had been hotly fought over, was snatched by stronger enemy forces, the units of the *SS Feld-Ersatz Bataillon* 31, I/ 80 and I/78 withdrawing northwards. The Soviets pushed on after them and penetrated into Udvar with infantry and 20 tanks. An armoured counter-attack to be carried out by Axis forces from woodland south of the village was caught in the flank by an enemy tank thrust while it was still in preparation and thus could not take effect. Fierce fighting unfolded.

Even in the new bridgehead before Kölked the Soviets did not remain idle. Units of the I/79 did tackle them, but in the face of the crushing superiority of the Soviets had to withdraw with casualties. Participants in the fighting recall:

St.R.:

> Middle of the night: Alarm! There were 13 of us, the assault unit of *SS-Sturmbannführer* Albrecht. It was black as pitch in pouring rain, we took *Panzerfäuste* and went towards some woodland south of Mohács, on the Kölked road. There were the Soviets. We tackled them. We thirteen men with three *Panzerfäuste* and two LMGs. Albrecht went forward and fired a *Panzerfaust* into a barn. The hay was ablaze. Now you could pick out the enemy well. The fight began. Albrecht gave his orders. Our left flank was soon shot to pieces. Albrecht gave the order to retreat. The Soviets didn't follow straight away. We went back to Mohács. As I later heard, many Soviets were also tackled by our unit from the side and pushed back into the Danube.

S. Gr.:

> The outpost has reported: Soviets have crossed at Kölked! Our company moved there directly out of Mohács and attacked the enemy, but they couldn't be thrown back any longer. In the fierce fighting the company leader, *SS-Untersturmführer* Alfred Berger, who always led from the front, copped it – seriously wounded! I - as his Adjutant – and the company bookkeeper, Julius Zink, a student from Obecse, worked our way forward, recovered him and brought

him back. Losing him was especially painful to us, because he was very popular and the two of us were really good friends.[3] As far as I know, in the fighting which followed the battalion commander, *SS-Sturmbannführer* Albrecht, was also wounded, in the arm.

Repeated attacks from the Béda Forest to the south-west of Kölked did not break through, the Soviets occupied the village, push on strongly and by 5pm were marching along the Mohács–Udvar road. This cut off the way to Mohács for the soldiers of the 31st SS Division (SS *Feld-Ersatz Bataillon* 31, II/78 and I/80) driven from the south and fighting around Udvar. They had to withdraw further westwards.

As a result of this advance the Soviets pushed forward northwards from the breakthrough area of Dubosevica/Dálvok, and were able to link up with their comrades advancing from Kölked and merge their small tactical bridgehead into a larger one. The forces of the 31st SS Volunteer Grenadier Division and the 44th Infantry Division 'Hoch und Deutschmeister' could not prevent the enemy from taking this step and had to withdraw to the line between the Kölked Tscharda and Sátorhelypuszta.

To the north of Udvar the enemy offensive was developing in two directions. The 20th Guards Rifle Division, the 10th Guards Airborne Division and the 32nd Guards Mechanised Brigade were advancing out of Udvar northwards along the Borza stream. The 41st Guards Rifle Division was pushing northwards out of the Kölked area on both sides of the Udvar–Mohács road, towards the town of Mohács. Both enemy attacks hit the units of the 31st SS Division: the I/78, II/78, I/79, I/80 and SS *Feld-Ersatz Bataillon* 31.

South of Mohács a fierce battle flared up between the units of 31st SS Volunteer Grenadier Division and the Soviets with their armoured support. The battle involved heavy casualties on both sides. The regimental commander of SS Volunteer Grenadier Regiment 80, *SS-Sturmbannführer* von Scanzony, was killed, together with the universally popular *SS-Oberscharführer* Hans Sator, who was shot in the head as the fierce and somewhat confused fighting moved over to the Uj-Istálló farm, where the Staff seem to have had their quarters. The Regiment, which had only one full battalion, involved in a fight to the death, was immediately taken over by *SS-Obersturmbannführer* Domes.

Eventually it was possible to halt the enemy attack directed at Mohács somewhere around the Fekete-Kapu high ground, 5km south of the edge of the town, where the armoured Soviet units were now faced with weak holding forces of the 31st SS Division (4th Company/Regiment 79 under *SS-Untersturmführer* Holderer). In order to avoid the right flank of the 31st SS Division being threatened, the units of the Division were ordered to withdraw along the general line Fekete-Kapu–Mohács.

---

3   *Untersturmführer* Alfred Berger came into a military hospital, then into a convalescent unit in Friesach/Kärnten, from where he then was taken in by a private family for further care at home. He was not able to return again to his unit, experienced the collapse in Kärnten, where as the result of a denunciation he became a British prisoner of war.

The enemy pushing west-north-westwards was also initially halted. The score sheet of 24 and 25 November on the LXVIII Corps sector of the front showed 14 Soviet tanks knocked out. But all this was only the prelude before the real great storm that was to break the next day and was designated as 'the defensive battle in southern Hungary'. With it, a new chapter also began in the war history of the 31st SS Division. In the fighting at the bridgeheads parts of the Division, it is true, those which, relatively speaking, had the greatest combat strength, took part, and these had to suffer significant casualties, but were also involved in important defensive successes. Now there began a greater test, the maelstrom of large scale fighting along the entire line into which the whole Division was to be swept.

CHAPTER 10

Defensive Battles in Southern Hungary, 26 November–6 December 1944

26 November 1944

After busy reconnaissance activity during the night, the morning saw the large-scale enemy offensive from the combined bridgehead continued with strong forces on a broad front. While the enemy in the Lug-Grabovac area, apart from some advances for reconnaissance, remained quiet, they continued their attacks with undiminished force against the front of the 44th Infantry Division 'Hoch und Deutschmeister'.

Two enemy divisions moved off in the direction of Kácsfalu/Jagodnjak and Keskend/Kozarac, two more stormed the villages of Hercegszölös and Karancs. A fierce battle flared up around both villages. Immediately, counter-attacks were made. In support the III/2nd 'Brandenburg', parts of *Gebirgsjäger* Regiment 99 and *Jäger* Regiment 750 were deployed in battalion strength. These, beginning from the Pélmonostor area, in a counter-attack from the north and from the south, threw back to the western part of the village the enemy who had broken through to Karancs, and later liberated the village. But in the afternoon, as a result of the strengthening enemy pressure, the Hungarian *Kampfgruppe* Balkay withdrew from Hill 243 (Steinberg, 4km north of Karancs), and this made the situation in Karancs itself unsustainable.

Popovac/Bán was lost on the night of 25 November 1944 to an attack by superior enemy forces. Further attacks, supported by armour, of the Soviet 113th Rifle Division south-westwards on Pélmonostor and Baranyavár, against Kamenec and in the heights south of the village, were repulsed by the parts of the 92nd (motorised) Brigade, the I/98th, the II/750th and *Aufklärungs Abteilung* 44. But the pockets of resistance were circumvented on the left by the Soviets with a further division. The 19th Rifle Division pushed forward from Bán south-eastwards against the commanding Hill 208. They took it and pushed forward west-north-westwards on a broad front between Baranyavár and Föherceglak. During the evening, this group of enemy forces reached the Ivándárda, Sárok, Bezedek and Lippó area.

In the sector of the 31st SS Division, in the area south of Mohács, the enemy was preparing to break through. They arrived on the historic battlefield of Mohács. It was truly an onslaught by latter-day Turks. And history repeated itself. As in 1526, so in 1944 the 'army of Europe' also lost the battle against 'the East' in this same place. The enemy breakthrough, with strong forces supported by armour was, in the face of weak elements of the 31st SS Division incapable of dealing with this type of large-scale battle, further widened to the north-west, west and north.

The fighting was continued on the edge of Mohács, the *Kampfgruppen* of the 31st SS Division (I/79) retiring by stages into the town.

By midday, the enemy attack carried out north-westwards had pushed the units of the 31st SS Volunteer Grenadier Division back to the line Ormánpuszta, to the south-western–eastern edge of Majs (the village was lost)–south-western edge of Töttös. There they were involved in desperate fighting with the 20th Guards Rifle Division that pushed up after them. In the evening they retreated behind the Karasica stream.

In the centre, i.e. between Töttös and Mohács, other units of the 31st SS Division were fighting against the 10th Guards Airborne Division and the 32nd Guards Mechanised Brigade, and were pushed back to the sector Nagynyárad north-west–Zsidopuszta–south-eastern edge of Lánycsók. Parts of SS Fusilier Battalion 31 were also thrown into the fighting here. In the afternoon the newly-formed security line of the Division ran on the approximate line west of Majs–Töttös–Nagynyárád and on to the high ground on both sides of Lánycsók, bending back from there to the southern edge of Mohács. This meant that the town of Mohács was surrounded on three sides, hence threatened with complete encirclement! The situation of the soldiers of the Division in the town (above all I/79 and II/79) was becoming precarious.

According to Army Group F's assessment of the situation at 4.45pm, the situation was, in general, very critical, but especially so on the northern wing, in parts of the 44th Infantry Division 'Hoch und Deutschmeister' and in the 31st SS Division. *Oberst* Bürker was of this opinion:

> Breakthrough widened as far as south of Mohács, westwards as far as Majs. At Beli Manastir counter-attack by us, small success, on northern wing with 44th Division and with 'Lombard' situation bad … Parts 'Lombard' ran away, gap opened up there, want to seal with help 71st Infantry Division. We will have to retire to 'Wieland Position' but order not yet given today; we want to hold north wing in district Mohács to Baja. Our intention to clear up situation with strong assembled forces 1st *Gebirgs* Division and 71st Infantry Division can no longer be carried out, we must deploy units as they arrive, that is to be expected. Certain consequences: withdrawal piece by piece…Enemy's intention: Push westwards and break through on to Fünfkirchen.

It was also pointed out that the broadening of the breakthrough would also have dire consequences for the Syrmian front, seriously endangering the supply lines for Army Group E. In addition to all this was the threat to Army Group South in Hungary. Things, he suggested, had become very serious and could no longer be sorted out with the forces to hand, rapid forces must be brought up to support the crumbling front – and that was a matter of urgency. The concluding statement read: "We are going to endure a quite severe crisis". That turned out to be true.

In Mohács, in the afternoon, the main line of resistance ran through the southern part of the town into which the 41st Guards Rifle Division had penetrated. The men of the 4/79, under *SS-Untersturmführer* Holderer, were putting up resistance on the small, elongated island on the Danube south of the town. Infantry guns of the 31st SS Division were in position and were shelling the Soviets from the flank. As well as the units of the 31st SS Division, there were in the town parts of *Ausbildungs und Ersatz* Battalion 135 and of the III/ *Ausbildungs und Ersatz* Regiment 44.

In command was the staff of SS Volunteer Grenadier Regiment 79; *SS-Sturmbannführer* Syr's command post was in the Korona inn in the middle of the town. At his disposal was a wireless detachment from SS *Nachrichten Abteilung* 31 under *Sturmmann* Fritz Mock. After hard fighting[1] the town was given up in the late afternoon. Just in time, because there was a threat of being cut off, and they only just managed to slip through! *SS-Oberscharführer* Hugo Krallmann from the staff of the *Nachrichten Abteilung*, on the orders of its commander *SS-Hauptsturmführer* Reimann, tried during the night on his 8-cylinder Mosch to provide wireless detachment Mock with rifle and machine-gun ammunition. He could find nobody there except Soviets.

S.R. a young ethnic German recruit of the 31st SS Volunteer Grenadier Division, recalled the experience:

> As our battalion commander Albrecht said, the situation was bloody awful, but not hopeless! We were in the lower town, my brother Adam on the Danube island with the infantry guns, but also my brother-in-law was not far away - he was serving in the Hungarian river patrol (Folyamörség). Things looked bad with the ammunition, for our machine-gun we only had 200 rounds, so the order was given to let the Soviets come to within 50m of us and only then open fire. We had gone round westwards, there was the threat of being completely encircled. Company commander *SS-Untersturmführer* Holderer withdrew without any orders from the regimental commander. He should have been shot by a firing squad for that… Our battalion commander… *SS-Sturmbannführer* Heinrich Albrecht was a daredevil, he could drive anything whether it was a car or an aeroplane and was always in front, in spite of being wounded in the leg. He just took a stick and put a slipper on his wounded leg. If everyone had been like him, no Soviet would have set foot on Hungarian soil! But then…! We had to withdraw, out of burning Mohács. Soviet aircraft had dropped incendiary bombs. Finally we were only just able to slip away out of the town through the gypsy quarter and so escape being encircled. But many men from my company remained there, many fellow-countrymen from our home village…after the war their bodies were exhumed and taken home.

After evacuating the town, the men who had been holding it withdrew north-westwards to the line Lanycsok–Hercegszabar. The enemy there only followed up slowly. The situation was nevertheless dangerous, because in the late afternoon the Soviets broke through the Ráctöttös–Nagynyárád security line, endangering their left flank. The units there withdrew westwards, as a result of which the area round Lánycsók, which was at first held, and the important road to Fünfkirchen, were endangered. The enemy was pushing westwards to Fünfkirchen, and at first did not turn northwards, while the enemy forces from the direction of Mohács had to wait for more units to be brought up in order to continue their attack northwards.

During the evening, fighting with heavy casualties developed between the withdrawing parts of the I/79, II/79, *SS Feld-Ersatz Bataillon* 31 and SS Fusilier Battalion 31 and the Soviets pushing up hard behind them on the main road to Fünfkirchen, at the village of Babarc. A.Gl. (I/79) recalled:

---

1   Not at all after "some exchanges of fire" as certain sources like to maintain.

Where the road from the village joined the Fünfkirchen–Mohács highway there was a bus shelter. Here we took up temporary positions, because the enemy was at our heels. At the edge of the road stood our horse-drawn carts, with us behind them. Since ammunition was very scarce, we had orders to let the Soviets come up close and only open fire from a safe short distance. They opened fire from a safe distance on us! They all had machine-pistols (Mpis), among us not one of us had a rifle. First, they shot up our horses, the poor beasts, running wild, over-ran us …Night, black as pitch, pouring rain …it was hellish! The fight was fairly short, we soon withdrew in the direction of Liptód. But many comrades were killed here, including fellow-countrymen from my home village. One got shot in the head right at the start. The second also got a mortal wound. The third got shot in the stomach and was left in a house in Bawarz where he then died. The fourth also copped it in the stomach, he also stayed behind, but survived and went home.

Twenty-four soldiers of the Division, mostly just eighteen years old, were killed there and were later buried by the parish authorities side by side in the same place.[2] They are lying there still today. The bodies were plundered by the Soviets, and their papers were scattered so that not all of them could be definitely identified. Most of them belonged to *SS Feld-Ersatz Bataillon* 31. There were among them also members of SS Fusilier Battalion 31, the I/79, the II/79, the I/80 and SS Artillery Regiment 31. This points to the fact that at that time the units of the Division

2   Their names, as far as these are known:
   1.   SS *Mann* Martin Fackelmann, from Elek/Hungarian Banat, born 1925.
   2.   Unknown soldier.
   3.   Unknown soldier.
   4.   Unknown soldier.
   5.   SS Grenadier Martin Fett, 4/SS Volunteer Grenadier Regiment 80, from Kaposfö/Somogy, b.1926.
   6.   SS *Unterscharführer* Julius Lazar, 4/SS Vol. Grenadier Regiment 79, from Gross-Lomnitz/Zips/Slovakia
   7.   SS Gunner Hans Kromer, from Apatin/Batschka, b.1927
   8.   SS Rifleman Franz Klein, from Szond/Batschka, b.1926.
   9.   Unknown soldier
   10.   Unknown soldier
   11.   Unknown soldier
   12.   Unknown soldier.
   13.   SS Grenadier Josef Pentz, Staff II/79, from Orszállás/Stanischitsch/Batschka, b.1905.
   14.   SS *Unterscharführer* Werner Bohnhoff, from Hamburg, b.1924.
   15.   SS Grenadier Philipp Diener, SS-FEB 31, from Tscerwenka/Batschka, b.1927.
   16.   SS Grenadier Jakob Arth, SS-FEB 31, from Tscherwenka/Batschka, b.1927.
   17.   SS Grenadier Hans Jauch, SS-FEB 31 from Tschonopol/Batschka, b.1927.
   18.   SS Grenadier Philipp Noe, SS-FEB 31.
   19.   SS Grenadier Philipp Fries, from Kisker/Batschka, b.1927.
   20.   SS Grenadier Kilia Schiffmann, SS-FEB 31, from Kiskér/Batschka, b.1927.
   21.   SS Grenadier Christian Dietrich, SS-FEB 31.
   22.   SS Grenadier Wendel Schoblocher, Staff I/79, from Vaskút/Batschka, b.1926.
   23.   SS Grenadier Georg Block, from Elek/Hungarian Banat.

had already become intermixed. Two NCOs were also killed there, *SS-Unterscharführer* Julius Lázár from Gross-Lomnitz/Zips and *SS-Unterscharführer* Werner Bohnhoff from Hamburg.

Generally, the situation was developing according to the breakthroughs on the right flank of the 44th Infantry Division 'Hoch und Deutschmeister', and at the point where the Division joined the 31st SS Volunteer Grenadier Division. The resulting gap in the front force led to the withdrawal of the entire front line sector of the 2nd *Panzer* Army on the night of 26 November 1944. They drew back to the general line Grabovac/Albertfalu – Kozarac / Keskend – Haljevokanal – Sumarina – Lapáncsa – Villány – Szederkény. There was strengthened enemy pressure from one Soviet and one partisan corps on the road from the northern edge of Esseg–Hercegszölös. There was also the loss of the Steinberg to the north of Karancs and of the village itself. This made it necessary for the left flank of the Division 'Brandenburg' to be bent back on to Kozarac/Keskend. The *Gebirgsjäger*, *Jäger* and Brandenburgers retired into the positions behind the Bellye–Keskend–Pélmonostor highway. Because of this on the one hand, and because of the breakthroughs into the Majs area on the other hand, the forces at Pélmonostor and Baranyavár, parts of 92nd (mot.) Brigade, 44th Infantry Division 'Hoch und Deutschmeister', 117th *Jäger* Division, together with *StuG Abteilung* 46, were forced to withdraw into the positions on high ground between Löcs and Villány behind the Karasica, after they had blown up the bridges over the stream.

The units of the 31st SS Volunteer Grenadier Division withdrew during the night from the line Tötös–Lánycsók. They were also incorporated into the Karasica position, and were directed to the sector Borjád–Mariakémend and further on as far as Késked. Army Group F was concerned about this gap in the line, which they intended to seal with the 71st Infantry Division. This had just arrived, and was at the same time to support the sector of the 31st SS Division, who were not yet reliable under fire. But of this eagerly awaited division, on that date only the advance command with 2 companies of I/Grenadier Regiment 194 had arrived in Fünfkirchen.

On that date the Army Group F's war diary mentioned that "parts of Lombard's Division have deserted". This sweeping statement did not entirely correspond with the facts. Nevertheless the fact was that many of the Division's recruits, distraught by the raging battle, neither properly trained nor properly armed, just took to their heels again. Of course, not over to the Soviets; rather, they tried to get home, to the villages of the Batschka. This became their undoing. They ran straight into Soviet hands and were taken prisoner. They crossed the Danube under strict Soviet guard over the pontoon bridge at Kisköszeg and soon found themselves in the Soviet collection camp at Temeschwar.

27 November 1944

On the southern flank the defensive fighting raged on with undiminished ferocity, some ground was lost and the administrative capital Dárda fell. In the centre, the enemy was advancing on the defensive positions on the Karasica. Lasting from about 10am until the evening was a mortar duel in the Lapáncsa–Magyarbóly or Magyarbóly–Virágos sector, between the units of the 44th Infantry Division

'Hoch und Deutschmeister' and the Soviets closing up along the security line. Several enemy units advanced against Villány but were repulsed.

Also on the left flank, in the 31st SS Division sector, north of Borjád, the Soviets were closing up from the breakthrough area Mohács–Majs up to the defensive position on the Karasica. Stronger enemy forces with armour pushed forward during the morning via Németbóly to the Mohács–Fünfkirchen road. They took Szederkeny and there crossed the new main line of resistance facing the weak security positions. The first parts of the 71st Infantry Division (2 companies, I/Grenadier Regiment 194) were placed in this defensive position. Weaker enemy forces turned south-westwards and took Kiskassa. Another group of them advanced along the Karasica valley northwards via Máriakéménd and occupied Hill 218. An armoured group, some 40 tanks strong, but without infantry, pushed westwards on to Fünfkirchen. Flak forces that had been brought up only 12km from the southeastern edge of Fünfkirchen destroyed 12 enemy tanks, immobilised 3 and brought the advance to a halt.

On the northern flank the parts of the 31st SS Volunteer Grenadier Division conducting the defence along the approximate line Lánycsók–Bár, whose will to fight was greatly flagging, gave way to the strengthened enemy pressure. They retired to the line Himesháza–Somberek–Dunaszekcsö. The result was that the enemy was able to take Lánycsók, Hercegszabar and Bár at the first attempt. The new defensive line was held until the evening. To provide the necessary cover for this sector of the front, parts of Grenadier *Ersatz* Training Regiment 44 were brought up. At Hercegszabar, the universally popular *SS-Oberscharführer* Helmuth Wenzel of the Divisional Staff was killed. On 27 November 1944 *SS-Untersturmführer* Franz Strich, leader 14/78, was listed as missing.

At Mohács, too, an enemy pontoon bridge was now built, over which on that day more large units crossed over the Danube. It was true that the day ran somewhat quieter and with smaller loss of ground than on the previous one. The Soviets were gathering their forces for the decisive breakthrough to Fünfkirchen and taking up their assembly positions, planned for this purpose, opposite the Karasica positions. But the situation remained extremely dangerous. The front was hopelessly over-extended and the available forces were too small.

According to the tactical textbook a Division should defend a 10km-long sector of front. From the northern edge of Esseg up to around Késked there were over 60km of main line of resistance, not counting the northern blocking position between Himesháza and Dunaszekcsö. The length of battle line was defended by only 5½ divisions. That number would have been about right if those were divisions at full combat strength. But they were battle-weary, varied *Kampfgruppen* whose forces had not been replenished. They only just retained the designation of Division and moreover had only arrived in dribs and drabs. The I/*Jäger* Regiment 750, the Staff *Jäger* Regiment 750 and the I/Grenadier Regiment 891 had only just arrived in the combat zone on 26 November 1944. At the same time the II/*Gebirgsjäger* Regiment 99 of the 1st *Volks-Gebirgs* Division had only just unloaded in Esseg.

The 31st SS Division was finally torn apart. One large section stood on the Karasica between Borjád and Keskend, the other on the line Himesháza–Dunaszekcso, while the rearward services of the Division were still in the Villány area (or in Fünfkirchen). The units had become mixed up. There were no longer any 'regimental lines of demarcation'. Thus, parts of Regiment 78 appeared in the area of Regiment 79, in Hercegszabar and Hercegmárok, and also in Szederkény and to the south. The *Kampfgruppen* had to hold a hopelessly over-extended front.

To the north there was a gaping hole in the front that seriously endangered the southern wing of Army Group South. Moreover, the Himesháza–Dunaszekcsö line was none too strong a wall against the onslaught of an enemy with strong forces. Army Group South therefore suggested that the OKH place their southern flank, located in the Bonyhád–Bátaszék–Szekszárd area, and the 3rd Hungarian Army in the same area, under the command of Army High Command 6, i.e. General Maximilian von Fretter-Pico. They had to bring up the LVII *Panzerkorps*, under *Generalleutnant* Kirchner, to the sector of the II Hungarian Army Corps. At first, however, no decision was made on the suggestion.

Since the fighting was raging only 15 to 20km from Fünfkirchen, during the day orders were given for the military and civilian evacuation of the town.

28 November 1944

The Soviets attacked with all their forces along the whole front and the battle raged along the entire line until evening. On the southern flank, the four attacking divisions, two Soviet and two partisan, after days of heavy fighting, succeeded in taking more ground. Division 'Brandenburg' and Grenadier Brigade (motorised) 92, together with the *Panzergrenadier* Assault Battalion of *Panzer* AOK (Army High Command) 2 (Rudno Assault Brigade), the only available units, had been thrown in at Fünfkirchen because of the deteriorating situation there during the course of the day.

As a result the front had had to be shortened. Ceminac/Laschkafeld, Jagodnjak/Kácsfalu fell, the new security line was formed between Point 87 (3km WSW of Bolmány)–Zeleno Polje (6km NNW of Bolmány)–Löcs and taken over by SS *Kampfgruppe* Hanke, which from now on was under the command of the 44th Infantry Division 'Hoch und Deutschmeister'. The sector between Bolmány and Nagyharsány was taken over by the two battalions of *Jäger* Regiment 750, the I/98 and *Aufklärungs Abteilung* 44.

The I/79 and the newly brought up III/99 of the 1st *Volks-Gebirgs* Division from north of Esseg and from Bellye O to Point 85 (3km SW of Dárda) formed a bridgehead position over the Drau, against which, during the afternoon, the enemy carried out several assaults without success. The enemy who had infiltrated into the marshy area south-west of Bellye were thrown back.

The Karasica position adjoining from the north, on which parts of the Division 'Brandenburg', the 1st *Volks-Gebirgs* Division, the 44th Infantry Division 'Hoch und Deutschmeister' and the 31st SS Division were standing from Löcs to Késked, was attacked during the early hours of the morning at two points.

The first point of concentration was the front of the 44th Infantry Division 'Hoch und Deutschmeister' west of Magyarbóly–east of Villány, where several strong attacks by the Soviet 19th Rifle Division were repulsed. A dangerous breakthrough was prevented by SS Volunteer Workshop Company 31. They were in Villány with other rearward services of the 31st SS Division, still forming up. When the breakthrough took place, they occupied, as alarm units, defensive posi-

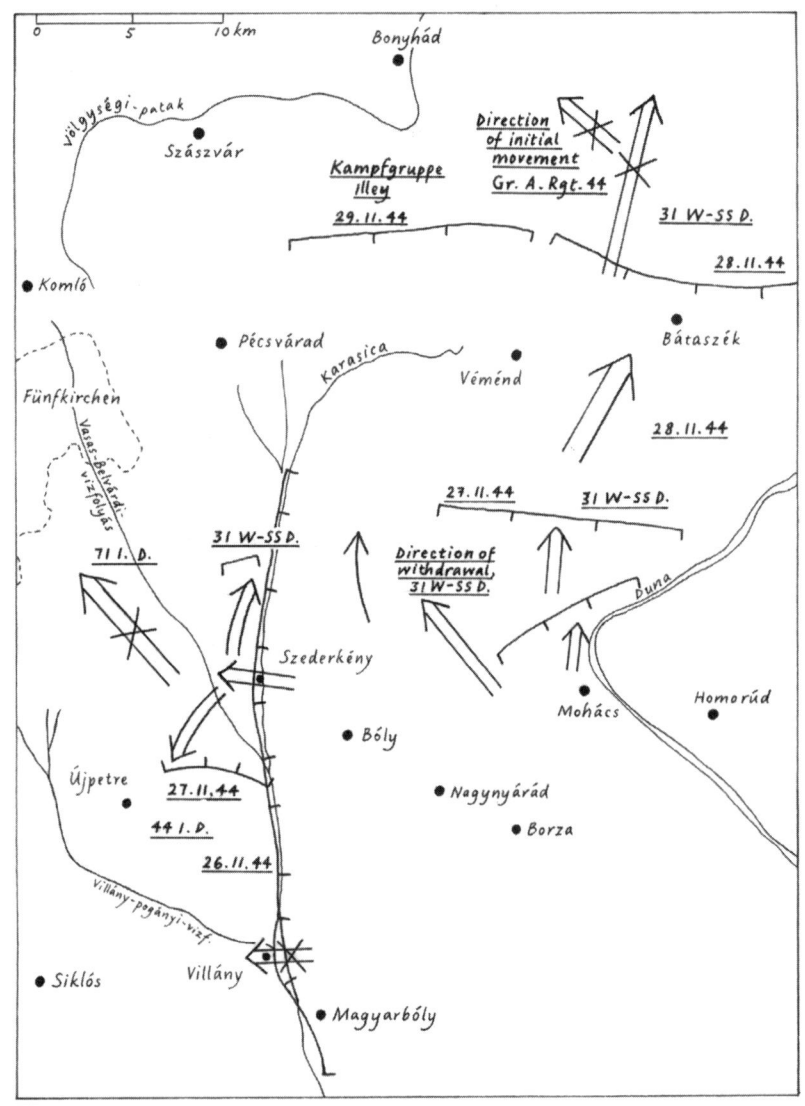

Map 2 Breakthrough east of Fünfkirchen on 27 November 1944, and the northern 'Riegelstellung', 27-28 November 1944.

tions in the endangered area and blocked the roads with minefields. The enemy breakthrough attempt was successfully halted. The heavy fighting at Villány lasted until the evening. The enemy wanted to take the road to Siklós so as to be able to push forward rapidly along it.

The second point of concentration was a little more to the north, to the west of Németbóly, between Szederkény and Kiskassa, where the Soviets had already crossed over the main line of resistance the previous day. The Soviets rebuilt the Karasica bridges between Villány and Villágos and brought the 3rd Rifle Brigade as well as two assault gun brigades after them into the breakthrough area. Here stood parts of the left flank of the 44th Infantry Division 'Hoch und Deutschmeister' and units of the 31st SS Division. They launched several counter-attacks against the Soviets in the area of Szederkény and Belvárdgyula, but were not able to halt them. The left flank of the 44th Infantry Division 'Hoch und Deutschmeister' was pushed back to Rácpetre, then right up to the northern edge of the range of the Villyáner Mountains, whereby their extreme left rested on Kistótfalu. The parts of the 31st SS Volunteer Grenadier Division positioned between Borjád and Szederkény withdrew in the direction of Fünfkirchen.

In the area of their breakthrough between Kiskassa and the Danube, the enemy were bringing up more new forces and were continuing to push forward north and north-westwards towards Fünfkirchen. On both sides of the Szederkény–Fünfkirchen road were the four battalions of the 71st Infantry Division (Infantry Regiment 184 with 4 anti-tank guns and one further battalion). They had arrived as the first stage of defence, the night before, in Fünfkirchen. They were immediately thrown into the fighting. The 71st Infantry Division was to come from Istria by express, but was late because of blown up railway lines.

Disaster was looming by noon. The left flank in the breakthrough area, i.e. the defensive line from Szederkény, about as far as Késked, was manned mainly by units of the 31st SS Division. These could not withstand the enemy pressure that was constantly increasing. Because of the critical situation in the breakthrough area, the *Kampfgruppen* retired in the general direction of Pécsvárad. As a result, firstly the road to Fünfkirchen became open, and secondly a large area of Army Group South's southern flank was exposed.

Added to this was the fact that the two army groups thought differently about the further intentions of the enemy. In Army Group F they were of the opinion that the enemy were concentrating their forces westwards, on Fünfkirchen. It was thought that they would then regroup their strong forces and in the process bring up new units from Bulgaria, in order to begin a general offensive across the Danube westwards. It was true that at that moment the main pressure was really on Fünfkirchen and less against the southern flank of Army Group South in the northern blocking position. That position was full of gaps, between Himesháza and Dunaszekcsö. On the other hand, Army Group F believed that the Soviets wanted to attack southwards across the Drau, which would create a very precarious situation in Croatia. If there was no setback here, the Drau front would become longer and longer. In this light, Army Group F was also taking countermeasures.

All the forces that could be used would be deployed to the west of Fünfkirchen and on the Drau. The intention was to hold up the enemy push westwards, or to repulse a southward advance over the Drau. Since the cover was already much too short, as on the northern flank south of Bátaszék, to where its area joined the southern flank of Army Group South, Army Group F was not able to bring up any more appreciable forces to support the units already there. Amongst them were parts of the 31st SS Division.

Army Group South assessed the situation somewhat differently. They agreed that the Soviets would attack along the entire Danube line. But they thought that the Soviets would advance in the Army Group South area, on Stuhlweissenburg, with the aim of invading Budapest from the west, as well as in the area of the 2nd *Panzer* Army towards the oilfield district at Nagykanisza. (This was correct, these were the real intentions of the Soviet command as already discussed). In this light, however, it was an absolutely urgent necessity to reinforce the junction between the two Army Groups, to stop up the wide gap caused by the withdrawal of the 31st SS Division and to secure the roads and passes in the mountains to the north of Fünfkirchen. Since Army Group F did not seem to be in a position to do this, Army Group South wished to bring under its own command the entire sector north of the Drau.

The Chief of Staff of Army Group South, *Generalleutnant* Helmuth von Grolman, at 10.55am rang *Generalleutnant* August Winter at OKW. He informed him that, in his opinion, contrary to that of Army Group F, the Soviet attack would continue to the north-west and the north. But Army Group F had nevertheless set up their defence to deal with an enemy push to the west. Army Group South, he said, therefore requested that the LXVIII Corps be placed under their command. *Generalleutnant* Winter was of the opinion that Army Group F must keep these forces, in order to have at their disposal the greatest possible fighting force north of the Drau. He believed that would bring the Soviet onslaught to a halt, but he wished to report the matter to *Generaloberst* Guderian.

Following their request, they did not believe that Fünfkirchen could be held for long, despite the fact that the 71st Infantry Division had been brought up. On the threatened southern flank were, as before, the weak forces of the II Hungarian Army Corps. In the first line between Pécsvárad and Pörböly was also the 1st River Brigade. Along with 6 Hungarian battalions, the Szekler IX Flak *Abteilung*, 3 light batteries, as well as the 4 battalions of Grenadier Training Regiment 44 were all on that day placed under the command of the River Brigade. Until then it had belonged to the 31st SS Volunteer Grenadier Division of Group 'Lombard'.

The mountain roads leading north were secured by the following units. The road between Pécsvárad and Mecseknádasd - III/Grenadier *Ausbildungs* Regiment 44 and the Hungarian *Kampfgruppe* Illey (2nd and 3rd River Patrol sections) - were secured with one battery. The road between Pécsvárad and Bátaszék was secured by the 135th Field Training Battalion, the 55th Hungarian Frontier *Jäger* Battalion, and the Neusatz police battalion with 3 batteries. In Bátaszék were one Hungarian Frontier *Jäger* company and the 16th Frontier *Jäger* Battalion with 4 anti-aircraft guns. On the railway between Bátaszék and Pörböly were the II/134th, I/486th and Hungarian II/139th. In the second line between Fadd and Bölcske were the eight battalions of the 23rd Hungarian Infantry Division with 11 anti-tank guns, 23 artillery pieces and a flak battery.

These forces were not sufficient to mount a sustained defence against a strong enemy attack. Therefore it was the intention of Army Group South to move the

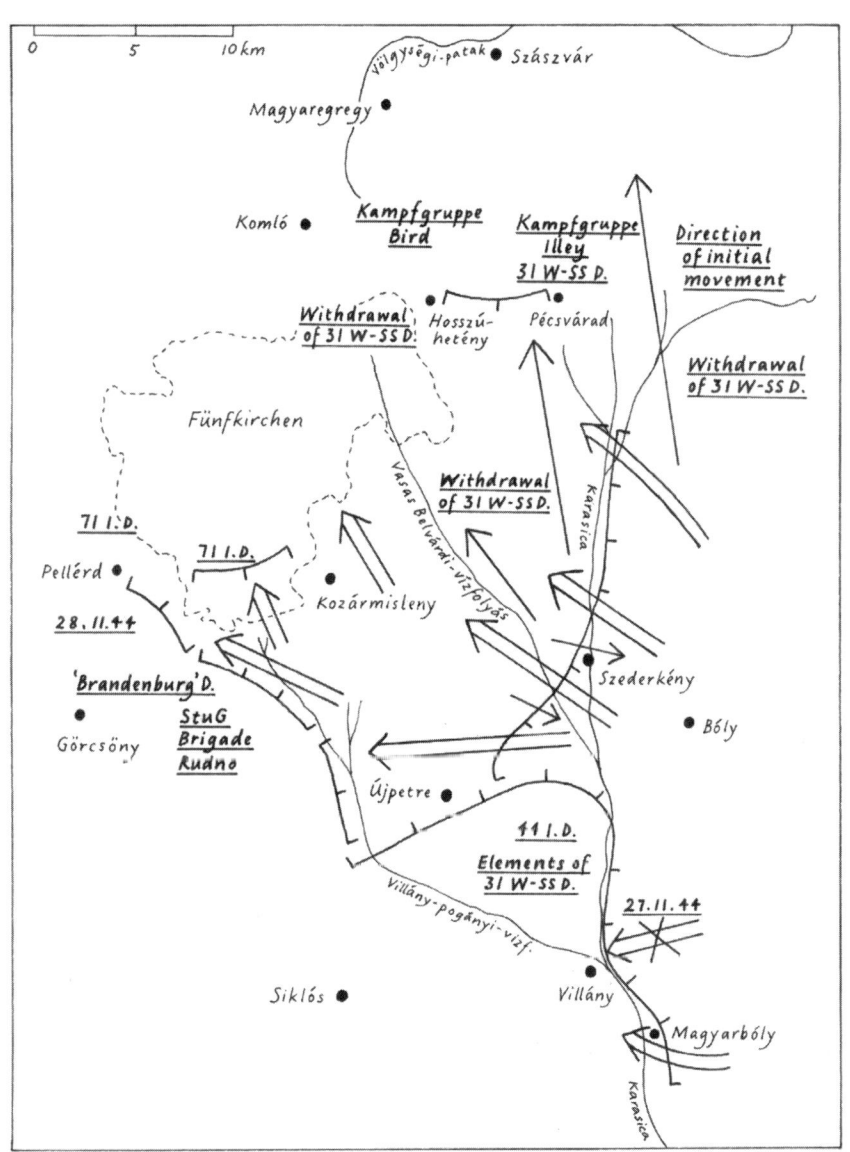

Map 3 The fall of Fünfkirchen, 28 November 1944.

LVII *Panzerkorps* (*Generalleutnant* Kirchner) to the junction point. In the early hours of the morning, parts of the 23rd *Panzer* Division were sent off on the march to Simontornya. The 1st *Panzer* Division was also prepared to be transferred into that area. In addition, artillery and flak units, assault guns and *Panzerjäger*, together with the 21 King Tigers of the 503rd *schwere Panzer Abteilung* were led into the depths of the endangered southern flank.

These precautionary measures were fully justified, as indicated by the events of the battle that began stormily at midday. At Army Group F, at mid-day, they still optimistically stated that "the situation at Fünfkirchen appears to be secured as a result of the arrival of a third of the 71st Infantry Division". However, the advance guards of the Division 'Brandenburg' (reinforced by parts of Grenadier Brigade (mot.) 92 and the Hungarian *Kampfgruppe* Balkay) on the Siklós–Fünfkirchen road 6km south of the town, were already meeting strong enemy forces and had to set up defensive positions. The closing of the gap between 44th Infantry Division 'Hoch und Deutschmeister' and southern flank 71st Infantry Division, for which these forces had been planned, did not succeed against an enemy advancing on a broad front. As a result, it became possible for them to invade Fünfkirchen from the south.

The Soviet 20th Guards Rifle Division, 10th Guards Airborne Division and 32nd Guards Mechanised Brigade pushed forward on to the town from the east and south-east. The regimental group of the 71st Infantry Division, reinforced with 4 batteries and flak, which had been already thrown into the battle, was thrown back to the eastern and south-eastern edges of the town. There, during the evening, fierce fighting was still raging with enemy infantry supported by tanks, during which it became apparent that Fünfkirchen would be penetrated from the south. At 8pm there was a fifteen-minute barrage on the defensive positions, then two enemy divisions with three armoured groups and a motorcycle regiment broke into the town. After some resistance, during the night of 28 November 1944 the rearguards of the 71st Infantry Division evacuated the town and withdrew in the direction of Pellérd and the railway line.

The enemy breakthrough westwards was blocked in a makeshift sort of way. As late as the next morning parts of the 71st Infantry Division held the security line Mecsekalja O–Point 593. To the south were adjoined, as far as Kökény, the Division 'Brandenburg' (now under the command of the 71st Infantry Division). They were engaged in a defensive battle against the enemy who continued to vigorously push forward. Between Kökény–Szalánta and Kistótfalu, the Rudno Assault Brigade (Grenadier Brigade (mot.) 92 plus *Panzergrenadier* Assault Battalion) was beginning to build a security line. The line guaranteed a hold on the cornerstone that consisted of the front of the 44th Infantry Division 'Hoch und Deutschmeister', running along the Villany mountains at Kistótfalu. They were able to close up the wide gap between the left flank 44th Infantry Division 'Hoch und Deutschmeister' and the right flank *Kampfgruppe* 71st Infantry Division, deployed at Kökény west of Fünfkirchen.

With reference to the succinct statement of Army Group South in its war diary that "Fünfkirchen was lost with the help of an uprising of communist miners" it was certainly not the case. There was actually some sniping activity and in the evacuation of the town ordered the previous day, some acts of sabotage undoubtedly took place. Among other things, these prevented Hungarian Field Hospital No.526 from being withdrawn to the rear.

While the Soviets were fighting their way through to Fünfkirchen, the withdrawal of the majority of the 31st SS Division from the northern flank of the breakthrough area north-westwards to Pécsvärad was taking place. It was mentioned in the war diaries as follows:

"31st SS-Division is shattered" (War Diary Army Group F); "The 31st SS Division on the northern flank of the Army Group was completely shattered." (War Diary Army Group South); "Situation in the area of the 31st SS-Division unclear because of the lack of any dispatches. How far the enemy has advanced there we do not yet know. We must reckon with the possibility that parts of the Division of combat strength no longer exist." (War Diary Army Group F); "Situation at Fünfkirchen disastrous, 31st SS in the general flood north-westwards." (Report *Luftflotte* 4)

Those statements were accurate. From then on the lack of training and the completely insufficient equipment and weapons exacted their price. The young, completely distraught recruits of the Division were in no way up to a large-scale battle against a greatly superior enemy. In addition, the Division was supposed to hold a sector of the front of the same size as was suitable for a Division at full combat strength. It was no wonder that the totally muddled groups of men withdrew. There were far too few combat-experienced officers and NCOs. In addition they had suffered painful casualties in the fighting of the past days and weeks. Their numbers were not sufficient to keep the retreat within a more or less orderly framework. The units were shattered. Many young recruits with homes in the area disappeared. Others stayed and were killed.

The majority of the Division tried to get to Pecsvarád, where during the afternoon they built up local defensive positions. In Pécsvárad, too, was the divisional command post. The enemy was hot on their heels and by afternoon were already 3km south of Pécsvárad. Army Group South sent a liaison officer to the Divisional Staff of the 31st SS Volunteer Grenadier Division to sound them out about the situation. The situation was not exactly encouraging. It was questionable whether the shattered units could withstand a serious enemy attack. In any case, security positions were prepared on the edges of the village and behind the road to Fünfkirchen and manned mainly by the men of the I/78, the I/80 and Regiment 79.

Other remnants of the Division withdrew, "some of them as if fleeing"[3] in the direction of Püspöknádasd, where the Hungarian *Kampfgruppe* Illey began to bring them under control. Remnants of the Division coming from the Hercegszabar–Himesháza direction also turned up there for the first time.

In the meantime, things looked bleak at Army Group F's northern blocking position on the line Himesháza–Somberek–Dunaszekcso. In this area, too, during the course of the day enemy pressure considerably increased, if not quite to the same degree as it did to the west. Heavy fighting developed and the weak parts of the 31st SS Division there had to retire further northwards. The retreat passed through Palotabozsok. To the south of Bátaszék a security position was again taken up by parts of the I/78 and Regiment 79, to block off the enemy breakthrough.

---

3 Quoted from the War Diary of Army Group South.

The thinly manned positions, at focus points only, stretched from around the southern edge of Mórágy to the community of Pörböly in the Danube meadows. Thus they formed the left flank of the similarly weak and uncertain security line of the 3rd Hungarian Army, formed from Hungarian blocking detachments and the remnants of the 3rd SS Replacement and Training Regiment 44. Together with flak and anti-tank units, they were supposed to prevent the northward infiltration of enemy forces on a broad front across the hilly landscape from Pécsvárad to Bátaszék. In command was the II Hungarian Army Corps. How thin was this cover was demonstrated by the fact that already on that day a Soviet cavalry reconnaissance unit advanced 7km east of Bonyhád. It had been repulsed, as was another, south of Szekszárd.

The end result for the day was not exactly promising. *Generalfeldmarschall* von Weichs, the supreme commander of Army Group F, informed *Generaloberst* Friessner, the supreme commander of Army Group South, in a telephone conversation at 10.25am, that the Soviet advance westwards had been temporarily blocked. The situation, even there, looked hopeless at best. For the northern sector, he said, no forces at all were available. Friessner replied that he would lead everything he could lay his hands on in this sector and that the main thing was to stop the enemy advance westwards.

Hopeless too was the situation of the 31st SS Volunteer Grenadier Division at the end of this black day in its young life. The Division was completely splintered and shattered. Individual groups of men were standing here and there on an almost 100km long curve from the Villány area via Fünfkirchen to east of Bátaszék. Of most of the remaining groups even the Divisional command had no news at all. S.Gr. (I/79) recalled the turbulent events of those days:

> After the loss of Mohács we retreated towards Versend, and then retreated again, towards Pécsvárad, we had no rest, events came one on top of the other. Many comrades were killed here, many quite close to their home villages, like the two Kress brothers. By the way, they were members of the 'Loyalty Movement' and had in no way voluntarily joined the SS, but nevertheless did their duty.
>
> Before Pécsvárad, in the village of Nagypál, there was a noteworthy event. On the march we were really bothered by the well-known Soviet 'sewing machine', also called UvD[4]. At Nagypál one of them got what was coming to it. We had an *Unterscharführer*, he was called Lachmut, a rough, red-haired man; he was a tough trainer. When he spotted the 'sewing machine', he sat down, instead of taking cover, behind a small apricot tree on the ground, propped up the machine-gun in a fork in the little tree's branches, took aim very carefully and then fired off a burst. Direct hit! Pouring out a lot of smoke, the aircraft went into a dive and was smashed on the ground.

29 November 1944

The Soviets broadened their breakthrough area both north-west and northwards. The German bridgehead on the Drau was narrowed on the night of 28 November

---

4   The PO-2 biplane, widely employed as a 'nuisance bomber' by the Soviets up until the end of the war.

1944. The Soviets immediately followed up and during the day kept the stretch of road in the bridgehead under lively mortar fire.

Between the Drau and the Villány mountains the Soviets, during the morning, pushed further westwards and reached Egyházasharaszti. By evening they were already facing the town of Siklós, which at midnight had to suffer a heavy barrage of Soviet artillery. Parts of *Jäger* Regiment 750 put up resistance until 3am on 30 November 1944, and then the town fell into enemy hands. The defenders withdrew to the line from the west of Siklós, west of Torjanci.

The northern point units of the enemy attacked during the morning. They swung from the area west of Villány into a northerly direction. Then they pushed forward, as far as Túrony, Bisse W, Szalánta SE, Németi W and Szökéd SW. In that area they concentrated their forces on the junction between the 44th Infantry Division 'Hoch und Deutschmeister' and 71st Infantry Division. There the gap between the left flank of the 44th Infantry Division 'Hoch und Deutschmeister' and the right flank of the *Kampfgruppe* 71st Infantry Division, deployed at Kökény (west of Fünfkirchen) had been sealed the previous day by the Rudno Assault Brigade.

Heavy fighting was also going on without a pause in the area surrounding Fünfkirchen. On the stretch of railway line at Péllerd to the south-west of the town, the Divisional Commander of the 71st Infantry Division was building a security line with a reinforced regiment of his Division and a *Kampfgruppe* from the Division 'Brandenburg'. On the western, north-western and northern edges of the town, rearguards of the 71st Infantry Division were putting up stubborn resistance and turned back many enemy attacks with armoured support. Also, parts of the 31st SS Volunteer Grenadier Division (probably I/80 and SS Fusilier Battalion 31) were still fighting at Pecsbanyatelep, Somogy, Vasas and Hird against the Soviet 10th Guards Airborne Division which was pushing up after them. It was supported by parts of Flak Regiment 231 and two Hungarian battalions (13th Reconnaissance Field Reserve Battalion and Battalion 'Mecsek'), which units also covered the subsequent withdrawal of these parts of the Division towards Kaposvár.

Other parts of the 31st SS Division (mainly from II//8 and Regiment 79) defended the important village of Pecsvarád at the junction between the two army groups. The roads on both sides of the village, running northwards, were secured by Hungarian groups, and reinforced with German flak units. Pécsvárad was attacked by the Soviet 80th Guards Rifle Division with strong armoured support. Several enemy attacks were repeatedly repulsed. Finally, however, towards 7pm, enemy superiority threw the weak parts of the 31st SS out of the village back to Puspoknadasd (today Mecseknádasd). Other parts (as for instance, the Staff of I/79) withdrew in the direction of Komló.

At the same time as the fighting for Pécsvárad raged, another point unit of the enemy attack (7th Guards Airborne Division) swung northwards along the eastern flank of the attacking Soviet Army Corps. In this area, at Püspöknádasd, Cikó and Möcsény, were the Hungarian securing forces with the remnants of the 31st SS Division and Grenadier Training Regiment 44, charged with the task of blocking the roads leading northwards and north-westwards from the Mecsek suburbs.

In order to clarify the command arrangements, at 8.45pm, Army Group South issued an organisational measure. The order said that all the scattered forces and remnants of units in the area, even if they belonged to Army Group F but were not in communication with the Army Group, were immediately to come under the command of the 3rd Hungarian Army. They were to be used to block the Mecsek suburbs. Through this order the remnants of the 31st SS Division, and thus the greater part of the Division with the Divisional Staff, located in the Püspöknádasd–Bátaszék area, came under the command of the 3rd Hungarian Army. Its II Hungarian Army Corps was in command on this front, while the parts of the Division in the area to the south of this remained with the LXVIII Corps.

According to unconfirmed information, command over the entire II Hungarian Army Corps (which only had command over the thrown-together Hungarian blocking units and the remnants of the 31st SS) was supposed to be transferred to the divisional staff of *Oberführer* 'Lombard'. The Divisional Staff 31st SS Division appear to have been located during this period first in the Szekszárd area, then in Dunaföldvár, then in Cece. Whatever was the case, various parts of the same 31st SS were with two army groups, in other words, a completely confused situation!

These measures for securing the Mecsek suburbs were it is true, still only in place at certain key points and were too thin to be able to prevent the enemy infiltrating between the blocking units. During the evening the Soviets were already appearing directly to the south of Rabenschwanz/Hidas-Felsö, directly in the rear of the *Kampfgruppe* in Püspöknádasd (I/79, II/79, *SS Feld-Ersatz Bataillon* 31). Bonyhád was also attacked and fell after a short battle in which two Hungarian battalions, a Hungarian battery, parts of Hungarian *Kampfgruppe* Illey and also parts of SS Volunteer Grenadier Regiment 79 and the II/78 were involved. The defenders were thrown back to the line Tevel–Zomba–Sióagárd. The course taken by the fighting in Rabenschwanz/Hidas-Felsö and Bonyhád forced the parts of the 31st SS Volunteer Grenadier Division which were still arriving in Püspöknádasd to withdraw after a few hours with further Hungarian units north-westwards towards Varalja.

Even at the northern blocking position at Bataszek fighting began again on the morning of the 29 November 1944. Weak enemy forces infiltrated between the blocking units (including parts of the 31st SS Division) and felt their way forwards northwards along the road in the direction of Szekszárd. A counter-attack by Hungarian units threw them back to Alsónána, but even there they were in the rear of Bátaszék. In the morning the town also fell. The I/134 was wiped out at Veránkapuszta. The weak Hungarian units, parts of Guards Regiment 39 with 2 police battalions from Debrecen and a battery, together with parts of the 31st SS Division (I/78 and parts of SS Volunteer Grenadier Regiment 79), fought a delaying action. They then withdrew in the direction of Szekszárd and built up a security line 6km to the south of Szekszárd–Ocsény–Donaubogen.

The end result of the day was a great loss of ground, especially to the north and north-west, together with withdrawal movements behind the Kapos and the Sió Canal with the enemy following up in strength. By evening the LXVIII Corps of the 2nd *Panzer* Army was positioned on the line Bolmány on the Drau–Siklós–Fünfkirchen West, but had no significant forces in the gap north of Fünfkirchen, where the Soviets were ensconced in Bonyhád and to the south of Szekszárd. The order of the OKW issued at 3am on 29 November 1944 to Army Group F to secure its links with Army Group South by a shift of forces remained simply a wish. The links between the two army groups were increasingly in danger.

This day of defensive fighting ensured that the 31st SS Division was completely splintered. Small remnants were all along the whole curve of the front extending over a length of more than 80km from Siklós to Szekszárd. There was no more contact between them, as most of these groups were in retreat.

30 November 1944

The large-scale battle continued along the entire line with undiminished intensity. At the narrowed bridgehead north of Esseg, during the course of the day several enemy attacks were repulsed. On the night of 30 November 1944 the bridgehead was evacuated after the Danube bridges had been blown.

On the shortened front of the 44th Infantry Division 'Hoch und Deutschmeister', to the west-south-west of Siklós, the enemy immediately followed pushed forwards. They continued to attack in the sector of *Kampfgruppe* Hanke (13th SS Division 'Handschar', now under the command of the 44th Infantry Division 'Hoch und Deutschmeister') on both sides of Alsószentmárton. A deep breakthrough to the south of the village was cleared, by bringing up III/ 750th.

In the area west of Siklós the fighting went on into the night. The enemy had pushed forwards westwards along the road to Harkány but was thrown back. The most hotly contested place was Szalanta at the junction between the 44th Infantry Division 'Hoch und Deutschmeister' and 71st Infantry Division. Numerous enemy attacks were repulsed, so that during the evening the place still remained in the hands of the *Panzergrenadier* Battalion.

The sector of Group 'Schneckman' consisted of the majority of 71st Infantry Division, parts of Division 'Brandenburg', *Gebirgsjäger* Regiment 99 and 54th Hungarian Frontier *Jäger* Battalion. Placed adjoining the north, between Szalánta and west of Fünfkirchen, the Group was in the midst of particularly bitter fighting, during which villages and hills changed hands several times.

In the area to the west of Fünfkirchen the enemy, in strength and with armoured support, was able to push back the troops of the 71st Infantry Division, only just thrown into the fighting off their transport, to the line Pellérd (7km SW of Fünfkirchen) Cserkút. During the course of this fighting three enemy tanks were knocked out. The enemy advanced north-westwards out of Fünfkirchen against weak Hungarian security forces and reached Abaliget.

The day was progressing even worse in the northern, from Püspöknádasd to Szekszárd. Army Group South was very worried. They recognised that the Soviet aim was to roll up the entire Danube front, to enable a further river crossing to be secured somewhere in the Paks Dunaföldvár area. But there was nothing available with which to fight off a strong Soviet push, northwards:

"The Hungarian blocking units and the 31st SS Division, as well as the 44th Grenadier Training Regiment, are no longer able to fight. The remnants of them, picked up by Hungarian units, are not capable of preventing infiltration of the enemy northwards on a broad front through the Mecsek mountains and east of there" – so read the war diary. Army Group South's hopes rested on the 23rd *Panzer* Division, and the 1st *Panzer* Division, which were on their way. But they had yet to arrive.

The difference of opinion between the two army groups concerning enemy intentions still continued. At noon, the Ia of Army Group F informed the Ia of Army Group South that the Drau–Fünfkirchen-West main line of resistance would be held for as long as possible. But if the enemy were to attack to the north of Fünfkirchen northwards, then "that sector would be in extraordinary danger". He said that Army Group F, however, maintained the view that they were trying either for a strategic breakthrough between the Drau and Lake Balaton, or for a political solution to be achieved through a large-scale offensive agreed with Tito (elimination of Croatia, as in Romania). Since the precondition for both of these, he continued, was a push westwards, then the enemy's point of concentration had to be to the west of Fünfkirchen. If the enemy had wished to find a solution to the north, he suggested, they would have long since smashed the weak Hungarian security forces. In addition, he concluded, Army Group F requested Army Group South to "prevent the encirclement" of their northern flank.

A real fear was that the northern flank would be encircled. The withdrawal which the *Kampfgruppe* of the 31st SS Volunteer Grenadier Division had been forced to make the previous day continued. After Váralja they reached Szasvar, where the point units of the Soviets who were pushing up hard behind them overtook the retreating groups and fired on them. There a short, but intense, exchange of fire developed between the enemy armoured units and the rearguard of the 31st SS Division. From there the journey continued, through Egyházaskozár and Mágócs behind the Kapos to Dombovár. There once again they took up positions.

The last remnants of the Division that were capable of fighting came from the direction of Szaszvár, Komló. In the morning they occupied the blocking position which had been prepared to some extent on the Kapos, between the village of Döbrököz and the town of Dombovár. To the north, between Döbrököz and Högyesz, the line was manned by the Hungarian units that had the previous day been pushed out of the Bonyhád area. Under their command were more fragments of the 31st SS Division, who also took up positions with them. How an attempt was made to organise in some way the retreating or scattered divisional troops was described in an account from A.Gl. (I/79):

> After the fighting at Babarc our crowd withdrew north-westwards. Only in Kaposszekcso was some order brought back into the ranks by *Hauptscharführer* Hans Zick. We got rifles, at last, for everyone. Ammunition was distributed. Soon we had our first contact with the enemy, it was a mounted reconnaissance detachment of three Soviets. We forced them to retreat. After more fighting of this kind we went to Dombovár.

The greater part of the *Kampfgruppe* of the 31st SS Division (principally from the II/78, Regiment 79 and *SS Feld-Ersatz Bataillon* 31) was brought up to defend Dombovár itself. A Hungarian combat unit from the 1st River Brigade, some 200 to 300 men strong, was with them there. The access roads to the town were blocked off. One great advantage for the defence was that the southern and south-eastern approach to the town was flooded by the River Kapos and this swampy ground could not be crossed by enemy armour. That facilitated the construction of a defensive line behind the Kapos. The three bridges, i.e. the railway-bridge, together with bridges V and IX, were blown up. To the rear the anti-aircraft guns of the I/231 took up positions.

The forward sections of the 80th Guards Rifle Division (with 10 tanks and 96 light assault guns) followed up hard and swung from the Fünfkirchen-Sásd road to Dombovár. They were already, between 5pm and 6pm, reaching the southern and south-eastern edges of the town. They began to shell the defenders with mortars and with their artillery took up positions on the hills at Mágócs and Csikóstöttös.

For the sector from Högyesz to Szekszárd the day brought even grimmer developments. During the early hours of the morning, Szekszárd was half encircled from the west and from the south-east, and was attacked. After short defensive fighting in the suburbs and in the town (in which remnants of the I/78 and SS Volunteer Grenadier Regiment 79 were also involved) the main Hungarian forces, after losing their artillery, withdrew behind the Sió Canal. The Soviets pushed up close behind them, penetrated, under assault gun support, into Tolna and pushed on further to Dunaszentgyörgy.

At the same time a battalion of naval infantry from the Red Danube Fleet landed at Gerjén (facing Kalocsa) on the western bank of the Danube and intervened in the fighting. The withdrawing Hungarian 51st Infantry Regiment had its line of retreat cut off on the line Paks–Nagydorog and was encircled. The Hungarian 42nd Infantry Regiment, however, was able to stop the Soviets so that the encircled men of the 51st could break out the next day.

The security front of *Kampfgruppe* Illey from the 1st River Brigade (with various units under its command, including some from the 31st SS Volunteer Grenadier Division), on the line Tevel–Zomba–Sióagárd, was attacked from the south. The weak securing units could offer no serious resistance and withdrew behind the River Kapos, especially since, after the loss of Medina and Szedres, their sector was also exposed and threatened to the east.

The Hungarian 20th Infantry Division which arrived in the Gyönk area the previous day, was already unloading under enemy artillery fire, and on 30 November 1944, was already fighting off enemy attacks on their hill position between Murga SW–Felsönana–Kölesd SE–Hidvég–Csapó–Tengelic. By then the situation was ominous. In practical terms there was no longer any firm link between Army Group F and Army Group South. In order to halt the Soviets, Army Group South decided to send in to attack, eastwards-south-eastwards on Tevel and on Bonyhád, those elements of the 23rd *Panzer* Division which had arrived in Simontornya. On the night of 30 November 1944, *Panzer Aufklärungs Abteilung* 23 began to counter-attack. They advanced as far as the line Högyesz–Mucsi. However, because of a shortage of petrol, they came to a halt and withdrew. Tevel and Bonyhád remained in enemy hands. The trouble spot at the junction between the army groups remained. The 120km wide, 60 to 80km deep area into which the Soviets had broken, between Drávaszabolcs and Szekszárd, threatened to develop into a strategic breakthrough.

1 December 1944

The defensive battle in southern Hungary on that day entered a new, decisive phase. The enemy attack across the Danube had been extended northwards beyond Dunaföldvár. The Soviets, deploying fresh forces, continued their attacks with un-

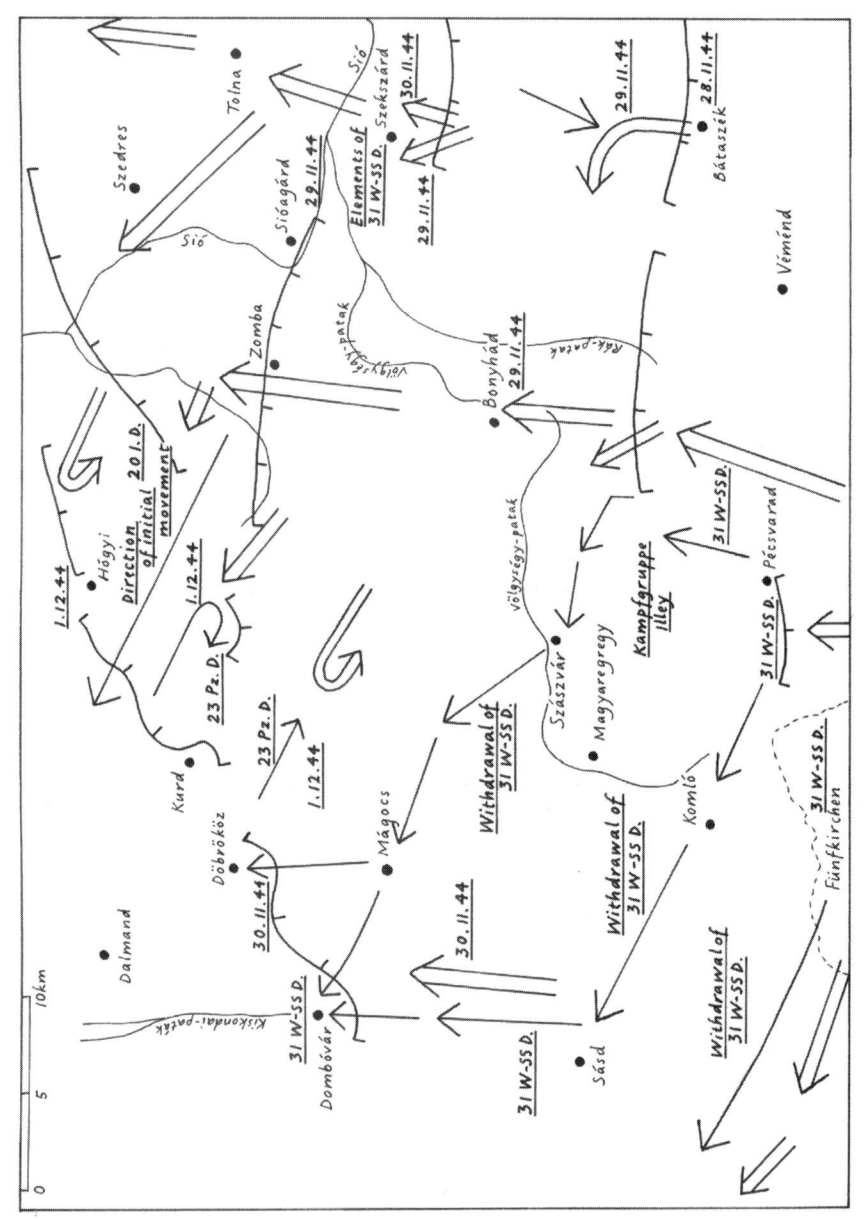

Map 4 Development of the situation north of Fünfkirchen, 29/30 November 1944.

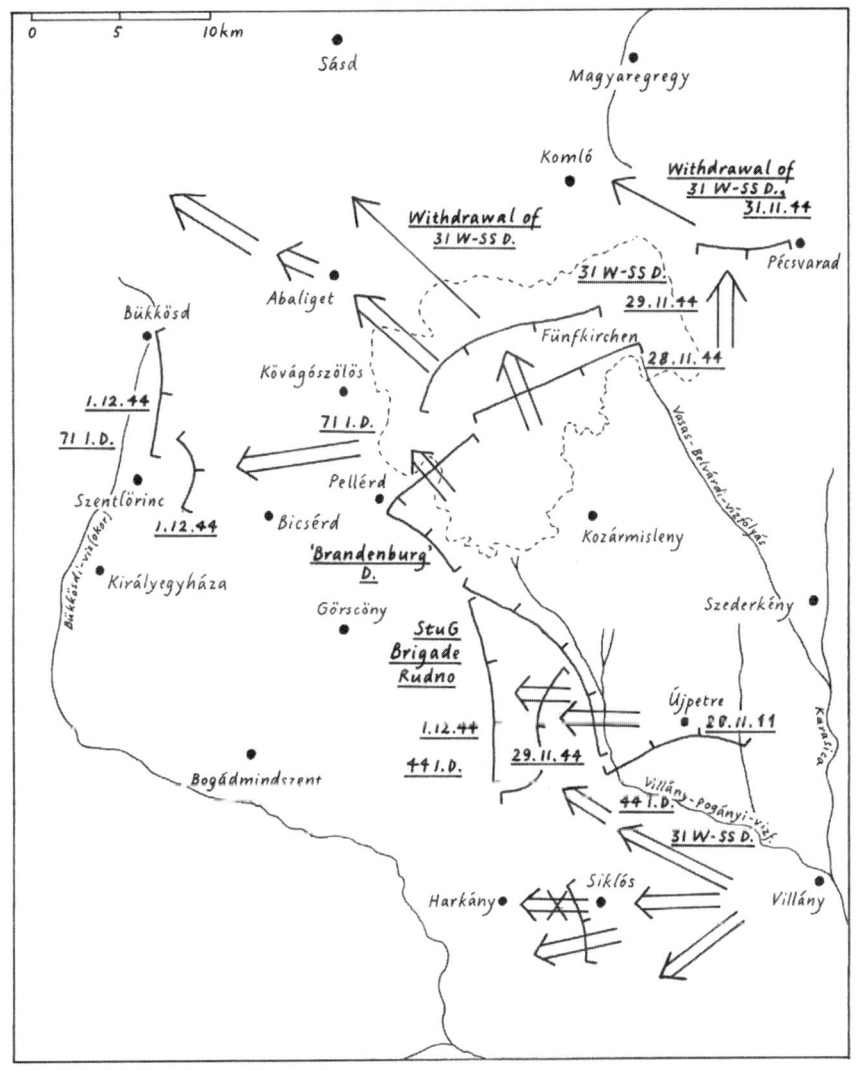

Map 5 Development of the situation south of Fünfkirchen, 29/30 November 1944 (partly also to 1 December).

diminished intensity. With a strong group of forces they attacked in the direction of the northern edge of Lake Balaton–Stuhlweissenburg. Then with another, equally strong, group in the direction of the southern edge of Lake Balaton–Nagykanisza–oilfields. The point units of the enemy attack, circumventing the northern flank of the LXVIII Corps, reached Kaposvár and the last suburbs of Mecsek. The counter-attack of the 23rd *Panzer* Division had not been carried out as planned and had not achieved the result that was wished for. The turbulent events of the battle developed as follows:

On the night of 30 November 1944, the Drau bridgehead north of Esseg was given up. The Soviets were not pushing across the Drau, but along the whole length of the river, changing over to defence against the XCI Corps.

In the area west of Siklós, the 44th Infantry Division 'Hoch und Deutschmeister' with its own 4 battalions, and 7 battalions under its command, fought off repeated enemy attacks. *Kampfgruppe* Hanke from the 13th SS Division 'Handschar', which still had all of 450 men, was relieved from the front on the night of 30 November 1944. Its positions were taken over by the III/750th of the 118th *Jäger* Division. While this *Jäger* battalion was able to maintain its positions on both sides of Matty against repeated enemy attacks, the enemy, advancing south-westwards to Siklós, forced a breakthrough to the road 8km NNE of Miholjac. The situation was cleared up by a newly-arrived battalion of the 1st *Volks-Gebirgs* Division.

As a result of the situation in the Kaposvár area becoming more acute (see below) the *Panzergrenadier* Assault Battalion from Assault Brigade Rudno was relieved from the Szalánta sector that morning, and sent to Kaposvár. Szalánta had been hotly contested, but was now occupied by the enemy. The main line of resistance was to the west of the village.

The main Soviet push, however, was directed against the sector of the front between Pellérd and Cserkút, on Szentlörinc, aiming at Szigetvár. Here the Soviets advanced in depth. By means of a concentration of 30 tanks the enemy, in regimental strength, broke through the front of the 71st Infantry Division on both sides of the Fünfkirchen–Szigetvár road. They could only be stopped east of Szentlörinc during the afternoon by alarm units. Further to the north, the Soviets were already at Okorvölgy. Therefore the 4th Battalion of the 71st Infantry Division, defending in that sector with the III/98, and individual remnants of the 31st SS Volunteer Grenadier Division, had to withdraw behind the Pécser and Okorwasser. They moved to the sector Szentlörinc, Korpád, Sásd and took up a new blocking position there.

In the Szentlörinc area the situation could again be reinforced. However, further to the north, in the area to the east of Kaposvár, in the gap between the left flank of the LXVIII Corps of the 2nd *Panzer* Army north-west of Fünfkirchen and the right flank of the LVII *Panzerkorps* of the Army Group Fretter-Pico, things looked bad. In the morning enemy tanks were already being spotted in the village of Gödre, moving towards Szentbalász and Santós. During the morning the village and airfield of Taszár 5km east-north-east of Kaposvár were attacked by Soviet cavalry and tanks. Enemy infantry with tanks had already pushed forward and were engaged in fighting with weak German flak forces 3km east of the town.

The *Panzergrenadier* Assault Battalion was rushed up, with a battalion from the 71st Infantry Division. The intention was, by extending these small forces in echelon, to stop the enemy push on Kaposvár. In the blocking position east of the town there were also small remnants of the 31st SS Division. They had been pushed back from the Fünfkirchen area and from Pecsvarád–Püspöknádasd and had been marched back through Godre towards Kaposvár. But the available troops were pitifully few, therefore the 2nd *Panzer* Army at 10.55am requested Army Group South to mount an attack from the Tamási area south-westwards on Dombovár. They aimed to hit the Soviets in the flank and thus to relieve the pressure on the weak forces holding Kaposvár. But Army Group South at the moment only had available the 23rd *Panzer* Division, and this had to be deployed against the advance of the Soviets to the north.

Along the north-western and northern security line from Dombovár to Högyesz behind the Kapos and from there to Paks, things also looked pretty precarious. The Soviet 4th Guards Army with 10,915 soldiers, 1,023 guns, 567 mortars, 10 tanks and 96 assault guns, on the morning of 1 December 1944 mounted their attack in the general direction of Stuhlweissenburg, against the front of the LVII *Panzerkorps*, XI Hungarian Army Corps and LXXII Corps. During the early hours enemy troops reached Mekénves, but counter-attacks by the 23rd *Panzer* Division threw them back. The Soviets made strenuous efforts to cross the Kapos at Kurd, however this dangerous attempt, which would roll up the entire Kapos defence, was for the moment repulsed.

East of Varsád, the Soviet attack was repulsed by the Hungarian 20th Infantry Division. But at Kéty N the Soviets succeeded in breaking through. The Hungarian 13th Infantry Regiment withdrew to the line Högyesz–Varsád. The enemy attacking from the Tengelic area threw the defenders back to the line Kajdács–Nagydorog. At 10pm the Hungarian 20th Infantry Division received the order to withdraw behind the Sió Canal. On the Danube, Nagydorog, Paks and Dunakömlöd fell. Between Harta and Dunapataj the Soviets made another crossing of the Danube.

On 1 December 1944 Dombovár was, without doubt, a cornerstone of the front. During the course of the day the main forces of the Soviet 80th Guards Rifle Division reached the town and attacked it. The war diary of Army Group South for 1 December 1944 noted:

Repeated strong enemy attacks in company up to battalion strength against Dombovár from the south are repulsed by the remnants of the 31st SS Volunteer Grenadier Division and remnants of Hungarian units, together with parts of a flak section ... South of Dombovár parts of the 31st SS Division which have been forced north repulse repeated enemy attacks.

And in the war diary of Army Group F for the same day: "The security line formed round Dombovár by weak parts of 31st SS Division was attacked by the enemy in company strength, without success".

The fighting lasted throughout the whole day. In the flooded outskirts the Soviets could not advance with too great a force on a broad front and their attacks bled to death. The flak of I/231 kept the enemy artillery and mortar positions on the high ground at Mágócs and Csikóstöttös under fire. In the late afternoon the enemy pressure increased. At 6pm *Generalmajor* Gaedcke, Chief of Staff of Army Group Fretter-Pico, reported to Army Group South:

> Against Dombóvár motorised Soviet armed forces are marching up. At this point they also surround the village to the west. The situation is also the same at Kurd, therefore the Army Group considers it necessary to bring back the 23rd *Panzer* Division into the area SW of Simontornya. In this situation the Dombóvár garrison is holding a hopeless position and must be withdrawn to Tamási. But this decision has wide implications, because as a result of it contact with the left flank of Army Group F will be broken. Now it is a matter of getting through the next few days somehow until new forces arrive.

The Ia of Army Group South informed *Generalmajor* Gaedcke at 7.35pm that *Generaloberst* Friessner agreed to the proposal and that "the Dombóvár garrison must set off on the march to Kaposvár to strengthen the combat commandant there."

So, after days of successful defensive fighting, Dombóvár had to be given up because of the deterioration in the situation on both flanks. The retreat was begun at about 10pm and proceeded in several stages. To deceive the enemy, a 'Wandergeschütz' was brought into play. It was a self-propelled gun that drove around the town firing, and thus gave the false impression that there were several guns. The rearguard of the 31st SS Volunteer Grenadier Division took up position in several places within the town. The largest rearguard was the remnant of a Hungarian police battalion that set up three anti-tank gun positions and several machine gun nests on the road leading from the railway bridge into the town and also on the Hunvadi-János Platz. The night remained relatively quiet.

The development of the situation during the day created a very critical situation. The strong enemy attack to the south-east of Kaposvár threatened to encircle the LXVIII Corps from the north and to force it to the Drau. If the southern flank of the corps at Szentlörinc–Drávacsepely held, then this could be avoided. But, on the other hand, if the southern flank was withdrawn to the fortified Margarethe Position between Gvékényes and Keszthely, it would open up a gap between the LXVIII Corps. The XCI Corps conducting the defence south of the Drau hoped to create a great gap through which the Soviet 57th Army could push unhindered to Agram.

The second danger was completely unacceptable. Therefore, the OKH gave the order that, in all circumstances, the Soviets must be prevented from breaking through between the Drau and Lake Balaton, and also prevent LXVIII Corps from being forced back to the Drau. In addition, it ordered them to keep the southern flank of the Drau under their own close control and at all costs to maintain contact between the two army groups. But the problem was that, to form a point of concentration on the left flank and at the same time to hold on the left, the necessary forces were not available. Certainly it would not be possible with only the 2nd *Panzer* Army. Army Group F was not able to throw any more forces into this sector of the front, at least not for the foreseeable future. The Chief of Staff of the 2nd *Panzer* Army, *Oberst* Bürker, called *Generaloberst* Friessner at 9.55pm and outlined to him the situation of the *Panzer* Army:

The LXVIII Corps is, during the evening, holding, with battle-weary units, the line Drau Crossing N Donji Miholjac (blown up)–Szentlörinc… The enemy attack on 1 December 1944, concentrating on the Fünfkirchen–Szigetvár road, was brought to a halt on this line. A continuation of the Soviet attack is to be expected in the early hours of 2 December 1944. The last Army reserves (remnants of the Rudno Assault Brigade and one battalion 71st Infantry Division) were sent off to Kaposvár to prevent the enemy's attempt at encirclement from the north through Kaposvár. Kaposvár is held only by alarm units. Neither the Army nor the Corps has any further reserves. If Army Group South cannot provide any forces then the LXVIII Corps has to free up more of its own forces and send them to Kaposvár in order to prevent the Corps being cut off. But the consequence of this will be that the main line of resistance of the LXVIII Corps will no longer be able to be defended strongly enough. Our conduct of the fighting under these circumstances has to be tough and delaying, with the aim of building up a permanent defence in the Margarethe Position. It is, however, questionable whether this can be achieved with the battle-weary units at our disposal. There are not sufficient artillery forces, *Panzerjäger*, and no pioneers. Forming a concentration at the necessary places is therefore impossible.

Then the state of the troops was described:

Fighting spirit in 44th Infantry Division 'Hoch und Deutschmeister' strongly diminished, 71st Infantry Division brought from Italy not used to conditions in the East, the otherwise good 1st *Volks-Gebirgs* Division has here only a reinforced *Kampfgruppe*, the Division 'Brandenburg' only consists of three weak battalions.

The 31st SS Volunteer GrenadierDivision in this report was no longer even mentioned, although it was still under the command of the LXVIII Corps and its *Kampfgruppe* was, during the day, still successfully fighting in Dombovár. So it appears that by 1 December 1944 the Division had been written off.

With this development of the situation, during the evening the OKW ordered fresh command arrangements that had been maturing for some time. The 2nd *Panzer* Army, with all its elements north of the Drau, with effect from 2.12pm, came under the command of Army Group South. The new line of demarcation between the army groups became the Drau, whose crossing points still belonged to Army Group F.

The command post of the 2nd *Panzer* Army was in Letenye. The line of demarcation was between it and Army Group Fretter-Pico. Under its command was the 3rd Hungarian Army. The demarcation line ran along the line of the SW tip of Lake Balaton–Kaposvár N–Baja N. The 2nd *Panzer* Army had one single corps, the LXVIII Corps, with its command post in Németlad, to which the following forces belonged: 71st Infantry Division with 4 battalions of its own and 1 other placed under its command (12 batteries, 4 heavy anti-tank guns, 2 *Panzerjäger* and 4 Italian assault guns); 44th Infantry Division 'Hoch und Deutschmeister' with 4 of its own battalions and 5 others placed under its command (19 batteries, 13 heavy anti-tank guns and 11 assault guns); parts of 1st *Volks-Gebirgs* Division with 3 of its own battalions and 2 placed under its command (10 batteries and 7 heavy anti-tank guns).

The remnants included 31st SS Division, 118th *Jäger* Division, Grenadier Brigade 92 (mot.), *Panzergrenadier* Assault Battalion, *Kampfgruppe* Hanke of the 13th Waffen SS Mountain Division 'Handschar', and finally, *StuG* Brigade 191. Still under the command of the *Panzer* Army was the General Command of XXII *Gebirgskorps*, which, however, apart from Pioneer Battalion 41 (mot.) had no troops. The last elements of the 1st *Volks-Gebirgs* Division were still being brought up.

At the same time as these organisational measures took place, others were under way. The General Command II Hungarian Army Corps of the 3rd Hungarian Army was withdrawn from the front. The sector it had manned was taken over, between Dombóvár and Cece, by the LVII *Panzerkorps*, and between Cece and Dunaföldvár by the LXXII Corps. As a result of this, the parts of the 31st SS Division that had been under the command of the II Hungarian Army Corps since 29 November 1944 came under the command of LVII *Panzerkorps*.

The task of the 2nd *Panzer* Army, according to a telegram issued by *Generaloberst* Guderian at 2.15pm on 2 December 1944, was:

> To prevent the further advance of the enemy between the Drau and Lake Balaton towards the Margarethe Position, and also to prevent the enemy taking control of the oilfields to the west of Kaposvár. The LXVIII Corps should not be allowed to be pushed south-westwards or southwards to the Drau. The breaking of contact with the forces of the Supreme Commander South-East located south of the Drau must, if necessary, be accepted. The intention to mount an attack southwards from the area west of Dunaföldvár with a strong *Kampfgruppe*, to hit the enemy in the Danube-Drau triangle, must be maintained.

The enemy intended to stay on the defensive on the Drau, but to thrust up hard on the heels of the withdrawing German units towards Kaposvár, Nagykanisza and Stuhlweissenburg in order to prevent the Germans making a stand in the Margarethe Position. The only question was whether there were enough forces to stop the enemy. The initiative continued to lie with the enemy who, by 5 December 1944, intended to reach the line Babócsa–Lábod–Kaposvár–Magyaratád. That would be the same as pushing the LXVIII Corps from the Margarethe Position and between the Mur estuary–Nagykaizsa–Lake Balaton south!

2 December 1944

Fierce fighting continued at all the hot spots. Szentlörinc was caught in the Soviet pincers from the south and north and attacked with assault guns. At 10am the village fell. The forces of the 71st Infantry Division, under whose command were probably also remnants of the 31st SS Division, were thrown back into the Kacsóta area. In the afternoon, counter-attacks were mounted south-westwards, but with little success.

Between Szentlörinc and Kaposvár the main line of resistance had more than a few gaps. Developments at Szentlörinc made the situation even more dangerous. An even more difficult situation was looming at Kaposvár. The defensive positions of the Division 'Brandenburg' to the south-east of the town were overrun by the Soviets in the early hours of the morning. The weak units gave way, and by 10am the town fell into the hands of a Soviet regiment with armoured support. A new security line was formed 5km south-west of the town by forces of the Division 'Brandenburg' in battalion strength. Orders were given for another battalion to be brought up. But in the afternoon the Soviets followed up as far as the Gige, Kissassond, Somogysárd, Hetes, Somogyjád road, and could only be stopped east of Kiskorpád (13km from Kaposvár).

North of Kaposvár, in the early hours of 2 December 1944, the front ran as follows: Kaposvár–gap–Dombovár S–gap–Dbrököz–gap–Kurd S–Mucsi S–from there on, eastwards as far as the Danube. More gaps, then, than support bases, and through the loss of Kaposvár the situation became even more difficult. The danger of the LXVIII Corps being cut off from the north was all the more precarious. In view of the developing situation, parts of *Gebirgsjäger* Regiment 99 and the Rudno Assault Brigade were thrown into the fighting, in the Somogyjád area, and the 3rd Cavalry Brigade, still on its way, was also ordered in.

The Kapos position, too, was penetrated in several places. During the morning the Soviets succeeded in forming a bridgehead at Kurd, on the western bank of the River Kapos, from which they thrust forward towards Tamási. A counter-attack mounted by the 23rd *Panzer* Division south of Tamási brought them to a halt. The group of the 31st SS Volunteer Grenadier Division in Dobrokoz (Regiment 79) was threatened by encirclement, and thus withdrew as ordered. At Szakály, too, the Soviets broke through the weak security line and stormed the positions of the 23rd *Panzer* Division and the Hungarian *Kampfgruppe* Illey on the line Tamási–Beleckska. The fighting lasted until the evening and ended with the loss of Tamási. Heavy fighting was also raging at Kisszkely, Vajta, Németkér and Dunaföldvár.

The town of Dombovár, already deserted by the main forces and only manned by rearguards, also fell on that day. The Soviet 80th Guards Rifle Division, supported by assault guns, pushed over the Szarvasd bridge, across the Kapos river and into the town. There it came up against the unexpected resistance of the rearguards of the 31st SS Division, and in particular, the police battalion. A Soviet assault gun was knocked out, and heavy fighting raged around the Hunyadi Platz and the Kossuth and Arany-Janos Strassen. At about 11am the German-Hungarian rearguards pulled back and left behind them a total of 20 German soldiers and Hungarian police killed. The Soviets suffered 28 casualties, including a regimental commander. The rearguard withdrew towards Siofok.

Through the withdrawal of these last forces from this area, a 65km-wide gap without organised resistance was now gaping between the northern flank of the 2nd *Panzer* Army and the southern flank of the 3rd Hungarian Army. The Soviets spotted their chance and immediately thrust after them in the general direction of Siófok.

Since the first *Kampfgruppe* of the 3rd Cavalry Brigade, still on its way, would only be ready for action on 5 December 1944, there was nothing available to prevent the LXVIII Corps being cut off, as had been threatened. Therefore 2nd *Panzer* Army decided to further withdraw the Corps' positions on the night of 2 December 1944. The forces of the LVII *Panzerkorps* and the LXXII Corps on the northern flank were also ordered back during the night into the so-called 'Eugen-Riegelstellung' (Eugen Blocking Position). The blocking position, which simply consisted of scanty field fortifications, between Siófok and Simontornya, followed

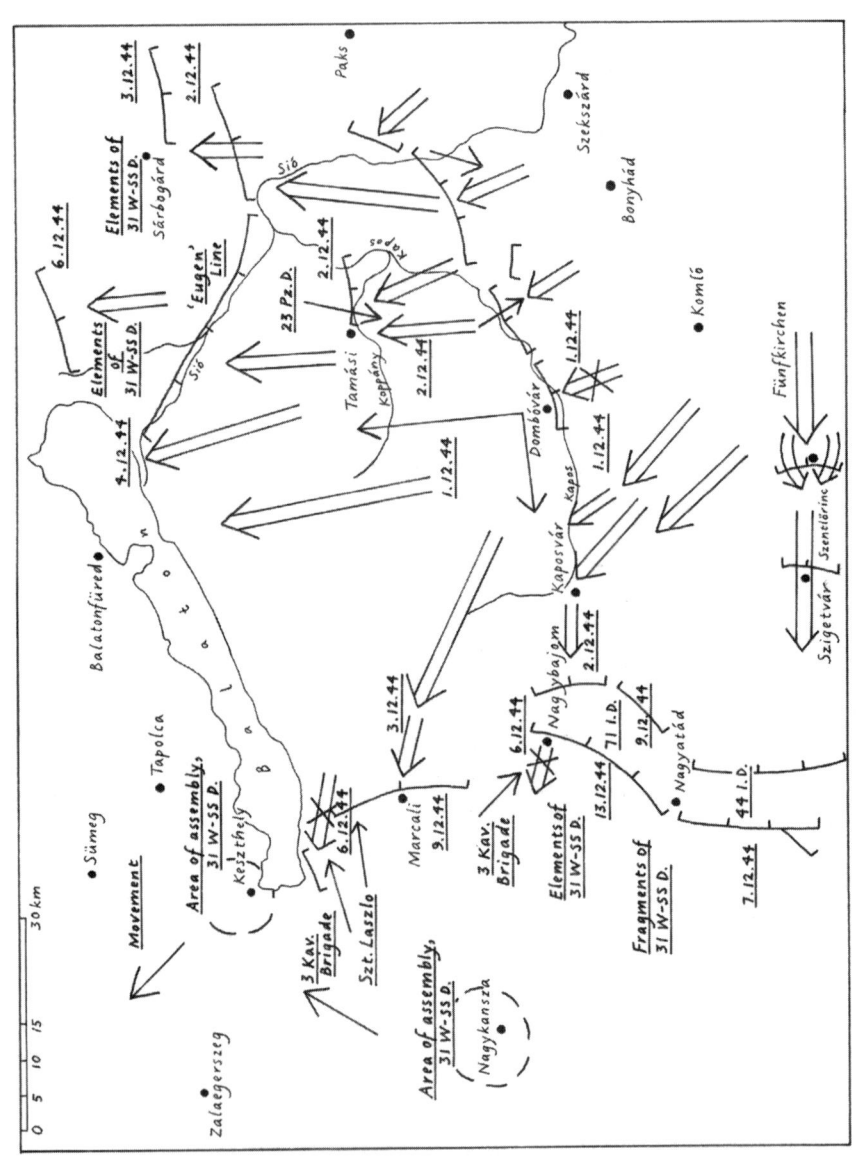

Map 6 Development of the situation from 1 December 1944 until the withdrawal of the Division from the Front.

the Sió Canal, but between Simontornya and Dunaföldvár had to make do without any natural obstacles.

The further course of the defensive battle up to the stabilisation of the front

On 3 December 1944 the front of the 2nd *Panzer* Army ran as follows: Szigetvár–gap–10km south-west of Kaposvár–western edge of Szomajom (today: Kaposfö)–gap as far as Siófok. In the sector of the 44th Infantry Division 'Hoch und Deutschmeister' heavy fighting was raging round Szigetvár, at Dencsháza, Botykapeterd, Csertö. The main line of resistance of the 71st Infantry Division to the north of Szigetvár was broken through on 3 December 1944. The 71st Infantry Division withdrew, so that the 44th Infantry Division 'Hoch und Deutschmeister' on 5 December 1944 was forced to give up the line Drávakeresztúr–Szigetvár, as well as the town of Szigetvár itself. They had to withdraw from the threatening encirclement on to the line Barcs–Lábod.

The 71st Infantry Division joined the line Lábod–Mike–Gige. The new main line of resistance held until 7 December 1944, with the Hungarian 54th Frontier *Jäger* Battalion (*Oberstleutnant* Szabó) surrendering of its own accord to the Bulgarians facing it, and Barcs being evacuated on 5 December 1944. The 44th Infantry Division 'Hoch und Deutschmeister' then withdrew behind the Rinya brook to the line Nayatád–Babócsa. Small remnants of the 31st SS Volunteer Grenadier Division were also supposed to have been present with them.

West of Kaposvár the defensive position of the Division 'Brandenburg', still only about 250 men, was broken through by the enemy, after fierce close quarters fighting in which 15 T-34s were destroyed. The Soviets were only brought to a halt to the east of Nagybajom. North of Kaposvár, as far as Lake Balaton, over an area of 50km, there were no longer any German troops and the enemy marched into this area as if it were peacetime. On 3 December 1944 Marcali was attacked. The newly brought up 3rd Cavalry Brigade received the order to hold the Soviet attack as far to the east as possible, to prevent the northern flank of the LXVIII Corps being outflanked and to close the gap between Kaposvár and Lake Balaton.

On 5 December 1944 the Soviets reached Lake Balaton at Balatonkeresztúr and threatened to push westward on the lakeside road. The 3rd Cavalry Brigade set themselves immediately to oppose this grouping of the enemy which, however, was too strong and could only be halted the next day to the east of Balatonberény. On 7 December 1944 Soviet reconnaissance units in the reed beds of the Small Balaton were already approaching the town of Keszthely! The enemy also gained further ground on 6 December 1944 at Marcali. The next day they were thrown back again by counter-attacks from the 3rd Cavalry Brigade and Division 'Brandenburg'. At Böhönye and Nagybajom the main line of resistance was firmly held.

On 8 December 1944 the enemy continued their attack on Marcali with strong air support, and took the village after hard fighting. Hungarian paratroops of the Division 'Szent Lászlo' took Kéthely. After fighting lasting until 9 December 1944, the villages of Balatonmária, Balatonkeresztúr, Balatonújlak were once again

firmly in Axis hands and the main line of resistance along the Balatonkeresztúr–
Marcali–Mesztegnyö railway line would hold firmly during the following weeks.

Further to the south swirling fighting was also under way. On 11 December
1944 Babócsa fell and ground was also lost at Szabás, Lábod and Rinyazentkirály.
On 13 December 1944 the main line of resistance in this area ran along the line
Drau – Heresznye W and N – Háromfa – Rinyaújnép E – Nagyatád –
Kónyjpuszta – Kutas – Nagybajom. Until 15 December 1944 this line was fiercely
fought over, with varying success. A farm at Háromfa, for example, changed hands
six times. Remnants of the 31st SS Division were said to have taken part in this
fighting between Nagyatád and Somogyudvarhely and suffered heavy casualties.
Then the fighting in this sector, too, subsided and the front finally stabilised.

From 3 December, heavy fighting raged along the Eugen *Riegelstellung*. It was
not possible to set up the position properly, because the enemy was advancing too
quickly. On 3 December 1944 the Soviets reached Lake Balaton at Szantód. The
'Immelmann' Stuka squadron prevented them pushing any further, but the false
rumour that the Soviets had succeeded in crossing the lake caused considerable dis-
turbance in the area behind the lines. At Simontornya heavy fighting raged. Soon
the entire southern bank of the Sió Canal had to be given up. Dunaföldvár was also
lost. The new main line of resistance could only be set up at Sárszentmiklós–
Dunapentele. On 4 December 1944 Siófok fell into enemy hands. In other places
too the Soviets broke through, including the Eugen Position on the Sió. The fighting involved very heavy casualties, so that on 6 December 1944, at last, withdrawal
to the Margarethe Position was allowed. The enemy, following up hard, was already penetrating this position in places. However, apart from some localised fierce
fighting, the front was stabilised and there was a break in the fighting.

Even if there is no more detailed information, it is certain that even in this
fighting, remnants of the 31st SS Volunteer Grenadier Division, under the command of various other units, were involved. Thus the staff of I/79 appeared in
Tamási, then in the Siofok area. *SS-Sturmbannführer* Albrecht, already wounded
several times, was seriously wounded just as he was about to bring down a sniper
from a roof. He had to give up his battalion, which was shortly afterwards taken
over by *SS-Sturmbannführer* Pachur. In this last fighting during the retreat *SS-
Hauptscharführer* Hans Zick was also killed.

An account by *SS-Rottenführer* Fritz Schuster of SS *Nachrichten Abteilung* 31
gives us an idea of what the situation was like during those turbulent weeks:

> At about the beginning of November, with another few chaps, I was assigned,
> from the telephone company, as a sentry, to the Army Corps' ammunition
> train. In this work we came to and fro through railway stations such as
> Szigetvár, Barcs, Nagyatád and others to receive water, rations and other things.
> Otherwise our everyday lives were quite monotonous. By day the train was
> camouflaged, parked motionless in some wood or other and we (a guard unit
> thrown together from every possible unit of the Corps, consisting of about 50
> soldiers under the command of an *Oberleutnant*) had to guard the train. But at
> night we moved and stopped on roads where the units then collected the am-
> munition from us in lorries. In doing this we were often attacked by Soviet air-
> craft and then it was mostly a matter of changing our position in a hurry. It was
> a very uneasy feeling sitting on such high explosive 'eggs'.

We had our quarters in one of the first class carriages and boredom caused some of my comrades to have a go at exploring the woods. In this connection I can still remember well one incident. I was lying in the window and watching the wood when I saw a soldier from our unit racing towards us without his cap and completely beside himself, on his last legs. Not far behind him was a raging bull. I opened the carriage door straight away and the soldier just about reached the step with great effort. Then the bull was there too and was trying to wreck the step. I got my rifle and shot it! That gave us a nice fresh roast.

Towards the beginning of December I came back to my telephone company in Nagykanisza and with my unit – all freshly assigned Batschka Germans – I went about operating the telephone exchange.

CHAPTER 11

The Division Is Withdrawn from the Front

A brief summary should once again be given of the action of the 31st SS Volunteer Grenadier Division in the defensive battle in southern Hungary. The combat units of the unprepared 31st SS Division, only half-ready for action, were brought up at the end of October to help secure the Danube. At that time no serious enemy attack was expected in that sector. At issue was Budapest, which the enemy was trying to reach in a more central direction. But in a few weeks things changed. The main target continued to be Budapest, but the Soviets, who held the initiative, decided from 7 December 1944 to seek a decision on the flanks. As a result, parts of the 31st SS Division became involved in a hotly contested sector of the front. The combat units of SS Volunteer Grenadier Regiments 78 and 80 at Kisköszeg became involved from 9 December 1944 in turbulent fighting against the enemy bridgehead. Meanwhile parts of SS Volunteer Grenadier Regiment 79 also had to repulse enemy attempts to cross the river on both sides of Mohács. In this fighting for the bridgehead, the Division was able to make its contribution to a defensive success.

After two weeks of unsuccessful efforts, the Soviets finally gambled everything on breaking through in one place. As this place they chose the south-western wing of the Hungarian front. The main strategic target remained Budapest. The Soviets tried to cut it off by a thrust from the south-western flank on Stuhlweissenburg. In addition to this were two further strategic targets. The oilfields of Nagykanisza would help to attain a favourable position to attack Croatia. Thus from 24 November 1944 the south-western wing became the main sector of the Hungarian front, the decisive focus of the battle. The units standing on this line had to face a decisive battle that the 31st SS Division was unable to handle. A large-scale battle flared up along the entire line and the German defensive front was pushed back, both northwards and westwards. It became, like a blister, increasingly stretched, until it finally burst on 28 November 1944 in the over-extended sector of the combat group of the 31st SS Division. From that day on events came thick and fast.

The Division was split up, and in parts shattered. The front became increasingly overstretched. One group, mostly I/80 and SS Fusilier Battalion 31, fought in the Fünfkirchen area. They then concentrated between Nagyatád and Kaposvár where they were involved in further fighting. The second group, I/78, parts of SS Volunteer Grenadier Regiment 79, took part in the defensive fighting in the area to the south and south-west of Szekszárd. From 2 December 1944 no further combat units worth mentioning from the 31st SS Divsion, turned up in the fighting as integral units. Certainly, shattered elements of the Division, under the command of other units including the LXVIII Army Corps and the LVII *Panzerkorps*, still took part in the defensive fighting. This occurred in several places of the widely extended front. However, the last action conducted by an integral combat group of the Division was the defence of Dombóvár.

Here it seems is the appropriate place to contradict a succinct statement that turns up, from time to time, for instance in *Generaloberst* Friessner's memoirs *Verratene Schlachten*. "The fact that the 31st SS Divsion flooded back in retreat in the area to the east of Fünfkirchen had placed the front under the most serious threat."

Right at the start it should be stressed that at the front there was not a '31st SS Volunteer Grenadier Division', but only a few inadequately trained, poorly armed units from it that were only half- ready for action. It is a fact that these, giving way to the enemy pressure, retreated. When the front line became too long, they lost contact with each other and with other units. But if a withdrawal, blameworthy or no, of a few battalions, could bring the front of an entire Army Group into a situation of very serious threat, then the causes lie deeper! The line was now too thin! Therefore recourse had to be made to all forces, even those in the process of formation. The same units that were barely sufficient to secure a river, would now have to maintain, in heavy defensive fighting, a frontline that became longer and longer. Such expectations were, of course, unreal.

The statement that the withdrawal of parts of the 31st SS Volunteer Grenadier Division was in some way their own fault, flies in the face of any evidence. They simply did what they could, but gave way just as others had to give way. To shift some kind of blame for what happened, on to this Division, would simply be cheap. On the contrary, the battle-hardened officers, NCOs and other ranks in the Division actually in no way fell short, neither in their spirit nor in their performance, of the standards normal for, and expected from, the Waffen-SS. It was just that in themselves they were too few! From the mass of the Division's recruits, however, there was nothing but good will. However, no battle can be won with just that. Their training and armament were completely insufficient, and this necessarily led to the Division being unable to live up to the expectations placed on it. That this fact had serious consequences for the entire section of the front was tragic, precisely because these consequences could be clearly foreseen.

However, in the final analysis, it was undoubtedly thanks to the soldiers of the 31st SS Divsion, among others, that the Soviets were so worn out at the Margarethe Position, that they were finally halted. They were no longer capable, directly from their march, of breaking through this last position before the Reich border.

From 1 December 1944 began the phased process of relieving from the front the mostly shattered remnants of the Division. The elements that arrived in Döbrököz on 1 December 1944 were overtaken by the order to begin to withdraw. On the same day the force holding Dombóvár was also withdrawn. The other fragments, too, were relieved in stages, as the situation at that time permitted. As the fighting, in all affected sectors had subsided by about 20 December 1944, the remnants of the Division were all relieved by this date at the latest. (The last men of Division 'Brandenburg', similarly withdrawn, left the frontline on 21 December 1944). As early as 12 December 1944, a telegram from Army Group South deals with the planned "transfer of the 31 SS Volunteer Grenadier Division, together with the 58th Waffen-SS *Gebirgs* Brigade (Tartar Nr 1), 25th Waffen-SS Grenadier Division 'Hunyadi' and the ethnic German Police battalions, if necessary, into Slovakia or the Reich area".

The remnants that had been relieved first arrived in Nagykanisza and its surrounding area. There they were directed into the area west of Lake Balaton, mostly to Keszthely, where the Divisional Command was also based. Then, villages in the Komitat Vas (Eisenburg) in the area surrounding Kormend and Vasvár, such as Olaszfa (where the Staff of SS Volunteer Grenadier Regiment 79 appears to have been), Pacsony and others were designated as collection points for the individual units. S.Gr. (I/79), a Hungarian German, recalls those turbulent days:

> A ceaseless retreat! That was our life in the last days of November and the first days of December 1944. Again and again taking up position, defying the Soviets, then withdrawing again. Püspöknádasd, Váralja, Szásvár, where we were fired on by enemy tanks, then Egyházaskozár, Magócs, finally in Döbrököz as rearguard. Here on 2 December 1944 orders reached us from Dunaföldvár that we should withdraw on the last train. As soon as I arrived in Nagykanisza the field police arrested me because I didn't have a written order. They spoke back to the Divisional Command, then I was released and sent off to Keszthely. We had been here for about two weeks before we moved to Olaszfa. In Keszthely, too, I met *SS-Oberführer* Lombard for the first time.

Not all parts of the Division came to the collection area on the route south by Lake Balaton, thus via Nagykanisza. In the case of many groups (e.g. Staff I/79) who had ended up in the Siófok area, they first went up to Odenburg and only from there to Eisenburg.

Many members of the Division, scattered in the combat area, were lost. They were incorporated into other German as well as Hungarian units and later shared their fate.

Even larger was the number of those who were taken prisoner by the Soviets and at this time were already sitting in the collection camp at Temeschwar. As a result of this fact a considerable proportion of the Divisional strength available at the Danube never arrived in Eisenburg. According to a source not confirmed in detail[1] the total strength of the Division, on 16 December 1944, was 11,000 men. It is, indeed, not clear what exactly that figure contained, but nevertheless the overall picture was clear. The casualties suffered by the Division in the Danube actions amounted to 2,000 to 3,000 men, and likely more, rather than less. Only a relatively small proportion of these casualties were killed or wounded. The figures relating to the 31st SS Divsion in the casualty report of the Supreme Commander South-East (Army Group F) for November, for his command area are below the real figures. These showed Officers: 1 dead, 5 wounded; NCOs/Other Ranks: 23 dead, 131 wounded.[2] This many killed are known from the one engagement at Babarc. In the casualty figures the missing seem to have predominated. The casualty report quoted otherwise speaks of merely 1 missing soldier, which is quite clearly nonsense.

---

1   Munoz: *Forgotten Legions*, p.367.
2   The explanation for this is to be found in the fact that from 28 November, at the latest, contact with parts of the Division was lost, so that individual *Kampfgruppen* of the Division were under the command of other units, even those of Army Group South.

According to research into the lists of missing held by the German Red Cross, the combat units of SS Volunteer Grenadier Regiment 78 (Regiment Staff, I and II battalions) and SS Volunteer Grenadier Regiment 80 (I/80) appeared to have suffered the greatest casualties. They were involved in fighting from 9 November 1944 at the enemy bridgehead at Kisköszeg. SS Fusilier Battalion 31 suffered extraordinarily high casualties. The I/79 was also quite seriously depleted. Affected to a greater than average degree were the groups of men with more recent dates of birth. That could be ascribed to the fact that it was men of this age, above all, who were in the combat units that were sent into action. With them the Division lost its most valuable human resources. Going beyond the casualties, it was clear that those who remained were also completely disorganised, and desperately in need of being re-formed.

The various Divisional units that had not seen action as combat units, such as the *Nachrichten Abteilung*, the Medical *Abteilung* or the administration and supplies services, experienced their own withdrawal. It took place with considerable casualties, from where they were quartered between Fünfkirchen and Mohács, to the new collection area in Eisenburg. SS *Nachrichten Abteilung* 31 marched back via Fünfkirchen and Kaposvár, landed at the southern bank of Lake Balaton, until they finally came to rest via Keszthely in the Eisenburg area. At that time *SS-Untersturmführer* Villier had a fairly uncomfortable experience:

On the march back to western Hungary, as far as Lake Balaton, I was detailed with *SS-Untersturmführer* Karl Stecker as officer in charge of the billeting party. We both rode on a motorbike. He definitely wanted to say goodbye to a lady chemist he knew in Pécs. We were sitting there with a liqueur when Soviet *Ratas* fired on the street. The lady chemist was beside herself with fear. I wanted to demonstrate to her how safe weapons can be and placed my pistol, which supposedly had the safety catch on, against my temple and was even about to pull the trigger. Karl said, 'don't be daft'. Then I held the pistol with outstretched arm above my head. I pulled the trigger and shot a lovely hole in the ceiling. The weapon's safety catch had been inadvertently left off. I had, through my own fault, nearly slipped into committing suicide!

The main dressing station of the 2nd Medical Company in Fünfkirchen withdrew on 28 November 1944, via Dombóvár, Kaposvár and Nagykanisza. They went at first to Zalaegerszeg, then to Szent-Gotthárd. The 1st Medical Company followed a similar route, but in doing so lost a lot of equipment and a number of men went missing. An account of the experience of the 2nd Medical Company of SS Medical *Abteilung* 31, in action and in retreat, was given by *SS-Rottenführer* Ernst Bennert:

At the end of October and beginning of November we moved from Mohács to Fünfkirchen and set ourselves up as a dressing station in a school close to the railway station. From the Wehrmacht we got a surgeon and a senior medical officer. So we were able to provide surgical treatment for the wounded who were arriving. They came not only from the 31st SS Division, but also from all the units in action in the Danube sector and even in Croatia. The treatment of the wounded and their transport away afterwards, worked excellently. The railway network was intact, and the Hungarians really co-operative. In Fünfkirchen we also got replacements, young and older Reich Germans, so that the company grew in size to some 70 men. Among them was also *SS-Unterscharführer* Hans Otter from Regensburg.

Our first patients were older Soviet prisoners of war, all wounded, curiously all in the feet. They looked very distraught, they'd landed up with the SS, from whom, thanks to the propaganda which had been hammered into them, they expected the worst kinds of atrocities. They were then very surprised when instead of knocking them off we took care of them. They were locked up in the first storey of the school where the main dressing station was housed, got blankets, rations and as far as was possible something to smoke, *Honvéd* cigarettes too, at that time very popular with us. As time passed they became more trusting. They had halted during the attack and had been helped on their way by their commissar with his machine-pistol – hence the same wounds in the feet.

Our first theatre assistant was *SS-Unterscharführer* Hans Gerber, an older original Berliner. Now, he was giving assistance in the care of the Soviets, to a Hungarian *Standartenoberjunker* who had studied medicine but had not yet qualified. The *Junker* asked for an instrument and Gerber gave him another. The *Junker* slung it back, and made his request again. Gerber gave him back the same instrument. So then the *Junker* looked at Gerber and said: "Very well, *Herr* Gerber, if you think so, I'll take this one.

Our plasterers, Bär and Rühl, both from a community in Transylvania, always played their own macabre jokes when they were putting on plaster. For instance, when applying plaster to the ribcage they would mould plaster breasts and with pelvic plaster casts they would mould plaster genitalia! Then they would mould Iron Crosses, and everything you could think of, on the chest, always taking care to provide us with some jollity.

The first decoration awarded in the Division, an Iron Cross of both classes, was received by a battalion medical officer, an *Obersturmführer* who came from the Batschka. His son served with us in the 2nd Medical Company, but his name escapes me.

At the end of November things got pretty hot in Fünfkirchen. On 28 November 1944 we had to evacuate our main dressing station. This did not proceed without difficulties, because we had no sufficient means of transport. Nevertheless, we succeeded in getting all the wounded to safety. We marched on foot and in horse-drawn vehicles through the Mecsek mountains towards Dombóvár. Once arrived in Dombóvár, we set up the new main dressing station. As soon as we had finished, the order came. We had to dismantle it all again. Then off we went, towards Kaposvár. Here it was the same. On we went to Nagykanisza. It was a fairly strenuous march. Once we managed 86km in one go, without stopping. It was cloudy weather. It drizzled, then in Mecsek it snowed. We arrived in one piece at Nagykanisza, where we were safe. On the way only a few ethnic Germans 'scarpered'. In contrast to us, the 1st Medical Company did not get away so 'scot-free'. They lost a number of men missing, and almost all their equipment.

From Nagykanisza the journey went on through Zalaegerszeg to St Gotthard. Here there was a bit of a rest. Then we were moved into Styria, into the area to the north of Graz. We gathered in Peggau, on the Mur, where we took up quarters. We brought our wounded with us. I can still well remember the 'Apple King' from Apatin who owed his nickname to the extensive orchards owned by his family. Another *Mujo*, too, accompanied us that far. We called him Franz. With his singing, even of Tito's partisans' songs, he really kept our spirits up. He was a charming fellow. Unfortunately we had to give him up in the Ostmark (Austria) to the Bosnian reserve unit in Leoben.

Pause for rest in Eisenburg

A short rest was granted to the parts of the Division gradually gathering together in the communities around Vasvár, in Komitat Vas/Eisenburg. There they took up temporary quarters. This, in and of itself, was already a difficult affair, because the villages in western Hungary, as 1944 drew to its close, were hopelessly over-crowded. German and Hungarian troops, refugees and all the Hungarian authori-ties who were still there, were crammed together. Despite that, for the disorganised units of the Division that above all needed reforming, the rest was very beneficial. Training was even continued, i.e. a bit of weapons practice in open country and some formal training. More than that was impossible.

On the other hand, during those days contingents of the young Hungarian-German recruits were gathered together and marched off to SS Pioneer Battalion 31 in Stiechowitz, near Prague. SS *Panzerjäger Abteilung* 31 went to Janowitz near Prague, and to SS Grenadier training. Reserve Battalion 35 went to Bruss near Konitz, West Prussia. From 1 December 1944 they were the reserve troop unit for the Division, apart from the provision of specialists. By means of these movements, the Pioneer Battalion and the *Panzerjäger Abteilung*, on the troop training ground of Bohemia, were now at their full complement. The men directed to the West Prussian troop training ground, to SS Grenadier Training and Reserve Battalion 35 were NCO applicants who had to pass the NCO course there. Probably mem-bers of the Division were also sent to other different schools and training units in the Reich.

But here it was not only movements and assignments that took place, much of the personnel long since marched off for the 31st SS Volunteer Grenadier Divi-sion, above all Reich German specialists, were only able to reach the Division dur-ing those days. *SS-Oberscharführer* Ernst Reimann, SS Supply *Abteilung* 31, described his own journey as follows:

> After the *Panzerfaust*[3] action on 15 to 20 October 1944 in Budapest, where I came away with a few scratches, I was sent urgently from *SS Jagdverband* South-East (Skorzeny) to SS Motor Vehicle Reserve *Abteilung* in Berlin. In November, I and other comrades were transferred to Berlin as driving instructors with the purpose of setting up a Divisional Motor Vehicle Driving School. I had already passed the examination as driving instructor and storekeeper at the Motor Ve-hicle Technical Institution in Vienna.
>
> My service rank was *Oberscharführer*. My comrades, transferred with me to the 31st SS Divsion, were *SS-Unterscharführer* Ernst Scholz (from Görlitz, later missing presumed dead, in Silesia), Fritz Mayer, Kurt Herdegen, Heinz Umbehauen and Hans Fritzenbach. We travelled by train via Budapest to Pécs, Fünfkirchen. It was about 25 November. At the station we asked the field police

3   Referring to Skorzeny's armed takeover of the Hungarian government infrastructure in Budapest to prevent that country leaving the war, or changing sides.

for the 31st SS Division. A jovial dog-handler gave the answer: 'What about the 31st SS Division! It no longer exists. No-one here knows what's left of it. But we could make good use of you. Report to so-and-so, we're forming an alarm unit'. With a crowd like that? We decided they could do without us!

From a Luftwaffe supply unit we learned that they had seen Waffen-SS with horses and carts on the way to Kaposvár. With our comrades from the Luftwaffe gone, we found the unit at Godre. We also found the 20 carts that belonged to the 31st SS Division. We now made the retreat with them as far as Vasvár near Körmend. We laid up, here and there, for days. During this time we did some training with the lads on the ground, weapons training. They only had rifles, nothing else.

Then in Vasvár things were on the move again. We arrived at the motor vehicle unit under the command of *SS-Obersturmführer* Herzog. There were cars and lorries. Only fuel was lacking! It was already around Christmas time. One day I drove with two *Untersturmführer* to Kapuvár to look for a fuel store. But on the journey the Opel's clutch went kaput. I was given a 'hard time' by the two *Untersturmführer*. At Kapuvár was a Wehrmacht workshop company, where they put in a new clutch. But the two *Untersturmführer* had to dig deep into their pockets and their 'smokes' were for other customers. The fuel dump having been found, we negotiated the petrol for the Division. The journey back went well, except for the fact that we had no snow chains with us. But that didn't matter.

The next day we drove in 3 lorries to Kapuvár to fetch some fuel. On the way, one driver, in the snow, drove his lorry into a ditch. Sump kaput! We towed it to a farm. The co-driver, a Batschka Swabian, stayed behind to stand guard. Spending the night in Kapuvár, in the morning we loaded the fuel, oil, petrol and diesel, on to the two remaining lorries. On the way back I also took the third in tow. At a great snowdrift, *SS-Unterscharführer* Scholz went into it at full pelt and the first lorry was stuck. With all the ropes we had, I pulled Scholz out. Start up a few more times, then pull again, till Scholz was free. But with the lorry in tow I got stuck in the end. Then Scholz pulled me out and through. Late in the night we arrived back in Vasvár.

The sequel came in two days. The one container we fetched had waste oils! *SS-Obersturmführer* Herzog said to me, "all of you go back to the fuel dump and sort it out". So we drove back to Kapuvár and gave 'Mr Fuel Administrator' a good piece of our mind. A *Hauptsturmführer* stood nearby, a tall, blond man, he saw and heard everything but didn't say a word. Then I had to go over to him and he said to me in a Berlin accent, "I'm glad that you've brought me back the fuel and the lorry. Otherwise it would look bad with our move to Maribor". He gave me his hand and said thank you.

During those days SS Reserve Battalion 'Transylvania', which was based in Janoshaza, was incorporated into the 31st SS Divsion. Very little is known about this battalion. It was, to judge by its name, intended as a reserve troop unit for SS Regiment 'Transylvania' that was formed for a short time during the first days of September. This regiment was an alarm unit and, at the same time, a last contingent of the Transylvanian Saxons. The regiment took part in the fighting in Transylvania and during this suffered considerable casualties. Then it was placed under the command of the 8th SS Cavalry Division 'Florian Geyer' and took part in the fighting withdrawal across the Theiss into the Budapest area, where it was finally incorporated into the 8th SS Cavalry Division. Whilst the strength was of the SS Reserve Battalion 'Transylvania' is not known, it can hardly have been more than weak company strength. According to one member of the battalion,[4] in it were men from all parts of Transylvania.

On 19 December 1944, an order from the *SS Führungshauptamt* designated Lower Styria as the new base area for the Division. The order stipulated: "31st SS Volunteer Grenadier Division is, on the orders of the *Reichsführer-SS,* to move from the area to the west of Lake Balaton immediately into Lower Styria to complete its formation.

> A new accommodation area is to be determined by the Division in direct agreement with the Senior SS and Police Commander Alpenland and the Reich Defence Commissioner… On arrival in the new area the Division is tactically and territorially under the Senior SS and Police Commander Alpenland and in service terms under the *SS Führungshauptamt.* The Division or units of the Division may only be deployed in action with the approval of the Chief of the *SS Führungshauptamt.*

The Divisional units were marched off from 21 December 1944. The move took place essentially on foot, although individual parts of the Division were moved by train or on lorries. At first SS Medical *Abteilung* 31 was shifted to the rear, into Styria. It moved on 20 December 1944 by a cross-country march via St Gotthard into the area to the north of Graz, where it took up quarters in Peggau, on the Mur. Then the other units followed, the move took until the first days of January 1945. SS *Nachrichten Abteilung* 31 was probably the last unit of the Division to set out, as it set out only in January.

The Temeschwar Collection Camp

Gradually, order returned to the groups of the shattered Division gathering in western Hungary. Many members of the Division had been taken prisoner by the Soviets, either in the fighting or as they had dispersed. They had been captured by the Soviets in their home villages, and were beginning their *via dolorosa.* That was the first, and for many the last station at the camp in Temeschwar. It is appropriate briefly to remember these men of the Division. St. R. gave this account:

> I was taken prisoner by the Soviets with several comrades on 28 November at Lánycsók. We were driven over the pontoon bridge at Kisköszeg back to Zombor. There we were at first used for digging excavations, but shortly afterwards put into wagons and brought via Szeged into the camp at Temeschwar. It was a great barrack camp on the road to Arad, 3km from the town, completely overcrowded. At least 35,000 to 40,000 people were held prisoner there. From time to time there were maybe even more. German and Hungarian soldiers were there, together with displaced civilians. Many women were also among them. We were not registered by name, only by number.
> Guard was, to a large part, mounted by Ruthenians who behaved with hostility and quite viciously to every German and Hungarian. There were no possibilities of work, which on the one hand had the effect of greatly dulling your

4 Source: H. Holzträger: "Das Regiment Siebenbürgen" in *Der Freiwillige,* vol 7-8/1992.

mental and spiritual sensibilities, but on the other hand provided a pretext for a quite dreadful level of rations. Our rations were the worst imaginable. Every day there were 200 grams of bread and twice a day a half litre each of thin cabbage soup, or more likely lukewarm water in which here and there swam some shreds of cabbage. A lot to die for, not much to live for. We were only able to drink out of polluted puddles, as a result of which dysentery soon broke out.

The camp was so terribly overcrowded that some of the inmates were soon separated and moved into a former riding school where conditions were even worse. At first we were shut into a large stall. The roof had caved in and the floor was nothing but puddles. Many of us clambered up on to the crossbeams to try to sleep there, only to fall back down on to those crouching on the floor below. Then we were crammed into a room so narrow that we could only stand or sit. And this was for weeks on end.

In the riding school there was at least good drinking water (horses are fussy about that), but there were still no washing facilities. We were de-loused and soon typhus fever joined the dysentery. We were very scared. We'd heard a lot from our fathers about the First World War when typhus had carried off more people than the front! The Soviets now tried to introduce some counter-measures, but it was too late. People were dying in droves. Every day there were 250 to 300 dead. In March there were at least 9,000.

In a former monastery a hospital was set up, but without medicine or other equipment, and also without doctors. Even those who survived the typhus died sooner or later of its effects. The high fever finished off their hearts, or they got oedema or became parched because their bowels had completely failed. Many went mad, or drowned in the latrines etc. The countless corpses were carried out on litters by their fellow prisoners. They were stacked up in a chapel used for a purpose for which it wasn't intended, and buried in graves in which the lying water was often so deep that the corpses had to be pushed under with poles. There was no recording of the dead by name, perhaps not even by number. I estimate that over 20,000 people must be lying buried on the road to Arad, 3km from Temeschwar.

It was in fact a hell where I survived 6 months. Then, in June 1945 we were loaded up and transported to Russia. I remained there until my release in 1950. I passed through various camps, but experienced none that was as hellish as the camp at Temeschwar had been.

Photographs

All photographs are from the author's collection except for the image of *SS-Brigadeführer* Lombard, which is kindly reproduced courtesy of Marc Rikmenspoel. The publishers' apologise for the poor quality of some of these images. However, due to their historical interest and rarity we have nevertheless decided to include them in this book.

SS-Brigadeführer Gustav Lombard, commander, 31st SS Volunteer Grenadier Division.

SS-Ostubaf. Sepp Syr, CO, SS Volunteer
Grenadier Rgt. 79, here as a *Feldwebel* in 1940.

SS-Ustuf. Alfred Berger.

SS-Ustuf. Alfred Berger with his company of Muslim soldiers from 23rd Waffen *Gebirgs* Division der SS 'Kama'.

SS-Ustuf. Alfred Berger and his company from 23rd Waffen *Gebirgs* Division der SS 'Kama'.

SS-Ustuf. Berger and his men.

SS-Uscha. Heini Knauer, from 4 April 1945 Btn Armourer, II/Grenadier Rgt 79 (here as a *SS-Mann*, October 1943).

A newly-recruited *Volksdeutscher*: Matschi Trapp, from Brestowatz.

Officers from SS Medical *Abteilung* 31 in Neu Werbass, August 1944: *SS-Rottenführer* Peter Glitza (left) and *SS-Rottenführer* Ernst Bennert.

Third from left is *Hstuf.* Günther Maaß, CO, IV *Abteilung*, SS Art. Rgt. 31. This photographs was taken at Jüterborg, 1940, when Maaß was a *Leutnant* in the *Schützpolizei*.

SS Hstuf. Albert Reimann, commander, SS *Nachrichten Abteilung* 31, in western Hungary, December 1944.

Men from SS *Nachrichten Abteilung* 31, Eisenburg, western Hungary.

SS-Ustuf. Hans Villier (left) and *SS-Ostuf.* Albert Vollenbroich (right),
Telephone Company, SS *Nachrichten Abteilung* 31, Eisenburg, December 1944.

1st (Telephone) Company, SS *Nachrichten Abteilung* 31, on the march from
western Hungary, Lower Steiermark, beginning of January 1945.

1st (Telephone) Company, SS *Nachrichten Abteilung* 31, on the march from western Hungary, Lower Steiermark, beginning of January 1945. The two officers at the head of the column are company CO, *SS-Ostuf.* Karl-Heinz Dreiucker, and commander of III Platoon, *SS-Ustuf.* Hans Villier.

Officers from SS *Nachrichten Abteilung* 31 in Gonobitz, January 1945. At right is *SS-Ustuf.* Otto Eichhorn; *SS-Ustuf.* Hans Villier is standing in the stream.

From left to right: *SS-Ustuf.* Hans Villier, *SS-Ostuf.* Karl-Heinz Dreiucker, *SS-Ustuf.* Jürgen Joost in the Lower Steiermark, January 1945.

1st (Telephone) Company, SS *Nachrichten Abteilung* 31, in the Lower Steiermark, January 1945 - *SS-Oscha.* Franz Vögtle is at far left, and beside him, *SS-Uscha.* Willi Pagel.

SS-Ustuf. Hans Villier (left), *SS-Ostuf.* Otto Eichhorn (right), in the Lower Steiermark, February 1945.

SS-Ustuf. Hans Villier, platoon commander, III Platoon, Telephone Company, SS *Nachrichten Abteilung* 31, Silesia, spring 1945.

SS-Uscha. Josef Holzinger, here as a sergeant in the Royal Hungarian *Honvéd.*

Men from the Division's *Nachschub Abteilung.*

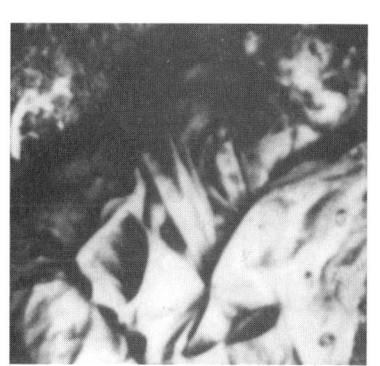

SS soldiers killed by Czech insurgents in the Königgrätz area, May 1945.

A three-man MG34 machine-gun team prepares to fire. The MG34 could be fired on semiautomatic or full automatic by use of double-crescent trigger. The weapon weighed just under twenty-seven pounds and could fire up to 900 rounds per minute. SCOTT PICK/SUMMIT PHOTOGRAPHICS

A German sentry well dressed for the winter cold. Early in the war, German forces were not nearly as well supplied, and many perished in the harsh Russian winter. SCOTT PICK/SUMMIT PHOTOGRAPHICS

A small patrol of German soldiers prepares to head out. Their white uniforms provide them with great camouflage, if not warmth. SCOTT PICK/SUMMIT PHOTOGRAPHICS

CHAPTER 12

Rest and Refitting in the Lower Steiermark

The land between the Drau and the Save, the Bacher mountains and the Croatian border formed, until 1918, an indivisible part of the Duchy of Styria and was called the Styrian lowlands or Lower Styria. The population of the towns was in the majority German. The rural population mostly consisted of Slovenians (Windischen) who maintained an allegiance to Austria. After the enforced annexation of the country into the new state of the Serbians, Croatians and Slovenians, a sharp end came to the hitherto peaceful cohabitation of the Germans and Slovenians. The old established 'Germanness' was exposed to harsh persecution on the part of the chauvinistic Yugoslavian power brokers. After the defeat of Yugoslavia, in a 12-day campaign, Lower Styria was again incorporated into the German Reich. But, as it had in the whole Yugoslavian area, soon there developed a movement of communist partisans. They were favoured by the wooded mountain landscape, and gained more and more ground. After the country fell in 1945, the partisans, who until then only dared to carry out their acts of terror under the cover of darkness, celebrated real orgies of murder, to which the German population in particular fell victim. After 1945, Lower Styria again formed part of Slovenia.

Into this country, fairly inhospitable because of the plague of communist partisans, and thick in snow during the harsh winter, there now marched the shattered units of the 31st SS Volunteer Grenadier Division. They had to complete, at last, the process of formation after refreshment and re-grouping. The Division was badly in need of a break. For over three months it had not been able to continue its process of formation because of the continuous retreat. At the same time the Division also had to take over security tasks in the area of the partisans. The protection of the immediate area in which it was based, was quite extensive.

Until the first days of January 1945 the units were arriving, mostly on foot, at their new quarters. The signal communication head of the Division was in Marburg a.d. Drau. A signals exchange was in an old castle nearby. The Divisional Staff similarly set itself up in a castle on the edge of Gonobitz, in the middle of the area in which the Division was based. The units were quartered in the area south of the Drau almost as far as the Save. They served for some short periods on the Mur. SS Artillery Regiment 31 was between Marburg on the Drau, and Windisch-Feistritz, widely scattered among the individual villages. The Staff of the Artillery Regiment was in Cilli, that of the III *Abteilung* in Kranichsfeld (15km south of Marburg) and the Staff Battery was in Pulsgau.

The grenadier companies of regiments 78, 79 and 80 were probably quartered in the central and southern parts of the base area. The *Nachrichten Abteilung* was first in the area Mureck on the Mur, then the telephone company moved into the villages round Gonobitz, the wireless company to Cilli. The supply services were based in the Bachern mountains between Marburg and Feistritz. The Medical *Abteilung* was at first to the north of Graz (the 2nd Medical Company in Peggau on the Mur, the 1st Medical Company 10km south of there). Then, in the middle of January the 1st Company moved to Gonobitz, the 2nd Company into the area between Marburg and Pettau, to march to Gonobitz at the beginning of February.

Accommodation was arranged mainly in improvised quarters, such as schools, guesthouses and others. They were fortified against the constant danger from partisans. There were, also, a limited number of private houses and barracks available. During this period the 31st SS Volunteer Grenadier Division, as a "large unit in the process of formation by the SS *Führungshauptamt*", was, in service matters, directly under the SS *Führungshauptamt.* Tactically and territorially they were under the Senior SS und Police Commander Alpenland (at that time *SS-Obergruppenführer* and General of the Waffen-SS and Police Erwin Rosener).

The main task of the units was to finish their formation. Accordingly their days were filled with instruction, exercises and guard duty. Individual groups, with tactical responsibility to the Senior SS und Police Commander Alpenland, were sent into action fighting the partisans. It was mainly the grenadier units that were used for these duties and in carrying them out they suffered very heavy casualties. There are no details of these actions, but an eyewitness account from E. Bennert (Medical *Abteilung*) should help to fill out this shortage of information:

> We often would go out on patrol against the partisans, but for the most part these patrols met with little success. Slovenian civilians observed us and told the partisans that we were coming. The partisans then withdrew to a respectful and above all safe distance. In one night patrol we were able to spot the signallers. We made out a house where several figures with petroleum lamps kept going out of one room and into another and walking up and down, which looked fairly suspicious, although we of course were not able to decipher the meaning of the signals which they had agreed between themselves. While the majority of the patrol went on, a 20-man-strong detachment remained behind and carefully stalked the house. At the right moment, quick as a flash they hit the busy signallers who were not a little surprised at these men seeming suddenly to spring up out of the ground. So they considered it advisable to give themselves up without a fight. In this way we neutralised the whole signals nest and took 14 partisans prisoner, among them also some former German soldiers who had deserted.

The enemy was everywhere and everyone always had to expect to be shot at from behind. In many places it was advisable only to pass through places in convoy with weapons at the ready. The area around Cilli was especially infested with partisans, practically ruled by them. In the town of Cilli they even plundered shops in German uniforms and with German Wehrmacht vehicles. Often the Division's quarters were surprised, and surprise attacks on soldiers travelling alone or in small groups were the order of the day. Many were killed, others abducted, and these either disappeared or if they were luckier came back completely cleaned out. SS *Mann* A. Glasenhardt recalled:

> We were standing guard in the woods, in darkest night. It was in Studenitz/ Brunndorf, near Marburg. Our teeth were chattering, not only from cold but also from fear. The previous day fellow-countrymen of our home village,

Berwinkl, Hans and Josef Hellebarth, had been taken prisoner by the partisans. The next night they were able to come back – stripped to their underwear. It was January, bitter cold! After a short hunt we succeeded in finding the partisans' trail and taking some of them prisoner. They were then handed in, bound, behind the car.

Or as the account of *SS-Rottenführer* Heini Knauer (in the Weapons and Equipment *Abteilung*) described:

Our battalion medical officer at that time, while giving medical aid in a smallish village near Marburg, was completely stripped and his driver, too. The MO was asked by a woman to have a look at her daughter who was suffocating. After several visits he saved the child's life. His thanks for this was that on his last visit he was chased 'butt-naked' out on to the street. It was only thanks to the intercession of the woman that he and his driver were left alive at all. They both came back half-frozen and as far as I know the MO then left us, seriously ill. I know of another surprise attack on our sentries in this small village. After three days we had got a number of partisans, in the process of which two of our comrades lost their lives in the exchanges of fire. But not a hair on the partisans' heads was touched. They were taken to Marburg and turned in to a camp there.

The Divisional Adjutant of the 31st SS Volunteer Grenadier Division while on a journey was also surprised in his Kubelwagen and shot, together with his driver. It is no wonder then that after this incident the senior commanders of the Division could only travel if they had sufficient security. The Divisional Staff were reinforced with motorcycle marksmen, flak and an armoured car.

There follows an account of an incident that indeed does belong to the less happy episodes. But it still does belong to the unit's history. Shortly before the transport away to Silesia, on 17 February 1945, a part of the signals detachment of the Staff Battery of SS Artillery Regiment 31 deserted, in Oberpulsgau, and went over to the Slovenian partisans. The group of deserters consisted of 29, for the most part very young, seventeen to eighteen years old Banat Swabians under the instigation of the detachment leader, the twenty-four years old *SS-Oberscharführer* Josef Ohl.

The motives for this step lay deeper than the well-known difficulties of the circumstances that the Division had to endure in the past months. It was a matter of Banat German schoolboys from middle-class families, who as early as 1943 to 1944 in the German senior school in Werschetz, had found themselves united by their rebellious behaviour. In September they too were drafted into the signals detachment of the reserve unit of the *DM-Standarte* 'Michl Reiser'. This detachment was, in the Batschka, without further ado incorporated into the 31st SS Division.

It proved to be a serious command error, to have brought up this unit *en bloc* as signals unit for the Staff Battery, instead of breaking it up and assigning the members of the detachment to different units. This did not even happen when some men from the Banat soon deserted. The detachment was immediately disarmed and temporarily treated as a punishment unit. But this only served to have precisely the opposite effect on those involved, and reinforced their intention to change sides. Towards the end of January 1945, Josef Ohl had established initial contact with Slovenian partisans through the woman who owned their quarters, the guest housekeeper Maria Mohorko. Little by little 29 men (including some stormtroops) declared themselves ready to go over to the enemy. Then, on the night of 17 February 1945, after careful preparation, taking along rifles, hand weapons and ammunition, they made off, in groups of four, into the mountains. When just one hour later the alarm was given in Oberpulsgau, a search for them was, already, in vain. After some days the deserters were sentenced to death in absentia by the court martial.

Reorganisation

During the Division's stay in Lower Styria, reserve transports were always on their way to it. Reserve personnel from the Reich area were brought up to the Division, partly from dissolved units of the Waffen-SS, partly from various training and reserve units. They included above all, skilled personnel, both officers and NCOs, but also other ranks. The SS Recruit Depot 'Kurmark' at the beginning of January assigned a larger contingent to refresh the 31st SS Volunteer Grenadier Division. As a result of this strong influx of Reich Germans, the proportion of ethnic Germans in the Division decreased. The Reich Germans then accounted for about a third, ethnic Germans from the Batschka a half, the rest of the ethnic Germans from other, mainly Hungarian, districts (e.g. from Swabian Turkey, but also from the Banat). The Reich Germans were more strongly represented in the Artillery Regiment, in the 13th and 14th Companies, in the *Nachrichten Abteilung* and the Panzerjäger *Abteilung*.

Weapons and equipment, and all sorts of heavy equipment, arrived so that at last the Division, more or less as it entered the sixth year of war, could be fully equipped. A member of the *Abteilung* Weapons and Equipment (WuG), *SS-Rottenführer* Heini Knauer, gave this account:

> On 6 January 1945 I was transferred from the *Waffentechnische Führerschule* Dachau with other comrades such as *SS-Unterscharführer* Tille, from Stendal, and *SS-Unterscharführer* Machek to the 31st SS Division. At first we had the task of sorting out the armaments for the Division's armouries with the chief armourer, *SS-Hauptsturmführer* Neubert. In four weeks we had assembled the technical armaments in Berlin and Naumburg and had finished the armament process around the middle of February. Nevertheless, later all sorts of materiel was still arriving in Silesia.

During the formation process the Division was at the same time reorganised into an 'Infantry Division type 1945'. The reorganisation was determined in an order of the SS Führungshauptamt dated 16 January 1945. It ordered:

1. For the 31st SS Volunteer Grenadier Division (similarly for the 27th SS Division 'Langemarck' (Flemish Nr 1) and the 28th SS Division 'Wallonie') the fundamental organisation of the Infantry Division 45 comes into force immediately.

2. The reorganisation is to be implemented immediately within the framework of the personnel and materiel available.

3. The Fusilier Battalion is to be considered as being transferred *en bloc* and completely to the infantry, the designation '*Aufklärungs Abteilung*' is discontinued.

4. As far as third battalions being formed in accordance with the basic Infantry Division 44 organisation hitherto in force, the implementation of this is to be con-

tinued. But in the event of the 31st SS Volunteer Grenadier Division currently under formation being deployed at the front, the third battalions will remain behind in the formation area of the Division at that time, at the special disposal of the SS *Führungshauptamt*. It is therefore in the interest of the 31st SS Division to expedite with corresponding care the further formation of the third battalions.

The essential points of divergence, between the organisation of the Infantry Division 45, and the Infantry Division 44, are summarised as follows:

1. Increase of the firepower of the Grenadier Company by incorporation of 2 assault sections with *Sturmgewehr* 44 in place of 2 rifle sections (retaining 9 MGs). The assault sections of the 31st SS Division were made up of Reich Germans, for the most part combat-experienced, tried and trusted soldiers and each numbered some 40 men. But it is extremely questionable whether every company provided 2 such assault sections, probably for the most part only one. They always formed the local reserves and proved their worth mostly as fire brigades.

2. Bringing together the large-calibre infantry weapons in the 13th (Heavy Weapons) Company.

3. Bicycle mobility for the Fusilier Battalion of the Division.

4. Increase of artillery firepower to 54 guns (including 18 M40 field guns)

5. Bringing together all supply units under a special regimental staff.

6. The discontinuation of the third battalions, mentioned above.

Whether and to what extent their formation really proceeded escapes our knowledge. But it is certain that the III battalions did not move with the majority of the Division to Silesia but remained in the Austrian area. Also, no Divisional *Kampfmarschverbände* were brought up after them, at most only individuals. All the indications point to the fact that these battalions comprised a majority of the older age ranges of the ethnic German military complement and in this way were removed from direct deployment at the front. Where exactly these battalions were, and what became of them, can no longer be determined. It is certain that their field post numbers were deleted in April 1945, and it is known that many battalion members (old men whose sons were killed with the majority of the Division in Silesia or were taken prisoner) came back in Summer 1945 from Austria to Hungary.

According to the reorganisation order the following new organisation was ordered, which formed the basis of the re-formation of the Division[1]:

Division Staff (19970)
    Mapping Office (19970)
    Field Police Troop (19970B)

SS Volunteer Grenadier Regiment 78
    Regimental Staff (45334A)
    Staff Company (45334B)
    I Btn with 1st-4th Grenadier Companies (36293)
    II Btn with 5th-8th Grenadier Companies (20797)
    13th Heavy Weapons Company (21356)
    14th *Panzerzerstörer* Company (21356)

1   The number in brackets represents the unit's field post number.

SS Volunteer Grenadier Regiment 79
    Regimental Staff (48865A)
    Staff Company (48865B)
    I Btn with 1st-4th Grenadier Companies (21714)
    II Btn with 5th-8th Grenadier Companies (37565)
    13th Heavy Weapons Company (46452)
    14th *Panzerzerstörer* Company (46452)

SS Volunteer Grenadier Regiment 80
    Regimental Staff (26445A)
    Staff Company (26445B)
    I Btn with 1st-4th Grenadier Companies (24378)
    II Btn with 5th-8th Grenadier Companies (33535)
    13th Heavy Weapons Company (40166)
    14th *Panzerzerstörer* Company (40166)

SS Volunteer Fusilier Btn 31 (22397)

SS Volunteer *Panzerjäger Abteilung* 31 (48064)

SS Volunteer Artillery Regiment 31
    Regimental Staff (38377A)
    Staff Battery (38377B)
    I *Abteilung* with Staff Battery and 1st-3rd Batteries[2] (34775)
    II *Abteilung* with Staff Battery and 4th-6th Batteries[3] (23497)
    III *Abteilung* with Staff Battery and 7th-9th Batteries[4] (47259)
    IV *Abteilung* with Staff Battery and 10th-11th Batteries[5] (32713)

SS Volunteer Pioneer Btn 31 43199

SS Volunteer *Nachrichten* Btn 31 39839

SS Volunteer Supply Regiment 31
    Staff (40349A)
    1st SS Volunteer Motor Vehicle Company 31(40349B)
    2nd SS Volunteer Motor Vehicle Company 31 (40349C)
    1st SS Volunteer Supply Column 31 (29101A)
    2nd SS Volunteer Supply Column 31 (29101B)
    SS Volunteer Supply Platoon 31 (30967)

SS Volunteer Motor Vehicle Workshop Company 31 (25211)
SS Volunteer Munitions Company 31 (44219)
SS Bakery Company 31 (48519B)

2   1st and 2nd batteries: 10.5cm light field howitzers; 3rd Battery: 7.5cm M40 field guns.
3   As note 1.
4   As note 1.
5   Each with 15cm heavy field howitzers.

SS Butchery Company 31 (48519C)
SS Administrative Company 31 (48519D)
SS Field Post Office 31 (27578)
SS Volunteer Medical Company 31 (42169)
SS Volunteer Motor Ambulance Company 31 (42169)
SS Volunteer Veterinary Company 31 (28248)

The formation of SS Volunteer Grenadier Regiments 78 and 79 proceeded well. SS Volunteer *Nachrichten Abteilung* 31 was also completed, and its recruits trained. SS Volunteer Artillery Regiment 31 was also for the most part completed, two batteries each per *Abteilung* had their 10.5cm light howitzers, the third *Abteilungen* their 7.5cm M40 field guns, the IV *Abteilung* their 15cm heavy field howitzers. To complete the artillery training, the *Abteilungen* were transferred (about the middle of January 1945) by train to Bohemia, into the Wamberg–Hollengrund area.

After the process of formation was ended, the III *Abteilung* was all of a sudden loaded up and transported right across Germany into the Heidelberg area, giving the impression that deployment on the Western Front was imminent. Perhaps there actually were such intentions on the part of the higher command. Then, just as suddenly, the transport was turned round, as a result of which it experienced the notorious British air raid on Dresden on 13 and 14 February 1945 at the Pirna railway station. Here the III *Abteilung* remained for 3 to 4 days, then, in accordance with a transfer order of 17 February 1945 it was reunited with the majority of the Division in Silesia.

Apparently, they dispensed with the reformation of the SS Volunteer Reserve Battalion that had been shattered in the action in Hungary, since the third battalions of the Grenadier regiments were intended to serve as field reserve units. SS Volunteer Grenadier Regiment 80 and SS Volunteer Fusilier Battalion 31 could, for personnel reasons, not be reformed. In Silesia, in place of these units, the Division later received other replacements. But the 13th and 14th companies of Regiment 80 were reformed and moved with the Division to Silesia. *SS-Untersturmführer* Gerhard Hiecke became company commander of 14th Company. Of the Fusilier Battalion not even the unit cadre was retained. Most officers and NCOs were probably distributed among other divisional units. The former battalion commander, *SS-Sturmbannführer* Ludwig Zeitz, was detached from the 31st SS Volunteer Grenadier Division and appeared in March 1945 as the commander of SS *Panzerjäger Abteilung* 3 of the 3rd SS *Panzer* Division 'Totenkopf'.

Meanwhile, the formation of the SS Volunteer Pioneer Battalion was under way (since October 1944) in Stiechowitz on the Bohemia training ground. By the end of February it too was completed. The majority of the battalion only rejoined the other parts of the Division in Silesia. Certain smaller units joined it while still in Lower Styria. The Divisional Commander, *SS-Oberführer* Lombard, had watched the Pioneer Battalion during their training at the training ground and was satisfied with their progress. An eyewitness account from A.Gl. gave a picture of what those weeks were like for the young Hungarian German recruits:

> In Pácsony some one hundred men, some of them volunteers, were selected and marched off to Prague to Pioneer Battalion 31. I myself did not volunteer, but

on the 'recommendation' of my cousin and of a good friend, Matthias Mandri, joined the transport. It was a gigantic training camp near Prague, which covered 36 villages. We were in Stiechowitz. There we were to be trained as pioneers. My group consisted almost exclusively of fellow-countrymen from my home village. They were Franz Kohl, Hans Berwinkl, Plassi Rutscher, Stefan Hellebarth, Michael Kling and others. The *Gruppenführer* was a Swabian from the Rumanian Banat, *SS-Unterscharführer* Josef Schilz. Contacts with the Czech population were strictly prohibited, but nevertheless many of us still bartered with the Czechs, because our rations were abominable. On the other hand we had enough smoking materials. As for the Czechs, their food was excellent. So, there, in the last year of the war, we could swap an entire ration card for a packet of tobacco!

Once I almost came badly to grief in such an 'action'. We were quartered in a school. Next to it was a bakery. That was too great a temptation for my cousin, who nevertheless didn't have the confidence to carry out such an 'action', and therefore persuaded me. While I was exchanging cigarettes for bread with the Czech, *SS-Untersturmführer* Schmidt from the 2nd Company spotted me and, when I had finished, caught me and 'turned me in'. Since I was not a member of the 2nd Company, but of *SS-Obersturmführer* Schröder's 3rd Company, Schmidt rang there and had me taken to my own company. However, *SS-Obersturmführer* Schröder wasn't there, the sarge 'took me over' and ordered me to report back in two hours to receive my punishment. So, in two hours I reported, but Schröder was still not there. Again, in the evening, he still he wasn't there. Then the sarge said: 'Call it a day, you've been lucky!'

SS Volunteer *Panzerjäger Abteilung* 31 had, since November 1944, been in the process of formation in the SS *Panzerjäger* School in Janowitz. Having finished its training it was now brought to the Division in Lower Styria. It consisted of the *Panzerjäger* Company (with 14 Jagdpanzer 38 'Hetzers') and its flak company. At first, the assault gun company was still in Bohemia. In fact it never arrived at the Division because it had been found another assignment. Under the command of *SS-Hauptsturmführer* Leihs, with 8 StuG IIIs, it was incorporated into SS *Panzerjäger Abteilung* 560 z.b.V. for some special use. The commander was *SS-Sturmbannführer* Wöst, then *SS-Hauptsturmführer* Markowz, who later participated in that unit's actions.

In connection with the basic organisation of the Infantry Division type 45, the *Abteilung* staffs of SS Volunteer Supply *Abteilung* 31 and SS Volunteer Administrative *Abteilung* 31 were dissolved and their companies were combined with the other supply units under a regimental staff in SS Volunteer Supply Regiment 31. In this process, using the available personnel and material, the 3rd and 4th mobile columns were reorganised into two motor vehicle companies. The Supply Company was assigned a lower organisational status as a supply *Abteilung*. The refitted SS Volunteer Motor Vehicle Workshop Company was also incorporated into the new Supply Regiment. A SS Volunteer Munitions Company 31 was, from January 1945, re-formed by Office VII of the SS *Führungshauptamt* and brought in to the Supply Regiment while still in Lower Styria.

The two medical companies merged, the Medical *Abteilung* was dissolved and a Medical Company formed under *SS-Sturmbannführer* Dr Otto Rohrs (a Schleswig-Holsteiner, earlier with the 'Leibstandarte Adolf Hitler', who had newly come to the Division. Under this arrangement the previous 1st Medical Company formed I Section under *SS-Hauptsturmführer* Dr Berger. The former 2nd Medical Company formed II Section under *SS-Hauptsturmführer* Dr Scherer, and SS Motor Ambulance Company 31 formed III Section under *SS-Obersturmführer* Keller. *SS-Obersturmbannführer* Dr Karl Matz remained the Divisional MO. Eventually, another surgeon was also transferred to the Division. *SS-Hauptsturmführer* Dr Konigsdorfer in civilian life ran a clinic in the Sudetenland. Both the new Medical Company and the Veterinary Company came under the Staff of SS Volunteer Supply Regiment 31. *SS-Hauptsturmführer* (later *SS-Sturmbannführer*) Wilhelm Morisse, who previously commanded the Supply *Abteilung*, became regimental commander.

Other changes of personnel also took place in the Divisional posts. The duties of Ib were taken over by *SS-Obersturmführer* Johann Lehner. *SS-Hauptsturmführer* Marzel Reichel became the new Ia (Divisional Adjutant). The new IIb (Divisional Orderly Officer) was *SS-Untersturmführer* Joachim-Hans Rahmel. Even the IVa, the old dashing uhlan *SS-Sturmbannführer* Karl von Turck left, and on Lombard's suggestion was appointed Commander of the SS Cavalry School that had moved from Göttingen to Prague. It was a last stronghold of the chivalric traditions of his time-honoured arm of the service. The new Divisional Intendant was *SS-Sturmbannführer* Dr Gustav Gewecke, then *SS-Hauptsturmführer* Rolf Werner came from the administration service. He occupied this post until 15 April 1945, when the Intendance was taken over by *SS-Sturmbannführer* Bruno Witte. *SS-Sturmbannführer* Wiegand also came to the Divisional Staff, later he became commandant of the Divisional Staff quarters.

SS-Obersturmbannführer Hermann Frimmersdorf, previously commander of the SS *Panzergrenadier* School Kienschlag, formerly commander SS *Panzerjäger Abteilung* 6 'Nord', relieved *SS-Sturmbannführer* Schneider, in the post of regimental commander of SS Volunteer Grenadier Regiment 78. Even battalion commanders changed. *SS-Hauptsturmführer* Theodor Clausen, commander II/78, was replaced by *SS-Hauptsturmführer* Emil Maitre, who was a tried and trusted troop leader from SS-Infantry Regiment 4 'Langemarck' and *Panzergrenadier* Regiment 4 'Der Führer', who led the battalion in Silesia until he was seriously wounded shortly before the end of the war. Clausen was to have received the II/78.

SS-Sturmbannführer Heinrich Albrecht recovered from wounds received in action in Hungary, but did not take over his old I/79. Toward the end of February 1945 he relieved *SS-Sturmbannführer* Ewald Schuhmacher at the head of the II/79. Albrecht led this battalion until the end of the war. Schuhmacher was transferred into the Protectorate. The I/79 was, from then on, led by *SS-Sturmbannführer* Kurt Pachur, who had taken over after Albrecht was wounded in December. During March 1945 he was posted missing and was replaced by *SS-Hauptsturmführer* Robert Gloning. Gloning served earlier in the 13th SS *Gebirgs* Division 'Handschar'. He was said to be battalion commander II/28, but this is improbable since he was only promoted to *SS-Hauptsturmführer* on 9 November 1944.

SS-Sturmbannführer Egon Zill appears to have left the Division at this time. His post as battalion commander III/79 was supposedly taken over by *SS-Hauptsturmführer* Werner Zimmermann who formerly served at the Moorlager training ground at Brest on the Bug. According to another source, he was replaced by *SS-Hauptsturmführer* Georg Petrus. The *Nachrichten Abteilung*, too, changed its commander. Instead of Reimann, *SS-Hauptsturmführer* Alois Kindshofer, the former head of the Supply Company, became *Abteilung* commander.

In the Artillery Regiment similar changes in personnel took place. At the beginning of January, or perhaps as early as the end of December 1944, *SS-Standartenführer* Hans-Kurt Kaestner became commander of SS Volunteer Artillery Regiment 31. He had been transferred from the Army to the Waffen-SS. *SS-Untersturmführer* Hans Michel Buehl became his Adjutant. The post of commander of III *Abteilung* was taken over on 7 January 1945 by *SS-Hauptsturmführer* Hans Dotterweich. He was a proven troop leader, who had also participated in the Volkhov action with the *Polizei* Division. Similarly, at this time *SS-Hauptsturmführer* Günther Maasz, who also came from the *Polizei* Division, became commander of IV *Abteilung*. The post of commander of II *Abteilung* was taken over by *SS-Sturmbannführer* Johannes Neugebauer, previously commander of the SS Artillery Reserve Regiment *SS-Sturmbannführer* Dehnen left on 5 January 1945.

In conclusion, there follow some of the experiences, told by comrades, of their time in Lower Styria. *SS-Hauptsturmführer* Hans Dotterweich, commander III/A.R. 31:

> I took over the III *Abteilung* of the Artillery Regiment on 7 January 1945 in Kranichsfeld, 15km south of Marburg on the Drau. It was a loose crowd, having apparently marched back from defensive fighting. The men came for the most part from the Batschka and the Banat. There were also ethnic Germans from Slovakia with them, I also had one on my Staff, an *Unterscharführer* from Pressburg. All my soldiers were extremely decent, there were never any disciplinary proceedings. The three batteries were in the villages round about, fairly far apart from each other. It was, incidentally, characteristic of the whole regiment that its units were stationed so far apart. In my estimation we covered an area of 50km, probably more. My immediate neighbour was II *Abteilung* under *SS-Sturmbannführer* Neugebauer. I scarcely saw him, since he was a good 20km or more away from me. All that I heard from Neugebauer, and I don't even know if it's true, was that from his *Abteilung* 10 or 15 men had vanished overnight into the mountains, never to be seen again.
>
> The batteries were commanded by *Untersturmführer*, as was customary in the sixth year of the war. One was called Klughart, one Meindel, a third was a Sudeten German. He left us during the night on the POW march in May, with the comment that he knew his way about in the mountains, and had relatives there. One, an *Obersturmführer*, came from the Batschka. The *Abteilung* Medical Officer, Dr Weber, from the Batschka or the Banat, was about fifty years old, a fine specimen of a man.
>
> We were not called upon for action against the partisans and did not come into contact with the partisans. With the Slovenian population we had a normal to good relationship. We actively pursued our training that lasted until the end of February. We were half horse-drawn, half motorised, with some 1.5–2 ton Citroen tractors and for the ammunition, 2 lorries. We had Light Field Howitzers 18/40, a new model, 4 guns per battery. Eventually we were fully equipped, with hand grenades, 98K rifles, etc. For directing fire the staff battery was

equipped with new model wireless sets Mark 'B'. IV *Abteilung* had their heavy stuff, 15cm heavy field howitzers.

Ernst Reissmann, Supply *Abteilung*:

Loading up in Körmend, there was a train journey to Marburg and Feistritz, in Slovenia. Here all the driving instructors were transferred to one place, somewhere in the Bachern mountains. We had to set up a driving school. Our quarters looked like a castle. The head of the school was an elderly *SS-Untersturmführer*. His name was Zichmann, Wichmann, or something like that. Here, contact with *SS-Obersturmführer* Herzog was broken. I went on some trips with *SS-Unterscharführer* Scholz to Graz, to get teaching and instructional materials from a Wehrmacht driving school. We had 6 cars and one lorry as the school vehicle, but no pupils as yet. They only came later, only in Silesia. 'Why' is a puzzle. There we certainly had enough time and opportunity to teach. So, apart from guard duty, setting-up and two actions against disturbers of the peace, it was a nice time down there.

SS-Rottenführer Ernst Bennert, 2nd Medical Company:

Arriving from Hungary, via ST Gotthard, in Peggau on the Mur, north of Graz, we took up quarters there. A part of the Reich Germans were now allowed to go on 'service trips', because there was no more leave. Thus I, too, was able to spend three days in Stettin, right at Christmas time. It was the last Christmas in Stettin, in our Pomeranian homeland. On the third day of Christmas I had to immediately begin my journey back, and on 31 December 1944 I was back with my crowd.

In Peggau we had little to do. Some men were sent to Berlin on the Short Medical Course, then came back. Thus towards the middle or the end of January we moved by foot or in horse-drawn vehicles, via Graz, to Marburg on the Drau. We took up quarters in a village south of Marburg, under fairly primitive conditions. There was no electric light or running water. Shortly afterwards we were moved again, this time to Gonobitz, a little place with about 2,000 inhabitants. There was wine growing and it had a small-gauge railway. The Divisional Staff was also there. On the way we spent the night in a barracks belonging to our artillery regiment. There, training was well under way. They had brand-new 10.5cm guns, horse-drawn. In Gonobitz we had to take over a guard base which had been prepared. It was a former school that was fortified by means of trenches, barbed wire, etc. Our main task consisted of having to keep guard over our Divisional Commander, *Oberführer* Lombard's, Fieseler Storch. Since there was only a few of us, it wasn't exactly easy to allocate guard duty. One day the pilot of the Storch, a Luftwaffe *Obergefreiter*, crashed and wrecked it completely. He turned it over when starting. We hoped that that meant the end of guard duty, because we only had a wreck to guard now.

There I saw our Division Commander, *SS-Oberführer* Lombard for the first time in the flesh. But the cause of this was a sad occasion. His adjutant and driver had been shot by bandits while on a journey. At the funeral I was assigned to the honour guard. Here a macabre incident occurred. Of course I had a carbine, but had not used it for a long time. It was a so-called exercise carbine, well oiled and polished. It had only one thing wrong with it, and that was that I couldn't get it to fire! At the final gun salute, there rang out the command 'fire'!

I followed along with the movement and acted as if I'd fired. But I didn't fire. And I did that three times! We had something to laugh about that evening!

In Gonobitz we had several times to suffer low-level attacks by American fighter-bombers. To defend against them, a 2cm flak gun was in position on the water tower, manned round the clock. One foggy day, some of our comrades were sitting up there with nothing to do, since you could scarcely see past the end of your nose. Since they were too lazy to keep going up and down stairs they made their calls of nature in a cardboard box. It was absolutely no weather for flying but, despite this, all of a sudden the sound of aircraft could be heard and the fighter-bombers were back again, dropping some bombs but causing no damage. Because of the poor visibility our flak didn't even come into action – at least not skywards. But earthwards they chucked their cardboard box with its contents down from the water tower. At any rate it was from an impressive height. Although in the drizzly fog the ground couldn't be seen they nevertheless almost scored a hit – on a passing *Sturmbannführer*. Fortunately for them it was only 'almost a hit'. It goes without saying that even days later we were still laughing ourselves silly over the incident.

CHAPTER 13

Transport of the Division to Silesia

The reformation or rather reorganisation of the units and the material equipment were not yet finished. The target strength in terms of personnel was not yet reached. However, on 17 February 1945, orders were given for the immediate transfer of the Division to Silesia, in the Görlitz area, for a planned offensive operation. The telegram from the OKH read as follows:

1. By order of the Führer, the 31st Volunteer Grenadier Division with all its components of personnel and materiel is immediately to be transferred by rail transport into the area around Görlitz. Sent ahead to 4th *Panzer* Army at Görlitz.

2. Parts of the Division ready for action are to travel as the first transports.

3. On arrival in the new area the Division is, until further notice, under the direct command of the *SS-Führungshauptamt*. Deployment in action, even if only of parts, is only to be carried out with the approval of the *SS-Führungshauptamt* (after a request to OKH).

4. Army Group Centre to provide a daily report of the parts of the Division that have arrived.

OKH/Army General Staff/Ops *Abteilung* (röm. 1a)

No. 2086/45 General Command

17.2.45

signed: Merk

General Staff Colonel and Deputy *Abteilung* Head

The move by railway arrow transport took until 28 February 1945. The units were loaded up in Gonobitz (e.g. *Nachrichten Abteilung*, etc), Marburg, Cilli etc. During the transport, individual parts of the Division suffered many air raids by enemy fighter-bombers. By far the most seriously hit was SS Volunteer Grenadier Regiment 78, on 20 February 1945, on the line between Klagenfurt–Maria Saal. It inflicted considerable casualties on the regiment. There was also some information from SS Volunteer Grenadier Regiment 79 about similar things happening. Some of the transports spent some days in sidings in Prague. That was bad enough in winter, but meant that the men had to cook their own food in the goods wagons.

After the departure of the 31st SS Volunteer Grenadier Division their quarters were taken over by the units of the 14th Waffen-SS Grenadier Division (Ukrainian Nr 1) who had set off on the march from Slovakia from 31 January 1945 and arrived in stages.

The units of the 31st SS Division had arrived in the destination area, unloaded in the town of Hirschberg, in the Riesengebirge, and assembled in the area

Hirschberg–Bad Wormbrunn. Gradually, there arrived the two battalions each from Regiments 78 and 79. The *Abteilungen* of the Artillery Regiment, the 13th and 14th companies of Regiment 80, the *Panzerjäger* and Flak Companies, the *Panzerjäger Abteilung*, the *Nachrichten Abteilung* and the Supply Regiment, plus SS Pioneer Battalion 31 were also unloaded at Prague and brought together, with the Division, in Bad Wormbrunn. The III *Abteilung* of the Artillery Regiment was similarly directed from Pirna to Silesia.

At first the units were quartered in the surrounding villages. Thus for instance, there were the Staff and II Battalion of Regiment 79 in Hermsdorf. Other parts of Regiment 79 were in Schreiberhau and Petersdorf. The *Nachrichten Abteilung* was in Bad Wormbrunn, the Staff of the Pioneer Battalion similarly in Bad Wormbrunn, and the 1st Company of the Pioneer Battalion in Maiwaldau. Parts of the *Panzerjäger Abteilung* were in Bobersdorf, and the Medical Company in Grunau, etc.

SS-Oberscharführer E. Reissmann gave this account concerning the short-lived Divisional driving school:

> We moved near to Hirschberg, in an inn of the community of Hain near Bad Wormbrunn. The Divisional Driving School was, at last, able to begin its work. Continually the driving trainees came from the Division to be trained. Then, around 15 April 1945, the Driving School was wound up. The vehicles were handed over to the various units of the Division. We driving instructors were moved back to the Motor Vehicle Reserve *Abteilung* in Wasserburg am Inn. At the end of the war we were engaged in the smaller combat actions against the Americans, through Munich–Achensee–Innsbruck, withdrawing to Landeck and surrendering there on 8 May 1945.

SS-Rottenführer Heini Knauer gave this account concerning changes in personnel and his munitions company:

> With the move to Silesia I was transferred, together with *SS-Unterscharführer* Tille and *SS-Unterscharführer* Machek, to Regiment 79. I took over the munitions company of II Battalion and also of 4th Company, which did not have its own ordnance NCO. *SS-Unterscharführer* Tille took over the same duties in I Battalion, while *SS-Unterscharführer* Marek, who was originally intended for III Battalion, joined the Staff, because the III/79 did not go to Silesia with the majority of the Division. Among other things, we became responsible for artillery weapons.
> Our first Silesian post was Hermsdorf – of the five Hermsdorfs in Silesia it was the one near Hirschberg. I myself had worked there in the battalion clerical office, because no machine would write. Our battalion commander of II/79, until that point, *SS-Sturmbannführer* Ewald Schumacher, took his leave of us there. He was transferred. His successor was *SS-Sturmbannführer* Heinrich Albrecht. He was a Berliner and had several children, of whom he often spoke. Battalion adjutant was *SS-Untersturmführer* Hundertmark, orderly officer was *SS-Untersturmführer* Bender, and paymaster was *SS-Obersturmführer* Bechsen, a dyed-in-the-wool bachelor.
> In the munitions company, where I commanded the sections for II/79 and the 4/79, we had working with us four comrades from Hungary and one from the South Tyrol. The South Tyroler was called Giomutzi. He came from

Sterzing (Vipiteno) and was a farmer, as well as being the father of six children. By using him in the munitions company we were able to protect him from front-line service.

The other Hungarian German's first name was Fritz, he was also a farmer and had already participated in a world war, so he was no longer the youngest. Later, in April, he was promoted to *Sturmmann*. He was very pleased about that because he could thus receive more pay that he could send to his family. In his thoughts he only lived with his family. I was often sorry for him when I saw that he had in his hand a letter or picture from his family and was crying. In March another comrade joined me in the munitions company. He had volunteered for the front again after a serious wound, we called him 'Bebberl'. His father was, he said, head of the SD in Linz.

Because many units of the Division had still not yet been fully equipped, weapons, including heavy weapons and equipment continued to be brought up. Fresh personnel, too, came with them, from weapons schools and reserve units. A smallish contingent of police from the city of Breslau, which remained outside the encircled fortress, was similarly incorporated into the Division.

After about a week, parts of the Division (probably from the two SS Volunteer Grenadier Regiments 78 and 79) were moved into the area between Goldberg and Schonau (for instance into the village of Konradswaldau) behind the area where the 10th *Panzergrenadier* Division was deployed. But no orders were given yet to go into action.

In the Hirschenberg area there were brought up to the 31st SS Volunteer Grenadier Division, the SS Police Regiment "Brixen" as replacement for the missing third Grenadier regiment, and the Hungarian Waffen-SS Grenadier Battalion 'Szálasi' as replacement for the missing fusilier battalion. These were incorporated into the Division as SS Volunteer Grenadier Regiment 80 and as SS Volunteer Fusilier Battalion 31. First of all we should glance at the previous history of these two units, and also, before describing the combat action of the Division, we should look at the general situation at this time on the front in Silesia.

Previous history of SS-Police Regiment 'Brixen'

After the treacherous Badoglio Putsch in July 1943, Italy broke its alliance with the German Reich. The German Wehrmacht occupied the kingdom in September and the Italian army was disarmed. South Tyrol, i.e. the provinces of 'Bozen', Trient and Belluno, went under the designation 'Operational Area 'Alpenvorland'. In practical terms they were separated from Italy. The *Gauleiter* of Tyrol, Franz Hofer, was appointed as Supreme Commissioner for this area. On 1 October 1943 orders were given for South Tyrolean police units to be set up to maintain order in the country. Responsible for forming the units was the newly set up post of the Commander of Order Police (*Befehlshaber der Ordnungspolizei*) Italy, under *Generalleutnant* von Kamptz, in San Martino, near Verona.

For forming these police units, first of all a core of 250 NCOs and other ranks was provided by the German police. At first the Police Regiment 'South Tyrol' was formed with volunteers in the Tyrol. The regiment was renamed Police Regiment 'Bozen' from the end of October 1943. A second police regiment came into existence much later, only in July 1944, and received the name 'Alpenvorland'. This regiment was now expressly formed from South Tyrol Germans. There was no longer any question of voluntary service. At that time there was a serious deterioration of the war situation in, among other places, Italy. There was also a worsening of the situation concerning bands in the operational area 'Alpenvorland', in October 1944. As a result, a beginning was made in forming two more South Tyrol police regiments. The third in the series received the name 'Schlanders', the fourth 'Brixen'. This last formation in the South Tyrol was the police regiment that would later join the 31st SS Volunteer Grenadier Division.

The formation of the regiment was ordered by the Chief of Order Police in his express letter of 12 October 1944. It read:

> *Befehlshaber der Ordnungspolizei* Italy had to set up a regiment, with a core personnel of Reich Germans, and with ethnic Germans from the South Tyrol. The regiment would bear the name SS Police Regiment 'Brixen'.

The regiment comprised a regimental staff with signals detachment. There were three battalions each with four companies, each fourth heavy weapons company being equipped with one MG section, one mortar section and an anti-tank section. The battalion staffs each had a signals section. A motorised column was to take care of the regiment's supplies.

The field post numbers were as follows: Regiment Staff, 31464; I Battalion, 01773; II Battalion, 18524; III Battalion, 05010.

The Police Administration of Innsbruck was designated as the home base of the regiment, the Police Weapons School I, Dresden-Hellerau as its reserve unit.

As core personnel, Reich German officers, NCOs and other ranks were provided from every corner of Germany. The required complement for Reich German personnel was 52 officers and 325 NCOs in certain posts. The remaining posts were filled with South Tyrolean. Post-holders were as follows:

Regiment Commander was *Oberstleutnant der Schützpolizei* Ernst Korn (b.1899), previously Commander of Order Police in Tirana/Albania.

Battalion commanders were *Hauptmann* Borgeest, *Hauptmann* Heinz Opitz, and *Major* Beussel.

Regiment Adjutant was *Hauptmann* August Schomburg, Regiment Orderly Officer *Oberleutnant* Dr Werner Ferch, Regiment Transport Officer *Leutnant* Otto Kaltschmidt, signals officer and commander of the *Nachrichten* detachment *Leutnant* Rudolf Krisch.

Battalion adjutants were *Oberleutnants* Heinrich Gaida, Erich Moller and Hans Niechoy, Battalion orderly officers *Leutnants* Hans Kock, Dr Rolf Kaiser and Eduard Ohmes.

Company commanders of the rifle companies were: *Hauptmann* Paul Aehnelt, Johannes Brings, Karl Fischer, Wilhelm Kupper, Leopold Steiner, *Oberleutnants* Johannes Quehl, Paul Somerfeld, Carl Meissner, Kurt Stelzer.

The heavy weapons companies were commanded by *Hauptmann* Horst Rutz and Heinrich Rickert, the third is unknown.

Platoon leaders in the heavy weapons company were *Leutnants* Ewald Kehlert, Franz Neumacher, Rudolf Krug, Bernhard Terwey, Werner Sucker and Leo Weth. Platoon leaders of rifle platoons *Leutnants* Erwin Dick, Kurt Lange, Waldemar

Gerwin, Gotthard Gelse, Helmuth Muller, Manfred Schwarz, Bruno Dittmar, Kurt Rosel and Walter Hollnagel.

Commander of the motorised column was Rev. *Leutnant* Klinke.

Detailed as administrative officers (Iva) were *Oberleutnant* Alwin Bauer (Regiment Staff) and *Leutnants* Hermann Bottner (I Battalion), Theodor Eckert (II Battalion), and Johann Veit (III Battalion).

The Master of Ordnance Assistance Reserve *Abteilung* of the *Ordnungspolizei* provided 3 ordnance assistants.

Other officers whose service posts are unknown to us were *Oberleutnant* Eberhard Clemens and *Leutnant* Ewald Strassburg.

By 12 October 1944, there were already 142 NCOs, and other ranks who had been marched off to Brixen, the place where the regiment was formed. Later, more were to arrive in train after train. Whether the full complement was reached is not known. Certainly personnel came from several reserve units and dissolved units. Thus, for instance, remnants of SS Police Regiment 26, that had fought heroically in the summer battle in White Russia under the Knight's Cross holder, *SS-Standartenführer* Bernhard Griese. They had been shattered in the maelstrom, as Army Group Centre collapsed. They were transferred to the South Tyrol to SS-Police Regiment 'Brixen' as core personnel (telegram, Chief of Order Police of 6 October 1944). By 12 October 1944 there were already 8 NCOs from the Troop *Nachrichten* Service, Regiment 26 and in the signals units of Regiment 'Brixen'.

The main complement of the regiment was recruited from South Tyrolean Germans. They were also joined by a small number of South Tyrolean Ladiners, who mostly spoke little German. The dates of birth ranged from at least 1902 to 1927. Thus comrades aged forty-two years were standing beside those aged seventeen years, i.e. a twenty-five year age difference. The picture was the same in the 31st SS Division. There were only a few volunteers among these South Tyroleans. Thus they were not designated and paid off as Volunteers of the German Police, but as police reservists, who were called up according to the provisions of the Emergency Law. (This was already the case in SS-Police Regiment 'Alpenvorland'). They were under SS and police jurisdiction.

As to the provision of equipment, the *Befehlshaber der Ordnungspolizei* Italy was also responsible for this, from their own resources. Motor vehicles were taken over from the *K-Staffel z.b.V.* Paris. Equipment with weapons, ammunition etc also had to be carried out by the *Befehlshaber der Ordnungspolizei* Italy from captured and 'other' sources. From the outset this did not bode well. Later, when in action, in fact, severe shortages in armament became noticeable.

The training of the newly set up regiment took place in the South Tyrol and lasted until about the end of 1944. What followed is fairly unclear. As a South Tyrolean police unit, the Regiment 'Brixen' would actually have been meant for security tasks or for fighting partisans in Upper Italy. That was actually the case with the sister regiment 'Schlanders' and with the regiments 'Bozen' and 'Alpenvorland'. In contrast to these, the Regiment 'Brixen' at the end of 1945 ended up in Silesia. They were joined with the 31st SS Volunteer Grenadier Division and thrown into the battle.

The circumstances of this move are unknown. A possible explanation for it could be that many of the South Tyrolean recruits, who did not opt for Germany,

were accordingly Italian nationals. They felt themselves to be 'compulsorily recruited', and refused to swear the oath to the Führer. That could have resulted in
the regiment being considered, by those at high level, as being unreliable and classified as such. As a precautionary measure, to eliminate the possibility of desertions
to home areas close by, they were moved to a distant sector of the front. Although
there is no concrete evidence for this, it is all the more possible in that this proce-
dure was often followed in the case of eastern units transferred to the Western
front. For instance, Georgians and other peoples of the Caucasus, who were sent to
France.

For whatever reason, the Regiment was transferred out of the South Tyrolean
valleys into the Hirschberg area. They were incorporated in the 31st SS Division, as
SS Volunteer Grenadier Regiment 80, as a replacement for the former's missing
third Grenadier regiment.[1] It was also designated as SS Regiment 'Schön', after the
new Regimental Commander, *SS-Sturmbannführer* Rudolf Schon. He took over
command of the regiment from *Oberstleutnant* Korn at a point unknown to us, but
in Silesia he was already in command of the Regiment. *SS-Obersturmführer*
Moeller became Regiment Adjutant, *SS-Sturmbannführer* Helmut Gantz, probably transferred from the Army to the Waffen-SS, became commander of I Battalion.

The 14th Company of SS Volunteer Grenadier Regiment 80 formed in Lower
Styria independently from Police Regiment 'Brixen' was under the command of
SS-Untersturmführer Hiecke and was incorporated into the new regiment. The situation, regarding provision of equipment and armament, was very bad for the regiment when it had to go into battle.

Waffen Grenadier Battalion der SS 'Szálasi' (Hungarian)

At the beginning of February 1945, the two Hungarian Waffen-SS divisions currently being formed i.e. the 25th Waffen-Grenadier Division of the SS 'Hunyadi'
and 26th Waffen-Grenadier Division of the SS 'Hungaria', were at the
Neuhammer/Queis troop training ground in Silesia. On account of the approach
of the front these two divisions, in terms of personnel, were at their full complement. However, they were only partially trained and equipped. With few arms,
they were put on alert on 6 February 1945. The divisions, with their greater part in
Strans, were exposed to a direct enemy attack. Therefore various alarm units were
organised. Membership was strictly voluntary, since in accordance with the agreements concerning the formation of the Hungarian SS divisions, these were, basi-
cally, only to be used for the immediate defence of Hungary. Under these
circumstances the Battalion 'Szálasi' was the first to be formed, probably as early as
7 February 1945. A former officer of the Division 'Hungaria', A.v.P., described the
birth of the battalion as follows:

> It mainly involved members of the (Hungarian) Arrow Cross Movement, they
> were Magyars, ready for a scrap, and arrived at the 26th Waffen Grenadier Divi-

---

1   According to Klietmann: *Die Waffen-SS. Eine Dokumentation* the 31ˢᵗ SS Division only
    retained one-third of the NCOs and sergeant-majors trained by Regiment 'Brixen'. But
    this does not appear to be correct. Perhaps here it was the case that a part of the
    regiment's core personnel were distributed among other parts of the Division.

sion SS 'Hungaria' (Hungarian Nr 2) in Neuhammer in black Arrow Cross uniforms. They also wanted to go into battle wearing these. They were already being loaded up at Oberleschen railway station when they were held back at the last minute by the Divisional Commander *SS-Generalleutnant* Jószef Grassy and had to change their uniforms. Lorries brought the field-grey uniforms to the station where the men changed in the open air. This was very important because the black Arrow Cross Party uniform was not recognised internationally as a uniform. Those wearing it were classed as non-combatants and in warfare would not have enjoyed the protection of the Geneva Convention, nor of the Hague Land Warfare Convention, that was promised to combatants. They could have been treated as guerrillas.

The battalion took the name of the leader of the Hungarian National Socialist Arrow Cross Party, Ferenc Szálasi. The strength of the battalion was about 250 men. In the battalion there were all Hungarian officers and NCOs, apart from a few German sergeants and paymasters. Command of the battalion was probably offered to *Sturmbannführer* Rudolf von Keitz. He had already played a part in the SS recruitment campaigns in southern Hungary and was at this time himself at the Neuhammer troop training ground, but he declined. So a Hungarian SS-Waffen *Obersturmführer* (*Oberleutnant*), name unknown, became battalion commander.

It should be added that most of the men were still young, without any combat experience and had only received a short period of training. They were joined by a few soldiers who had only a little frontline experience. On the evacuation of the Neuhammer/Queis troop training ground, on 8 February 1945, the battalion was marched off with the group of Hungarian SS divisions towards Dresden. From there, in a further march, they reached the Zwickau area. Between 14 and 21 February 1945 they rested between Reichenberg where they received immediate orders to go to the Görlitz area. On 21 February 1945 they left the command of the Hungarian SS divisions.

On the way to their ordered destination they were diverted into the Hirschberg area, where they arrived at the end of February 1945. There they were probably, at the qualifying date 1 March 1945, incorporated as SS Volunteer Fusilier Battalion 31 (field post nr 22397) into the 31st SS Volunteer Grenadier Division. Their original fusilier battalion, the *Aufklärungs Abteilung*, had been wiped out in the fighting in Hungary. They had not been reformed in Lower Styria. This incorporation probably took place in Schreiberhau.

Here the battalion received some new *Untersturmführer* from the SS *Junkerschule* Prague, as well as German NCOs. At this time there were no longer any Hungarian officers in the battalion. A little later, *Untersturmführer* Zvonimir Bernwald, who had similarly newly received his *Leutnant's* commission in Kienschlag on 30 January 1945, was given command of the battalion. He recalled:

> It was somewhere near Waldeburg, where I took command of the battalion of the Hungarian Division 'Hunyadi'. When we eight to ten *Untersturmführer* arrived from Prague at the divisional command post, the orderly officer gave each a glass of cognac. Only he forgot me! I interpreted this as a good sign for the future.

Loaded up in Waldenburg, the battalion was transferred into the Strehlen area, where it remained until 8 May 1945. They took part, within the Division, in the defensive fighting over that area. In retreat over the Eulengebirge, into the area south of Langenbielau, it was almost completely wiped out by pursuing Soviet troops. The remainder were killed by Czech partisans, so that there were hardly any survivors.

The men of Battalion 'Szálasi' of the Hungarian Fusilier Battalion of the 31st SS Division were volunteers. They embodied the ancient Magyar soldiers' blood lineage that had so often withstood the onslaught from the East. They held high the Hungarian military virtues of ancient renown. But there was one thing more. There was a new pan-European spirit that urged them into battle although so far from home. That spirit bade them stand firm as iron in the fray. It caused them never to doubt that there, in far-away Silesia they were defending the whole of Europe as well as their homeland. At that time, most of their long-suffering homeland of Hungary was lost. In spite of that, they did not give up, for they knew full well what their fight meant. Their soldierly spirit surmounted the unfortunately very limited circumstances of the state of their training and their armament. For that reason their sacrifice had all the more weight. They did not waver and did not ask the reason why. Nor did they ask for any reward. In the end they did not even ask for victory. So they held, and so they died.

The continuing development of the situation in Silesia

On 12 January 1945, after an enormous preparatory artillery barrage, the deployment of many fighter-bombers and an almost inexhaustible stream of armour, the Soviets broke through the German Narev-Vistula Position in several places. In several attacking groups they prepared to advance westwards. At the beginning of February, advance units of Soviet armour were already at Küstrin on the Oder, and thus at the 'front door' of Berlin. On the southern frontier of Lower Pomerania and East Prussia, a new German defence was formed with its front facing south. Then, by the end of March, East and West Prussia as well as Lower Pomerania were lost. The new front in that area stood on the lower Oder.

At the same time, the Red Army in the south moved out of the Vistula bridgehead of Baranow-Sandomierz against Upper Silesia. The centre and northern wings of Army Group A (on 25 January 1945 renamed Army Group Centre) were shattered and their remnants flooded back westwards. Especially badly hit were the 4th *Panzer* Army (Gräser) and the 17th Army (Schulz). The Soviet thrust continued without a pause on the shattered front between Tschenstochau and Lodz/Litzmannstadt. It was scarcely halted by individual pockets of resistance that formed, again and again, under determined German commanders. The newly appointed Supreme Commander of the Army Group, *Generaloberst* Ferdinand Schörner, a Bavarian of robust constitution and sanguine temperament, was again placed by Hitler at the most critical places on the Eastern Front. He was able in the first days of February to stiffen the morale of the completely disorientated troops and to weld them together into units ready for combat.

On 17 January 1945 Cracow fell. On 21 January 1945 the southern offensive group of the 1st White Russian Front (Marshal Konev) broke into Upper Silesia. On 24 January 1945 Oppeln and Gleiwitz fell. The 1st *Panzer* Army (Heinrici) had to give up the front in eastern Slovakia and took up a new position to the east of Mährisch-Ostrau. On 26 January 1945 Kattowitz fell and on 27 January 1945 *Generaloberst* Schörner, without seeking the approval of the Führer HQ beforehand, ordered the 17th Army to evacuate the Upper Silesian industrial district, the great armoury of the Reich. Army Group Centre thus had the chance of being able to succeed in defying the Soviet assault with the forces released on the Oder front.

The Oder line already had several enemy bridgeheads. In the first days of February the bitter fighting along the whole line swung to and fro. The Soviets brought up reinforcements with them, formed a concentration at Steinau, and on 4 February 1945 also linked their smaller Oder bridgeheads at Schurgast and Ohlau with the large Brieg bridgehead. From there on the following days they thrust southwards and westwards through Grottkau. On 8 February 1945 they also moved on to the offensive from the bridgeheads on both sides of Steinau and Lebus. While there was some success in repulsing the enemy at Grottkau, Oppeln and Ohlau, from the Steinau bridgehead, they broke through the defensive front southwards and westwards and pushed forwards in both directions. South-eastwards the Soviets penetrated into the western and north-western outworks of *Festung* Breslau, with which move the decisive battle for Silesia's venerable capital began. The Silesians affectionately called it 'Gruss-Brassel'. Moving westwards, they quickly gained ground, and on 9 February 1945 took Liegnitz, on 10 February 1945 Primkenau, on 11 February 1945 Bunzlau, and on 11 February 1945 encircled Fortress Glogau.

On 12 February 1945 the Soviets attacked once more with strong forces from the Brieg bridgehead and on the same day were able, in very heavy fighting at Jordansmühl, to join hands with their comrades pushing forward out of the Steinau area. The pincers from Steinau and Brieg had now closed round Breslau and, in spite of the deployment of three *Panzer* divisions (19th, 20th and 8th *Panzer* divisions), were not able to open again. It was true that on 14 February 1945 there was some success in forcing open the ring for a short time, but on 15 February 1945 the trap finally and definitively snapped shut. Within it was a city with still some 80,000 civilians and 45-50,000 soldiers in 5 regiments and 26 *Volkssturm* battalions set up for a long-term defence. Playing a large part in the fighting which attended the encirclement of the city were the 269th, 208th and the 17th infantry divisions, divisions with which the 31st SS Volunteer Grenadier Division later came into close contact.

At the same time as the fighting for Breslau, the Soviets advanced, westwards and south-westwards, further in to the Lower Silesian plain. At the Neuhammer troop training ground between Bober and Queis the Hungarian Waffen-Alarm-Regiment der SS (*Standartenführer* Peinlich), supported by an Estonian company, put up a stubborn and successful resistance. In other places, however, the Soviet forward thrust met no opposition. On 13 February 1945 Goldberg fell, on 14 February 1945 Sagan fell and on 15 February 1945 Naumburg. On 16 February 1945 the Soviet 3rd Guards Tank Army attacked with renewed impetus in the gap between the 17th Army and the 4th *Panzer* Army. They took Löwenberg and reached the area to the west of Lauban. Further to the north the Soviets were in Neuhammer, Rauscha, Halbau and 10km east of Guben. On 17 February 1945 the Görlitz area, and thus Saxony, were already in great danger!

Because things were 'hot' everywhere in Silesia, the reserves were not sufficient, and reinforcements had to be brought up. One of these reinforcements was
to be the 31st SS Division. On 17 February 1945 the OKH order reached it concerning transfer by express transport into the threatened area.

On 18 February 1945 the 8th *Panzer* Division carried out, from the
Greiffenberg area, a surprise thrust northwards against the enemy forces which
were moving from Löwenberg against Lauban and Görlitz. This stopped the enemy push on Görlitz. It was a decisive contribution towards the setting-up of the
line on the Lausitzer Neisse, which henceforth from Rothenburg (north of Görlitz)
to the Neisse estuary north of Guben became the fighting front of the 4th *Panzer*
Army. With the intended deployment of the 31st SS Division in the Görlitz area,
while they were still on their way, the position became untenable.

But despite this there was no shortage of possibilities for going into action. At
the end of February the wide Lower Silesian plain was for the most part in Soviet
hands. The vital rapid traffic artery, the *autobahn*, was lost. Breslau was encircled
and caught in a battle to the death. After the failed Oder defence, they were at the
northern edge of the foothills, and surrounded by the far off, just visible mountains
of the Germanen, the Zobtenbergit. It was now simply a matter of 'scratching' in
the Silesian soil, there to build a new wall.

The situation in this command area of the 17th Army, in the last days of February 1945 looked as follows. After the preceding heavy fighting involved in the encirclement of Breslau and on the flanks, German resistance, with the protecting
mountain chain to the rear, stiffened along the approximate line Penzig–Lauban–
Lowenberg–Jauer–Striegau–Zobten–Strehlen–Cosel. That front could certainly be
held at first, but in the longer term its state was thought to be not very reassuring.

Between Striegau and Jauer there were plenty of gaps. Even in other places the
main line of resistance was only fairly thinly manned. Lauban and Striegau were in
enemy hands, each only just an hour on foot behind the frontline. Beyond this
nothing could be known, at the present, as to how things would go. During those
days a large-scale enemy attack was expected in the Army area. For this reason the
17th Army was reinforced. The 1st *Panzer* Army sent the 359th Infantry Division
and the 545th *Volksgrenadier* Division and now also the 31st SS Volunteer Grenadier Division was placed under its command, i.e. directly under AOK (Army High
Command) 17 as Army Reserve. Parts of the 31st SS Division were directed into
the area between Goldberg and Schönau.

The task of the 17th Army was to hold the front to the south-west of Breslau,
They had to be close near enough to the *Festung* to provide a good jumping-off
point for a later attack that would restore communications with the city. In addition, an enemy breakthrough north of Schweidnitz had to be stopped by both defensive and offensive means. The connection to the edge of the mountains west of
Striegau, i.e. in the direction of Jauer–Goldberg, had also to be maintained.

At higher command levels, in the OKH and FHQ, they nurtured even more
far-reaching plans, and large-scale offensive intentions. A telegram of the OKH
Ops *Abteilung* to Army Group Centre, dated 21 February 1945, stated:

> The task of Army Group Centre and the Vistula is to prevent further enemy ad-
> vances beyond the line Görlitz–Schwedt. The task is to keep a firm hold on the
> Moravian-Silesian industrial districts and the area of fighting in Pomerania and

West Prussia. Thus we must create the conditions for a transition on to the offensive.

In addition, Army Group Centre has to conduct the action in such a way that, in the Schweidnitz–Hirschberg area, the necessary ground is to be retained north of the Sudeten. That will enable an attack to be mounted through the area on both sides of Liegnitz, northwards, against the flank of the main enemy offensive groups.

Thus, a giant pair of pincers, from Pomerania in the north and Silesia in the south, was to cut off the Soviets who were standing on the Oder just 90km from Berlin! It was a completely feasible operation, which gave a bad headache to the Soviet marshals, who retained a terrific respect for their opponents. What they could not know was that the forces needed for this operation had long since been unable to be mustered.

Thus for Army Group Centre (HQ in Salzbrunn, then in Josefstadt) at that time there was unfortunately no longer any question of strategic ideas. The Army Group judged the situation as follows. On the basis of the forces available to it, the task of Army Group Centre could merely be to defend its existing front, only occasionally offensively.

The Soviet attack on Berlin, seeking a decision, was soon to be expected. By contrast other attacks against the long-extended front of the 17th Army, however threatening they may be, were peripheral, serving the purpose of tying forces down away from the main front and thus precluding any threat to the Soviet flanks. Thus of decisive significance was the sector of the 4th *Panzer* Army between Görlitz, Muskau and Guben. On the other hand, the area of the 17th Army was a peripheral front, although at the beginning of March an enemy attack was considered to be quite possible even here.

Added to all this was the question of Breslau. The Army continued to harbour the intention of relieving this heroic fortress. (Not only Army Group Centre but also the Führer Adolf Hitler, according to a file note of 26 February 1945, maintained the intention of an attack in the direction of Breslau!) But since the forces of the 4th *Panzer* Army were tied down in the Görlitz area, and those of the 1st *Panzer* Army around Mährisch-Ostrau, the last reserves at the beginning of March had to be deployed elsewhere. That was following the liberation of Lauban and Striegau. In March, the troops necessary for such a strategy were not available. Although as time went on, the gaping discrepancy between what was intended and what was possible grew greater and greater, no-one ever gave up the intention of relieving the fortress.

A further distinctive circumstance in the area of the 17th Army, at the beginning of March, was the pause in enemy operations. That gave the continually over-extended German troops and their commanders the pause for breath that they needed, in order to regroup their units. At first it seemed quite inexplicable. Only after the war was the puzzle solved. The license given to the Red Army troops, by their highest command, to rob, burn, murder, plunder and rape had caused the strict order and discipline of the Red Army to come apart at the seams. Communications, supply functions, and also the carrying out of orders had all come to a standstill. The Soviet Army's ability to strike was crippled!

Out of all these circumstances, considerations and possibilities, there crystallised the task of the 17th Army, mentioned above.

CHAPTER 14

Deployment of the Division in the Jauer Area, March 1945

Out of the situations and considerations described in the previous chapter came the 31st SS Volunteer Grenadier Division's orders for action. On 28th February 1945 the *Reichsführer-SS* gave General Krebs his verbal approval to make the Division available for action.

After this release for action had been given, the Army envisaged using the Division in the area south-west of Jauer. As a result of the dislocation of Army Group Centre from 1 March 1945, parts of the 31st SS Division (combat units of SS Volunteer Grenadier Regiments 78 and 79) were in the area between Goldberg and 'Schön'au. Meanwhile, all the other parts of the Division were still in the Hirschberg area, in the order of battle under the direct command of the 17th Army as Army Reserves.

The exact course of the 17th Army front, during the first days of March, appeared to be as follows. Directly to the south was Lauban, a town in enemy hands since 26 February 1945, and Löwenberg, a town lost since 16 February 1945. Along the line Neuland–Hagendorf–Nieder-Görisseifen–Ober-Mais, it went north of Schmottseifen–Zobten near Löwenberg–Lang-Neundorf. Then it went between Goldberg and 'Schön'au along the line Harpersdorf–Steinberg–Wolfsdorf–Prausnitz–Haasel (including these places). From there it went on to Hermannsdorf–Kolbnitz–Peterwitz (including these places). Then it went past the southern edge of Jauer, a town in enemy hands, to Poischwitz–Dornberg–Häslicht. In the area of Striegau it followed the line Fehebeutel to the western and southern edge of Striegau, a town in enemy hands since 12 February 1945. It continued to Haidau–Muhrau–Saarau, and from there it lead to the Zobten mountain and further on to Strehlen.

In the Lauban–Löwenberg area were XXXIX *Panzerkorps* and LVII *Panzerkorps*. Between Löwenberg and Goldberg, was the *Kampfgruppe* 408th Infantry Division. Between Goldberg and 'Schön'au was the 10th *Panzergrenadier* Division. On both sides of Jauer, was the *Kampfgruppe* of the 269th Infantry Division. They had been hard-hit after the fighting outside Breslau.

In the sector near Striegau was the 208th Infantry Division i.e. the four divisions under the command of the XLVIII *Panzerkorps*. Between Striegau and Zobten were the *Kampfgruppen* 19th *Panzer* Division and 359th Infantry Division. At Zobten was the 20th *Panzer* Division (these three under the command of XVII Corps). East of Zobten was the 254th Infantry Division. On both sides of Strehlen was the 100th *Jäger* Division. South-east of the town was the *Kampfgruppe* 45th *Volksgrenadier* Division. These three were under the General Command of VIII Corps.

In Upper Silesia the LVI *Panzerkorps* was with the 168th Infantry Division, the 18th SS Volunteer *Panzergrenadier* Division 'Horst Wessel' and the 20th Waffen-SS Grenadier Division (Estonian Nr 1). Out of all those large units virtually none was a full-strength division. All had to a greater or lesser extent taken a beating. The divisions with greatly weakened fighting strength were designated as *Kampfgruppe*.

The parts of the 31st SS Division transferred in the last days of February to the sector between Goldberg and 'Schön'au (the line Harpersdorf – Steinberg – Neukirch – Wolfsdorf – Prausnitz – Haasel) at first also remained there. The majority of SS Volunteer Grenadier Regiments 78, on 1 March 1945, was amalgamated as a *Kampfgruppe*. They moved via Ketschdorf – Bolkenhain – Rohnstock into the sector on both sides of Jauer, from where it moved into the positions at Seichau – Hermannsdorf – Peterwitz – southern edge of Jauer – Poischwitz – Dornberg – Häslicht and relieved the 269th Infantry Division. The 269th Infantry Division, thus relieved, marched into the Zobten area, and the 10th *Panzergrenadier* Division into the area of north-west Neisse.

SS Volunteer Grenadier Regiment 80 (former Police Regiment 'Brixen', also designated as SS Regiment 'Schön') moved into the area east of Striegau, relieved Grenadier Regiment 337 of the 208th Infantry Division and on the night of 5 March 1945 took up positions on the line Haidau–Muhrau–Saarau. *Oberstleutnant* Albinus, regimental commander of Grenadier Regiment 337, described how it was relieved, as follows:

> Grenadier Regiment 337, until then deployed in the sector Saarau Haidau with its front to the north, was relieved, on the night of 5 March 1945, by Regiment 'Schön' of the 31st SS-Division. This SS Regiment 'Schön' was a police regiment from the Tyrol and consisted of Ladiners with German core personnel. The Ladiners had been brought from their Alpine valleys. For most of them, being transported there was the first time they had been on a railway train. They were peaceful 'children of nature', but completely distraught. They didn't understand what tasks faced them in this country. If you said that their weapons were from Andreas Hofer's time, then strictly speaking that was an exaggeration, but it hits the nail bang on the head. The core personnel were thrown together. As they relieved us, this regiment, which at first had hardly any weapons, received hand arms and machine guns. Strong rearguards from our unit remained until the morning of 7 March in the positions with the honest Ladiners in order to prevent a disaster. A disaster was to be feared if the enemy had attacked now – without such supporting 'corset stays'. Thank God they didn't.[1]

The *Abteilungen* of the Artillery Regiment, together with the flak and *Panzerjäger* companies of SS *Panzerjäger Abteilung* 31 were similarly deployed between Jauer and Striegau. The *Nachrichten Abteilung* assigned wireless and telephone troops and posts to the units. But the parts of them which were not yet ready for action had first to be equipped, so even the light signals column was only formed at this point. *SS-Oberscharführer* Hugo Krallmann became column commander.

---

1   Quoted in Ahlfen, *Der Kampf um Schlesien.*

SS Pioneer Battalion 31 was not deployed as a complete unit. Every third platoon of the companies was assigned to the individual regiments that within their organisation did not have any pioneer companies proper to the regiment. Thus the III platoon of the 3rd Pioneer Company joined SS Volunteer Grenadier Regiment 80. The III/2 Pioneer Company and III/1 Pioneer Company joined SS Volunteer Grenadier Regiments 79 and 78 respectively. *SS-Untersturmführer* Bernd Pabel, platoon commander II/1, was moved to one regiment as pioneer commander. His II/1 was now taken over by *SS-Untersturmführer* Max Stubenrauch. The 1st Pioneer Company at first marched on foot into the Lauban-Löwenberg area, then it too came into the Jauer area, with quarters in Blumenau. The baggage remained in the Hirschberg area. The Medical Company set up a medical collection point in Ketschdorf.

The 31st SS Volunteer Grenadier Division was placed under the command of the XLVIII *Panzerkorps*. But this was qualified by the fact that it would not be deployed as a quite complete unit. Because of the 208th Infantry Division being boxed in, in the north-west of Striegau, and already concentrating for a counter-attack, no direct communications existed. Thus, between the *Kampfgruppe* of SS Volunteer Grenadier Regiments 78 and 79, they were deployed on both sides of Jauer. The SS Volunteer Grenadier Regiment 80 was east of Striegau. Therefore, from time to time, individual units of the Division would be placed under the command of other divisions. Thus, for instance, in the survey of 10 March 1945, one battalion from SS Volunteer Grenadier Regiment 78 or 79 appeared as being under the command of the 269th Infantry Division. But on 15 March 1945, four battalions that were evidently the reinforced *Kampfgruppe* brought up to retake Striegau appeared as being under the command of the 208th Infantry Division.

As far as the combat strength of the 31st SS Division and their personnel were concerned, there was a full complement. No exact strength is known, but according to recollections there were 10-12,000 men. But if only this is taken into account, a false picture is given of its readiness for action.

The combat strength of the three battalions of SS Volunteer Grenadier Regiment 80 and of Hungarian SS Fusilier Battalion 31 was fairly questionable. There were greater numbers in the four battalions of SS Volunteer Grenadier Regiments 78 and 79. Their assault detachments were certainly high-quality units. SS Artillery Regiment 31 had reasonable numbers, but often suffered from a shortage of ammunition. SS Pioneer Battalion 31 had several months of training behind them. But no-one could foresee how the young Hungarian Germans would conduct themselves in a battle. Later, when it came to it, they proved themselves outstandingly. SS *Panzerjäger Abteilung* 31 was fully ready for action.

Thanks to the continuing deliveries of weapons and materiel, the 31st SS Division were finally no worse equipped than were their neighbouring divisions. In parts, perhaps, even better. These, too, had for the most part, their most important striking force, in the formation of the assault detachments. These, too, were topped up with young recruits. A not inconsiderable number of the Hungarian Germans of the 31st SS Division had already got a 'whiff of powder' in the fighting in Hungary. Actually, the 31st SS Division was not able to achieve the quality of the old SS divisions. But then, during the last few months, even they were only a shadow of

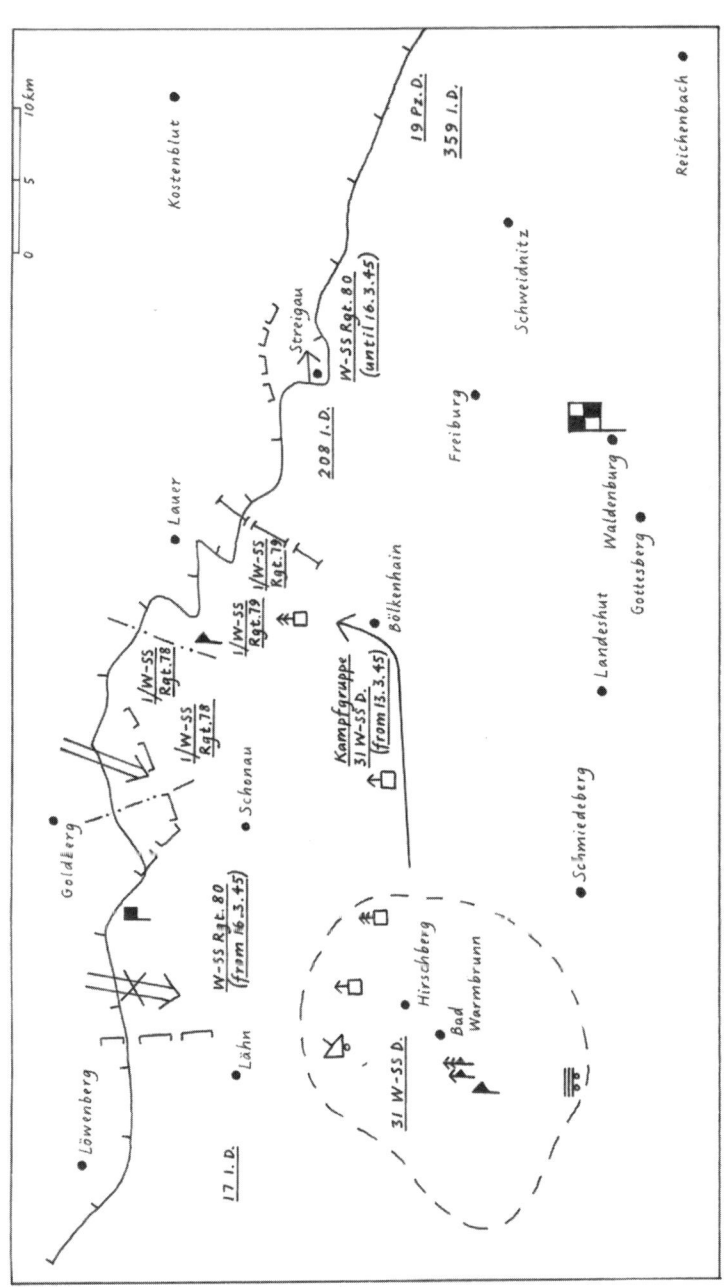

Map 7 Battles of the 31st SS Volunteer Grenadier Division in Lower Silesia, March 1945.

their former selves. During the last months of the war the combat value of the 31st SS Division, whatever it was, rated more above, than below average.

Of the combat activity of the 31st SS Division in the Striegau–Jauer area few details are known. There is a complete lack of official records for this period. Only first-hand accounts can be relied on. It is certain that, in March 1945, in that sector, sometimes heavy fighting took place. Then, towards the end of March 1945, the main line of resistance more or less hardened. From this point in time there were no more large-scale battles. There was certainly local fighting, and attempts at 'sounding out' and the like. There was a levelling of forces. Both sides were concentrating their forces in the wider situation, principally on Berlin. In the narrower situation, i.e. in the Army Group command area, on the Görlitz area, and towards Upper Silesia, the Soviets beyond this were facing *Festung* Breslau. From the fighting to and fro in the central sector, north of the protecting wall of mountains, there stood out the two great counter-attacks of the 17th Army at Lauban and Striegau.

Army Group Centre then considered its most important task to be the retaking of the lost stretch of railway at Lauban and securing it at Striegau. The very efficient railway line running north of the mountains and south of the fighting front of Mährisch-Ostrau via Neisse–Kamenz–Glatz–Hirschberg–Lauban–Görlitz was the backbone of the armies fighting in Silesia. With the aid of the transport trains they could quickly move their units from one wing to another or bring up the corresponding supplies. Then, in February, Lauban and Striegau were lost and as a result the western stretch of line from Görlitz to Greiffenberg was no longer usable. The similarly efficient Königszelt diversionary line at Striegau was greatly threatened. Therefore the liberation of both towns was now the first priority. The counter-blow at Lauban had the further and not inconsiderable significance of tackling or at least disrupting the enemy lodged in the general area of Görlitz.

Counter-strike at Lauban

The 1st Company, SS Pioneer Battalion 31, under *SS-Obersturmführer* Gerhard Hillmann was, shortly before, directed into the Lauban–Löwenberg area. That was the combat area of *Panzerkorps* 'Grossdeutschland'. There the 1st Company had to erect barriers on the main traffic routes. They had also to strengthen bridges and street crossings to enable them to be used by heavy armoured vehicles. A short account is here given of the counter-attack at Lauban, although no other units of the 31st SS Division, the majority of which were far away from this area, were actively involved in it.

Two armoured *Kampfgruppen* were standing by for the operation. The right-hand group consisted of the LVII *Panzerkorps* (*General der Panzertruppen* Kirchner) with the 'Führer Begleit' Division from *Panzerkorps* 'Grossdeutschland', the 8th *Panzer* Division and *Panzer* Brigade 103. The left-hand group was formed of the XXXIX *Panzerkorps* (*General der Panzertruppen* Decker) with the 19th *Panzer* Division, 16th Infantry Division and the *Führer* Grenadier Division from *Panzerkorps* 'Grossdeutschland'. Since the Supreme Commander 17th Army, *General der Infanterie* Schulz, had been seriously wounded shortly before, *General der Panzertruppen* Troops Nehring took over command. He carried out a counter-attack that was planned as a classic pincer operation.

The counter-attack began on the night of 1 March 1945. It surprised the enemy and thus quickly gained ground. But then it stuck in some places in the face of tough enemy resistance. Instead of the planned large encirclement, a smaller one closed off the incident. Thus, on 4 March 1945 the *Führer* Grenadier Division thrust eastwards over the Queis and linked up with the 8th *Panzer* Division at Logau. With that, the battle had in practical terms been successfully fought to its conclusion. The 89th Soviet Mechanised Corps was encircled, 230 enemy tanks and 48 enemy guns were destroyed or captured, and Lauban was liberated on 5 March 1945.

The Recapture of Striegau

The operation to recapture the town of Striegau was carried out by the Brandenburg 208th Infantry Division (*Oberst* Berger). They were supported in this task by a reinforced *Kampfgruppe* of the 31st SS Volunteer Grenadier Division. In the survey of the command relationships for 15 March 1945, 4 battalions of the 31st SS Division appeared as under the command of the 208th Infantry Division. That was the *Kampfgruppe* mentioned. One part of the *Kampfgruppe* was formed by the SS Volunteer Grenadier Regiment 80 (Regiment 'Schön', formerly Police Regiment 'Brixen' with two or three battalions under *SS-Sturmbannführer* Rudolf Schön). They defended a sector outside the town and only entered the town after the fighting inside was finished. The other part of the *Kampfgruppe* (1 or 2 battalions), that was also involved in the street fighting in Striegau, was probably assigned from SS Volunteer Grenadier Regiment 78 or 79. But it was not possible to be absolutely clear about this. Probably they were also reinforced by artillery and *Panzerjäger*. Since there are no details concerning the activities of the *Kampfgruppe* of the 31st SS Division, recourse to the description of events from the viewpoint of the 208th Infantry Division has been made (described in Ahlfen's *Kampf um Schlesien*), alongside a few pieces of information concerning the 31st SS Division.

After Grenadier Regiment 337 had been relieved in the Saarau-Haidau sector by SS Volunteer Grenadier Regiment 80 on the night of 5 March 1945, it assembled to the north-east of Striegau to counter-attack. The targets of the attack were the town. It had been fortified by the enemy like a *Festung* and included the commanding heights to the north-east, i.e. the Järischau Mountains and the Streitberg. It was decided to carry out a 'one-sided' encirclement operation. More precisely, that was a one-jawed pincer operation with a steady right-hand jaw formed by SS Volunteer Grenadier Regiment 80 and a left-hand jaw formed by the 208th Infantry Division. They had to thrust forward, get to it quickly, and snap shut. The attack began on the night of 8 March 1945, still in darkness. Without a preparatory barrage, and by surprise, from the Kreuzberg, directly to the north-west of Striegau, I/337 advanced on the right, II/337 on the left. Fusilier Battalion 208 was in the centre.

Generalmajor von Ahlfen related the events:

> *Strasse* 115, leading north, was crossed without contact with the enemy. I/337, which according to the plan was to turn south-westwards. On the road at first it stuck in the face of tough enemy resistance in confused garden terrain. On the other hand, II/33 encountering virtually no resistance advanced through the

railway housing and the Järischau Mountains right up to the outskirts of Järischau. They set up for defence on the Järischau Mountains. Fusilier Battalion 208, too, had quick success without any hard fighting. Turning south-westwards between the I/ and II/ it had taken Muhrau from the north and established contact with SS Regiment 'Schön' south of the Striegauer Wasser. Then, between Mührau and the southern edge of the Järischau Mountains, it, too, organised itself for defence with its front facing eastwards. The neighbouring unit on the left, Grenadier Regiment 309, had according to plan taken the commanding line of high ground Sperlingsbruch – Katzenberg – Streitberg. Thus the encirclement of Striegau met with very quick success.

This account described quite succinctly how SS Volunteer Grenadier Regiment 80 in its sector on the Striegauer Wasser between Haidau and Saarau came to play the part of a 'steady jaw'. But now the encirclement that had begun fairly easily was to be followed by heavy localized fighting to free the town from the enemy hiding there. Once again, the events are recounted by von Ahlfen:

> The enemy (in Striegau), an anti-tank artillery regiment, reinforced by infantry, with many 5cm anti-tank guns of American make at its disposal, defended itself in bitterly conducted street and house-to-house fighting. The I/337, eating in from the north and Pioneer Battalion 208 attacking in the southern part had heavy casualties.

The once quiet streets were stormed. House by house, block by block they were recaptured. Parts of the *Kampfgruppe* of the 31st SS Volunteer Grenadier Division appear on that day and the next, on 10 March 1945, to have been thrown in from the south into this local battle. However, the parts of SS Volunteer Grenadier Regiment 80, located between Haidau and Muhrau and released by the successful encirclement operation, appear to have been brought into the town to secure it, only after the fighting there was finished.

Again von Ahlfen related what happened:

> The Soviet wireless operator called for help. 'Hold on, we are coming!' was the reply. On the afternoon of 9 March 1945, for the first time, enemy counter-attacks running up against the mountain line of Grenadier Regiment 337 and Grenadier Regiment 309 failed. On 10 March 1945 the former Divisional Reserve, Grenadier Regiment 338, took over the difficult house-to-house fighting in Striegau. The I/337, released by this move was deployed to the south of the Järischau Mountains, between Fusilier Battalion 208 and II/337. Once again heavy counter-attacks with strong artillery and armoured support were repulsed with heavy casualties on both sides.
>
> Furthermore, on 11 March the weather was bleak and foggy, with snow showers, only zero degrees and dreadful slush. Again, fierce relieving attacks began, with 2 fresh divisions. After uninterrupted firing on the woodland, and on the quarries situated on the southern and northern edges of the Järischau Mountains, the enemy broke in. They were thrown out again soon afterwards.
>
> During the night of 11 March the forces occupying Striegau broke out, north-eastwards to Järischau, and to the north. 'Wild Sow' was the name of such a push by massed forces. In the light of car headlights the break-out was in part bloodily gunned down, but many parts escaped in the snowstorm.

On 11 or 12 March 1945, I Platoon 1st Company, SS Pioneer Battalion was ordered to Striegau. The platoon commander, *SS-Untersturmführer* Heinz Hummel, gave this account:

> While the attack was still under way, my company commander (*SS-Obersturmführer* Gerhard Hillmann) and I were ordered into the town, in which, however, the fighting had already finished. We were to reconnoitre a blown-up bridge. Using a dispatch rider I had my men brought up. In the grounds of the nearby monastery, woodland trees were felled for building the temporary bridge. The trunks were transported, by the horses of an Army unit, to the ruined bridge. Since we were dealing with a medium-sized stream, it was sufficient to build one pillar. This was set in the middle of the stream, on the ruins of the old stone bridge. The bearing capacity was calculated to carry armoured vehicles.
>
> As we were bringing up the railings for the bridge, an Army general drove up in his Kubelwagen. I gave my report. When he heard scraps of Hungarian from the lips of the men engaged in building the bridge, he wanted to know more about our unit. He also spoke to these men with the help of an interpreter.

A Divisional wireless station for the 31st SS Division was also set up in Striegau under the command of *SS-Untersturmführer* Lambert Randenrath. They had the task of maintaining communication between the *Kampfgruppe* and the Divisional Staff. But back to the crisis point and *Generalmajor* Ahlfen's account:

> On 12 March, too, the enemy relieving attacks did not abate. G.R. 337, exhausted and weakened by casualties, was assigned a battalion from another Division and deployed to relieve the I/337. On 13 March, again after heavy preparatory fire, the enemy pushed into the woodland of the Järischau Mountains, where the battalion from another Division had suffered badly from 'Baumkrepierer' (shells bursting in the crown of trees). And finally, in the afternoon the enemy broke out of this woodland for a push westwards. But by the fire of a Hetzer *Abteilung* – assigned to us just in time – and by the counter-attack of the I/337, tank and infantry attacks were beaten off.

It is feasible that the "battalion from another Division" which was spoken of here could be one from the *Kampfgruppe* of the 31st SS Volunteer Grenadier Division. The parts of the Division between Haidau and Muhrau were indeed free. The *Hetzer Abteilung* may have been SS *Panzerjäger Abteilung* 31. In March 1945 they did receive another 6 *Hetzers* and they were in this area. Even so, these assumptions are not directly confirmed.

The Saarau-Muhrau sector continued to remain quiet, but meanwhile the defensive battle in the Järischau Mountains went on:

> At that time the II/309 was, on 14 March 1945, placed under our command for the counter-attack. The enemy had again been reinforced during the night of 13 March 1945 in that notorious stretch of woodland. With daybreak their attack was expected. However, at 4.30am on 14 March, completely surprising them, our barrage from the mortars of 4 battalions began. The woodland was so systematically and effectively combed through by this barrage that our own action of pushing into it, cleaning it out and pushing through it went smoothly and quickly. The entire hill was again in our hands. But towards midday the en-

emy suddenly attacked to the west of the northern quarry against the forces that there were only weak. Quickly, *Oberstleutnant* Albinus with his last reserves, such as dispatch riders and clerks, formed a holding position between hills 237 and 230. Then, to turn the crisis up to boiling point, enemy fighter-bombers turned up in the blizzard. The fighter-bombers suddenly turned inward, certainly on their mission to catch us on the slopes. But they had not spotted how far their own infantry had already advanced. So then they smashed their own attack with their bombs and machine guns. It was a decisive success for us.

In Nowarra's *Nahaufklärer 1910-45, Das Auge des Heeres* this event was portrayed as follows:

Soviet 'Stormoviks', Ilyushin Il-2s, were to support a counter-attack by their troops. In the confusion of the fighting the unit commander lost track of what was going on and directed his flights to dive-bomb their own troops. Craft from *Nahaufklärer Gruppe* 2 could see this and informed the 31st SS Division who, immediately exploiting these circumstances, was able to re-take Striegau.

Even if the last half-sentence is not exactly accurate (Striegau was taken two days earlier and not only by the *Kampfgruppe* of the 31st SS Volunteer Grenadier Division), the account still hits the nail on the head. This event had made an essential contribution to the success of the operation. *Generalmajor* von Ahlfen continued:

The enemy infantry were shattered and turned round. Our pioneer detachment pushed after them frontally, and II/337 in a flanking movement from the quarry, so that there was no more stopping for the enemy. The old front was again completely restored, while after this shock the enemy attacks stopped. When on 15 March the sun rose and brought the first warm day of spring, it shone on a battlefield which had now become peaceful, had been taken successfully and been fought with dogged bravery.

Striegau was now liberated again. But how things looked in the unhappy town with its beautiful 14th Century Church of St Peter and Paul and its 15th Century Protestant church, which took the breath away from even old, hardened veterans of the Eastern Front. Werner Bänsch gave this account:

Of the approximately 6,000 people who had stayed in the town, we only found 56 alive when we re-took it. The majority of the others had been driven away eastwards like cattle. We found 148 people murdered. Actually the number of those murdered would have been much higher. But since, as we re-took the town, many houses were burning down, we were not able to determine the number of dead in them. Among those murdered were only six men – all killed by a shot in the back of the neck – and four or five children whose heads had been kicked in. All the others were women and girls who, to judge by appearances, had been raped to death. The schoolgirl Herta W. and her entire family were murdered, her brother, her parents, her grandfather. The youngest of these victims was 12, the oldest 78.

These facts were also confirmed by soldiers of the 31st SS Division. *SS-Untersturmführer* Hummel commented:

The sight which met us in the town was hellish. Between dead Soviet and German soldiers, including many of the fallen from our 31st SS Division, in the streets, there were lying, one after another, raped and murdered German women, and little children with their skulls smashed in. We assumed that there was no-one left alive in this town which we had re-taken. But, little by little, a few women came out of their hiding-places. They were almost out of their minds and asked for a doctor because they had been raped by the Soviets. Then we heard that Striegau had been a town with 25,000 inhabitants, and in addition the same number of refugees had come there when the town had been taken by the Soviets.

The experience of the suffering of refugees and the news of atrocities practised by the enemy since they had set foot on German soil created a great bitterness. That was still held in check. To the German soldiers, the horrors of Striegau completely changed that calm. In his measured cast of mind, the decent ordinary soldier was deeply shocked. What had been previously thought of as 'only propaganda', was now brought before their very eyes by the Bolshevik enemy. There, they met face to face, in the flesh, such as could never have been imagined. They saw real subhumanity. They saw every kind of despicable behaviour that had been goaded on by words of hate, and taken to the very extremes of bestiality. In truth, the Horsemen of the Apocalypse had arisen, to swallow up the world. Is it any wonder that these shameful, murderous acts sowed hatred, and the desire for revenge and retribution? "Think of Striegau!" In spite of all that, the soldiers of the Wehrmacht and the Waffen-SS tried not to let themselves be carried away in revengeful acts, however great their fury at the sight of the Soviet atrocities. H. Knauer (Staff II/79) recalled:

Again and again, even in the orders of our battalion commander Albrecht, we were reminded and warned to treat prisoners well and not to try to wreak retribution for atrocities by doing the same. As we were brought up to do – we did not let ourselves be carried away to such extremes.

Further battles of the 31st SS Volunteer Grenadier Division in March 1945

After Striegau had been retaken, the new main line of resistance ran along the line Streitberg–Järischau Mountains–Muhrau Saarau. The line would be held until the surrender.

On 16 March 1945 SS Volunteer Grenadier Regiment 80 was relieved in the Muhrau-Saarau sector by Grenadier Regiment 337 of the 208th Infantry Division. After a short pause in Striegau they moved to a threatened front between Löwenberg and Goldberg, to the sector somewhere between Lang-Neundorf–Wolfsdorf. The regimental command post was in Neukirch. There the Soviets attacked on the line Zobten near Löwenberg – Lang - Neundorf – Harpersdorf – Steinberg – Neukirch with strong armoured forces. They threw SS Volunteer Grenadier Regiment 80 back behind the village of Sussenbach where there was an important road intersection. Only there could the enemy attack be held, the enemy armour knocked out and the situation cleared up again. Süssenbach was re-taken and the earlier main line of resistance was for the most part restored. But

Harpersdorf and Steinberg, as well as half of Neukirch remained permanently lost. In that fighting SS Volunteer Grenadier Regiment 80 suffered heavy casualties.[2]

SS Volunteer Grenadier Regiment 78 attached itself to the right of Regiment 80 and occupied the sector between Konradswaldau and Hermannsdorf. I/78 was on the left, II/78 on the right, apparently at Seichau). SS Volunteer Grenadier Regiment 79 adjoined to the east, between Hermannsdorf and Poischwitz, with I/79 and II/79 whose battalion command post was in Jagendorf. Between the units there was still a lot of pushing to and fro, according to the situation. The right-hand neighbour of the 31st SS Division was the 208th Infantry Division. The line of demarcation between them was formed by the Neisse. The left-hand neighbour was the 17th Infantry Division in the Löwenberg area.

On that sector of the front there was changing fighting, during which the villages of Wolfsdorf, Prausnitz and Haasel were lost. Particularly heavy fighting took place for the Sargberg near Konradswaldau, in which the units of SS Volunteer Grenadier Regiments 80 and 78 that had been brought up lost and re-took the mountain several times. By May 1945 the Sargberg would have changed hands seven times. Along the whole line continual, often very fierce, fighting was going on. Many villages changed hands several times, but the main line of resistance was always essentially restored.

SS *Panzerjäger Abteilung* 31, too, went into action successfully several times in these sectors. This however always depended on not having to turn back from pursuing the Soviets because of a shortage of petrol, as happened from time to time.

Two eyewitness accounts recalled this fighting. First the account of A. Gl., at that time Pioneer Section, SS Volunteer Grenadier Regiment 80:

> The command post of our regiment was in Neukirch. Our pioneer detachment was also there as intervention reserve. We were always thrown in at the hot spot at any given time. So we were immediately prepared to counter-attack when the Soviets broke through at Süssenbach. The Soviet armour was already in fairly deep behind our lines. One of our Tigers, which was standing carefully camouflaged in waiting, knocked out their advance unit and forced it to turn back. Then we were able to re-take Süssenbach in a counter-attack. In the village we found that an old man and two young women, who apparently had not let themselves be evacuated earlier, brutally murdered. Apart from them, there was not a soul.
>
> Our detachment also went into action many times at the Sargberg. This mountain, not too high but commanding the landscape, was long, in the shape of a coffin and really deserved its name – and not only because of its shape! It was even attacked several times daily, lost, and then re-taken in a counter-attack.

SS-Rottenführer Heini Knauer, armourer II/79, gave this account:

> Our first action took place in the Jauer area. From our first standpoint I could see into the town of Jauer. We, the 'fighting impedimenta', were always located fairly close to the main line of resistance, now 1 to 2km, now only 500m behind it. But I would often stop at advanced observation posts to test the newly re-

2 Information from comrade A.Gl., as well as from Becker, *Die Flucht. Niederschlesien 1945*, p. 251.

ceived, newly collimated equipment. The fighting changed a lot. Many villages changed hands several times. Often we suspected that the Soviets were withdrawing deliberately, in order to catch us in a trap by enticing us from behind.

During the course of that fighting, and by the end of March 1945, a new main line of resistance had developed directly south of Harpersdorf and Steinberg. It continued on through the centre of the village of Neukirch, along the railway line and a further kilometre to the north of Hermannswaldau. Then it went north of Konradswaldau, north-west of Willmannsdorf, north of Seichau, by the Breiteberg to the south of Schlaup, to the north of Peterwitz, by the firing range south-west of Jauer and to the north of Poischwitz. On that front the units of the 31st SS Volunteer Grenadier Division held their positions until the end of April, when they were relieved.

The changing fighting, and the extension of the defensive sector that was far too great for one division, necessitated frequent changes of position. Units were directed again and again to the place on the front that was threatened at any one time. Or they would be sent to a gap in the front, in which process they suffered considerable casualties. But the sector of the front was kept firm as a result of this fighting. When, at the beginning of April 1945, the 100th *Jäger* Division occupied the line Hermannswaldau–Poischwitz, the sector between Goldberg and Löwenberg was first taken over by the 17th Infantry Division. Then the Estonian 20th SS Division took over. The fighting died down. This line, from Goldberg to Poischwitz and also the one from there through Dornberg and Häslicht as far as Striegau, was, in its essentials, held until the surrender.

Quite specially, SS Pioneer Battalion 31 served again and again as fire brigade and was thrown in wherever there was a current 'hot spot'. Besides carrying out pioneer tasks that were also ordered by the General Command of XLVIII *Panzerkorps,* the pioneers were essentially used for infantry actions. *SS-Untersturmführer* H. Hummel, platoon commander I Platoon/1st Company, recalled:

In Blumenau, in the Jauer area, our company was assigned the Division's punishment platoon. Besides commanding my platoon I was charged with giving the punishment platoon pioneer training.

For one of the pioneer tasks, together with the village blacksmith, we built a pile-driver. Then we drove in a barrier out of posts that we further reinforced with sandbags to dam the waters of the Kleine Neisse outside the village. A great expanse of ground was flooded by this means and thus formed a natural obstacle.

Each evening we would march, laden with mines, towards Jauer. The main line of resistance ran close to the town. In front of it, under cover of darkness, we laid our mines. The roads were secured with T-mines, the open country with S-mines. In one of these actions the commander of III Platoon, my friend *SS-Oberscharführer* Werner Rauner had a fatal accident, despite being an experienced pioneer.

After we had carried out our mission, with the recapture of Striegau, we were moved into the Zobten Mountains. Here we were set to work building defensive positions. In the distance we could hear the sound of battle from the fighting at Breslau.

In March, the Division's rations situation on the Jauer front was satisfactory, because it was also possible to 'live off the land'. Many local inhabitants, evacuated earlier, returned for the spring tilling of the fields, and always liked to give something from their stock to the soldiers.

In conclusion, an account from *SS-Rottenführer* Ernst Bennert (Medical Company) should complete the picture of the Jauer front:

> Moved at the end of February, from Gonobitz to Hirschberg in the Riesengebirge, we took up our quarters in Grunau, 6km east of Hirschberg. Now we were only one company, with two platoons and the Ambulance Platoon. Here at last we got ambulances, but not motor vehicles, only horse-drawn ambulances. I had never seen anything like them in my life. I felt as if I had been transported back in time to 1870/71 or the First World War. Nevertheless, in Hirschberg things got going. Men from units that had been dissolved, heavy weapons, armoured vehicles were brought up to the Division.
>
> In March we moved to Ketschdorf and were supposed to set up a main dressing station in a deserted house. After checking the premises, however, our officers refused to set up the main dressing station there, because it was such a bug and lice-infested building. So there was only a collection point in the Piasten Hospital in Ketschdorf. There we also took care of Estonian Waffen-SS men from the 20th SS Division, which, after heavy fighting in Upper Silesia, had broken out of enemy encirclement.
>
> On 3 April we in Ketschdorf experienced a sad event, which happened as follows: We had in the company a *Rottenführer* from Stuttgart, his name was Bachmann and he came from the Luftwaffe. He was already fairly tired of war and often had made derogatory remarks about the Führer, the German people and the Fatherland, although we had told him time and again to keep his trap shut. But despite our warnings, as we were unloading in Gonobitz he went too far and was denounced by two *SS-Unterscharführer* (sent by the *SS-Führungshauptamt* to us for frontline experience, but who had otherwise suffered nothing), so that he went before the court-martial. He was sentenced to death for subverting military strength and this sentence was carried out in Ketschdorf on 3 April, Good Friday.

Development of the situation in March in other sectors

It was planned to deploy the forces that had been released after the battle at Lauban to relieve the encircled *Festung* Breslau. A start had even been made with corresponding troop movements in the assembly area Frankenstein–Reichenbach–Schweidnitz. But the Army Group was soon forced to change their plans. Observation of enemy movements suggested that within a short time the Soviets would begin a large-scale attack in Upper Silesia aimed at breaking through into the Mährisch-Ostrau industrial district and on into Bohemia. Therefore the armoured forces (8th, 16th, 19th and 20th *Panzer* divisions also the 10th *Panzergrenadier* Division and 'Führer Begleit' Division) had to move to Upper Silesia to reinforce the 1st *Panzer* Army. The 254th Infantry Division, too, (*Generalmajor* Richard Schmidt) followed later. Giving up these divisions not inconsiderably weakened the 17th Army, and naturally had the consequence that a greater load was placed on the divisions that remained, including 31st SS Division.

Then, on 10 March 1945, fighting began in the area south of Gleiwitz and east of Ratibor. The Soviets stormed the Sohrau-Schwarzwasser sector, aiming for Mährisch-Ostrau. The Supreme Commander of the 1st *Panzer* Army, *Generaloberst* Heinrici, was already expecting the offensive. Because of this, on the evening before, he had his troops withdraw from the front line to a so-called 'large-scale battle, main fighting line' somewhat further to the rear. That was to protect them from the usual Soviet bombardment that preceded an attack. The plan worked. The combat strength of the troops remained intact. Because of this they were able, in very heavy fighting until 20 March 1945, proudly to achieve a successful defence. They successfully barred the way through to Bohemia for the Soviets, who were only able to gain 5 to 8km of ground.

Outside the Mährisch-Ostrau industrial district, one strongly needed, and much desired Soviet objective was to grind down the forward curve of the front at Oppeln. Their approach march could be seen perfectly from the 718m high Zobten and also from the 393m high Rummelsberg near Strehlen. The Soviet intentions were clear. A thrust from the north, starting from Grottkau, was directed southwards on Neisse and south-eastwards on Neustadt. The forces attacking from the Cosel area were to go westwards with the same general target of Neustadt. The two jaws of the long pincer arms were to close, and encircle the German forces. According to this plan, then, this second large-scale enemy offensive began on 15 March, and proceeded more or less according to plan. On 18 March 1945 the two jaws of the Soviet pincers closed at Neustadt and encircled 4 German divisions. They were the 344th Infantry Division, the 168th Infantry Division, the Hungarian German 18th SS Volunteer *Panzergrenadier* Division 'Horst Wessel' and the Estonian 20th Waffen-SS Grenadier Division.

At first, until 24 March 1945, the town of Neisse was held. However, counter-attacks by *Fallschirmpanzer* Division 'Hermann Göring' did not break through. A dangerous breakthrough out of this area, through Leobschütz to Jägerndorf, i.e. in the rear of the heavily fought-over Schwarzwasser sector, was able to be stopped by XXIV *Panzerkorps*. On 19 March 1945 the 344th Infantry Division and the 18th SS Volunteer *Panzergrenadier* Division, on their own initiative, began to break out of the Oberglogau pocket towards Deutsch-Rasselwitz. They succeeded magnificently.

Through the gap broken through at Deutsch-Rasselwitz many refugees, women, children, and old people were also able to escape with most of the soldiers. But because the bridges on the Hotzenplotz and the Braune were already destroyed, the majority of the heavy weapons had to be left behind. In the same way, parts of the 168th Infantry Division were able to break out north-west of Neustadt on the night of 20 March 1945. The Estonian 20th SS Division, as early as 17 March 1945, began to break out westward from the Falkenburg pocket, an action in which their brave commander, *SS-Brigadeführer* Franz Augsberger, was killed. The fact that these divisions (especially the 168th Infantry Division and the 20th SS Division) were now very seriously shattered had left behind most of their materiel and heavy weapons, once again weighed very heavily against the combat strength of the 17th Army. In fact, it was more severe than the loss of the area Cosel–Oppeln–Grottkau–Neisse–Neustadt.

On 24 March 1945 the Soviets extended their attacks to the Strehlen area where, from about mid-February, the 100th *Jäger* Division had already repulsed numerous strong enemy attacks over a broad sector. Their main line of resistance ran from Rothschloss, through Karzen–Plomühle–Saegen, and a little to the north of Strehlen–Ohletal–Knirschwitz–Hermsdorf–as far as Louisdorf. Under the command of the 100th *Jäger* Division was SS *Kampfgruppe* Delfs. It was a *Kampfgruppe* of about 800 men from SS *Panzergrenadier Ausbildungs und Ersatz* Battalion 4, under *SS-Obersturmbannführer* Hermann Delfs, once stationed in Wohlau. They stood on the approximate line Brosewitz–Wansen–Mechwitz.

As soon as it became light on 24 March 1945, after massed artillery fire, the Soviets broke into the main line of resistance at Plomühle with tanks and pushed the defenders westwards. Towards noon another group of tanks reached Karschau. The *Jäger* carried out a counter-attack from Gollschau and by evening liberated the village again, destroying many tanks.

The enemy also broke through the main line of resistance at Kuschlau and Saegen. During the course of the day they turned up at the northern outskirts of Strehlen. The civilian population had, thankfully, already been long since evacuated. Strehlen fell finally on 25 March 1945, at about midday when a platoon of Pioneer Battalion 100 had given up the quarry on the western edge of the town. Parts of SS *Kampfgruppe* Delfs had given up the sugar factory and the little village of Niklasdorf.

Heavy enemy attacks were repulsed on 25 March 1945 at Dobergast. But at Karzen and Rothschloss things remained quiet. Towards evening on 25 March 1945, the enemy ceased their assault and did not renew it. On 26 March 1945, SS *Kampfgruppe* Delfs too came to rest, after it had fought through heavy defensive battles around Ohletal–Glambach–Ruppersdorf. The Divisional command post was at Mehltheuer (Podiebrad). The 100th *Jäger* Division achieved a fine defensive success in preventing the enemy breaking through to Frankenstein and Glatz. Their new main line of resistance then ran from Kurtwitz, through Karschau–Dobergast–Striege to central Mehltheuer (Podiebrad)–Riegersdorf, as far as Schönbrunn (11km south-east of Strehlen), including all those places. In essence this was the line that the 31st SS Division was to take over two weeks later.

At the end of March the Supreme Commander of the 17th Army, *General der Infanterie* Friedrich Schulz, was given command of an Army Group in central and southern Germany. That was a great disappointment to him. He was a strong, native-born Silesian for whom the fight for Silesia was especially close to his heart. Showing his personal bravery, he often came up to the most forward line and eventually was wounded. He was succeeded at the beginning of April 1945 by another native-born Silesian, *General der Infanterie* Hasse.

CHAPTER 15

Deployment of the Division in the Strehlen Area, April 1945

After the changing defensive fighting in the area Goldberg–Jauer–Striegau, in which its units had suffered heavy casualties, at the beginning of April 1945 the 31st SS Division was moved into the Zobten–Strehlen area. They had exchanged with the 100th *Jäger* Division that had been fighting there up to that point. They had similarly suffered many losses. The *Jäger* occupied the 31st SS Division's old sector at Jauer, while the 31st SS Division took up their positions from around Rothschloss, as far as Prieborn to the south-east of Strehlen. The exchange of the two divisions took place between 2 and 9 April 1945.

At the same time the 31st SS Volunteer Grenadier Division was removed from the command of the XLVIII *Panzerkorps* and at first placed under the command of VIII Corps, as it appeared from the survey of 5 April 1945. But after a few days the areas of command of the General Commands also changed. The General Command of XLVIII *Panzerkorps* was removed from the front. Its sector before Jauer with the 17th Infantry Division, 208th Infantry Division and the 100th *Jäger* Division, which was just relieving the 31st SS Division, was taken over by the VIII Corps. The command area of XVII Corps, which hitherto had only included the Zobten area, was extended to cover the area of the VIII Corps before Strehlen. The 31st SS Division, was just relieving the 100th *Jäger* Division, the 45th Infantry Division. Meanwhile the 45th Infantry Division was taken over by the XXXX *Panzerkorps* adjoining the right. Thus from 9 April 1945 until the end of the war the 31st SS Division was under the command of the XVII Corps, together with the 269th Infantry Division and the 359th Infantry Division.

SS Volunteer Grenadier Regiment 79 took the section that was in Prauss. SS Volunteer Grenadier Regiment 78 took up positions somewhere between central Mehltheuer/Podiebrad and Prieborn. The Hungarian SS Volunteer Fusilier Battalion 31 was pushed in between the two regiments into the area before Striege (i.e. directly opposite Strehlen).

There were no precise details concerning SS Volunteer Grenadier Regiment 80, but based on testimonials it was clear that it similarly came into the Strehlen area and did not remain near Jauer. There were also indications that this badly weakened regiment was divided between the other two. This was not probable, although in the surveys of April 1945 the 31st SS Division often appeared as '*Kampfgruppe* 31st SS (5 battalions)'. For example, that could mean 2 battalions each, Regiments 78 and 79 plus a Fusilier Battalion.

The frontline that the 31st SS Division had to hold was beyond its capacity. Its divisional area between Rothschloss and Prieborn was over-extended. It was 35 to 40 kilometres long. Thus, according to the tactical manual, three times the recommended length for a division. But in 1945 it was more the rule than the exception.

It resulted in the divisional units being far apart and having virtually no contact with each other. On the left adjoined the 269th Infantry Division in the Zobten area. On the right the 45th Infantry Division of XXXX *Panzerkorps* was in the Neisse area. But those links, too, were fairly loose. The villages that the 31st SS Division occupied were empty. The Strehlen *Kreis* was evacuated according to plan as early as the end of January 1945 and in February 1945. Many farmers returned there, in March 1945 and April 1945 and tilled their fields, just a few kilometres behind the front.

There could be no question of a defensive system arranged in depth. From time to time even artillery *Abteilungen* had to take over their own defensive sectors. Otherwise the artillery was divided about equally along the long front line. The III *Abteilung*, for instance, was in the Zobten area.

SS Pioneer Battalion 31 was also not deployed as a whole unit. The quarters of the 1st Pioneer Company in Steinkirche are known. There was also the command post of the Telephone Company. The individual detachments of the Telephone and Wireless Companies were located in different villages, and also often changed location. Precise details were not available for SS *Panzerjäger Abteilung* 31. There were even indications that it was only much later, on 3 May 1945, that it followed the greater part of the Division into the Strehlen area. The Divisional command was first quartered in Frankenstein, to move then at the end of April further to the south, into the town of Glatz.

The Medical Company ran a collecting station for wounded in Gnadenfrei and, from as early as 3 April 1945, a main dressing station in Frankenstein. In Nimptsch, a school building was set up as a Divisional convalescent home in which slightly wounded or convalescing soldiers could recover, not far from their units. Finally, the baggage trains and the supply services moved into the Glatz area.

As far as the armament and equipment of the Division was concerned, thanks to the considerable efforts of the responsible service authorities, they were continually being improved. They were brought to a status that, in spite of shortages, in the penultimate month of the war, was really impressive. It was true that precise details concerning equipment were not available. There were enough indications that heavy weapons from the weapons schools were in fact being brought up in sufficient quantity, and also first-hand accounts gave an approximate picture.

The artificer of the II/79, *SS-Unterscharführer* H. Knauer, gave the following account:

> It's true that I can only give an account of things in my own regiment, but I know of nothing that was lacking in equipment here. I was frankly run off my feet with work. We were continually receiving new weapons and never before have I had to collate so many mortars and infantry guns as I did at that time. It was the same with our observation and survey equipment. Everything needed was there. Perhaps that was one more reason why the Soviets facing us kept relatively quiet.
>
> I also quite clearly remember, from a battalion meeting, hearing it said that our Division was also assigned tanks, 20 of the Tiger type. Later in the retreat through the Eulengebirge I did in fact see some Tigers which had crashed down ravines. These were said to be from the 31st SS Division.

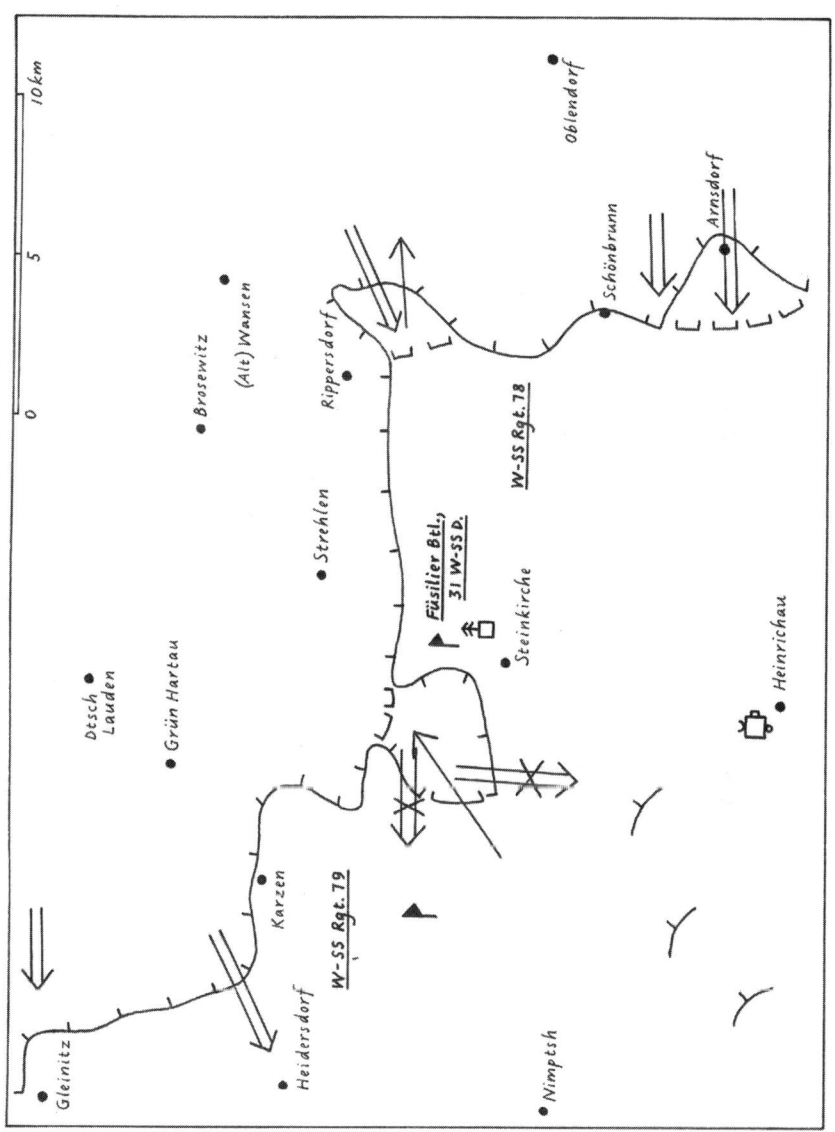

Map 8 Actions of the 31st SS Volunteer Grenadier Division in the Strehlen area, April 1945.

Whether the Division actually did get tanks was not confirmed but also cannot discounted. It could have been a matter of a *Panzer* unit placed under the command of the Division. On the other hand, it was clear that SS *Panzerjäger Abteilung* 31 was well equipped with assault guns. It is true that its *Panzerjäger* Company received, in March 1945, in addition to its 14 *Jagdpanzer* 38 Hetzers that it had had since December 1944, another 6 of the same type. The Flak Company was similarly supposed to have been fully equipped.

Fully armed and equipped were also the artillery *Abteilungen*, according to *SS-Hauptsturmführer* Dotterweich, Commander II/A.R. From time to time, things were more difficult with ammunition. Once again, H. Knauer commented:

> With the chief stores administrator, *SS-Unterscharführer* Stöckert, I had to take charge of procuring ammunition and it wasn't always easy. From time to time we covered many places, as far up as Hirschberg, until everything was sorted out.

Special equipment, such as signals equipment, medical vehicles etc, was the subject of considerable shortages. It can be said of the supply situation that, as time passed, it became worse and worse. Supplies were held up, principally because of lack of fuel.

Fighting at Strehlen

As the Division was about to occupy the new front line, it first had to fight free some of the positions, because as soon as the 100th *Jäger* Division pulled out, the Soviets thrust up behind them and achieved a not inconsiderable gain of ground. The sector of the front that the 31st SS Volunteer Grenadier Division found began to the east of the Zobten area. The positions were directly to the south of the town of Zobten that was in enemy hands. Zobten Mountain, including the northern faces, was in German hands. The front ran eastwards to about 400 metres outside Jordansmühl. There it turned southwards and to the west of Gross-Jeseritz. Occupied by the enemy since February, it ran out into the district of Rothschloss-Heidersdorf. From that area the front again turned eastwards, ran through Karzen and north of Nass-Brockuth, where east of the village it turned southwards to the Kleine Lohe and ran along the stream to the east of Kurtwitz. There it again ran eastwards. But between Karschau and Dobergast was a sack-shaped area of enemy penetration. It was cordoned off, in a makeshift way, reaching through Gollschau to Leipitz and Sadewitz. Then the front ran between Strehlen and Striege, to the north of Mittel-Mehltheuer, and on, directly north of Mückendorf.

At the beginning of April 1945, Knirschwitz too, far to the east of Mückendorf, was also in German hands. There was a sack-shaped salient in the front, the corners of which were enemy-occupied Ruppersdorf (occupied since 25 March 1945) and Eisenberg (occupied since 19 March 1945). At Mückendorf the front once again turned southwards and ran on along the line Riegersdorf, Krummendorf, Schönbrunn, Prieborn (including these places) and, at the beginning of April 1945, also to the east of Arnsdorf to Deutsch-Jägel.

As the front was fairly long both the German and Soviet forces were insufficient to hold it firmly. It could not be described as a classical main frontline. It was held at every metre. It was rather a main area of fighting in which distant villages could be freed of the enemy just as closer villages could be occupied. Particularly confused was the situation in the threatened areas of Rothschloss–Heidersdorf, Karschau–Sadewitz–Dobergast and Knirschwitz.

Particularly at Karschau–Sadewitz–Dobergast the enemy advance created a dangerous turmoil that the arriving parts of the 31st SS Division (SS Volunteer Grenadier Regiment 79) had to clean out. Stronger enemy forces were already arriving at Prauss in the west and at Kaltwassertal (=Leobschütz) in the south. Fighting was flaring up here and there, in which even more distant villages like Gross-Kniegwitz, and others, were coming under fire and being bombarded. After hard fighting the units of the 31st SS Division finally threw back the enemy, blocked the breakthrough area and restored the old main line of resistance Karschau–Dobergast. The Karschau pillar continued to be fiercely contested, but at first was able to be kept in German hands.

At Rothschloss–Heidersdorf too the situation had to be cleaned up. The village of Heidersdorf was stubbornly attacked by the Soviets. The loss of that important road intersection between Nimptsch–Breslau and Reichenbach–Strehlen was to have a great effect. It affected troop movements and supply movements, both on the Zobten and the Strehlen fronts. There was also the danger that the Soviets would push forward from there to Gross-Kniegwitz. If they could join up with their comrades they might make their way forward from the Prauss area, to capture the entire front from behind at Karzen and Kurtwitz. Heidersdorf must thus be held and for this reason a fight for it was now going on. After fighting with varying turns the German forces gained the upper hand and threw the Soviets back to Rothschloss, where they dug in. Heidersdorf remained in German hands until the end of the war.

Fighting also continued at Knirschwitz and its neighbouring village of Hermsdorf. But there the Soviets were able to win control of the villages. The loss of Knirschwitz, however, was more useful than damaging, because as a result the front became significantly shorter. It ran through the firm, supporting pillar of Mückendorf. Heavy fighting was also in progress on the other wing, in the area leading up to the Zobten massif where, among others, fierce fighting was taking place for the Johnsberg. But the front was held.

Even if the fighting in those places was relatively fierce and changing, it still remained (not only from the point of view of what was happening in Silesia as a whole, but also from that of the narrower Zobten–Strehlen area) limited to local areas. Thus the sector Karzen-Kurtwitz on the Kleine Lohe remained relatively quiet, as did the line south–south-east of Strehlen. Even before the Strehlen sugar factory, the target of such heavy fighting in March, the war seemed to be standing still. The same was also true of the sector Mückendorf–Deutsch-Jägel, in which, however, at the beginning of April, Arnsdorf was lost, and fighting continued for Deutsch-Jägel.

After the battles already described in the first ten days of April 1945, in general the engagements along the whole front died down. From that time until 8 and 9 May 1945 the front which had been cleaned up by the 31st SS Division ran from north-east of Heidersdorf, north of Rothschloss, through Karzen, past Nass-Brockuth to east of Kurtwitz. From there it went on through embattled Karschau, between Striege and the Strehlen sugar factory. It continued on through Mittel-

Mehltheuer (Podiebrad) and Mückendorf (including both), then southwards, 800 to 1000 metres outside Riegersdorf and close by Krummendorf. Then it went directly east of Schönbrunn, one-and-a-half kilometres east of Prieborn and on southwards to Deutsch-Jägel. It continued in the direction of Neisse. Later in April, Karschau too was lost, but by then the front finally stabilised and was held until the surrender.

The task of the 31st SS Volunteer Grenadier Division was now to consolidate this line, to fortify it by minefields, barbed wire barriers, etc, to set it up for defence and secure it. The Soviets facing them also showed no intention of attacking. They, too, were digging themselves in, outside Rothschloss and Karzen, in Peterwitz and Niklasdorf, in Ruppersdorf and Eisenberg. Although the sector of the front was no longer the target of fierce fighting, it was also never completely quiet. Reconnaissance activity, mortar attacks, artillery duels, and attempts at sounding out on the part of both sides were the order of the day.

There was much more fighting in the sectors of the 31st SS Division's neighbours, such as at Deutsch-Jägel in the south-east which was being defended by a police unit reinforced by armour. From 29 March 1945 this village changed hands seven times, until it was finally lost on 5 May 1945. There was also fighting on the extreme right flank of the 31st SS Division, to the east of Prieborn, but the enemy got no further there before the surrender. The most significant fighting was in the neighbouring sector to the left, outside Zobten. There, right up to the surrender, the positions were constantly embattled, in the process of which individual villages changed hands up to eight times. The important road intersection of Jordansmühl was fiercely contested, but it too remained in German hands until 7 May 1945.

The Soviets, however, did not always use firearms, they also used loudspeakers. A lot of enemy propaganda in German, spoken by treacherous Germans of the so-called 'National Committee of Free Germany', rang out over to our positions, encouraging troops to give ourselves up and desert. For the most part it was cheap and primitive stuff: "Naked women are promised to deserters", as Comrade A. Gl. (Regiment 80) recalled. But there were only very few who were taken in by these stupid words and decided to commit the cowardly act of desertion. On the other hand – and this was not a little surprising – there were many people on the Soviet side who even in these last, hopeless weeks, still believed in the 'Nemetzki' and deserted!

SS-Unterscharführer H. Knauer (Staff II/79) gave this account of the defensive fighting which was still costing the Division all kinds of sacrifices:

> At the end of March we were taken out of the positions at Jauer, after days of driving around. We were, truly, almost always on the move, and always in the night, so as not to give too great an opportunity to the busy Soviet 'sewing machines'. We finally ended up, II/79, in Prauss. In this area we relieved the 100th *Jäger* Division, which in some places had to give way before the constant Soviet attempts to advance, so that in several places our units had to clean up the front line before they could take up their positions. Even in Prauss the Soviets, in one corner, had to be beaten back before we received our positions there.
>
> I set up the armourers section in the castle in Prauss, in which the battalion's chief stores administrator, *SS-Unterscharführer* Stockert, resided. We were there until 8 May 1945. The front ran quite close to us, barely a kilometre away.

Up there was a village. Our men were in the upper half, the Soviets in the lower half. We, Stöckert and I, on the first day of Easter, only just missed driving into the Soviet lines there, had we not been stopped by our last sentry. The weather was so bad in the night that we missed the crossroads.

We were able to repulse every Soviet breakthrough attempt, so that later they too gradually stopped trying. We had in our battalion an assault unit, about 40 men, Reich Germans and for the most part old soldiers. They too were with us in Prauss to the end, in a large farm opposite my service post. They were very well armed and at the farm also had two tanks under cover. The assault unit, a kind of iron reserve, was only sent into action once during the whole period. That was when the Soviets broke through and were already behind our battalion command post, which was in bunkers in some woodland. A Soviet battalion was completely beaten back, in short order, by these men. It was indescribable what they did. Afterwards we had complete calm there until 8 May 1945.

Since there was a shortage of weapons, among the units of personnel with technical training, I was often travelling about to catch up with these tasks. Once I was in the same quarters as a Hungarian *Leutnant* from the Fusilier Battalion. With us he had the rank of a *Hauptscharführer* and was a very good rider. I myself was promoted during the course of April to *SS-Unterscharführer*, something that, after the training course in December, was long overdue.

Around 26 or 28 April I was in Heidersdorf with a technical task. There, there was also a Luftwaffe unit, the members of which, all decorated, old soldiers, wanted to persuade us to try to get through to the West with them because they didn't want to become prisoners of war of the Soviets. We declined. Our unit didn't waver right up to the end, and to the last hoped for a change in fortune.

But during the last days many baffling things happened, which I can't explain even today. Thus a meeting took place between a *Sturmbannführer* of ours, whom I didn't know, and a Soviet officer. It was in the first days of May, in a wood quite near to our battalion command post. The two officers, escorted by a couple of soldiers, approached each other in this woodland path in no-man's-land. The sentries had to stop about 50m away from the marked meeting place. When the two met, they suddenly vanished into the twilight, while the sentries came back as they were ordered.

The following personal accounts should round off the picture of the Strehlen front.

Deployment of Hungarian SS Fusilier Battalion 31 'Szálasi'

The battalion commander, *SS-Untersturmführer* Zvonimir Bernwald, gave this account:

We were occupying a very long sector directly south of Strehlen which we took over from the 100th *Jäger* Division. Both to the right and to the left the sector stretched on, forever. It could only be called a thinly manned security line, a long chain of foxholes, separated and far apart. The battalion command post was located in about the centre of the wide sector, in the little village of Striege.

Directly in front of us was the Strehlen sugar factory, which was already in Soviet hands.

We were a weak battalion, the NCOs mostly Germans, the other ranks all very young Hungarians, most of whom had barely completed 8 weeks of training. We had no heavy weapons apart from some heavy mortars. Far to our left, from Zobten, we heard the thunder of guns. In front of us was Breslau, just 40km by the Strehlen-Breslau railway line. By night it was always bright over the Silesian capital. It was clearly lit up and the noise of battle could also be clearly heard.

But in front of us the front kept quiet, even the enemy seemed to be weak in this sector. There were no large engagements apart from some advances for reconnaissance carried out by both sides. I also had no communication with those higher up, so we were gripped by a strange sense of being deserted, everything was so shadowy, so ghostly.

In no-man's-land there were still five to seven dead from the *Jäger* Division. We brought them out. In the meantime, during the night lads had disappeared, we couldn't explain it. It then turned out that the young lads had, during the night, through nervousness and inexperience, fired shots hither and thither. Then the Soviets crept up and lifted them one by one out of their foxholes. Since they were too young and completely insufficiently trained, we continually had problems with them.

Then there were also language difficulties that, even with interpreters, were hard to overcome, although I personally had a first-class *SS-Unterscharführer* as interpreter. Casualties kept within limits. Now and then the Soviets sent us some shells. At one time I would have chased them and asked for a little artillery support from the rear, but because of shortage of ammunition only 10 rounds were made available. I gave up on that, it would only have given away our weakness. Either show off or don't!

Then I too 'copped it'. On 13 April I was carrying out reconnaissance in the advanced fighting line and, on a small estate, we were fired on by enemy mortars. My runner, an *SS-Unterscharführer*, was killed. I too received some scratches. At the Division's main dressing station in Frankenstein I was treated by a doctor, but then came back again to my unit. So about 5 or 7 May I was ordered away, as quartermaster, to look for possible accommodation in the area to the rear.

Deployment of the III *Abteilung* SS Artillery Regiment 31

The III/AR. 31 had its own way. During the course of March it was already in the Zobten sector. The *Abteilung* commander, *SS-Hauptsturmführer* Dotterweich, gave this account:

From the Pirna area we arrived, at the end of February, at the Silesian front. Most of the 31st SS Division was already there, but I had no personal contact with the Divisional Staff and also no kind of communication with other units. We were completely without any kind of information. Even on the railway station at our destination, which we found out from a railway official, there were no responsible people there. I was assigned, in writing, the area where we would be deployed and set up my batteries accordingly.

We took up a defensive position in about the centre of the Striegau–Strehlen sector, in front of the towering Mt. Zobten. My command post was located about 300 to 400m behind the main line of resistance, in a small village, or rather a hamlet, consisting of a few houses. Our forces, both artillery and infantry, were so far apart that they perhaps covered three times the proper span of a division. Information and communication between each other were nil.

For the Soviets it must have seemed no different. In front of my sector the front kept very quiet. We were facing an enemy who remained veiled in secrecy. Here there was mainly only very weak combat activity, so that the *Abteilung* had no casualties at all.

The *Abteilung* was at full combat strength, was fully trained and armed. After we left Lower Styria there were no more reserves arriving. The men were very well-behaved and maintained order up to the last minute. Something which became worse and worse was supply. In the last weeks it dwindled down to nothing. The Supreme Commander of Army Group Centre, *Generalfeldmarschall* Schörner, strictly forbade slaughtering a cow or picking up something from the land. There were, it seemed, enough ownerless cattle in the district. We truly had the feeling that we had been left in the lurch by everybody.

Deployment of SS Pioneer Battalion 31

Accounts of the deployment of the Pioneer Bataillon during these last days were given by its members. Hans Leben, who was transferred to the 31st SS Volunteer Grenadier Division at the beginning of March 1945, wrote:

Our task was mainly laying mines, mostly at night. We also built barbed wire obstacles, positions, bridges and crossings among other things. It was a really dangerous business clearing enemy mines, doing it there were several accidents with tragic results.

After I returned to my unit, after three weeks' convalescence in the Divisional convalescent home, it was already the beginning of May. During the last days we were still building anti-tank barriers outside Steinkirche under the protection of a grounded Stuka. The enemy side was relatively quiet. After we had finished our task we finished off a bottle of rum with *SS-Untersturmführer* Hummel and two other men. The end was very close, it was already in the air.

SS-Untersturmführer Heinz Hummel continued:

I recall the following unusual event from the days of our last deployment at Steinkirche. On the way to one of our regiments for whom we were to lay mines, I was spying out the land from a skylight. In doing so I became witness to the action of a field court-martial. A Hungarian (or Hungarian German) *Oberscharführer* from the regiment (not from the Pioneer Battalion) was accused of desertion. He had tried to persuade the men of his platoon to desert to the enemy. But they didn't agree and reported the incident. The *SS-Oberscharführer* was sentenced by the field court-martial to death by hanging. Before the sentence was carried out, the men of his platoon were each asked by the Divisional Commander whether they wanted their platoon commander to live or die. Without exception they decided for the death sentence. Afterwards the sentence was carried out. The man died bravely, still crying 'Long live Hungary!'

About the beginning of April, a group of the 1st Pioneer Company was ordered by the Supreme Commander of Army Group Centre, *Generalfeldmarschall* Schörner, to keep guard over arrested officers. These had left their units without leave and were about to clear off in the direction of the West. In connection with discipline it should be made clear that in the units streaming *en masse* westwards there were no longer any coherent units. With the exception of our unit that kept together, maintained discipline, and fulfilled its duty right to the end, no similar units from other parts of the Army were to be seen.

At the beginning of April there suddenly appeared in Steinkirche, unannounced, the Divisional Medical Officer, a *Standartenführer* [Author's note: Dr Matz]. He inspected the quarters. My I Platoon was in an inn. He checked not only the rooms but also the kit. There were no causes for complaint. At this time it was the death sentence for plundering!

At the end of April I was transferred to the Battalion Staff and appointed Battalion Adjutant. My I Platoon/1st Company was taken over by *SS-Hauptscharführer* Hoffmeister. In the same way to the Battalion Staff came *SS-Obersturmführer* Hans Bahr, previous commander of 2nd Pioneer Company, as officer for special purposes. His 2nd Company was taken over by the previous platoon commander I/2, *SS-Untersturmführer* Schmidt.

How strict the punishment was for plundering the property left behind by the evacuated Silesians, was outlined by an eyewitness, A.Gl. (III/3 Pioneer Company):

We had in the Pioneer Battalion a cycle platoon of Magyars. One of them had nicked something from somewhere, and it was found on him. For this he was sentenced to death! The entire company had to parade in a square to be present at the execution, by firing squad, in front of a railway embankment. His ten best friends had to carry out the sentence. His last request was: 'Shoot straight, mates'!

Deployment of SS *Nachrichten Abteilung* 31

Ustuf. Villier (platoon commander, III Platoon, Telephone Company) recalls:

After we had been unloaded in Bad Wormbrunn, we were quickly deployed at the front. We were continually changing positions, because again and again we had to close other gaps in the front. First we were in the Jauer area, later we moved into the Strehlen district. The last place I was deployed was Steinkirche, where we were somewhat to the rear, in the village of Heinrichau. We detailed telephone detachments to the units in front of us, among others the Hungarian Fusilier Battalion.

Our equipment was not complete when we went into action, pieces of equipment were still arriving. Thus, for instance, *SS-Untersturmführer* Jürgen Jost (officer for special purposes in the *Abteilung* staff) still had to go to Berlin to fetch quite a few motor vehicles. The parts of the *Abteilung* were not yet ready for action. But only those in the Nimptsch area received their training. But even so, at least as far as the telephone company was concerned, we didn't even have half of our proper complement of equipment. With personnel, however, we had our full complement. However, some people still kept arriving individually. *SS-Untersturmführer* Gerd Lingner from Transylvania, during the last days, came straight out of war school.

Close to the village of Steinkirche was a large estate, it belonged to the Saxe-Weimars. The main line of resistance ran close in front of an estate building in which the leader of my listening unit, *SS-Rottenführer* Frits Schuster, had his quarters. The owner of the estate had had a miniature railway built in the park for his children. Once, Fritz got up steam in the locomotive and – at night, because of the possibility of the enemy spotting us by day – drove me round the park. Childlike experiences of a soldier!

In front of us was also the Strehlen sugar factory. It was in enemy hands but easily observable. On 20 April 1945, as it was becoming light, we saw, covering almost all of its chimney, a poster on which a fist was holding the head of Adolf Hitler, dripping in blood. Underneath in German: 'Congratulations on your last birthday!' I couldn't and didn't want to imagine that it could be the last. Emotionally we were so entangled that, even now, we ourselves didn't want to admit that the war was lost. But reality said differently. Soon followed the surrender and with it our retreat. And while our company in the trench warfare in Silesia had almost no casualties – I only recall three men being killed – and my platoon none at all, it was soon to be different in the Czech 'witch's cauldron'.

SS-Rottenführer Fritz Schuster, commander of the listening detachment in the Telephone Company, continues the account:

Around the end of February I was given command of the 31st SS Division's only listening detachment. I got a detachment of about 12 men, and a Listening Apparatus 34 which looked like a small communications indicator board, with many tuning switches and a listening loop (4km cable drums). These had to be taken from the apparatus through no-man's-land, i.e. between the fronts, and led back to the apparatus. With this equipment you could listen in to earth currents, such as earth return circuits, field telephone lines within a radius of 16km, while being able to concentrate on particular sounds through the tuning switches. I also had an interpreter-stenographer with me who was to listen with me. So in personnel terms I was under the command of III Platoon/Telephone Company, but as far as the signals service was concerned I was responsible to the Ic (Defence Officer) of the Division, to whom I had to make a daily report.

Unfortunately the results we gained were almost nil, because the Red Army was building no field telephone lines but using the postal network. They were using double circuits to which we couldn't listen in. But for all that we were able to listen in to some conversations and it is true that among them there were some even of Secrecy Level 5.

My last post was in Steinkirche, where the main line of resistance ran quite close by. It was annoying that, from a stationmaster's house, the Soviets controlled the railway line which ran towards us with a stream running parallel to it. I wanted to blow up this post in order to be able to set my listening line in the stream. By night I went barefoot through the stream and was about to smoke out the Soviet post with hand grenades. But the Ivans had laid a tripwire through the stream and I suddenly got a good hiding from all their machine pistols. Thank God, I remained unhurt and landed streaming with sweat, soaked to the skin, but still in one piece, back in our position.

But finally we struck lucky with the listening in. Indeed I had been able to earth a telephone A-mast, through which we were able to listen in to some Soviet conversations right up to Army status. Unfortunately they no longer helped us to victory. Whether they were in fact of any use at all, looking back, I am unable to judge. For me personally, in Soviet captivity, they brought the accusation of espionage, for which I was supposed to hang in 1946.

Deployment of SS Medical Company 31

SS-Rottenführer Ernst Bennert gave an account of the Medical unit. It was well-known that things were always different from other units:

> At the beginning of April we moved, in two night marches, from Ketschdorf to Frankenstein. There the greater part of the Division had found itself. We set up a main dressing station in the town's monastic hospital. Our Hungarian medical students, from Budapest and elsewhere, were still with us. They were very popular and knew their stuff. The Divisional pharmacy also moved to Frankenstein. *SS-Obersturmführer* Geiger; *SS-Oberscharführer* Schröder from Vienna was, at the same time, NSFO of the Medical Company and in this capacity was very reasonable, nice and friendly. *SS-Unterscharführer* Schulte from Hamburg, my friend *Sturmmann* Peter Glitzar from Danzig, and *Schütze* Horst Sczorar from Kassel were also there.
>
> Most of the Division's sectors here were completely quiet. Casualties kept within reasonable limits, so the main dressing station was not overloaded. Once, five or six seriously wounded Hungarians from the Fusilier Battalion were brought in. They had wanted to bring out a wounded man, but in doing so all of them got into a minefield. They had probably all been at the front for a long time, some of them wore the Infantry Assault Badge and other decorations. For two of them I gave my German blood. Unfortunately they did not recover, and all died.
>
> Cases of self-inflicted wounds also turned up. There were not too many, but mostly they were young seventeen to eighteen year old lads. Otherwise, it wasn't a very demanding time. I can still remember well one amusing incident. Our Divisional MO, *SS-Obersturmbannführer* Dr Karl Matz, came from Stralsund. He was thus a Pomeranian like me, and when there are two Pomeranians in one crowd… Shortly before the end of the war, all the officers were sitting in the bunker when a runner came and wanted to hand over a message to the company commander. Since he wasn't used to such high-ranking 'creatures', I took the message from him. With my steel helmet on I handed it, according to the book, to the company commander. Then off with the steel helmet and I poured myself a glass full of the schnapps that was on the table, and said: 'Permission to drink to the *Obersturmbannführer's* health!' Everyone just looked at me with a bafflement mixed with curiosity. But Dr Matz said: 'Yes, do that, do that'. Then, after half a minute, I asked him for one of his commanders: 'Yes, who is it then?' whereupon Dr Matz said: 'Don't you know him? He's Bennert from Stettin!'
>
> During the two-and-a-half months in Silesia, a song spread more and more within the Division. Everyone knew it and it was often sung with great pleasure. It was the *Schlesier-Lied*, the homeland song of the province which we were de-

fending. Our Batschka German comrades changed the song around a little and instead of Silesia sang Batschka and instead of Oder, Danube:

'One day I'll come back again to my homeland, early in the morning, when the sun is rising, then I'll look down into the valley, where at every door a girl is standing. There she sighs quietly, so quietly, and whispers gently: My land of Silesia/Batschka, my homeland, so by nature, nature as of old: we'll meet again, my land of Silesia/Batschka, we'll meet again, by the banks of the Oder/Danube.'

The significance of the fighting in Silesia

The fact that the 17th Army stood its ground was very important. Even after the focus of the enemy attacks had been shifted exclusively on to both flanks of Army Group Centre, thus to the Moravian Gate and into the Lausitz. Since 25 March 1945 (loss of Strehlen), it had no longer been attacked on a large scale. It did not exactly seem enticing to the Soviet command to run up against the broad, high mountain walls of Silesia. However, because it was a firm stronghold, in addition to protecting the important east-west railway line, it protected the roads used by refugees leading through the mountains to Bohemia.

The extent of refugee movement was enormous. Of the 4.7 million population of Silesia, 1.6 million fled through the Protectorate. Another 1.6 million fled by indirect routes into the still free areas of the Reich, mostly to Saxony, Thuringia and Bavaria. The total number of people fleeing, however, was even larger, because, from the end of 1944, Silesia itself was a sought-after reception area for refugees from the bombed-out German cities. Because of this it was called 'Germany's air raid shelter'. It was also used for evacuated ethnic Germans from the south-east. It must be remembered that the fleeing population of the Batschka also found a temporary refuge in Silesia. Finally, the refugee columns from Poland also travelled to and through Silesia.

The great humane task of the 17th Army (and of Army Group Centre *per se*) was to secure an area in which to flee and to make the necessary time for the movement of these millions. Over and above this, the area being protected was the home of more millions of German people. The Sudetenland had 3 million Germans and another 1.5 millions of people who had stayed behind. The columns of refugees, coming from the parts of Silesia already occupied by the enemy, were still staying, for the most part, until the surrender. They were in the free Silesian districts and in Bohemia, where they had been held up, until the middle of April 1945, in the area to the south of Karlsbad.

It should not go unmentioned that of the Silesians evacuated in February and March 1945, at the beginning of April many men returned to their home villages. That was in order, in true devotion to their home soil, to carry out the spring tilling of their fields right up to the edge of the front line, with all the dangers that this involved.

However, the enemy from whom it was necessary to protect these people, was only too well known to the soldiers of Army Group Centre, including those of the 31st SS Volunteer Grenadier Division. Most recently, in Striegau, they had come to know the Soviets who claimed, as their right, murder, arson and robbery, rape, torture and deportation. There were many, in fact too many 'Striegaus' among the population, who had remained at home. They could not or would not flee, even in the first days of peace after the surrender.

Generalmajor Hans von Ahlfen, in his book *Der Kampf um Schlesien,* certainly expressed most eloquently what a spirit of sacrifice the troops had shown:

> The southern flank of the Army Group, the 1st *Panzer* Army were in Moravia. The centre, the 17th Army, still held the territory in front of the mountains. The 4th *Panzer* Army in the north bent back as far as the Dresden area. Thus Army Group Centre stood there like a human body, with its torso and its arms bent backwards, placing itself protectively all around the eastern half of Bohemia and Moravia. It was round the escape area of the Silesians escaping to freedom.
>
> The soldiers, grimly doing their duty, fought to the uttermost where Silesia's mountains, crowned with forest, rise up to heaven. There, conditions became more and more difficult, serious, even bitter. Their sacrifice, before the greatness of which we fall silent in reverence, saved the route to new life for the millions of Silesians moving westwards. Only those whose terrified eyes have seen burning and blood, death and horror, overrun homesteads, columns of refugees shot to pieces and crushed, know the horrors that were averted. Only those whose agonised ears have heard suffering cries to heaven, will now be able to realise from what horrible death and from how much suffering, the fight for Silesia, with its sacrifices, preserved those escaping to freedom.

In this fateful, heroic battle, the 31st SS Division, increasingly as the war went on, was an important and reliable element on the extended front of the 17th Army. As the months passed, the 17th Army's forces shrunk more and more. It had to release its divisions to the flanks of Army Group Centre. They were under greatest threat. It had to release divisions to the 1st *Panzer* Army and 4th *Panzer* Army, without its own defensive zone becoming any shorter. Thus, the increased importance, and a longer, more thinly manned line, fell to the lot of the divisions that remained.

But during these weeks the 31t SS Division became more cohesive. It was not only materially reinforced, but was also, inwardly, brought together and strengthened even more. Therefore in the last weeks, there came into existence a Division which, of course, did not attain the level of excellence of the old SS divisions, but which could be relied on even more firmly. All that happened at a time when, in many Wehrmacht divisions, definite signs of break-up were appearing. The 31st SS Division maintained order until the last minute. This was also confirmed by many contemporary eyewitness accounts. Its last great action in Silesia, in which it performed brilliantly, was its participation in the last large-scale German counter-attack at Zobten.

Action of the 31st SS Volunteer Grenadier Division in the last counter-attack at Zobten

The 17th Army had a task that never lost its importance, that was to be the relief of Breslau. This operation was endangered from the flanks. Two enemy fronts, the southward facing security line, relatively weakly manned, and the ring of encirclement around Breslau, had to be penetrated. It required strong and mobile forces.

However, every time the necessary concentration of forces had been laboriously brought together, they always had to be used as a fire brigade to extinguish the flames of attempted enemy breakthroughs on other weakened parts of the front.

In the first days of May 1945 a concentration of forces was at last available once more. It was decided to attack in the territory facing Breslau. With luck, this attack, by creating a corridor, would restore communication with the encircled city. At the least it would win some breathing space for the defenders. But things turned out differently. The circumstances changed considerably before the attack to relieve Breslau could be begun. The strength of the fortress was approaching its end. On 3 May 1945 the Commandant of Breslau, General Niehoff, was already considering a surrender.

However, a surrender was strictly forbidden by the Supreme Commander of Army Group Centre *Generalfeldmarschall* Schörner. He advised that an attack to relieve the city was imminent. But on 5 May 1945 it was already clear that Breslau, unconquered after a quarter of a year of heroic fighting, must lay down its arms. On that day there also arrived in Breslau the last telegram from the 17th Army – "we are lowering our colours in proud mourning to the heroism and self-sacrifice of the defenders of Breslau".

So the decision was taken on 5 May 1945. It was only on 6 May 1945 that General Niehoff established communication with the Soviet General Glusdowski and accepted his honourable conditions for surrender. Thus on 5 May 1945 an attack to relieve Breslau had already become pointless. The significance of the heroic defence of the city was that it tied down strong enemy forces. As a result of the town falling, the situation in the territory was saved before it became precarious. That was because of the release of enemy forces.

Immediately, some units, of about divisional strength, were released by the Soviets. They set off on the march southwards, in the general direction of Zobten, and against the weak German defensive front. To halt their rapid advance, to forestall the threatening disaster of an enemy breakthrough into the eastern Sudetenland, and also to severely disrupt the broad stream of Soviets flowing towards Berlin, the assembled grouping of German forces prepared to attack.

The bulk of this grouping of forces was formed by the 31st SS Division. Parts of SS Volunteer Grenadier Regiment 79 and probably also of the other Grenadier regiments, but not of the Pioneer Battalion, were brought up. Artillery support was given by the III *Abteilung* (Dotterweich) of SS Volunteer Artillery Regiment 31. But other *Abteilungen* were also involved. Since all the Army's armour capable of combat should have been assembled for the planned attack to relieve Breslau, SS *Panzerjäger Abteilung* 31 must also have taken part in the operation.

Apart from the 31st SS Division, the 100th *Jäger* Division also made forces available, while the 18th SS Volunteer *Panzergrenadier* Division 'Horst Wessel' with all its assault guns contributed, in *Kampfgruppe* 'Dirks', to the counter-attack. It was first to be unleashed during the early hours of the morning of 6 May 1945 on the town of Zobten. Very little is known about this last German counter-attack. However, considering that it took place 3-4 days before the surrender, it was certainly not insignificant and also not unsuccessful. Therefore we have to rely on scanty accounts from those who took part.

SS-Unterscharführer Heini Knauer (Staff II/79) gave this account:

On the night of 5 May, hellish fire from our artillery and flak came over us to break on the completely surprised Soviets. They had no longer expected this kind of firepower from us. Moving towards us from Breslau, an entire enemy division was kept under fire the whole morning. On the dot at 6 am the artillery fell silent and the attack of our infantry on Zobten began. It came from three sides, from the assembly areas to the south, the south-east and the south-west of the town. The approach road looked ghastly. The Soviets, especially the units marching up from Breslau, suffered high casualties as a result of our artillery fire. Towards 11am came the report: Zobten in our hands, taken by the men of our Division!

SS-Hauptsturmführer Hans Dotterweich (Commander III/A.R.31) who provided the artillery support, recalled:

Our push into the deep area by infantry, accompanied and supported by the III *Abteilung*, proceeded well and met no significant Soviet resistance. It would have been easy to push through to Breslau. Some individual assault units even got as far as the Breslau-Berlin autobahn, on which the Soviets were marching as if in peacetime.

However not everywhere did things go so smoothly. In other places the attack met strong enemy resistance and ground to a halt. The chronicle of the 18th SS Volunteer *Panzergrenadier* Division 'Horst Wessel', *im letzten Aufgebot* by Tieke & Rebstock, described this counter-attack from the viewpoint of *Kampfgruppe* Dirks as follows:

The *Kampfgruppe*, formed for the most part from 2/SS *Panzer Abteilung* 18 and led by *SS-Obersturmführer* Dirks was assembled and refreshed in Bober-Röhrsdorf (north of Hirschberg). It was to go into action in the planned relief of Breslau. On 28 April 1945 eight assault guns i.e. all those in the *Abteilung* capable of combat, were brought together in *Kampfgruppe* Dirks, and loaded up.

SS-Oberscharführer Schilb gave this account:

On 3 May 1945 departure from Schweidnitz to Zobten. After short preparation in the area north-east of Zobten, in the morning hours of 5 May [author's note: actually: 6 May!]1945 the attack began together with infantry of the 100th *Jäger* Division. On the right of *Kampfgruppe Dirks*, Hetzers from an Army *Abteilung* were attacking.
    After only about 400 metres the first Hetzers were on fire. I couldn't see where the defensive fire was coming from. As I later found out, it must have been Stalin tanks lying in wait in a good position. It thus became clear that the Soviets had made the ring of encirclement around Breslau extremely strong and that from the beginning our attack was doomed to failure. In the meantime we had good cover due to a rise in the ground and our *Kampfgruppe* had no casualties. The attack was broken off and we rolled at top speed back to where we started and a little later back to Schweidnitz again.

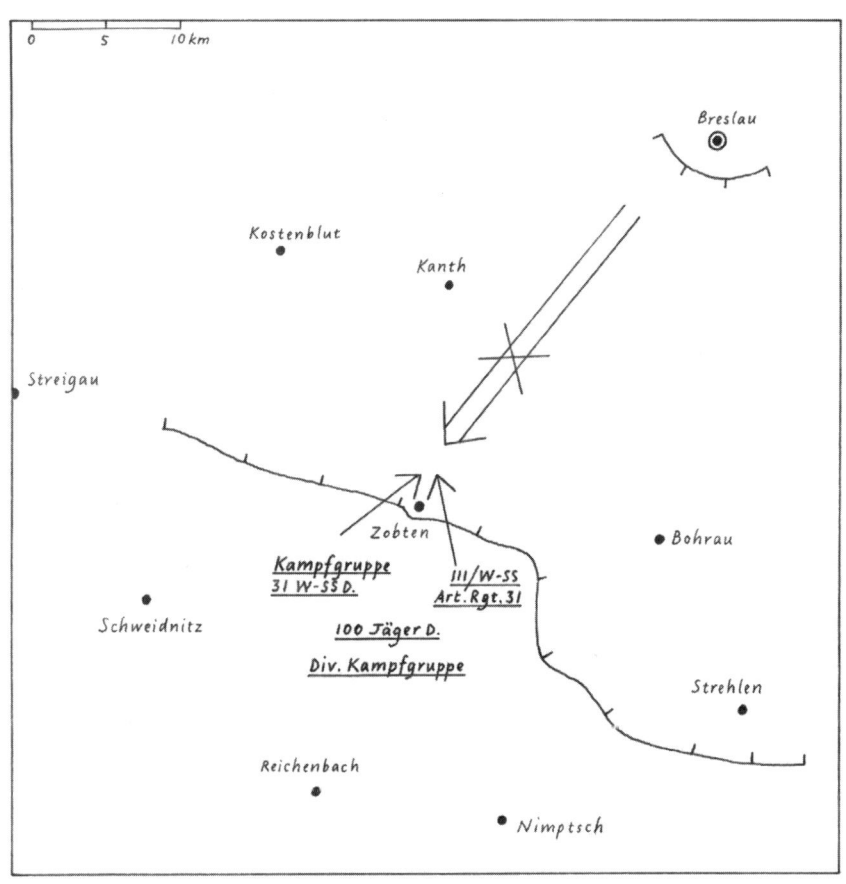

Map 9 The final counter-attack and recapture of Zobten, 5/6 May 1945.

Whether there was in fact any intention to continue the attack seems, however, to be improbable. The Soviet offensive formation moving up on the defensive front was shattered in the counter-attack, thus averting the danger of a breakthrough. Zobten was retaken, thus strengthening the defence. On the penultimate day of the war this was success enough. The German offensive group, including the units of the 31st SS Division, returned to the positions from which they had started. The next day the general retreat began.

CHAPTER 16

The Surrender and Retreat of the 31st SS Division

The overall situation during the last days and the surrender

On 16 April 1945 there began the large-scale Soviet offensive aimed at Berlin and the Elbe. That also affected the left flank of Army Group Centre. The front of the 4th *Panzer* Army was broken through on 16 April 1945 between Muskau and Guben. The enemy was aiming to move through Spremburg and Cottbus and on to Berlin, while another grouping of forces was attacking towards Bautzen. They were constantly moving and very heavy fighting opened up. It ended with a clear defensive success on the part of Army Group Centre. But even this could not turn away the disaster looming over the Reich capital. With the Soviet assault against the Seelow Heights, which commanded the battlefield of Berlin, in practical terms the fate of Berlin was sealed.

On 25 April 1945, advance units of Soviet armour reached the Elbe between Risa and Torgau. There, near the village of Leckwitz, where they carried out the atrocious massacre of a column of refugees, they joined up with the Americans for the first time. The Oder sector to the south of Stettin, collapsed under the weight of the Soviet offensive. The 3rd *Panzer* Army withdrew towards Mecklenburg.

Also on the right wing of Army Group Centre, in the Mährisch-Ostrau, Troppau and Brünn area, heavy fighting had continued to rage since mid-April. The 1st *Panzer* Army stood fast like iron. It was in the Brünn area that the Soviets, in a second battle of Austerlitz on 26 April 1945, suffered such heavy casualties that they temporarily halted in their attacks, although Brünn had to be surrendered. The battle for Breslau continued with undiminished severity. The 17th Army front along the Silesian wall of mountains continued to remain relatively quiet.

In the meantime Berlin was in a fight to the death. Alongside the Wehrmacht, the *Volkssturm*, Hitler Youth and SS volunteers from many European nations braced themselves against the Soviet 'flood'. The last citadel was the Reich Chancellery, which held out until 4 May 1945. On 30 April 1945 the Führer and Reich Chancellor, Adolf Hitler, chose to commit suicide. As his successor he designated Grand Admiral Dönitz, who had to take all measures which the situation required.

The Grand Admiral immediately decided to end the war against the Western Powers, but to continue the war against the Soviet Union. That would be for as long as it took for the soldiers and civilians to get there who might have a chance of getting behind the lines of the Anglo-Americans. The decision was vague. It aimed for a staggered surrender that would proceed in stages. But it did not at all suit the intentions of the Allies. It was an armistice between Germans and Anglo-Americans that Stalin particularly suspected and feared. But for the Grand Admiral it was a question of rescuing hundreds of thousands of German people. Therefore he tried, with great energy and determination to take that narrow path.

Right at the beginning of that task Dönitz did something that was later to prove to be a serious mistake. In fact he often admitted it. The consequence of it was to fundamentally determine the fate of the 31st SS Division. For when Dönitz, in his first discussion with *Generalfeldmarschall* Keitel and *Generaloberst* Jodl, on 1 May 1945, wished to immediately give the order to *Generalfeldmarschall* Schörner's Army Group Centre to withdraw to the American line, the two OKW Generals opposed him. They thought that the Army Group would collapse if it had to carry out this serious order for withdrawal at that point. He conceded. Keitel and Jodl were able to have their way. For all that, the issue of an order, on 1 May 1945, for a withdrawal of Army Group Centre to the West might have been possible and perhaps also advisable.

It would have been unnecessary to consider any effects of endangering the Army Group's neighbours, because the northern neighbour was the front at Berlin, and the southern neighbour was Army Group South. They were already far away to the west, in fact west of Vienna. It was precisely Army Group Centre, protruding far out to the East, which would be most entitled to begin moving to the West. By using the natural characteristics of the terrain, that with its many narrow mountain passes was extremely favourable to a withdrawal, there would not be too much need to fear the enemy pushing up immediately behind them.

But other considerations came to the fore. Consideration was being given to holding on to Bohemia and Moravia, with their virtually unscathed industry, as a self-sufficient fortress. Perhaps too it might also be a security for later negotiations. Another possibility was the thought of a joint attack on Bolshevism, along with the Western Allies, as being still in the air. At that time it did not by any means appear as eccentric an idea as post-war historians like, rather dismissively, to label it. It was precisely that idea of which Stalin was always afraid.

For all these considerations, the situation of Army Group Centre, seen from the wider perspective, was deadly serious. It simply projected out too far to the east, like a balcony. This was especially true of the XXXX *Panzerkorps* and the XXXIX *Gebirgskorps* (le Suire) of the 1st *Panzer* Army: the latter was still in the Beskiden! To secure the withdrawal of the *Gebirgskorps*, the town of Olmütz had to be held. The task was entrusted to General Hax with his 8th *Panzer* Division. He carried out his task, too, and on 8 May 1945, with his orderly officer, was the last man to leave blazing Olmütz, on a motorcycle. At the same time the XXXX *Panzerkorps*, bending back its right wing to Klein-Mohrau, withdrew its main line of resistance to the prepared position on the crest of the Altvater Mountains. By that process it retained communication with the 1st *Panzer* Army, prevented the Soviets breaking through into the Glatzer Kessel and was even able to keep a Division (1st Ski *Jäger*) as reserve.

The front of Army Group Centre then ran south-west of Brünn, where at first loose communication with the 8th Army of Army Group South still existed. From there it ran through Prossnitz and Olmütz up to the crest of the Altvater Mountains. Then it descended through Zuckmantel, between Neisse and Ottmachau, to the south of Strehlen. It continued on through Zobten, then north of Striegau and Lauban into the area to the north of Görlitz. From there the line ran through

Bautzen, and to the north of Dresden over into the Erzgebirge. The western front of the Army Group facing the Anglo-Americans then consisted of a loose security line, from Chemnitz through Eger as far as Weiden.

The deadly serious situation of his Army Group was also well known to the Supreme Commander, *Generalfeldmarschall* Schörner. He was of the same opinion as the OKW, namely that Army Group Centre would collapse if it gave up its well-constructed Sudeten position. But he proposed another plan by which to snatch as many as possible civilians and troops from the grasp of the Soviets. Instead of an immediate withdrawal, he wanted a well-prepared, phased operation. However, that would require a longer period of time. Therefore Schörner requested that the planned withdrawal to the West be deferred until 18 May 1945. He wished to give as many refugees as possible time to flee and he wanted to lead his soldiers as a coherent unit to the Western side.

His proposal was put forward by the Chief of Staff of Army Group Centre, General Natzmer, on 3 May 1945, on the occasion of a bilateral examination of the situation at Dönitz' Reich Government in Mürwik. He requested that an armistice should only be concluded when the majority of Army Group Centre had gone far enough to the West to fall within the custody of the Western Powers and not that of the Red Army. In other words, according to the calculations of Army Group Centre, on 18 May 1945. Even if Natzmer's proposal and his requirements were acknowledged, Grand Admiral Dönitz, in the light of the overall military and political situation, could still not give any firm guarantee that the date of 18 May 1945 could be kept. But Natzmer was assured that Army Group Centre could count on its requirements being met. It was ordered to immediately begin all preparations for the withdrawal, but at first to remain where they were.

Later the question arose as to why the Reich Government and the OKW did not order Army Group Centre to withdraw immediately. It is true that it was not impossible, although uncertain, that it all depended on the Reich Government being able to conclude the armistice on 18 May 1945. But was this not a risk? Nevertheless, it is true that it was believed to be the lesser risk, compared to that of a rushed withdrawal. This was not only because of the opinions expressed by the High Command of Army Group Centre, but other considerations also played a part.

Firstly, very promising negotiations concerning a partial surrender were under way with the British commander, Montgomery. On 4 May 1945 these also bore fruit, in that all German troops facing the front of Montgomery's 21st Army Group, including those in Holland, Frisia, Schleswig-Holstein and Denmark, could be handed over to them. At the same time it was agreed that members of the German armed forces who came from the East to Montgomery's front, and wished to surrender, would also become prisoners of war. Thus, a successful partial surrender was concluded, and it was pretty well along the lines of that intended by Dönitz. That success was encouraging and it led to the hope that events would proceed along the same lines. Reflecting those hopes it also seemed quite possible that the deadline of 18 May 1945 could be achieved.

Secondly, it was hoped that the Americans would occupy Czech territory, which would have been directly possible and which also would have met the wishes of the overwhelming majority of the Czechs. It was even hoped to meet the Americans and the Reich Protector of Bohemia and Moravia, Karl Hermann Frank. He sent over to the Americans a delegation of Czech civic politicians with the task of handing Czech territory over to them. But the mission failed since the Americans did not give it a hearing.

Thirdly, plans were in existence for the Reich Government to move from Mürwik near Kiel to Prague. Since north-west Germany was, by means of the partial surrender before Montgomery, handed over to the British, it now depended upon them whether the Reich Government could henceforth govern from Mürwik or not.

Thus there were convincing reasons for holding the frontline in Moravia and Silesia, by which, and this should be emphasised, orders were also given to carry out, with all possible speed, the preparations for a withdrawal to the West. But the divisions of Army Group Centre still had a task to carry out. The background circumstances must be described. They illuminated quite clearly that these units, including the 31st SS Volunteer Grenadier Division, during the last days, were by no means holding a lost post, but a post from which very much was expected, even at the highest political level.

In accordance with those tasks and orders, Army Group Centre fought and worked on during the first week of May 1945. In the Brünn area and at Mährisch-Weisskirchen a breakthrough by superior Soviet forces was once again repulsed. At Bautzen, Kamnetz and Königsbrück, as well as to the north-west of Dresden the enemy was thrown back. Breslau continued its heroic defence.

In the meantime, the preparations were under way for the planned withdrawal, for which the terrain offered extremely favourable tactical advantages, provided that the withdrawal began at the right time. The 200km-long mountain front of the 17th Army was extended in depth. From the main line of resistance on the northern edge of the foothills, over the mountains and passes, to the southern edge of the mountain country in Bohemia and Moravia, it stretched to the distance of 40 to 70km, as the crow flies. Skilfully used, it was tactically an ideal terrain for a withdrawal directed according to prepared plans. The preparations for this tactical use of terrain, especially of the passes, were everywhere under way. Thus, for instance, at Glatz the commandant of the planned *Festung* Glatz, *Generalleutnant* Boettcher was carrying out extensive preparations for blockade. But also immediately behind the Strehlen front of the 31st SS Division, entrenching work was already fully under way. At Tarchwitz and Krelkau, as well as at the entrance into the Eulengebirge at Quickendorf, Silberberg and Herzogswalde, anti-tank trenches and trench positions were being dug.

On 5 May 1945 the arc of the front, south-east of Mährisch-Ostrau, was drawn back according to plan. On 6 May at Olmütz, repeated Soviet attacks were repulsed. *Festung* Breslau succumbed to enemy superior force. A last counter-attack at Zobten, which has already been extensively described, successfully threw back the enemy once again. The front was held with iron resolve. Rumours were spreading that the overall surrender, including the Eastern front, was imminent. These were refuted by a telegram from the High Command of Army Group Centre, in order to combat the possible rise of panic.

On 6 May 1945, a wireless message arrived from OKW that announced an overall surrender. In other words, it was a surrender to the Soviets. The time of this surrender was not stated in the wireless message, negotiations were still in progress. But it added that withdrawal movements towards the American front had to be begun as quickly as possible. That wireless message was relayed by the Army Group to the armies and corps in the Group. Thus the order was given to withdraw and retreat. A little later this message was also fully confirmed when, on 6 May 1945, the order for surrender arrived. According to this the armistice, for all forces, came into force from 8am on 9 May 1945. Shortly afterwards that OKW wireless message was amended to the effect that the armistice applied to the entire front from midnight 9 May 1945.

In the midst of the race against time, to secure the planned withdrawal of the troops and the refugees, the surrender order hit Army Group Centre like a bomb. The race against time was lost! Now it was completely out of the question to still be able to surrender the majority of the troops to the Western Powers. A mere two days were not enough for the armies in the East to be able to reach the American lines. Soviet captivity stared hundreds of thousands in the face!

But how did things suddenly come to pass on that surprising 9 May 1945? Despite very skilful negotiation, on 6 May 1945 the Reich Government, still trying to achieve a partial surrender, were given a choice by Eisenhower, by way of an ultimatum. The choice was either immediately to sign an overall surrender, or the fronts of the Western Allies would be closed to those German soldiers who were trying to give themselves up individually, and all negotiations would be broken off. There was no other way out, only to sign, which is what happened at 2.41am on 7 May 1945. But how many soldiers of the 1.5 million-strong Army of the East would reach the Western front in just 2 days? Grand Admiral Dönitz now realised that he had been wrong when, on 1 May 1945, at the discussion with Keitel and Jodl, he had conceded to their objections against the immediate withdrawal of Army Group Centre. They were now in especial danger.

Verbal orders, for proper implementation of the surrender conditions, were given by Army Group Centre, on 7 May 1945, by telephone and wireless. On 8 May 1945, at 8am, they were in a meeting of Army commanders. The orders were for units to cease fighting at midnight and to halt at the place which they had reached at that point. All heavy equipment had to remain where it was and the divisions had to withdraw in groups, as quickly as possible, in a general south-westerly direction. All that was in order to be able to bring back as many people as possible. All available vehicles and every drop of fuel had to be used for this purpose, regardless of material. All troops and staffs were to be free to withdraw, on their own initiative, as far to the west as possible.

To secure this movement, the Erzgebirge front was not, under any circumstances, to lay down its arms before the parts of the Army Group to the east of them had crossed the Moldau. These orders from *Generalfeldmarschall* Schörner could easily have clashed with the order for surrender, but as he stressed: "No order can force troops to leave their comrades in the lurch!"

At the same time, the High Command of Army Group Centre brought up the fact that, as a result of the Czech insurrectionary movement, and the rapid progress of the ordered withdrawal, there were now scarcely any possibilities for exercising command. It would not be possible everywhere to prevent complete disorganisation and non-compliance with the conditions of surrender.

This was the position. Army Group Centre's formal orders for surrender, given on 8 May 1945, could no longer reach the majority of the divisions. Communications with service authorities from General Command upwards (i.e. to the armies and to Army Group Centre) had been completely severed from the early morning of 8 May 1945, so that the Army Group's last orders and instructions could get through to the troops. This collapse of the command structure was mostly caused by the uprising of the Czechs that flared up on 5 May 1945 in Prague. It then overflowed into the country.

The divisions that on 6 and 7 May 1945 for the most part were still in their old positions facing the enemy, followed the order for withdrawal received on 6 and 7 May 1945 and found themselves in retreat. For the most part they did not have any clearer idea either about the overall situation, or about the insurrectionary movement that in the meantime was dangerously gaining ground in Czech territory. More and more, events were churning into a 'witch's cauldron' the hospitable country of only a few days before. Nor was there much of a clue, regarding the extremely important question as to where the Americans actually were. Some of them at first had not much idea as to when exactly the surrender came into force.

The withdrawal of the 31st SS Volunteer Grenadier Division

It was necessary to explain, in the above detail, the background details and interrelationships at the political level and also those of Army Group Centre in order to make comprehensible the events surrounding the 31st SS Division. They undertook, carried out, and suffered the consequences of decisions taken and tasks assigned at high level. How the 31st SS Division itself experienced these turbulent events, or rather how it was damaged by those events, will be illustrated by the following authentic account by the Divisional Commander, *Brigadeführer* Gustav Lombard:

> The Supreme Commander of Army Group Centre, *Generalfeldmarschall* Schörner, received on 6 May 1945 the following wireless message from OKW: 'Eisenhower appears, in line with his political task, only to be allowed to conclude an overall surrender. Hence, surrender of the forces facing the Soviets. Nevertheless, he is prepared to negotiate, concerning partial surrender, with all forces facing his American front. Therefore operations are immediately to be conducted so as to bring the front facing the Soviets as quickly as possible within Eisenhower's sphere of influence. This is with the aim, as in Mecklenburg, to be absorbed into the American front. Report intentions. (signed: Keitel)'
>
> A little later this wireless message was received, through our superior command authority, the XVII Corps, at my Division. With only the instructions to act accordingly, the wording of this wireless message gave my Staff and me the unforgettable impression: We are standing alone, there is no longer any command structure. In line with the desperate situation I decided to issue the following orders:
>
> 'Right up to the time of surrender, destroy all heavy weapons, including machine guns. Only hand weapons to be retained, although shooting after surrender is murder, both for the defeated and for those who are victorious'.
>
> 'Destroy all secret documents'.

'Immediately begin to detach from the enemy in groups, in units, or individually as the situation dictates'.

'Try to reach the Pilsen area – with the exception of Prague! According to the OKW wireless message the possibility exists there of being taken prisoner by the Americans. Anyone who cannot, or does not want to do this must let themselves be overrun'.

This order was issued to all commanders who could be reached, or to their deputies. With the instruction 'let themselves be overrun' we wanted to make things easier for the some 200 Hungarians and also for our Tyroleans, who were now becoming 'Italians'.

The 3rd US Army under General Patton was actually in south-western Bohemia. On 6 May 1945 it took Pilsen but, with that, halted its further advance into Bohemia. The fact that the agreements made between the Allies did not allow Patton to march any further could not, of course, have been anticipated on the German side. That was why later, even in command authorities, various suppositions and rumours arose as to how he would approach Jungbunzlau or Hohenelbe. The rumours were all to turn out to be terrible disappointments. But Patton actually was in Pilsen. Then it was a question of reaching that area.

The withdrawal of the Division from its positions began on 7 May 1945 and proceeded according to plan and without significant enemy pressure. *Brigadeführer* Lombard recalled:

> We succeeded in detaching ourselves from the enemy better than we had thought possible. Our enemy had orders not to push on after us. The Soviets certainly knew what OKW and the Army Group had, unbelievably, not suspected, that control of the Protectorate of Bohemia and Moravia was immediately taken by the insurrectionary Czechs, who at the time of the surrender no longer even existed. Added to this is the fact that the high command of our 'opposite numbers' were, of course, aware that on 9 May 1945 a Soviet Army would advance from Dresden to Prague, and thus cut in half the pocket in which we found ourselves.

While the greater part of the Division was withdrawing on various route marches over the Eulengebirge to Bohemia, rearguards were left behind. They had a double task. On the one hand, of rendering the bridges, and narrow points in the road, impassable to the enemy, after the troops and refugees had passed through. On the other hand, if possible, of holding up, by force of arms, the enemy that was pushing up close behind. The rearguard forces were fairly small. There was no longer any question of being able to man the rearward trenches that had been so carefully prepared during the previous weeks.

Even if in most places the Soviets did not take up pursuit, for the most part they very quickly occupied the vacated area. In the process, more or less heavy rearguard fighting developed. Deutsch-Jägel, having changed hands seven times since the end of March, was evacuated on 5 May 1945 and occupied by the Soviets. A little later Schreibendorf, situated to the south-west of Deutsch-Jägel, fell. On 7 and 8 May 1945, the Soviets took possession of Datzdorf, Durr-Brockhuth, Karlsdorf, Prieborn, Rothschloss, Waldneudorf, and Wammelwitz all, for the most part, without any fighting.

On 9 May 1945, when no soldiers were any longer there, Deutsch-Tschammendorf, Reichau, Prauss, Gollschau, Kummelwitz, Rummelsdorf, were taken and other places well known from the actions of the 31st SS Division. Also, in the sector adjoining to the south-west, from 7 May 1945 the Soviets immediately felt their way carefully but doggedly after the withdrawing German forces. During 8 May 1945 the main route of their march was on the main Münsterberg–Kamenz–Wartha and Münsterberg–Frankenstein–Silberberg highways leading westwards. But many villages in the Frankenstein *Kreis* were only occupied on 9 May 1945. Thus the Silesian *Kreise* of Strehlen, Reichenbach, Breslau-Land and Frankenstein, in which the Soviets had been held back from their advance for almost a quarter of a year, only finally fell after the surrender.

The various units of the Division withdrew along the following routes of march:

Nimptsch–Frankentein–Silberberg–Glatz–Nachod–Josefstadt–Königgrätz: Most of SS Volunteer Grenadier Regiment 79, SS Pioneer Bataillon 31, Medical Company, SS *Panzerjäger Abteilung* 31 (?), Div. Staff (?).

Nimptsch–Reichenbach–Langenbielau–Brauna–Trautenau: Parts of SS Volunteer Artillery Regiment 31.

Reichenbach–Langenbielau–Braunau–Nachod–Josefstadt: Telephone Company of SS *Nachrichten Abteilung* 31.

Hirschberg–Bad Warmbrunn–Trautenau: The rearward services still stationed in the Hirschberg area.

Not all parts of the Division began the retreat on 7 May 1945. For most of them, especially for the combat units, it only began on 8 May 1945. Thus, for example, the II/79 only evacuated their positions on 8 May 1945, at 8pm. Their combat detachment left behind as rearguard only left them at 10pm, at about the same time as the Pioneer Battalion covering, as last rearguard, the retreat of the Division.

Many of the units withdrawing on 8 May 1945 became involved in a fighting withdrawal, with the Soviets following up behind. Especially significant engagements were at Lauenbrunn and Kobelau (parts of SS Volunteer Grenadier Regiment 79), where there were even greater casualties on both sides. There were actions in Dittmannsdorf, around the Kamenz railway junction, in Schonwalde and in the Eulengebirge passes at Wartha, Silberberg and Lampersdorf (parts of SS Volunteer Grenadier Regiment 79 and SS Pioneer Battalion 31). At Wartha, *Volkssturm* too were involved in the fighting with them, while from the Neudecker Pass German artillery (SS Artillery Regiment 31?) was still firing. A stalling skirmish was said to have taken place in Glatz.

During the last night the Pioneer Battalion, as last rearguard, blocked the roads through the passes into the Eulengebirge behind the withdrawing columns of the Division. The commander of 3rd Company SS Pioneer Battalion 31 was appointed as combat commandant of the Silberberg that had been declared a fortress. But no combat actions developed around the fortress. Only on 9 May 1945, as the pursuing Soviets reached Silberberg, he blew up the road leading over the mountain, past the fortress, and thus prevented the enemy following up quickly and overrunning the retreating refugees and soldiers. Finally, he could do no more fighting that day.

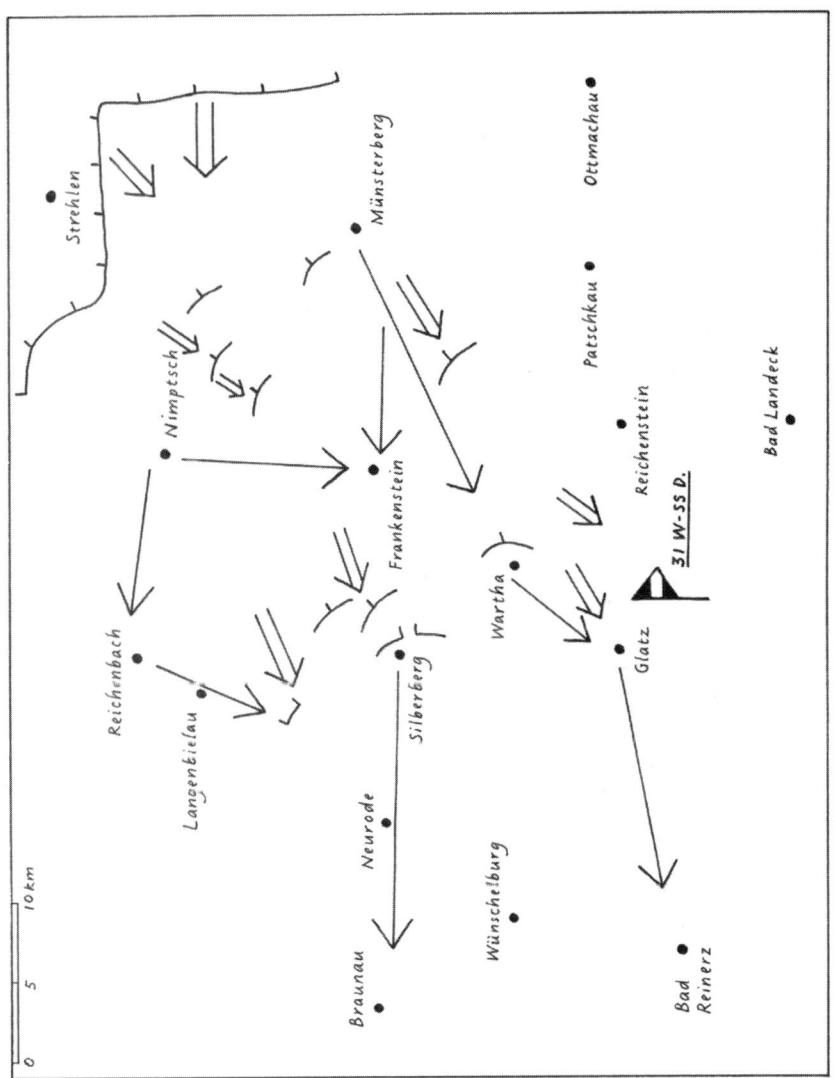

Map 10 Retrograde movement of the Division, 7/8 May 1945.

In conclusion, a Silesian, Pastor Hübner from Lampersdorf, described what sort of days his home village, which had lived for months under the protection of the 31st SS Division, had to undergo after the Division had retreated:

> When at the beginning of May Breslau fell, the fate of our villages was sealed. On 8 May, we saw another engagement during the retreat, between SS and the Soviet troops. Through it our village remained unscathed. In the early morning of 9th May the Soviets moved in. The majority of the village inhabitants had remained in their houses. Those who had fled into the mountains and the forests were plundered by the Soviets. In the village the Soviets took from the farmers most of their horses and carts. Many women and girls were raped.

CHAPTER 17

The 'Great Death' of the Division

The first day of peace dawned. It was a beautiful May day. But instead of bringing calm and peace, 9 May 1945 opened up for the soldiers of the 31st SS Volunteer Grenadier Division a *via Dolorosa* that eclipsed everything they have previously experienced. On that day the units of the Division crossed the Eulengebirge and the majority of them found themselves more or less deep in Bohemian–Sudeten German country, somewhere in the area between Braunau and Königgrätz. But this country was like 'a witch's cauldron'!

On 5 May 1945 an uprising broke out in Prague that soon spread to the country. Everywhere groups of insurgents were forming whose only purpose was to torture and kill everything German they could lay their hands on. They did not remain within the boundaries of the Protectorate, but immediately snatched at the Sudetenland. That was on the basis of the Munich Agreement, still completely valid in terms of international law. It was German Reich territory, and soon the Czech flag was also waving on the Schneekoppe.

What went on in Czech territory was beyond all manner of reason. The reason why the otherwise good-natured and friendly Czechs turned, *en masse*, into raging monsters lies in the fact that for six years they were the most enthusiastic collaborators with Hitler's Germany. They made an exemplary contribution to the production of the Reich's war industries. They also made achievements in agriculture that exceeded many German ones. The Czech administration, from police to ministerial civil servants, also remained at their posts and loyally served the government authorities of the Protectorate determined by the Germans. For this reason the Czechs had a bad conscience and were afraid, after the tide of war had turned, that they would not be on the side of the victors. To make up for this they saw, during the first days of May 1945, but only after the surrender, that their time had come. In their enthusiasm to give a few more kicks to the dying lion, they made themselves guilty, *en masse*, of appalling crimes. The motive for them was the most cowardly and dishonourable of the war.

Into this country in full revolt, there came the 31st SS Division without heavy weapons. From the 7 and 8 May 1945 when it crossed the Czech frontier, it had had to undergo constant engagements with the insurgents. At first the retreat of the 31st SS Division in the general direction of Königgrätz took place in fairly coherent individual and, whenever possible, in partly motorised units. By the time of the latest in the area of Josefstadt–Königgrätz, however, it was no longer possible to move in that way. The shortage of petrol was preventing it. The result was that the units dissolved in accordance with orders. Gradually most individual groups, smaller groups and individual men would be forced by the Czechs to surrender their arms. Most of them were assured of free conduct to the Americans. That was a lie, a transparent pretext by which, sadly, very many Germans were taken in. They then had

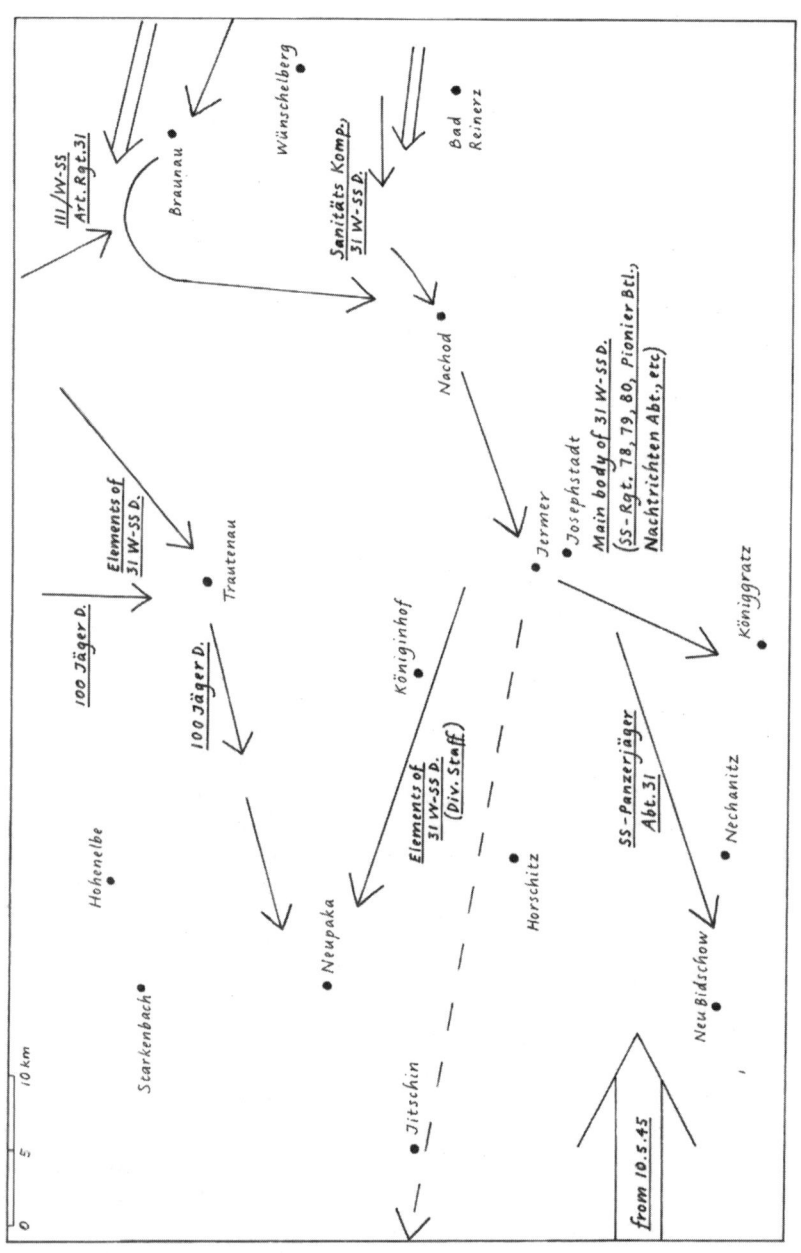

Map 11 Surrender and break-up of the Division, 9 May 1945.

to let themselves be taken into custody by the Czechs, with their own weapons, that they had just surrendered.

On 9 May 1945 the Soviets pushed forward southwards from the area west of Dresden on the Elbe. They occupied Prague on 10 May 1945 and with armoured forces came up against the several German divisions in the Königgrätz–Josefstadt area. Among them was the 31st SS Volunteer Grenadier Division. So the way to the Americans was blocked! The German forces were cut off, and taken prisoner by the Czechs, then handed over to the Soviets.

The Czechs instituted a formal hunt for German soldiers, especially for members of the SS. Most were killed. This Czech lust for killing was the undoing of many members of the 31st SS Division. Many officers, NCOs and men who fell into the hands of the insurgents were brutally murdered.

Only the arrival of Soviet troops saved many men from certain death at the hands of the Czechs. So it came about that although everyone was struggling to reach the Americans, in order to go into American rather than Soviet captivity, many were saved from a worse fate by that very Soviet captivity.

Thus the Division ended up with most of its force in the Josefstadt–Königgrätz area, with parts at Neu-Bidschow, Kolin and Jungbunzlau. Only a few succeeded in breaking their way through to the West or the North and becoming American prisoners of war, or not prisoners of war at all. Those taken prisoner by the Soviets then went back to Silesia, into the Breslau-Hundsfeld collection camp.

The fighting with the insurgents and with the Soviets exacted many sacrifices. The Czech lust for revenge, and Soviet captivity, exacted even more. All in all the casualties of the 31st SS Division in the last two days of war and the first days of peace were thought to be about 4,000 killed in action, or murdered, or missing. So the Division suffered the greatest casualties of its history, not in the field, but after the war had ended, in Czech territory.

At this point it may be permitted to consider the decisions of the Divisional Command during the last days. For after the war Lombard was, from time to time, reproached that with ordering the disarmament and dissolution of his Division, still almost half intact, he had done away with the last chance of reaching the American lines. However, this reproach cannot be regarded as well-founded.

Firstly, his order went back to an Army Group order and ultimately to the imminent unconditional surrender of the German Wehrmacht. That the order would prove to be unworkable and thus would entail serious consequences was apparently unknown even to Army Group Centre. *Brigadeführer* Lombard, however, could have had absolutely no idea of this. The order that he gave was the same as that given by all other Wehrmacht and Waffen-SS divisions in the area. The eventual disarmament and surrender of hand weapons was not ordered by him, but by the leaders of the various units under Czech pressure. That was in so far as they gave way to it.

But whether or not the idea of making a way through insurgent Czech territory to the Americans in Pilsen, still armed, was correct must, in considering this question, take into account at least four sets of circumstances.

There was the enemy. They were faced by the Soviets who on 9 May 1945 pushed from Dresden into Czech territory. These were the Soviets from whom they had just detached themselves in Silesia and who were following up slowly but surely behind them, and the insurgent Czechs were all around.

There was the time leading up to the surrender coming into force, and there was the distance from the county of Glatz to the Pilsen area. In no way would time have been sufficient to reach the Pilsen area with the entire Division before the armistice came into force. But, after the surrender, the order was given forbidding the use of arms. While it was possible to force the Czechs to give way merely by threat of arms, this would in no way have been possible against the Soviets. It would have come down to fighting in which, in the long term, the Division would sooner or later have succumbed to superior Soviet force. Through fighting after the armistice it would also have been deprived of any rights under the conventions of war.

(Of course it is difficult, in the light of the known circumstances in Czech territory, to still speak in terms of 'the conventions of war', and it is also a fact that many units or groups, including some from the 31st SS Division, fought their way through by force of arms. But it is an entirely different thing when a small group does this, than when it is done by a large unit. And even the groups making their way by force of arms for the most part did not succeed, the distance was simply too great. Sooner or later they also realised that it was better to lay down their arms).

There were the agreements reached between the Allies, under which the German soldiers were to be taken prisoner by the last opponents against whom they had been fighting. This meant, for the 31st SS Division, Soviet captivity. Only individuals still had any chance of being captured by the Americans. The attempt to hand over the entire 31st SS Division to the Americans is also unlikely to have succeeded. It could have been handed over to the Soviets without further ado, which was often the case with other units. (But here it should be mentioned that there were also American commanders who did not hand over their prisoners, especially in the Pilsen sector, because of the tensions between Soviets and Western troops).

Lombard was also reproached with having disguised himself, instead of leading the Division through. This does not hold water at all. He only disguised himself when he narrowly escaped with his life from a Czech massacre. In addition, he no longer had any possibility of exercising command, since his staff had also fallen prey to the killing. Shown here, as the result of these investigations, should be the comments he made on this subject at his later interrogation in Russia:

> The mass murders in Czech territory gave everyone a shock such as they had never had before. Not only we, those who were affected, but also many on the other side…Whoever knows me will know that I would never have allowed my Division to be detached from our Soviet opponents if I had even suspected that the OKW order of 6 May 1945 was unworkable. Fate had spoken and one should make no effort to contradict it.

In actual fact it was a shock. That the Czechs would murder in such a crazy and brutal way, as they did, could perhaps only have been guessed, in advance, by those Germans who had known them from the Hussite wars. The Austrians or Sudeten Germans might have guessed, but never Reich Germans. They only knew the friendly Czech in the *Bierstube*. Certainly Lombard, a Prussian aristocrat and gentleman as he was, would not have expected such actions.

It is not possible to describe the end of all units of the 31st SS Volunteer Grenadier Division in detail and in chronological order. Nevertheless, this last act of the tragedy must be described, by those who were involved in it, from the general to the ordinary soldier. The accounts give a multi-faceted picture of the fate of the one-time 31st SS Division. The starting points are the respective last positions in Silesia.

First the Divisional Commander, *Brigadeführer* Lombard, gives his account. The Divisional Staff set off from Glatz, apparently as early as 7 May 1945. As far as can be deduced from Lombard's account, he tried to circumvent Prague in quite a wide arc to the north, in order then to swing in from north-western Bohemia to the Pilsen area. In this way he travelled north past the Josefstadt–Königgrätz area and in Neu-Paka came up against Czech insurgents. It did not need much for him to have shared here the fate of the 4,000 men of his 31st SS Division who were murdered! His good luck allowed him to escape and to break through quite a long way further westwards, where he was taken prisoner by the Soviets.

> We, i.e. the Divisional Staff of the 31st SS Division and I, also the regimental commander of our artillery regiment and his orderly officer had attached themselves to us when went in our motor vehicles over the Eulengebirge into 'Czech territory'. In Neu-Paka, where there was already a column of the 100th *Jäger* Division[1], the next-but-one neighbouring division on our left, with its Divisional Staff, we were stopped and surrounded by a horde of heavily armed Czechs. The ringleader with a white armband came up and asked me to surrender the vehicles and to surrender for my Division. When I asked whether this would mean captivity, he replied: 'No! My word of honour as an officer that all of you and others from the Army who are already waiting in the side-streets will be allowed, immediately you have surrendered and given up your arms, to travel on to the Americans. The way there is guaranteed by agreement between German high command authority and the Czech authorities'.
>
> My officers and I had to go into the parish house and I surrendered for the 31st SS Division. In a side room, unnoticed by the Czechs, I met *Generalmajor* Schury, commander of the 100th *Jäger* Division, to whom exactly the same procedure of giving up arms and surrender had been applied. When we were outside again, they had in the meantime pushed a lorry with soldiers of the 100th *Jäger* Division behind my car so that I no longer had any visual contact with our second car, the Ia and his orderly officer and certainly not with those behind. My escort officer, *SS-Untersturmführer* Achim Rahmel, wanted to protest, but got a slip of paper which said (anyway that's what they told us, because none of us understood Czech) that I was transport leader of the whole column. We set off, but even before we could get out of the village our column was attacked. My driver and the driver of the lorry behind us were still able to put their foot down, but only mine managed it. The others we never saw again. Apart from me, my driver, the Ia, the Divisional MO, and the dentist, no-one was able to escape. Almost all the others were murdered. (Author's note: the regimental com-

1   he 100th *Jäger* Division set off during 6 May from Bolkenhain through Landshut towards Trautenau and from Schönau through Rudelstadt to Schatzlar, in the process of which, on 7 May, heavy fighting developed on the retreat at Ober-Lauterbach by the Katzbachgebirge. The Division Commander, *Generalmajor* Schury, announced the surrender in Arnau. Immediately afterwards his columns fell into the trap in Neu-Paka, not far west of Arnau, and the events described by Lombard occurred, taking place, according to him, on 7 May.

mander of SS Artillery Regiment 31, *SS-Standartenführer* Kaestner, his adjutant, *SS-Sturmbannführer* Wiegand were not murdered in this bloodbath, they were seen later, when the Czechs handed them in to the prison in Jitschin, 15km south-west of Neu-Paka, and later transported them on from there. But since then there has been no further trace of them).

Later, as a Soviet prisoner of war, I met *Generalmajor* Schury again, who told me that at that time in Neu-Paka, in contrast to me, they did not let him travel on, since, so they told him, generals were, as soon as they were captured, immediately to be handed over to the Soviets. From this we deduced, Schury and I, that the Czech with his 'word of honour' had wanted to have me, as a Waffen-SS man, 'done in', unnoticed in the chaos. At least I escaped with my skin.

On both sides of the road along which we were driving lay a terrifyingly large number of corpses of murdered German soldiers. In each case they had been ambushed, it wasn't the work of snipers, because always several dead men were lying in one place. Once our way was barred by four Czechs. Two of them came up to us, I wanted to show the slip of paper to the one who was speaking to me, but at the same moment the other hit me with the butt of his rifle. I fell on to the driver, the two others pulled me up, shocked, and the four Czechs had run away.

The Czechs were in control of all roads and paths. We couldn't fight their lust for killing. During a short rest in a wood I thought over our hopeless situation and gave my last order: 'Every man is to try on his own initiative to reach the Teplitz-Schönau railway station!' It wasn't far. To hell with the Eisenhower front in Pilsen. Whether a train is still stopping at the station which goes in the direction of home will decide our fate. Herbert Bartel, my batman, said out loud that he couldn't leave the old man on his own, and we could see in Achim Rahmel what he was thinking, that without him we would be really lost. Despite this the boys had one last time to obey my order.

The next night but one I met Achim Rahmel again at the Teplitz railway station, from now on disguised as *Leutnant* Werner of the *Gebirgsjäger*. I was now Major of Reserves Elmut (without an 'h') Mueller ('ue', not 'ü'). (I carried out this change of name deliberately, for in 1941, in Russia, I had got to know a Captain Helmut Mueller. I knew that after his transfer to the Western front at the beginning of 1942 he had been killed in action as Major of Reserves. That was something that I had reliably heard from a mutual acquaintance. I couldn't disguise myself with more absolute certainty, unless I was betrayed. In any case, I wouldn't have put a Müller in any danger.

Achim gave me a sign that he agreed with my disguise. We spotted the last train to Dresden. It was packed to bursting point with women, children, and soldiers travelling alone. At last the train departed, but moved remarkably slowly. A few times I thought that it's just going to stop. And in fact, one time it did stop. Loud yelling. Screams. Commands. Everybody out! Hands up! The Soviets! We were prisoners! We ended up in a reception camp and were registered by the Soviets. A few days later the staff officers, and hence I too, were transferred from this tented camp by railway to Görlitz and three days later also met there the others captured with us coming by route march from Teplitz. The heavy strain caused considerable casualties, but no-one was murdered by the Soviets. It was only with the Czechs and Titoists that that happened.

The disciplined manner in which the units of the 31st SS Volunteer Grenadier Division held together, to the last, even after other units were completely disintegrating, indeed, the determined manner in which they kept going as long as possible, may be illustrated to us in an account, dramatic in its simplicity, from A.Gl. from the Pioneer Detachment of SS Volunteer Grenadier Regiment 80:

> Our regiment marched through Silberberg and crossed the frontier at Braunau. At the frontier we were challenged by armed Czech civilians to lay down our arms, but our commanders vigorously refused to do so. Army units for the most part didn't do that. They handed over their weapons or threw them down. Although the Czechs had in this way got hold of many weapons, our regiment still represented a fighting force to be reckoned with, so that they didn't think it advisable to hold us up by force and they let us go on. We moved on in a motorised march towards Josefstadt. From the town we could see that caution was needed. We got out of the lorries and secured the column in extended order with rifles at the ready. Thus we advanced towards the town.
>
> In the market place, a great mob of people had banded together, and was listening to a Czech. We, of course, didn't understand a word, but from his demeanour and way of speaking we could deduce that it was a really inflammatory and rabble-rousing speech. Our weapons commanded enough respect for us not to be attacked as we marched through the town. Only when we had the town behind us did shooting begin in our rear from roofs and similar hiding-places, but at first this didn't bother us much. The end came when after a short stretch on the road our petrol ran out completely! Finish! The troops were dispersed, each was sent on his way with a slap on the back and advised to try to break through on his own initiative. We were thanked for our loyalty and wished 'safe home'. But things were to work out differently. In Königgrätz most of us were taken as prisoners by the Czechs.

Because the Czechs were especially on the hunt for members of the SS, many men took their unit insignia off their uniforms and tried to merge unobtrusively in the mass of Wehrmacht members. But many fell victim to their trusting nature. A.Gl's account went on:

> Taken prisoner by the Czechs, we were driven to Königgrätz to a barracks square. A huge number of German soldiers was already there, both from our Division and from Wehrmacht divisions. On the barracks square they had us fall in and the command rang out: 'SS step forward!' Some fifteen or sixteen men stepped forward, I wanted to, too! To my good fortune the man next to me, my *Gruppenführer*, Josef Schilz from the Banat, with whom I was good friends, hissed to me: 'Stop there!' So I stopped where I was. The men who had stepped forward were immediately put up against the wall and simply gunned down by machine-pistol.
>
> From Königgrätz we had to march to the Breslau-Hundsfeld camp. It took five whole days on foot. It was a proper hunger march, because we got nothing to eat! Many, very many, fell victim to the hardships of this march. Anyone who couldn't keep up, and fell, was shot dead by the Soviet sentries. There were several of us from my home village and it was our good fortune that one of them, a medical orderly, had with him a good portion of Transensis saccharin. We dissolved it in water and drank it. It gave us some energy. On the fifth day we got

some rations. One loaf for 32 men! We spent about a month in Breslau, then, about the end of June, we were transported off to Russia.

Not only on the hunger march, but also in the Breslau-Hundsfeld camp, death reaped its harvest. Every day 150 to 200 men died. Especially vulnerable were the older, the sick, and wounded soldiers who could no longer bear up under such hardships. The weeks-long, often months-long stay of the physically weakened and malnourished prisoners in the open air, even though it was summer, caused considerable casualties. The great number of prisoners (in this camp at times there were up to 300,000 inmates) made it difficult for the Soviet military authorities to feed them and provide them with medical care. Even mental and physical exhaustion often resulted in death.

The majority of SS Volunteer Grenadier Regiment 79 also perished in the Königgrätz area. The blood flowed in streams. P.D., runner with the Regimental Staff, gave this account:

> After we had handed over our weapons, the Czechs forced us with the same weapons to strip and to dig holes in the ground in a clearing. Everything was ready for the execution when we were freed at the last minute by a high-ranking Soviet.

One group from the regiment (Baggage II/79) succeeded, by determined action and also in part by use of arms, to escape from the hell of Königgrätz. They broke out further to the West, into the Jungbunzlau area, where it was thought the Americans were. It was a fairly widespread supposition that the American-Soviet demarcation line would be drawn on the Elbe or Moldau. This hope was not fulfilled. The group was taken prisoner by the Czechs at Jungbunzlau, driven to Melnik an der Elbe into a death camp, and those who survived were handed over to the Soviets. The horrors that H. Knauer (II/79) describes will have been experienced by most of those who were there:

> According to the order to withdraw, the II/79 left its defensive positions southwest of Strehlen on 8 May 1945. The staff left Prauss at 8pm, the rearguard only followed at 10pm. I had the task of taking the baggage out of its position. On 9 May at midday I received orders to destroy all the battalion's papers and to act in accordance with a code word which had been kept secret until then. According to this order I had the task of leading my people as far as Jungbunzlau in Czech territory and there, of going into American captivity.
>
> We travelled, following the greater part of the Division, through the Eulengebirge towards Königgrätz. During the afternoon of 9 May, I once again came across *SS-Sturmbannführer* Albrecht with his smaller staff, *Untersturmführer* Bender and Hundertmark, and his driver. He suggested that we travel with him, since we had the same route, but I declined, because my people had asked me to stay with them. What then happened to him and those with him I can't say, but it is a fact that from the end of the war he was posted as missing. As we were travelling through the Eulengebirge, in several places we saw vehicles that had crashed over precipices lying at the bottom, beside them bodies of soldiers, also several high-ranking SS commanders. It cannot be ruled out that Albrecht, too, that first-class officer, met his sad end in this way. Other vehicles, beside which no dead men were to be seen, had probably been tipped

over the edge by the men themselves because of the shortage of petrol which was becoming more and more evident. We also saw tanks that had ground to a halt, some of which could not even be driven off the roads.

When we arrived outside Königgrätz we found a veritable hell! I personally was punched in the face by a Czech, another pointed his machine-pistol at me because I defended myself. At this moment some comrades shot out the lights there which made it possible for us to drive away in the vehicles. Then in Königgrätz we shot our way through by sweeping the streets with a machine gun. The Czechs had certainly not reckoned on a vehicle coming by which still had weapons on it. The greater part of our Division remained stuck in Königgrätz and was taken by the Czechs (there were still no Soviets there) and driven together to the barracks. Only smaller groups like mine got out, provided that they acted with determination. Indeed, many small groups and individuals were simply 'bumped off' by the Czechs!

Once we had broken our way past Königgrätz, we then got through, without firing another shot, to Jungbunzlau. Here we found not a single American, but only an empty barracks and Czech insurgents. We were forced to leave all vehicles and to surrender all weapons, or else, since the surrender had already come into force, we would no longer be protected by the international conventions and the Red Cross.

Well, unarmed, defenceless, and on foot as we were, we saw no trace of any protection by international conventions, but plenty of the horrible atrocities which the Czechs carried out on captured soldiers. This happened even as we had run through the first villages, on the march from Jungbunzlau to Melnik. A group of about 50 comrades, including some from the Wehrmacht, we had to run on specified roads.

In one place after Jungbunzlau we saw SS comrades, stripped to the waist, clearing anti-tank barriers. On their backs had been branded SS runes 10cm high! We wanted to help them in their work, but were driven on and shot at.

After that same village we had to turn off the road into a field where there were several men. As we got closer we saw how three SS officers, still in full uniform, were digging holes. When the first had dug the hole deep enough he had to strip. Four of the men standing around (there were also Germans standing there, and indeed, as we later found out, entire families brought there by force by three armed Czechs) had to hold up the comrade in the air by his hands and feet with his belly upwards. Two other men who had to be ready at one side, were given sticks in their hands and with them they had to beat the comrade on the belly. When these men didn't want to do it, one of the Czechs brutally beat a man to the floor and another man had to take the stick. Two Czechs now demonstrated how to do the beating, always on the belly, and the men had to copy them. The comrade was soon unconscious, when suddenly one of the other two German officers drew a pistol out of the leg of his boot and fired at the two Czechs. The third threw down his machine-pistol and ran away, but wasn't hit. What happened after that I don't know, because the three comrades didn't come with us. One of them lived nearby.

In another place we saw, on an open SS vehicle, two or three dead comrades. Czechs came and dragged up two half-unconscious Red Cross Sisters. I of all people got the order from a Czech in some kind of uniform that we had to take the girls with us to Melnik. When we had gone a few metres outside the village we saw at the roadside a burnt figure. As we then found out from the Red Cross sisters, this was one of the comrades from the vehicle who had survived. He was doused in petrol there and set on fire. The two women had to watch it all.

In Melnik we were driven into a camp which was set up in the grounds of a sugar factory. I led my group in order into the camp and we were lucky enough at first not to be recognised as members of the SS and to be able to slip through the first checkpoint, since a larger number of members of the Wehrmacht had joined us on the way.

But after two days the game of hide-and-seek finished, because all the inmates of the camp were examined again individually. Each one had to step over a stretched rope with their left arm raised, as a search was carried out for the "bird under the arm". Thus it happened that not only SS members were unspeakably beaten there, but also soldiers on whom was found a mark or something else showing a swastika.

What later went on in the camp in Melnik cannot be described. Every morning piles of dead lay in the meadow. They were those who had died during the night, because machine guns were always being fired over the flat terrain and whoever stood up was instantly a corpse. There were many dead on the Elbe bridges and in the waters of the Elbe.

In Melnik some high-ranking officers, including Wehrmacht officers, were tortured to death and beaten. The men were placed by the Czechs with their faces to a wooden fence and had to put out their tongues on which a coin was placed. If the coin fell off, the Czechs beat the man with their rifle butts until it was back on his tongue. These procedures did not last long, because the coin fell off more and more often and it was not long until those who had been tortured like this were lying on the floor until they died there. I saw there a Wehrmacht *Oberst* die in that way. He was about seventy years old.

Here it should also not be forgotten how the Czechs dealt with women. We had to watch, as some open lorries, with naked women, were driven round and round in circles through the town. Facing outwards, the women stood completely naked on the lorries, their hands tied behind their backs and fastened to the vehicle so that they couldn't fall over. On their breast hung a placard that read, 'I am a German whore'. Despite this, it was astonishing how bravely these women took such humiliation, because there were hardly any of them to be seen crying.

Our salvation was, in fact, soldiers of the Red Army who came into the camp one evening and brought an end to the madness that the Czechs carried on there. Finally the Czechs were chased away, some even shot dead. The wounded prisoners, even members of the Waffen-SS, were treated by medical personnel.

Here, at last, our group ceased to hold together because we all had to fall in according to districts. The foreigners too were similarly split up according to their homelands. Thus, the same night, we set off again in the direction of Prague where we arrived at daybreak. It was said to us that we would be taken to the goods station in Prague and from there released to go home. For whatever reason, this didn't happen. Two days later we were back to Melnik, but at least not in the old camp.

On the march to Prague we often had boiling water poured on to us from the windows of the houses. These 'water pourers' were all Czech women. On the march back this performance ceased, because when they saw it the Soviets simply fired into the windows and the cries of pain gave away the fact that they had also hit their target. After we had Soviet guards we were as a rule no longer attacked by the Czechs. It is clear to me that if the word 'liberation' can ever be properly used of us Germans, then we were actually liberated from the Czech hordes by the Soviets.

But it was no 'life insurance' to be among the Soviets. On the march to Prague, and back to Melnik, it had come to be amusing, to some Soviet sentries, to treat to a bullet those comrades who, because of dysentery or because of general weakness, could no longer march any further on their own. They were left lying, in open graves, by the roadside. Two Mongols were particularly enthusiastic in this practice. We reported it in Melnik to a senior Soviet officer who was inspecting us there. What he did then I don't know, but it's a fact that we didn't see those sentries again.

After another two days in Melnik we were transported in the direction of Saxony and arrived in a camp in Zittau. I was then in two further camps, in Christianstadt where in Autumn 1945 the camp was taken over by the Poles, and in Sagan. I have to say that I was mistreated neither by the Soviets nor by the Poles, although in the meantime it had become known, through betrayal, that I was a member of the Waffen-SS.

That I was able to return home from captivity early, as early as December 1945, is due to particular circumstances. I helped with the camp theatre group, which brought me into close contact with the camp commandant. He was a Jew who had in 1932 emigrated from Berlin to Poland, an actor by profession. Although he was a Jew, he had a good attitude even to us. He said to me: 'There's no blood on your hands and as a prisoner you were always honourable, you denied nothing'. That brought about my release. Of course, years later this didn't stop the GDR authorities from accusing me of slander of the state, on the simple grounds that: 'His education in the Waffen-SS has made him into an enemy of the state of the first order, so that he may expect a heavy punishment'. They then kept this promise. I was in custody for over 6 months and was so badly maltreated that I suffered permanent damage.

SS-Hauptsturmführer Hans Dotterweich (*Abteilung* Commander III/A.R. 31) gave an account of how his command came into Soviet captivity as early as outside Braunau, thus sparing them suffering and murder at the hands of the Czechs:

We were in the Zobten–Strehlen area when on 7 May the regimental commander, *Standartenführer* Kaestner, a very decent man, asked if we had a civilian suit in our backpacks, to which of course we said no. We heard from him that Germany was surrendering on 8 May. On the evening of 7 May we marched as a unit over the Eule, blew up our guns in Neudorf on the Eule, and moved with small arms in the direction of Braunau. The column grew bigger and bigger. In the end I had some 1,000 men in the column which I was leading. Many officers and men too, from the Batschka, surrounded and exhorted me not to flee, or panic would break out.

The Soviets met us shortly before Braunau. I took over the surrender on 9 May 1945 at 2pm. Our *via Dolorosa* began. As prisoners of war we had to march to Breslau to the Hundsfeld camp. In our first transit camp in Waldenburg we met women from the surrounding villages who wept terribly and complained about constant rapes by the Soviets. I was in Hundsfeld until the beginning of September, when we went on by rail into the prison camps in the Soviet Union, at Polozk, and Minsk. Then, after my sentence to 25 years' hard labour, I was sent to Stalingrad. I was released in 1954. What reassures and satisfies me is that in the last months and even in the last days I didn't negligently risk the life of any man in my III *Abteilung*. In actual fact I did not lose a single one. My unit, consisting for the most part of Batschka Germans, was also brave and maintained good order right up to the last minute. Even as prisoners of the Soviets we stuck together with iron resolve.

SS-Untersturmführer Heinz Hummel tells of the fate of SS Pioneer Battalion 31, with particular reference to the battalion staff in which he was working as Battalion Adjutant at the time. He himself was one of those who were able to escape north, to Silesia. But many members of the battalion met their death in the bloodbath at Josefstadt. Those who were able to escape this fate were taken over by the Soviets and driven through Trautenau into the Breslau-Hundsfeld camp. On the transport to Russia, and in the camps there, many died. After long years only a few members of the former SS-Pioneer Battalion 31 were able to see their homes again. Among them was the battalion commander, *SS-Sturmbannführer* Otto:

> The last Divisional order was given verbally to the Divisional units, in fact to the commanders who could be reached or their representatives. I received the verbal order at the Divisional Command Post in Glatz, on behalf of the Pioneer Bataillon. The order was for the destruction of the heavy weapons, immediate detachment from the enemy, and to set off on the march in the direction of the Pilsen area.
>
> The Pioneer Bataillon detached itself from the enemy on the night of 8 May 1945 and was rearguard for the Division. We had orders to blow up bridges and transformer stations. We prepared charges on certain sectors of road. Blowing up roads proved to be impossible since they were full of soldiers flooding to the rear and, of course, refugees. Our withdrawal from the Strehlen area took place in the direction of Glatz, over the Eulengebirge, Bad Kudowa, and the Nachod frontier crossing, towards Königgrätz.
>
> After I had conveyed the Divisional orders to the 1st Pioneer Company, I drove on my motorbike after the battalion staff. When I arrived at the frontier in Nachod it was already manned by armed Czech civilians with red armbands. Only those who were unarmed were allowed to pass. I destroyed my machine-pistol, but hid my pistol for safety under my riding coat. My journey continued towards Königgrätz. Outside Jeromir (near Josefstadt) I then found the battalion staff which was led by *SS-Obersturmführer* Bahr. The duties of protective escort for the battalion Staff had been taken over by a platoon of the 2nd Company led by *SS-Untersturmführer* Kiebauch. The location of the Battalion Commander, *SS-Sturmbannführer* Otto, was unknown. After the war it turned out that he had been left behind with engine problems in his VW-Schwimmwagen.
>
> I rode on my motorbike out in front of the column to scout out conditions in Jeromir. At a crossroads in the town stood the Divisional MO with his driver and Kubelwagen. A Czech policeman was asking him whether the roads to

Prague were free. For the information the policeman was given a packet of cigarettes. As the MO's car drove from the block of houses to the next crossing, suddenly from both sides Soviets attacked the Kubelwagen. I turned my motorbike and drove back at full speed to outline the situation to *SS-Obersturmführer* Bahr. We tried to turn the vehicles, but it was no use, we were in the trap. Evidently only I was able to escape on my motorbike because all the enquiries which I made, after the war, as to where these men were, remained fruitless.

I drove out of the town and warned all the soldiers and refugees I met. Again and again I was stopped by Czechs who didn't want to let me go on. Explaining that I was fetching up another unit, I was able to continue. Three kilometres outside I turned into a field track and now tried to 'disguise' myself. While I was doing this I was surprised by five, armed, young Czechs, who took away my motorbike.

When I returned to the road, masses of people, soldiers, refugees were snaking in the direction of Königgrätz. Suddenly I saw on a motorbike our Battalion MO, *SS-Hauptsturmführer* Herrmann, and his battalion SDG, *SS-Oberscharführer* Simang. After I had explained things briefly to them they got rid of everything that could prove a burden in the situation. We left the road and marched across country north-westwards. In the late afternoon we heard the sound of tracks. The Soviets were there. We heard shots and women screaming. When it got dark our long march into uncertainty began.

For some 14 days we were on the move, running by night, by day creeping into the forest. Hunger got bad. By day we fed ourselves on the young shoots of the spruces, and if at night we found a field of potatoes, we dug for seed potatoes which we ate raw. As a result we became so weak that we had to keep lying down because our knees were trembling.

In Libau in Silesia we reached Reich territory. At a farm we got jacket potatoes with salt, for us a celebration meal, and marched on over the Riesengebirge. Around Marktlissa the Soviets were holding open season on everything male and German. Unknowingly, we too ran into their hands. Those who were caught were driven together, in Marktlissa, where I met a *Gruppenführer* from my platoon, *SS-Unterscharführer* Dielschneider. He had, like us, fallen into the trap. Inhabitants of Marktlissa who wanted to bring us something to eat and drink were chased away by the Soviets. The next day we were moved into a nearby former camp for *Ostarbeiter*. It was a barrack-block camp with a kitchen and canteen. Every day the Soviets brought in new prisoners and in the afternoon we had to parade. Under heavy guard the men marched to Sagan.

We didn't let ourselves be registered and every day mixed in with the newcomers. But Dielschneider reported in and then disappeared. He spent four and a half years in the coalmines in the Donets Basin.

After a week we decided to flee, but the risk was too great for *SS-Oberscharführer* Simang. The following night we 'scarpered', despite the moonlight. In a barn close to the camp we hid ourselves and slept until the afternoon. Then we went to the farmhouse and asked for food. As we were sitting at a table, our comrades were passing by on the highway. Simang spent five years in Soviet captivity…

We moved on. At Görlitz we crossed the Neisse unchecked, then on we went to Bautzen, with a fork or rake over our shoulders. When we arrived one afternoon at my parents' house, the first goal was reached. After three months, I had to go off on my travels again, this time to West Germany. The doctor, Albrecht Herrmann, a quite outstanding person, with whom fate had joined me in a close friendship on our adventurous flight, died in 1995.

SS *Nachrichten Abteilung* 31 met a no less horrible end. Parts of the Wireless Company in the Schweidnitz area were supposed to have withdrawn through Bolkenhain to Bohemia. Many members of the section were brutally murdered by the Czech insurgents in the Josefstadt area. Others died on a death march from Josefstadt to Königgrätz. An account of these events was given by Hugo Krallmann, leader of the Light *Nachrichten* Column:

On the morning of 8 May 1945 we moved out of the Nimptsch area in good order, without panic, to the Czech frontier. On 9 May 1945 we then went on without machines and material. We doused everything with sulphuric acid at the frontier and tipped the wreckage into an open air swimming pool. We crossed the border towards Josefstadt. The road was crammed with refugees without any possessions, and thousands of ordinary soldiers.

In Josefstadt we were disarmed and had to leave behind all vehicles. They sent us completely indiscriminately and without any order or guard on to the road in the direction of Königgrätz. We split up, put on drill or Wehrmacht uniforms, which were lying about in wrappers, and disappeared into the crowd so as not to be noticed. *SS-Untersturmführer* Karl Stecker set out on his own before we got to Josefstadt, because as a native of Olmütz he could speak the local language. *SS-Oberscharführer* Josef Vossen, who stammered slightly, also left, since he was at home in Silesia. *SS-Untersturmführer* Jürgen Joost was shot by civilians with a burst of machine gun fire, between Josefstadt and Königgrätz. After the Czechs fired indiscriminately into the crowd with machine guns, the wireless operator *SS-Oberscharführer* Alfred Schulz and I threw ourselves into the ditch. Afterwards we lost each other. I went on, until 10 May, to Josefstadt together with *SS-Obersturmführer* Schwalbe. He told me that he wouldn't be made a prisoner but would shoot himself and suggested that I did the same. After a while he went off with three men into a nearby wood. Shortly afterwards I heard three shots. I never saw them again. *SS-Untersturmführer* Bantelmann was also there.

The following account by *SS-Untersturmführer* Hans Villier, platoon commander in the Telephone Company, illustrated particularly strikingly what German people had to suffer in the first days of peace in Czech territory. It can be seen as representative of the experience of many members, not only of SS *Nachrichten Abteilung* 31 but also of the 31st SS Division as a whole, and even of the entire Wehrmacht.

On 8 May we received orders to change position again, but this time with the additional instruction to, as far as possible, dismantle all field cable still in use and take with you all signals equipment. Up to this point all material was, whenever possible, exchanged with the unit following into the position.

Then came the order to march. At first we withdrew over the Eulengebirge to Neurode. It was a great problem crossing the Eulengebirge. I, with my horse-drawn platoon, was quite good at it. From hairpin bend to hairpin bend we rolled on and turned up the Serpentine. Again and again horses had to go back to relieve weaker animals or even to pull motor vehicles that were out of petrol.

These were supposed to be important but, in the end, had to be left behind. The horses were fainting with weakness, not only because of over-exertion but also because we couldn't give them enough to eat. While we were still on the eastern side of the mountains Paul Kuhn brought me the news from the company commander. 'The war is lost'. Armistice on 9 May 1945! For me a whole world fell apart. I went into some nearby bushes, I didn't cry, I bawled in complete bewilderment. Until then I had still believed that, like Hindenburg in 1918, we would be able to march back home in good order. Soon I was taught 'to know better'.

At the moment I was pleased that I was able to keep together most of my platoon, from Steinkirche through Gnadenfrei and Langenbielau to the foot of the Eulengebirge. On the roads through the passes it would no longer be possible to prevent my column becoming split up. With bitterness I had to recognise that, in this situation, the leaders of the two sections of my platoon were taking to their heels, together with the sarge. For me that was desertion, even when the war was over. We had always said we would bring our men back to Germany. But at least the three got home OK, as I found out from the sarge after the war.

But even today I think, full of gratitude, of our company commander, Karl-Heinz Dreiucker, that, as long as it was possible, he stayed with us. Later in Polish captivity he was put to work in a mine and died there. I also think with pleasure of the loyal troop leader Paul Kuhn from Iserlohn. What a pity that he was lost through a mistake. While we were still in Silesia I had ordered him to bring up our field smithies for the horses. But he must have lost his way because, though he was seen along the route of march of another unit, he didn't find his way back to ours. But Listening Unit Schuster (Fritz Schuster + 1 man) joined us. Without being equipped with any vehicle they had been in action until the last day, listening in to enemy telephone conversations at the most forward point of the line. But for this march they had 'organised' a landau with horse, on top of which a goat was sitting!

So we reached Neurode where, following orders, we dropped all the signals equipment we still had into the swimming pool. Then we marched on westwards through Bad Kudowa to Bohemia. Meanwhile the fleeing Silesian civilian population had queued up behind us. Suddenly the word was that the Soviets were 5km behind us, which unleashed panic. Everyone wanted to go on as quickly as possible and thought that in Czech territory they would be safe from the Soviets. But what followed then were atrocities and acts of inhumanity the like of which I, as a soldier, had never seen or experienced.

We crossed the frontier over a little river bridge east of Nachod. On the signs set up there it read: Surrender your weapons voluntarily, we laughed at first, but not for long. In Nachod we had to pass through an anti-tank barrier. In front and behind it Czechs in every possible kind of fantasy uniform, even bits of German uniform and steel helmets were there. They were armed to the teeth. Beside the barrier were even standing two Tiger tanks, manned by Czechs. The weapons evidently came from the previous units that had been disarmed, a process that now we too were not to escape. Even today I am amazed that the company commander's order: 'Make your weapons unusable and only then hand them in', was carried out. I myself still had the courage to smash my binoculars right in front of the eyes of a Czech who wanted to have them, only to find out later that others who had done the same kind of thing had been killed. Following that, my courage too, for such actions, was gone.

Our beaten column, consisting of members of our 31st SS Division, the 100th *Jäger* Division and civilian refugees, had to march along a prescribed route in an endless column through Josefstadt, Smirschitz and Königgrätz to Pardubitz. Again and again searches were made and everything of use was taken from us. In this process I saw how some in the column swallowed rings and watches, something I could never have managed. And time and time again, defenceless as we were, we had to watch how, for no apparent reason, comrades from the Army, too, were picked out of the column, beaten, kicked and killed or shot.

Suddenly a new thing was checking under the arm. They were looking for the tattooed blood group sign of members of the SS. Anyone caught was led away. This had the result of making us get rid of all external emblems. Since I found it dishonouring to take off my epaulettes, I threw away my whole tunic without further ado. It was an officer of the 100th *Jäger* Division who recommended to us to intersperse our unit throughout the column.

For one last time I brought the men of my platoon together and told them, if questioned, to say that they were members of the 100th *Jäger* Division. To help them with that, I told them the most important facts about this Division, e.g. places where it had seen action, important officers, etc. On the march we often saw men who had swastikas painted in oil paint on the upper half of their bodies. They had to carry out various kinds of work and were whipped as they were doing so.

When our column crossed the Elbe bridge at Pardubitz, again and again the Czechs grabbed soldiers out of the column and threw them in the Elbe. Laughing hideously they shouted after the unfortunate men '…eil…itler'. The height from the bridge to the river was about 20m and the Elbe also had a pretty strong current, so that scarcely any of these comrades could have survived. Crossing this bridge I was more afraid than I had ever been in my life.

In Pardubitz we saw the first full Soviet formation, a Stalin Organ battery. The Soviets, mostly drunk, were greeted effusively by the Czechs and threatened us with their fists. Encouraged by this the Czechs then had new tortures ready for us. We, and the Red Cross Sisters too, were beaten with sticks and pokers and not a few had their hair torn out. When the ordeal was over, we could set off on the move again. We arrived west of the town at a 'Disarmament Area', surrounded by all possible kinds of uniformed men, i.e. Czechs and Soviets. Our long march out of Silesia was here at an end.

Next day all ethnic Germans had to report and were led away *en bloc*. Here we parted from our loyal Hungarian German comrades. Then, on this ground, a small miracle took place. A comrade, Ernst, and two Silesian girls attached themselves to me. Especially through the patient pleading of the two girls, we received a pass from a Czech clerk. And what was a very much greater miracle, because the girls had said that they were pregnant and sick, they even gave us a small cart and 2 completely lame nags. This Czech must, in contrast to most of his fellow-countrymen, have had a kind heart. So we were able to leave this area. The pass helped us further and further on, except that we two men, because nothing useful was found on us, had to put up with a lot of mistreatment. As long as we were together, the girls were spared this.

Our next destination was Kolin. On the way, time and time again, we witnessed terrible cruelty that the Czech rabble inflicted on German soldiers and civilians. We were scared sick when once, in the middle of the night, a Soviet column passed us and an officer came up to our cart. He said something we couldn't understand and then went away again. Certainly he thought we were Czechs.

Once arrived in Kolin we underwent the usual ordeal and as bad luck would have it the blood group was discovered on Ernst and me. The two girls and two Austrian medical troops who had attached themselves to us shortly before, were allowed to go on. But the two of us were brought to a kind of police station and in the night were beaten many times with truncheons.

The next morning we were taken away in a jeep. Very soon a halt was called in the middle of a wood. I believed with certainty that the worst awaited us there. So both of us summoned up superhuman courage and cunningly made use of the next opportunity to flee. We certainly began the 10km to the West 'at the double', running into the wood. During the next days we always marched by night, avoiding every path, and going northwards. I found out that actually, you can live off grass and brook water.

After some days we arrived in Seiffen in the Erzgebirge and were overjoyed to be in Germany. We said who we were and were immediately warned not to do that because there were many Germans who would immediately betray us to the Soviets. A BDM Leader helped us on and brought us to a doctor, Dr Gockel, who scraped away our blood group tattoos. For three days we were welcomed on a large estate and well looked after, until one evening a horde of Soviet soldiers appeared and raped all the women, there, before our eyes. It's terrible to be defenceless. We were so anxious to be gone that we set off the very same night on our way from Seiffen.

In Oelsnitz (Erzgebirge) we got a certificate to say that we had arrived there in a hospital train, and I became a lance-corporal of the 100th *Jäger* Division. Holding this certificate we steadily marched into the Harz, where we separated. Outside Nordhausen I was nabbed by the Americans and locked up in Sangerhausen in a school building. During the night you could hear great cries of pain from the cellar. SS men were being 'treated' in the same way as in Czech territory. I was not discovered to be a member of the SS. Later I also found out how those classed as being incriminated politically were tortured. They had to put their hands behind their backs and fall forward, just like a plank, until they hit their face on the floor and were thus badly injured.

One day I was, quite unexpectedly, summoned and was given my certificate of release. Compared to many comrades I had the unbelievable good luck to get away from captivity and to be home quite soon. But in any event it still, even today, seems a miracle to me, that I was able to get out of the Soviet/Czech area at that time.

SS *Panzerjäger Abteilung* 31, on 3 May 1945 was moved from the Hirschberg to the Strehlen area, and set off from there through Glatz in the direction of Königgrätz. It laid down its arms. Since it was suspected that Soviet troops were already in Königgrätz, as they approached the town (or they were already there, the accounts do not give clear times) the column turned carefully westwards. At Neu-Bidschow (Novi Bizdow) it came across Czech insurgents who, with few exceptions, butchered the unarmed men, so thoroughly that from this section of the 31st

SS Volunteer Grenadier Division hardly any (including the *Abteilung* commander, *SS-Sturmbannführer* Landwehr) survived.

One of them, Adam Stoffner, told of the murder:

> We began the retreat towards Königgrätz. I was seriously wounded and being transported on a lorry. Because the Soviets were already in Königgrätz, our section turned west and in Neu-Bidschow came across Czech insurgents who immediately opened fire on our column with rifles and machine guns. When the lorry on which I was being transported had been brought to a halt, one man after another was taken down and immediately shot. When, out of the 40 men in the vehicle 18 had already been killed, a British motorised unit came by. They saved the remaining 12 men, but immediately handed them over as prisoners to the Soviets. Of these 12 men I was the only one to come back from Russia.

SS-Obersturmführer Heinz Sebastian, at the time Adjutant of SS *Panzerjäger Abteilung* 31, confirmed this account of the events in the terrible massacre:

> The route of the *Panzerjäger Abteilung* led from Hirschberg through the Strehlen and Glatz areas in the direction of Königgrätz. On the orders of our commander we laid down our arms and at Neu-Bidschow, unarmed, met Czech partisans, The three staff lorries which were driving at the front, immediately came under their fire, but were able to escape. The first vehicle of the column following us, which evidently similarly escaped direct hits, nevertheless positioned itself diagonally across the road and prevented the other lorries from driving on. The Czechs immediately stormed these vehicles. Despite looking for ten years for former comrades and asking after them, I found no trace of them, so they must have all met their deaths in the bloodbath. The three staff vehicles that had got away also didn't get far. Shortly afterwards, we were once again faced by insurgents and the majority of our personnel were murdered. We couldn't even defend ourselves since we had all laid down our weapons before setting off.

After the war *SS-Sturmbannführer* Landwehr was criticised for having ordered the *Abteilung* to lay down their arms. The circumstances can no longer be clearly established. Apart from the relevant commands from senior authorities, it is known, and is evident from the accounts of other units, that retreating German military columns were only admitted into Czech territory by the insurgents after they had laid down their arms. That was obviously the case with the *Panzerjäger Abteilung*. The fact is that the *Panzerjäger Abteilung* column recognised the danger at Königgrätz and tried to avoid this area. It still had enough petrol, the shortage of which was disastrous for many units, to carry out these moves. That speaks for the careful precautions and perceptive leadership of *SS-Sturmbannführer* Landwehr.

Medical Company 31 withdrew from Frankenstein on 8 May 1945 in the direction of Glatz–Bad Kudowa. Even in this area they were prevented from marching on by a Soviet armoured unit, upon which the company dispersed in the Heuscheuer Gebirge. Many members of the company were classed as missing from that time, but some managed to break through. Among them was *SS-Rottenführer* Ernst Bennert, to whom we owe the following account. He immediately slipped through northwards to Reich German territory and in that way escaped Soviet captivity.

The order to surrender reached us at our main dressing station, in the convent hospital in Frankenstein, on 8 May. No panic broke out, the troops remained disciplined, and prepared for the march early next morning towards Glatz. The company marched on foot or on horse-drawn vehicles, some of which were still from the Batschka. A single lorry carried the orderly room. Glatz was reached in the evening. It was as quiet as if it was completely at peace. We stopped at an estate. During the night, two comrades suggested to me that we should 'scarper' since it was all over. I said 'no'.

In the middle of the night there was an alarm. We had to move off quickly, towards Bad Kudowa. Our retreat, at first disciplined, was beginning more and more to turn into hopeless flight. In the morning, as a bright sunny day dawned, we reached Kudowa and wanted to go on in the direction of Trautenau. Suddenly we spotted that the exit from the valley in which we were marching was blocked by about 12 Soviet T-34s. All stop! What now? A comrade from Hungary grabbed a *Panzerfaust* and wanted to knock out another T-34. I was able to dissuade him from this by saying that if the Soviets had opened fire they could have created a bloodbath. Our column was mixed with civilians. So now the company was dissolved, and the members of the company dispersed in all directions, into the deeply fissured rocks of the Heuscheuer Gebirge.

I similarly disappeared into the woods with my comrade Steiner from Heidelberg. We stalked along a road and scouted out the situation. We spotted armed Czechs. Later another five comrades from the company joined us and we held a council of war. My view was that a march to the west, to the Czechs, was too dangerous, and I suggested going north. I also recommended proceeding very carefully, always scouting out the situation, making sure and then marching by night. In no way, should we act impetuously. In this way we, seven men, armed and with rations, had a good chance of getting through. The five comrades were unfortunately too impatient and made off during the night. The worst thing was that they took our rations with them. Luckily I had vitamin tablets on me with which we two could stay alive.

For several days we remained hidden in the woods. From the south we heard the sound of heavy fighting. One day we were able to get in contact with a farmer who brought us something to eat and also a very detailed walking map. Thus we were able to continue with more certainty on our way north-north-westwards. At Ullersdorf, south of Liebau, we reached German Reich territory and stopped at a farm. There we found out that there were Soviets in the village, so we marched on and got into the Riesengebirge. We were also able to march, unobserved, by day. The Soviets didn't have the confidence to go into the woods, where it was suspected that there were still German soldiers. In fact, there we met scattered Estonian SS men who were still carrying on a mini-war, on their own!

Soon we reached the vicinity of Ketschdorf am Bober, where we had once been quartered. From a secure hiding place we saw a road with a lot of traffic, and in the Rosenbaude a Soviet headquarters or something similar. All of a sudden two Soviets were facing us. We were very shocked, and they were too, they had their machine-pistols on their backs, while we had ours at the ready. They ran away like rabbits! Stupidly we than ran into a patch of woodland that had a diameter of about 50m, and around us were Soviets. There we waited out the night and marched on. It's well known that at night all cats are grey! That was how we ended up on a Soviet military airfield. Surviving even that, safe and sound, we arrived in Ketschdorf to find it was full of Soviet horses. It was impossible to reach the people we knew, so in the streaming rain we slipped back into the woods.

Next day we came to a weekend home, where the lady of the house gave us somewhere to stay, and food. We recuperated there for eight whole days. We also got civilian clothes and took off our uniforms, from which we had earlier removed the badges of seniority. We also 'deposited' our machine-pistols. The woman was a great fortune-teller and laid out her cards for us. For me she saw no problems coming, but when it was Steiner's turn she burst into tears and warned him to be very careful. At the time we laughed about it, but whatever you might say, Steiner never arrived in Heidelberg and was posted missing.

After a week we marched on. In the Riesengebirge we were guided further by foresters. We passed the Teichmannsbaude, Robert Ley's last headquarters, then the Kochelfallbaude that I knew from earlier, and past the Goldene Aussicht Warmbrunn. Upstairs was a tourist café where we got turnip soup – and had to pay for it too. Since I wanted to get to Stettin my hometown, and Steiner on the other hand to Heidelberg, here we parted.

Further on in my journey, I helped out for a few days with a farmer, then with a miller. Then the Poles came and drove out the German population who lived there. With a column of these people who had been driven out I reached the area west of Lauban. There the Poles directed the column into a field and robbed the refugees even of their last goods and chattels, as they only let them carry on with 20kg of baggage. With a scythe over my shoulder and a whetstone at my belt, I arrived at the Neisse at Görlitz. I swam across, and marched on towards Muskau, Cottbus, etc.

In the villages, 'Antifa' (Anti-Fascist) people had talked themselves up into mayors. They, of course, sent me out of the villages. On a farm at Briesen on the Berlin–Frankfurt/Oder *autobahn* I spent a longer time, until at the end of July, the district began to crawl with NKVD because Stalin was expected at the Potsdam Conference. I took up my pack again and reached Blumental, *Kreis* Uckermunde, where an uncle of mine was a forester. In the meantime, Stettin was occupied by the Poles. My parents found refuge in Glücksburg.

With 50% common sense and 50% luck, I had succeeded, until then, in avoiding captivity. It was 1946, Good Friday, when I was denounced in Berlin and arrested by the British. After being in various camps and prisons, I was shipped to England, where I was only released in December 1948.

While a greater many members of the Division managed to break through north-north-westwards to Silesia or Saxony, most of them ended up as prisoners of the Soviets. A very few managed to get diagonally through Czech territory into the Pilsen area originally expected to be held by the Americans. One of them was *SS-Obersturmführer* Zvonimir Bernwald, battalion commander of the Hungarian SS Fusilier Battalion 31:

> Shortly before the war ended, about 5 to 7 May I was ordered from my battalion to the rear, in order, as quartermaster, to look for possible quarters. Since I didn't return to the Hungarian battalion, I in fact know nothing of what happened to it afterwards. The order to retreat reached me in Nimptsch. It was left open to us to break through, in groups or alone, to the Yanks. In Kamenz, in fact, we

dispersed, and I decided to make my way alone. I reached the town of Braunau on foot, where I came across Soviets for the first time. I went on, through Bad Kudowa to Josefstadt. There I found out in the post office that, from midnight on 8 May the weapons on all fronts had been silent. I heard that the Americans were supposed to be in Hohenelbe, so I marched off in that direction. On the way, some Dutchmen joined me, and we went on together.

The Czechs were raging round us with terrible brutality. My only good fortune was that I could speak perfect Croatian and good Russians, so that I could make myself understood to them. They were also unsure about the Dutchmen, evidently they didn't really know who and what they were. In Hohenelbe I met the former pastor of Slavonisch-Brod, my home village. He explained to me that some Yanks had in fact been there in Hohenelbe, but had only briefly landed in an aircraft and then flown back again. So, some Job's comfort! I now had to try to reach the Pilsen area.

Under fantastic adventurous conditions I made my way with effort through to Prague, where traces of the Czech mania for terror were still quite fresh. Everywhere, on the lamp-posts, Germans were hanging, terribly mutilated. Until just before Pilsen I travelled by train. Getting off there I made my way on foot as far as Cham, where I could cross the frontier. At the end of June I became a prisoner of war of the Americans, and was sent into the Regensburg camp. So my adventurous, but in the end successful flight, through Czech territory, lasted about six weeks.

The former IVa of the Division, *SS-Obersturmbannführer* Karl von Turck, also had an adventurous flight. In December 1944 he was ordered from the 31st SS Division and appointed as *Standartenführer* and Commander of the Cavalry School in Prague. He also deserves a mention here. He left Prague in time, accompanied by his Adjutant and Orderly Officer, in the direction of Budweis. Von Türck, even then, at a time when everyone was trying to get rid of their uniforms, especially those of the SS, was immaculately dressed, as he had been all his life. Naturally he was wearing his long riding boots, which made running sheer hell for him.

At Budweis the three were captured by Czech insurgents. The complete elegance of von Türck, and the high decorations of the others, certainly made an impression. They were not killed straight away, but locked up, half-undressed, on the first floor of a school to await the proper execution that had been promised them. The building was being guarded by a solitary Czech. They thought up a vague plan to escape. After it had gone dark the orderly officer jumped out of the window on to the neck of the Czech sentry who in this way was eliminated. He was undressed, the orderly offer put on the 'partisan costume' and then escorted the two others, the 'evil fascists', in the direction of Krumau. Here von Türck met a former comrade officer from the Austrian uhlans, a Count, who could get them civilian clothes in which they were finally able to cross the border. Despite, or perhaps because of, his considerable rashness he had an incredible run of luck!

From SS Volunteer Grenadier Regiment 78, from SS Fusilier Battalion 31 and from the Supply Regiment there are no individual accounts, but these units, too, ended in the same way and under the same circumstances as are very strikingly illustrated by the above descriptions.

In its great death in Czech territory, in the first days of peace, there comes to an end the history of the 31st SS Voluntary Grenadier Division, the last contingent of the Danube Swabians. Far from their homeland from which they had marched out to defend, their fate, and the fate of their Reich German, South Tyrolean, Hungarian and other European comrades they reached its fulfilment. Their living and dying, their sacrifice, are at the same time a warning and an obligation.

> There, where the last graves in the world
> Bear witness to death and to deeds,
> The monument is set up for you,
> Comrade!
>
> There breaks out of darkness, out of death and destruction,
> Above disaster, above dying,
> Your light, comrade.
>
> There, where the last graves of deeds
> Arch up in the light,
> There grows your life, comrade:
> To be an heir!
>
> There grows from the graves, there grows from the craters,
> There grows from the horror of a thousand faces
> Your duty, comrade!

(Hans Jürgen Nier)

CHAPTER 18

What Became of Them?

To ask what became of people is, it is true, a question always related to individuals, but what became of German soldiers after the Second World War has a more common basis. Moreover, what became of former members of the Waffen-SS is characterised by the fact that they were branded as criminals - the Waffen-SS was declared a criminal organisation by the Nuremberg Tribunal.

Because of this the former members of the 31st SS Volunteer Grenadier Division met a particularly harsh fate. For most of those who were able to escape Czech brutality, there began for the most part a year-long *via Dolorosa*, as prisoners of war of the Soviets. Many of them died, while they were still behind the barbed wire, and are buried in mass graves or camp cemeteries. Although many of the youngest and oldest members, who could not work well, were released relatively early, the overwhelming majority only saw their homeland again after 8 to 11 years.

One of the very last members of the Division to be released was *SS-Rottenführer* Fritz Schuster, who only saw German soil again in 1956:

> Taken prisoner in mid-May 1945 at Kostomlati near Aussig, I then got the opportunity of getting to know large parts of the giant Soviet empire. Because of my activity as commander of a listening unit in SS *Nachrichten Abteilung* 31, during the last days of the war, I was accused by the Soviets of 'espionage', for which I was to be hanged in 1946. I escaped this sentence by an adventurous attempted escape from the Altai Mountains. I went right through three prohibited districts as far as Sverdlovsk in the Urals, where I was captured and terribly beaten. Then I was taken back into my camp where an entire garrison finished the job. There was hardly a part of my body in one piece. I was unconscious for three days and couldn't move for a year. But this saved my life. The death penalty was rescinded in May 1947. But I was still only released in January 1956, considered as 70% seriously war disabled. That was after just eleven years as a prisoner of war.

After their return home there then began a raw struggle to earn a living, both for the Reich Germans and the ethnic Germans. Things were even harder for the latter because, like the Germans from the areas in the East, now under Polish, Czech and Soviet rule, they too were robbed of their homeland. The ethnic Germans from the Yugoslavian Batschka were murdered, *en masse*, in death camps. Those from Rumanian Transylvania and the Banat were dispossessed and banished for years to the Baragan steppes. Those from Hungary were dispossessed, some of them driven out, some left in the country, but interned and put under political surveillance. The South Tyroleans were stripped of political rights and persecuted. Despite all that, those who were driven out, those who remained and the Reich Germans, set about with all their power rebuilding their own lives and their homeland. Thanks to their hard work and decency, after a time, their private lives and

221

their country began to improve. They, who suffered the war in all its harshness, could have no more ardent wish, than for a just peace among their peoples.

As Soviet prisoners of war

The following account came from a simple ethnic German SS man, A.Gl. who loyally did his duty in the 31st SS Volunteer Grenadier Division from the first minute to the last. His fate was the fate of thousands of Hungarian Germans and can here be taken as being representative of them all.

> At the end of June 1945 we were transported away from the Breslau-Hundsfeld camp in the direction of Russia. There were 32 of us in the cattle wagon. We hardly got anything to eat, but what was a lot worse was the heat. We had only very little water, so that when it was raining we held out a spoon from the wagon ventilator to drink the water we caught in this way.
>
> At first we had to work in Kovel, unloading wagons. In November 1945 we travelled homewards. We were hoping soon to return home, as the Soviets had also promised us. But then things turned out differently. Hungary didn't want to have us and sent us back! So the SS members in Mármarossziget were sorted out again and taken into the Carpathian Mountains for tree-felling work.
>
> We were forbidden to write letters home. A comrade, a Swabian from Temeschwar, established contact with a Rumanian and he smuggled out a letter in which we, all fellow-countrymen from W., had written our names in order to give an indication that we were still alive. The letter arrived in W. and the women and mothers replied. Suddenly, one day 18 letters arrived in the camp, the next day 60. But the Soviets then got wind of the letter smuggling, caught the Rumanian, and beat him up badly. We were very sorry for the man.
>
> We three men, Franz Hauser, the Swabian from Temeschwar and I, decided to escape. Only a few days before we had planned to do it, we were loaded up into wagons and transported to Focsani. Then we arrived in the port town of Constanza where we were put on a ship and taken across the Black Sea to Batumi. We got to Tiflis, where we were split up into different camps. I went to Rustavi, 40km from Tiflis. 18,000 prisoners built an entire town there. In Tiflis we were with our former commander, *Brigadeführer* Lombard. He pretended to be *Major* Mueller. Of course we recognised him, but none of us gave him away. As I heard later, however, an officer betrayed him to the Soviets. He was put on trial in the place where he had had his command, although the Soviet inhabitants all spoke up for him, because they were best off under his command.
>
> In 1948 the Reich Germans were released from Rustavi. We ethnic Germans from Hungary and Yugoslavia remained. Shortly after this a transport was assembled in which I was, and a Jewish major spoke to us. He said we would also be released and were going to Germany. In fact we went as far as Brest-Litovsk. But here we changed wagons and were transported to Minsk.
>
> In Minsk we went, not into the big camp, but into a separate smaller one. From time to time Soviet girls came, the guards even let them into the camp on Sundays. One Sunday an officer came across the girls in the camp, whereupon we were immediately transferred into the big prison camp. Here there were some 4,000 prisoners, including 23 generals and many members of the 'Totenkopf' 'Wiking' Divisions, all sentenced to 25 years' penal servitude.

Some 90 women were also in the camp, mostly from the Rumanian and the Yugoslavian Banat. They were civilians who had been deported.

For a while we worked in Minsk on construction work, then we were loaded up one day and transported to Voronezh. But we were only another month there until, in 1950, we were released, by the Soviets, to Hungary. When we arrived in Budapest we were put in a prison, the so-called remand house. Now it wasn't the Soviets, but the Hungarian authorities of Rákosi's 'People's Republic', who directed us into the hard labour camp at Tiszalok on the Theiss. Others went into similar camps in Kazinbarcika or Debrecen.

In Tiszalök we worked on the big dam and the power station. 'Achievements of the workers of the People's Democracy', in actual fact, it was a feat of construction by Hungarian Germans! We weren't allowed to write any letters, only to receive them, that is if, in the first place, our nearest and dearest knew where we were, the returnees from Russia! Conditions in Tiszalök were worse than in most Soviet camps. In the first two years we spent there, we only got beetroot, nothing but beetroot. On the other hand, in the third year we only got beans, every day! The guards treated us like criminals, and talked to us like criminals, too.

One day I was asked where I wanted to settle down. In Germany, I replied. You can't do that, was the answer. Then in my home village. You can't do that either, was the reply. I lost my temper: 'Here, then!' Then I was beaten. I wanted to move to Germany because I believed that my family was there. Finally I heard from my father and found out that the family was still at home.

At last on 18 September 1953 I was released to go home! In November, that was shortly after my release, mutiny broke out in the Tiszalök camp. Those who wanted to move to Germany, and were kept inside because of this, instituted a hunger strike, withheld their labour and barricaded themselves in their barracks. The guards could only regain control of the situation by armed force. There were several men killed (Author's note: 5 – and their names were: Georg Gazafy, Matthias Geistlinger, Josef Schulz, Hans Tangl and Josef Wildhofer). There were also a number of wounded. But the resistance had not been in vain. Within 10-15 days they were all released to go home.

Now at last I was physically free, but not, by a long way, a free man. I wasn't allowed back to my home village, since it was in the so-called border zone. At first I had to report to the police station in the town of Baja. 'Hearty' welcome, foul-mouthed cursing, yelling at the 'war criminal'. Within 48 hours I was to report my permanent address! But how could I know who would give me accommodation, as I was not allowed into my village and I did not know anyone in Baja! It was the commandant's female secretary who took pity on me and called me back. Now I was allowed to visit my village and I had four days to find lodgings in Baja. Finally I did find some, with a great-aunt. I was also able to get work, odd jobs as a casual labourer. I have no profession. I'm only a farmer. Often I also did a bit of 'black' work in the village I wasn't allowed to visit. Occasionally I found work there, at harvest and suchlike.

I was 'of course' under strict police surveillance. A curfew was imposed on me. I had to be in the house between 8pm and 5am, and this too was checked often enough. On Sundays I had to report to the police. All that lasted another three years and only in October 1956, when the revolution broke out, did they

stop it. Only after that did I at last become free and, 12 years after joining the
31st SS Volunteer Grenadier Division, went home to my home village.

The life story of *SS-Brigadeführer* Gustav Lombard

Gustav Lombard was born on 10 April 1895 in Kleinspiegelberg, *Kreis* Satzig, in
the Uckermark. His father was lord of the manor. The ancestors of the family were
Huguenots who, fleeing religious persecution in France, found a new home in
Prussia. He was educated at the college in Niesky/Oberlausitz. In 1913, following
the instructions in the will of his father, who had died early, he travelled to the
United States to maintain contact with relatives living there. He writes in his cur-
riculum vitae:

> There I first attended the Agricultural High School in Missouri, from which I
> also received a basic military training. The outbreak of war kept me there and as
> a result of my propaganda activity in the German-American clubs was interned
> as a 'troublesome foreigner'. When in 1919 I was able to go to Amexco in
> Koblenz, I immediately seized my chance and returned to Germany. I worked
> in automobile construction and by 1931 was in a managerial position at the
> Chrysler car factory. Since then I have been an independent businessman. Since
> 1932 I have been the leaseholder of one of the large garages in Berlin. I am also
> chairman of the Reich Association of Garage Owners of Germany and chair-
> man of the specialist Transport Committee in the Berlin Chamber of Industry
> and Trade.

In May 1933 Lombard was accepted into the SS, and with his entry into the
Berlin *SS-Reitersturm* – the 1st *Sturm* of the 7th *Reiterstandarte*, the so-called 'Dip-
lomatic *Reitersturm*' – his career as a soldier began. On 15 September 1935 he became section leader with the service rank of an *SS-Untersturmführer* and
commanded the special sections on the occasions of the state visits of Mussolini, of
Prince Regent Paul of Yugoslavia and of the Reich Administrator Horthy. After exercises with the reserves in Cavalry Regiment 4 and in 'Reiter 9' and after completing a Reserve Officer course in the Senne camp, on 13 September 1936, he was
promoted to *SS-Obersturmführer* and appointed commander of his 1st SS
Reitersturm Berlin. In the same post, on 11 September 1936, he was promoted to
SS-Hauptsturmführer.

After three and a half years, on 1 March 1940 he entered the *SS-Totenkopf-
Reiterstandarte*, and shortly afterwards entered the SS reserve troops remaining at
disposal, where he was charged with forming a 'mounted *Abteilung*' in one of the
two planned cavalry regiments. From 18 March 1940, he was *Abteilung* Commander in SS Cavalry Regiment 1. After a quiet year of building up the unit, at the
beginning of the Soviet campaign he went into action with his section in the
Lomscha area. On 21 June 1941 he was promoted to *SS-Sturmbannführer* and was
now involved in forming the SS Cavalry Brigade. On 5 August 1941 he was given
command of SS Cavalry Regiment 1, and soon also confirmed as its commander.
At the head of this regiment Lombard proved himself against a Soviet Cavalry Division which had broken through and later, under the command of an Army Infantry Division, at Selisharewo on the Volga. In the first winter battle in the arc round

Rzhev the SS Cavalry Brigade achieved dazzling success in defence and won high-level recognition of its achievements.

On 16 March 1942 Lombard was promoted to *SS-Obersturmbannführer*, with seniority of rank from 1 March. In May 1942 he was decorated with the German Cross in Gold. Under *Brigadeführer* Wilhelm Bittrich in Summer 1942 there took place the formation of the SS Cavalry Division, which with Army Group Centre, from Autumn 1942 chalked up outstanding successes both in attack and in defence. Here Lombard's cavalry regiment, far out in front of the Division, left to its own devices, on the sole initiative of the commander barred the way to a very dangerous Soviet breakthrough. Medvedevo and Knasche to the south-east of Toropez were the places which remain unforgettable to every man of Cavalry Regiment Lombard, because they became symbols of how a soldier should do his duty and how he should die bravely. But through this battle the XXXXI *Panzerkorps*, under the command of which the SS Cavalry Division was, succeeded in destroying six Soviet divisions. Lombard, on 30 January 1943 promoted to *SS-Standartenführer*, on 10 March 1943 received for his decisive action on his own on-the-spot initiative the Knight's Cross of the Iron Cross.

Here, a section from his own memoirs should be inserted to give a clearer idea too of him as a man:

> … Shortly before midnight a Soviet counter-attack with the reinforcements already assembled… and the poor terrified pioneers took to their heels, the company commander after them, wanted to catch them up, stop them. Thus it happened that he was swept along with them. Model demanded a court-martial 'for cowardice in the face of the enemy'. Bittrich tried to talk him out of it. In vain! Even the familiar words were heard 'we need a death-sentence to discourage the others'. But 'Lombard could be put in as an observer, which would certainly have a calming effect'. That is what happened. But I wrote a letter to Hitler, asked him to reprieve the company commander. I wrote that I had been brought up in my parents' house to consider the circumstances in considering guilt. It took getting on for six weeks. The death sentence was rescinded. He was reduced to the rank of *Oberfeldwebel*, and transferred to a pioneer battalion with Army Group South. While a prisoner I got to know the *Oberleutnant's* brother, I heard from him that his brother had been killed in action, as a *Hauptmann*, a fortnight before the war ended.

Towards the end of the second winter, the SS Cavalry Division was sent into action in the Pripet Marshes against a 'partisan corps' which was led by a Soviet general who is still well-known today. Afterwards the Division, and hence Lombard also with his regiment, joined the 8th Army, south of Kharkhov. Heavy defensive fighting and eventually the withdrawal of Army Group South on to the western bank of the Dnieper characterised this period.

After two and a half years on the Eastern Front, Lombard then received a different mission. From October to 28 December 1943 he replaced *Brigadeführer* Hansen, while he was ill, in his post as commander of the 1st Italian Volunteer Assault Brigade, *Milizia Armata*. Ordered on 28 December 1943 to the Command Staff *Reichsführer-SS*, he soon returned again to the Eastern Front. On 15 January 1944 he was ordered to 'Stossgruppe (shock group) *SS-Obergruppenführer* von dem

Bach-Zelewsky', which was responsible for defending the traffic junction of Kovel, endangered by the Soviets' advance and declared a *Fester Platz*.

He became Chief of Staff of *Kampfgruppe* Kovel, was still able to reach the town on the highway and very judiciously organised the defence by the weak forces that were available. After Kovel was encircled by the Soviets, at the end of February the newly-appointed commander, *SS-Gruppenführer* Herbert Gille, was flown in. *Fester Platz* Kowel held out until it was relieved at the beginning of April by General von Saucken's 4th *Panzer* Division. In the meantime, on 12 March 1944, Lombard was promoted to *SS-Oberführer* and taken into the active service of the Waffen-SS. After the relief of Kovel he came back to the 8th SS Cavalry Division.

From 14 July to 23 August 1944 Lombard was ordered to Hirschberg in the Riesengebirge for the 12th Divisional Commanders' Course. He was there on 20 July when the assassination attempt on the Führer took place. As a consequence of the attempt, many senior officers, on whom there fell only the slightest suspicion of being connected with the conspirators, were arrested. This happened to General Staff Colonel Count Kielmannsegg. Lombard, who had known the irreproachable soldier Kielmannsegg well, set all the wheels in motion to have him released. After intervening personally with Himmler he went to the Head of the Gestapo, Müller, to exercise direct influence on him. After a long period of persuasion, Müller finally condescended to grant Lombard's requests and released Kielmannsegg. "There are five more officers under arrest who have laid themselves open to suspicion", Müller said to Lombard, "you can take them with you". In the course of these releases, even *Generalmajor* Heusinger, who was among the group, was released.

After the Second World War, Count Kielmannsegg became a general in the Bundeswehr and Supreme Commander of the land forces of Nato 'Europe Centre'. Adolf Heusinger became Chairman of the Nato Strategic Planning Staff.

After he had completed the course, it was planned for Lombard to become commander of the Waffen-SS Cavalry School that was in the process of being formed. But he felt the urge to go to the front. Again to quote from his own words:

> …But I rebelled against this, even with Himmler. There's nothing that can be done about it now, I was told. 'Personally signed by the Führer!' Eventually I asked General Burgdorf to understand my objections and he helped me to face the others with a fait accompli. Only one hour later his agreement was secured for the man I suggested who would replace me. Hitler had certainly never come across anything like that, and if he had, it would certainly have not mattered to him.

So, on 23 August 1944 he was given command of the 6th SS *Gebirgs* Division 'Nord', but he was never to take up this post, because by 1 September this order had been cancelled. Shortly before the end of September, he was nominated as commander of the 31st SS Volunteer Grenadier Division that was to be formed. It was a command which, in the battles on the Danube and in Silesia, he held right up to the bitter end. For the manner in which he stabilised the situation, for his energy in the crisis of Reich Administrator Horthy's attempt to break with Germany on 15 October 1944, as well as for his action in evacuating the Batschka, the Supreme Commander of the Hungarian *Honvéd* awarded him a high Hungarian decoration. He was informed of this decision by telegram in April 1945.

On 1 April 1945 he was promoted to *SS-Brigadeführer* and *Generalmajor* of the Waffen-SS. Like the majority of his soldiers, Lombard also became a Soviet prisoner of war and for over 10 years found himself in various Soviet camps. How he, in disguise, became a prisoner, was described in the previous chapter, but his experiences as a prisoner are now told on the basis of his own recollections.

In the Görlitz collection point, set up in the grammar school, I was so strictly guarded that it was impossible to establish contact with the outside world. They revealed to us that we would soon be transported away to the Soviet Union, to 'rebuild again the country we had destroyed'.

I recall particularly two meetings, one with *Generalmajor* Schury, the commander of the 100th *Jäger* Division, passed off without problems. The other, with a young SS man, could have had serious consequences. When he saw me, he stood to attention and stammered 'Heil Hitler, *Brigadeführer*!' 'You're making a mistake, dear fellow, my name is Mueller and I'm a *Major* in the reserve'. We exchanged winks, he had understood and quietly went on his way.

Surprisingly, my batman, Helmut Bartel, also turned up. To my delight the German doctors succeeded in getting him released early on the grounds that he was completely unfit. My escort officer, Achim Rähmel, who survived not too badly the march on foot to Görlitz, despite having his ribs broken in Czech territory, was transported away with other comrades. Now it was only the driver that was still missing, but I only saw him again after my return home to Munich in 1955. [Author's note: Rähmel also survived, he died in 1995 in Berlin].

Weeks later I was transported away to Hoyerswerda. Thousands of prisoners there were guarded by the NKVD. Then came the day that was to lead 100 of us into an uncertain fate in the Soviet Union. Next to me in the wagon was the Catholic chaplain of the 17th Infantry Division, the Division that had been our last neighbour. I was lucky. Beside me was a ventilator through which you could look out. In Upper Silesia the train stopped on an open stretch of line and I saw a roebuck, undisturbed. With my left hand I drew the chaplain to me, I lifted my right hand in an oath, and said: 'Reverend Father, hear me. Blessed Hubertus, if you bring me back again to Germany, then I shall never again pull the trigger on deer, roebuck or wild boar'. I have kept the oath, too". [Author's note: In fact, Lombard was invited to go bear hunting in Canada, where his grandson was serving as a naval officer, and did indeed go, but not on the hunt].

At the end of October we were at the destination of our endless journey. We were in the Caucasus. High up in the mountains we were received into the Kudaish camp. It was a punishment camp for Waffen-SS and the Division 'Grossdeutschland' – so it was said. Mind you, a correct German camp leadership presented itself to us, the newcomers. Of course, under pressure, an 'Antifa' Group of a few opportunists had been formed, but the majority of all inmates remained soldiers in bearing and in spirit. As one of the older men, fairly unfit to work, I was given the job of sentry, under the supervision of a NKVD man. One day I was ordered to the 'boss'. Because I couldn't answer the questions put to me in Russian, I was hit on the head with a rifle butt. That was in December 1946. As I later found out, they already knew who I was and the blow with the rifle butt was a first warning.

Soon afterwards I was moved to Tiflis. There began interrogations for hours on end, by day and by night. Everything was swimming round me, but I remained 'Mueller'. When the interrogations were over, I was moved from the barrack block into a dog kennel. It was wide enough, but only breast-high. There I lived for several weeks, until I was taken away and brought into the town to the NKVD headquarters. At a long table sat 5 NKVD officers. One asked, 'How are you, Lombard?' I didn't answer. I remained Mueller. Whereupon the door was opened and a German General Staff officer, who knew me from before, acknowledged to the relevant question that I was really Lombard. So now they knew who I was. Then they took me back to the camp, but not into the dog kennel again, but into a barrack block in which some 20 Hungarian officers were quartered. They were all wearing their uniform, but things were no better for them than for us Germans.

Days later I was taken away and brought to the NKVD chief of the region. He greeted me and asked me to sit down. We both thoroughly scrutinised each other. First he wanted to know whether there had been *Wachtmeister* in the Wehrmacht who hadn't been police officials. I was able to explain to him that the sergeants in the cavalry and the artillery were actually called *Wachtmeister*. The result was that some days later a *Wachtmeister* came to me and informed me that proceedings had been begun against him.

With his second question he wanted to know the reason for my disguising myself. I told him 'the obvious reasons'. Without going into this any further, he explained to me that anyone from General Staff, major upwards, was under suspicion of being a war criminal. They had already known for a long time who I was, and also that in Autumn 1941 a Lombard had been sent by *Feldmarschall* von Kluge to Hitler with the request not to use any troops from the Army and Waffen-SS for police actions. The man was in fact me, but I had made the case to *Obergruppenführer* Jüttner, not to Hitler. 'You will now be tried, but not here, but in Mosyr in the Pripet Marshes, where the atrocities were carried out'. I nodded my agreement. The four-star general asked 'Is there anything else you want? Ask if there is anything else you want to know!' I pointed to the wall, where three magnificent sets of antlers were hanging. 'Where did you shoot those?'

Some three weeks later I was transported away to a camp near Mosyr, the town where my 'atrocities' took place. The prosecuting attorney expected from me written statements, as to where and in what capacity I was active in Mosyr. My interpreter expressed what good luck I had, namely that the supreme commander in the Caucasus did not know how a German general was to be treated – 'namely, a quick trial right where he is captured!'

One day I was taken out, dressed in civilian clothes, and had to go in to a room in which nine men, dressed like me, were already gathered. The ten of us had to stand in a line. Then a woman was brought in. She scrutinised each of the ten. When she stood in front of me she gave a start. She had recognised me, and said that I was the commander of the Germans who had been in her village an entire week. She added excitedly: 'Never in the entire war were things so good for us in the village!' I didn't turn a hair, the score was 1:0 for me. Then a man came in and, beaming, cried 'the General!' As to his answer to my question where and when he came across me in the war, I had to 'report' that at that time I was not yet even a colonel, never mind a general.

But nevertheless, a little later, on the basis of the notorious order from Stalin, I was sentenced in a quick trial, without any testimonies from witnesses, to 25 years' punishment camp. When I asked why, the judge lectured me: 'Stalin has ordered that every general who did not refuse to obey Hitler in 1941 is a war criminal'.

In the middle of January 1948 I was transported to a camp to the south-east of Moscow. In it there were Soviets sentenced on political grounds. For instance, there were those such as Boris Simonowitsch, Lenin's chief interpreter in Switzerland, a Polish Jew from Bialystok and from his youth a convinced communist, together with Estonian, Latvian and Lithuanian senior officials.

In this camp I associated with Polish clergy for whom, as commander of *Fester Platz* Kovel in the winter of 1943/44, I had made it possible to get out to the West. The later Cardinal Slepoi was also one of them. He sent me his best wishes again from Rome at the beginning of the Sixties.

In October 1949 I suddenly had to be admitted to the hospital with facial paralysis and bad headaches. Only gradually did my condition improve. Shortly afterwards I was moved to another camp where conditions were very bad. I was put to heavy hauling work and suffered a hernia. In February 1950 I was operated on in the hospital. Afterwards my condition deteriorated rapidly. The surgeon had himself been sentenced to 25 years' punishment camp for 'collaborating with the Germans'. During the operation, against his better judgement, he had to follow the instructions of the NKVD medical staff! I was dying! One morning an NKVD general threw open the door to ask how I was. Half an hour later I was operated on again, this time under general anaesthetic. Two weeks later I was certified as healthy. But this was not quite true. I had constant trouble until I returned home in 1955, but I then trusted my own staying power more than the Soviet medics. In 1956 I went for treatment in Munich. Afterwards the surgeon, a well-known authority, said that he 'would never have touched it if he had seen in advance how things looked in my belly'.

A little later I was transported away again and brought together once more with German prisoners of war, after two and a half years. Then I was transported to Stalingrad, later to the Asbest camp. From then on things for me were the same as they were for all other German soldiers who fell into Soviet hands at the end of the war.

Lombard, like all captured generals, was only on 10 October 1955 allowed to return home from the Woikowo camp. Until his retirement he ran his own agency for Allianz insurance in Munich, in which he was very successful. He was distinguished every year as the best Allianz representative.

To his one-time comrades Lombard always remained true. He remained to the last a loyal member of the Munich local association of the HIAG and the Cavalry Divisions' Veterans' Association, attending every meeting. Nor did the Danube Swabians forget the time when he came to the rescue in evacuating the Batschka. The General, already an old man, replied to their vote of thanks in these words:

> I saw it as my duty as a man, to help my German fellow-countrymen in the Batschka. I also had in my mind my own time of internment in 1917 and 1918 in the United States.

Gustav Lombard reached a blessed old age. He died on 18 September 1992 in his 98th year, shortly after the death of his beloved wife, a famous opera singer. With him the senior member of the Waffen-SS in Munich was borne to the grave. Rider, hunter and soldier – these were in him the three manifestations of a great power, of a freshly daring, enthusiastic and natural man. He was once called a fearless, impeccable rider. He was not only that, he was also an exemplary officer, concerned for the welfare of his soldiers. He was a man who proved his worth in war, in times of need, and in the post-war years, a man eager to help.

His last wish was that at his funeral his admirers, instead of spending money on wreaths and flowers, should make donations to the 'Paul Hausser' social work scheme.

The youngest in the Division

The youngest soldiers of the 31st SS Volunteer Grenadier Division deserve remembrance in a special chapter. At fifteen and sixteen years old, they were imbued only by the intention, in their love for their homeland, to throw what was most precious to them, their young lives, against the advancing enemy.

There were forty of them. They came from the large German Batschka community of Tscherwenka and formed their own 'youth platoon'. They were treated particularly gently and found a home in SS Volunteer Artillery Regiment 31. The following account came from one of them, Rev. Dr Roland Vetter, and was published in the local newspaper *Unser Tscherwenka*:

> Our home parish of Tscherwenka was involved more than average in the three SS advertising campaigns. On 4 October 1944 another, fourth recruiting campaign took place. The local commandant called upon the fifteen and sixteen year old lads of the town and some forty responded. In that way, without call-up and medical examination, they became the last contingent from Tscherwenka.
>
> Whenever in history army commanders mobilised old men and children, the greatest danger was imminent, since for the most part these operations perished without success. Neither Napoleon's Hundred Days' Army, with its old men and children, nor Hitler's *Volkssturm* and Hitler Youth, were able to turn round the fortunes of war. So, too, the little group of lads from Tscherwenka was not in a position to save their beloved homeland. It was not some idea, nor was it excessive nationalism that gave them the impulse to make the effort. Nevertheless, they tried, by making the ultimate sacrifice, the sacrifice of themselves, purely for love of their homeland.
>
> Even if their sacrifice might have been 'senseless', love is never endowed with too much sense, nor is love of homeland. It is part of love's essence to be and to exist beyond logical categories of thought. Nor must love necessarily be unreasonable. It simply exists in a state beyond reason, as it does beyond unreason. So the following lines can neither be written without this love, nor, if they are read without it, can they be properly understood.
>
> On the morning of 4 October 1944 an officer, who was known locally, appeared as representative of the local commandant in the *Volksheim* and requested the call-up of those who were sixteen years old. Straightaway about forty lads were informed, they were mostly born in 1928. But there were also some among them born in 1929 who were thus only fifteen years old.
>
> From the *Volksheim* they were first taken to the clothing depot at Fuchsglasers Eck, where they put on a rough and ready uniform, since various

items were lacking. Armament was also really scarce. They were quartered in the Lelbach building near the former Elektrana, north of the Hohe Brücke.

To the youth platoon were assigned three Reich German soldiers, *Sturmmänner* and *Rottenführer*. On the very next day drill began on the cobbled yard of the Lelbach House and the *Volksheim*. On the second day the recruiting officer appeared again, followed by some civilians. Some parents had insisted that the lads should be offered another opportunity to change their hasty decision. In the event three of the young soldiers took advantage of this offer.

On 8 October 1944 the evacuation of the parish was ordered. The local inhabitants set off in refugee columns and an exodus began the like of which had never been seen before. Even the military stationed in the village, and thus also the youth platoon, marched off in the direction of Sombor. On the road was also a pitiful group of emaciated, Jewish, forced-labourers from Bor.

In the dawn light of 9 October 1944 the youth platoon from Sombor marched off in the direction of Bezdán, where it crossed the Danube. In weeks of marching through Transdanubia, interrupted by stops for several days in various villages, the unit reached an area close to the Reich border. During these weeks the youth platoon received temporary training, and was now also inspected and sworn in. One group of twelve lads was ordered away to the Protectorate for training, while the majority marched with the rest of the 31st SS Division to Slovenia.

After artillery training at the troop training grounds of Seltschan and Beneschau near Prague, the special group came back to their unit in Slovenia and was brought together with the whole 31st SS Volunteer Grenadier Division to take up action in Silesia. In May there began the retreat through Czech territory, during which almost the entire Division became Soviet prisoners of war. Some friends were killed, while others were afterwards missing. The remainder were scattered, but a little group of lads from Tscherwenka stayed together.

After a journey lasting weeks this group reached Kovel in the Ukraine to be put to work for eight months. They were lucky to be released as early as the beginning of 1946. Others remained prisoners for longer and only much later came back to the West as so-called *Spätheimkehrer*. In Germany and Austria they found their nearest and dearest. So ended an odyssey in what was once the motherland of the emigrants.

We must be ready,
To defend what we love.

Someone might come,
Wanting to take it away from us,
Wanting to besmirch it
And destroy it.

We must be ready,
To defend what we love,
Even if our strength
Is small and our
Weapons are of wood.

(Ernst von Dombrowsky)

The Division's old 'warhorses'

There were many such old 'warhorses' in the 31st SS Volunteer Grenadier Division, old officers and NCOs from the former K.u.K. Army, soldiers to the marrow of their bones, who could not endure being in the background when the enemy was standing on the threshold of their homeland. In memory of them, shall stand here the journey of *SS-Unterscharführer* Josef Holzinger who was certainly one of the best of them.

Josef Holzinger was born in 1897, in Sellye/Swabian Turkey, as the offshoot of a family of craftsmen who had emigrated to Hungary in the 18th century. The Holzingers had been carpenters for as long as anyone could remember. His three brothers were drafted into the army right at the beginning of the First World War. He reported for duty a year later, 1915, as a volunteer. He fought on the Tyrol and the Carpathian fronts as a wireless operator. After the Great War ended he went back home and worked again as a carpenter in his father's workshop. In 1938 he was drafted in to the Hungarian *Honvéd* as a specialist. As a trained wireless operator he joined the wireless unit of a transport battalion. He was a born soldier and in 1940 had his active service status extended for the duration of the war. He became leader of a wireless unit with the rank of sergeant.

He had already volunteered earlier for the Waffen-SS, but his application was only accepted in autumn 1944. He was forty-seven years old. He was medically examined in Szentlászló and taken on with his rank reduced by one grade, as *Unterscharführer*, with the remark that after completing a wireless unit leaders' course in Unna he would be promoted to *Oberscharführer*. But, due to events, nothing more came of this. At first he went to Neu-Werbass and was employed with the staff of the III/79. As a good chess player he soon became friendly with the battalion commander, who also played chess.

He participated in the defensive fighting of the 31st SS Volunteer Grenadier Division on the Danube and as the front drew near to his home village, he was given leave and promised a lorry to get his nearest and dearest out. But this did not happen. The parish public notary spoke out against evacuating the population, and for the most part they listened to him. When Sellye fell into enemy hands, Holzinger's mother and sister were still in the village and were deported by the Soviets.

Then he went with the 31st SS Volunteer Grenadier Division to Silesia. When Police Regiment 'Brixen' was brought up he was excited, since within this regiment were also incorporated the remnants of SS Police Regiment 26, in which his son was serving. But at that time he wasn't able to see the young Holzinger, who in 1942 had applied for the career of an active officer in the police and had completed studies at the Tölz *Junkerschule*. Young Holzinger had been captured by the Soviets in the summer battle in White Russia.

The ageing man was no longer up to the hardships in Silesia and he became ill and was taken into a military hospital in Hirschberg. On the retreat, in the area of Königgrätz, he was taken prisoner by the Soviets, being released from captivity in September 1946. When he returned home he found himself, like all Hungarian

Germans, expelled from property and justice and Fatherland and branded as a war criminal. He was convicted in Fünfkirchen and spent two years in prison, and afterwards was under police surveillance for seven years. His son, who had similarly survived war and captivity, had settled in Germany. They were only able to meet again in 1967. He earned his living working in the office of a friend and died in his home village of Sellye in 1976, aged 79.

I know affliction and I know death,
And yet I follow the ban,

I bear a heavy weight of old scars,
And yet I stand in the grey army.

My youth is wasted in the field,
Yet today I bear the sword as a man.

My dreams were not of battle and war,
I am lured not by fame, nor easy victory.

One thing only I know: the land wastes away and dies,
Whose people no longer stand in arms.

Only those who put up a fight are worthy of life,
So here I stand and wield the sword.

And stand with soul, blood and body,
Before house and land and child and wife.

And if fate should undo me:
Blessed is he who knows for what he dies!

I am no leaf fluttering in the wind;
I die for my child and my child's child.

(Walter Berger)

CHAPTER 19

The Reserve Units of the Division and Their History

By decree of the *SS-Führungshauptamt* dated 1 December 1944, SS Grenadier *Ausbildungs und Ersatz* Battalion 35 (until 15 November 1944 SS *Panzergrenadier Ausbildungs und Ersatz* Battalion35) was henceforth designated as the appropriate *Ersatz* unit for the 31st SS Volunteer Grenadier Division. This responsibility extended to cover the Divisional Staff of the 31st SS *Volunteer* Grenadier Division, the staffs and staff companies of its Grenadier regiments, the staffs of its Grenadier battalions, as well as all its Grenadier, Fusilier and heavy weapons companies, excluding the specialists.

SS-Grenadier *Ausbildungs und Ersatz* Battalion 35 was based at the SS Troop Training Ground 'Westpreussen' in Bruss, near Konitz. It consisted of the battalion staff and 5 companies. In addition to the 31st SS Division it was also the responsible *Ersatz* unit for the command staff and Escort Battalion of the *Reichsführer-SS*, the SS Commandant Obersalzberg, SS *Jäger* battalions 500, 501 and 502, SS Parachute Battalion 600, the Waffen-SS Grenadier Division (Russian Nr 2) - later changed to 30th Waffen-SS Grenadier Brigade (White Ruthenian) - various special service companies of the *HSSuPoF* Russia Centre and Russia South, as well as, from 15 December 1944, the 25th Waffen-SS Grenadier Division 'Hunyadi' (Hungarian Nr 1). The Battalion commander at that time was *SS-Sturmbannführer* Arthur Plorin.

After the 31st SS Division had been relieved from the south Hungarian front, and had assembled in western Hungary, a number of Danube Swabian recruits were selected. Before the end of December they were marched off to *Ausbildungs und Ersatz* Battalion 35, in Bruss, for further training and to complete a NCO course.

With the breakthrough of the Soviets into the eastern part of the Reich, the situation at Troop Training Ground 'Westpreussen' became precarious. From 2 January 1945, *Ausbildungs und Ersatz* Bataillon 35 set up at short notice an alarm unit, the so-called SS *Kampfgruppe* Joachim. It was 3 companies strong, and formed from the officers, NCOs and other ranks of the battalion at Friedrichsbruch, to the south of Bruss. *SS-Hauptsturmführer* Helmut Joachim became commander, and *SS-Untersturmführer* G. Steinmaier, former commander of 2nd Company *Ausbildungs und Ersatz* Bataillon 35, became Adjutant. Also with them was a certain *SS-Untersturmführer* Bruns.

The *Kampfgruppe* moved on 22 January 1945, via Könitz–Kamin–Zempelburg–Vandsburg, into its destination in the Flatow area. There, on the night of 22 January 1945, it was ambushed in a wooded district occupied by Polish partisans. They suffered considerable casualties. The commander of the 1st Company, *SS-Untersturmführer* Jacobs, was killed. On 24 January 1945 Group

Diedrich from the SS and Waffen-NCO School/Troop Training Ground 'Westpreussen' were brought from Reckow to the *Kampfgruppe* as its 3rd Company, and the *Kampfgruppe* was reorganised.

On 26 and 27 January 1945, the *Kampfgruppe* moved into the Immenheim and Grünhausen area and stood at the disposal of the XVI SS Corps (*Obergruppenführer* Demelhuber), who placed it under the command of the 15th Waffen Grenadier Division of the SS (Latvian Nr 1) (*SS-Oberführer* Ax). On 27 January 1945, it carried out defensive fighting in the Immenheim area, in which it established connection with the 15th Latvian Waffen-Fusilier Battalion (*SS-Sturmbannführer* Pomrehn). After the fighting it withdrew to the line Immenheim-Wiesengrund and defended Immenheim. Withdrawing in the night through Runau (Runowo), on 28 January 1945, it took up defensive positions east of Wilkenwalde, where it was in defence until 29 January 1945.

On 29 January 1945 it withdrew, defended Wilkenwalde and covered the withdrawal movements of the 15th Waffen Grenadier Division der SS (Latvian) to Dorotheenhof (withdrawal to the Kujan sector). On that day, *SS-Hauptsturmführer* Joachim rode out and did not come back. Apparently he was killed. The command was for a short time taken over by the adjutant, *SS-Untersturmführer* Steinmaier.

In the following five days the *Kampfgruppe* carried out a stubborn defence in the Küddow sector. After the fighting withdrawals to Flatow, it moved to Jastrow and secured the village until 31 January 1945. On 1 February 1945 it cleaned out the woods, east of Jastrow, of enemy forces that had trickled through. On 2 February 1945, it carried out a counter-attack, broke through to Flederborn and tried to retake the Flederborn-Wallachsee road. On 3 February 1945, it broke through to Landeck and then in this area defended the Küddow sector.

It was thanks to the successful defensive fighting of the 15th Waffen Grenadier Division der SS (Latvian Nr 1) and the units under its command - *Kampfgruppe* Joachim, SS *Panzergrenadier* Regiment 48 'General Seyffardt' (Dutch Nr 1) and Army Grenadier Regiment 59 – against crushing superiority, that a rapid enemy breakthrough north-westwards was prevented. The enemy advance to Pomerania was delayed. A breakthrough from the ring of encirclement at Flederborn and the shattering of an enemy division outside Landeck were achieved. For that feat of arms, the divisional commander of the Latvian 15th Waffen Grenadier Division der SS, *Oberführer* Adolf Ax, was awarded the Knight's Cross. The Ia from the same Division, *SS-Sturmbannführer* Erich Wulff, who was later killed in action at Landeck, and the regimental commander of the Dutch SS *Panzergrenadier* Regiment 48 'General Seyffardt', *SS-Obersturmbannführer* Siegfried Scheibe, were also awarded the Knight's Cross

Kampfgruppe Joachim, which made an essential contribution to this defensive success, was split up in the battle during which there were many casualties. A group under *SS-Hauptsturmführer* Diedrich, left to fend for itself, fought through on about 5 February 1945. They moved in the direction Landeck–Gross-Born and into the Falkenburg area, where they were received by the SS Escort Battalion of the Reichsführer-SS (*SS-Obersturmbannführer* Pertsch) and incorporated into the battalion. The other group, under *SS-Untersturmführer* G. Steinmaier, remained fighting up to 5 February 1945. Along with the 15th Waffen Grenadier Division der SS (Latvian Nr 1), they were relieved from the front. They moved, first to Schlochau, then to Bruss. From here the remnants were moved to Denmark. *SS-Untersturmführer* Steinmaier recalls his part in the action:

> The *Kampfgruppe* was deployed under the worst conditions. No-one knew exactly under whose command we were. The daily fighting withdrawals were very much disrupted, not least through our helping refugees. The whole front was in a process of continuous withdrawal. It never stopped. In addition to that, the armament of the *Kampfgruppe* left a lot to be desired. What exactly happened to *SS-Hauptsturmführer* Joachim, after he rode out, no-one knows. What he had said the evening before, concerning family matters, led one to suspect that he had anticipated his death – or had deliberately gone out to meet it.

Those parts of the battalion which did not join *Kampfgruppe* Joachim, but remained at the Troop Training Ground were shunted off to SS Reception Camp 'Kurmark' in Jamlitz (*Kreis* Lüben: railway station Lieberose) from 1 February 1945, to which the other movements were diverted from this time. As in *Kampfgruppe* Joachim, members of the 31st SS Division were also in this part of the battalion moving to Jamlitz. Later they went into the alarm units formed from this unit, which were for the most part finally brought up into the 32nd SS *Panzergrenadier* Division '30 Januar'. That was the reason why former members of the 31st SS Volunteer Grenadier Division turned up individually on the Oder front and in the Halbe Pocket and were killed there.

It goes without saying that, as a result of these developments, hardly any of the members of the Division who had once marched off to *Ausbildungs und Ersatz Bataillon* 35 ever came back to the 31st SS Division. They shared the fate of the 'lost' alarm troop that they were in at the time.

On 1 April 1945, a new *Ersatz* unit was designated for the 31st SS Division. It was SS *Panzergrenadier Ausbildungs und Ersatz Bataillon* 36, which had been in Ahlfeld/Leine since November 1944. This unit was from now on responsible for all members of the Division, with the exception of specialists. In addition to this it also retained its earlier responsibility for the Grenadier units of the 28th SS Volunteer *Panzergrenadier* Division 'Wallonie'. Whether any movements from the *Ersatz* unit to the field unit, or vice versa, were actually still taking place, in this last month of the war, can no longer be established with certainty because of lack of evidence.

An account of a 31st SS Division comrade, the Danubian Swabian Sepp Gratwohl, about his experience in *Kampfgruppe* Joachim, shall serve here by way of conclusion:

> When the shattered 31st SS *Volunteer* Grenadier Division gathered together again in western Hungary and a little order came out of the chaos, 200 men, including me, were marched off. It was Christmas Eve. We went to the training battalion at the Könitz troop training ground in West Prussia, where we arrived on 1st January 1945. Here we had to do an NCO course. The chief of our NCO training company was *SS-Obersturmführer* Reiner. In January another letter reached me from my former commander, *SS-Untersturmführer* Alfred Berger, from a military hospital in Austria. He wrote that as soon as he was better and back with the unit, he would sort out for me a transfer to his unit so that I could be his Adjutant again. Sadly, this didn't happen.

Scarcely had we made ourselves at home in Könitz, in the midst of the huge forested area of the Tucheler Heide, than the Battalion set up *Kampfgruppe* Joachim that was to be deployed against the approaching Soviets. A good half of the battalion consisted of Hungarian Germans from the Batschka and elsewhere. In the same way we were also very strongly represented in the *Kampfgruppe*. On 23 January 1945 we set off in the direction of the front. We marched for days, until we arrived in Nakel. Then we were deployed in the Bromberg area, at Jastrow and Flatow, shoulder to shoulder with Latvian comrades. Our three companies had a 10-12 mile-long sector. We didn't even know exactly where we were, we only saw woods and meadows, and had virtually nothing to eat.

Then on 3 February 1945 I was badly wounded in an attack. I was shot in the stomach! I lay there unconscious, while my comrades stormed on forwards. After a short time I was picked up and brought to the dressing station, but I didn't know any of these men. I was transported with other wounded to Danzig, from there somewhat later by ship to Denmark. I wound up in the Convalescent Company that carried out guard duties in the little towns of Nyköbing and Nystedt. The commander was a tall, imposing SS commander, *SS-Untersturmführer* Steinmaier. I'd seen him in the fighting of *Kampfgruppe* Joachim outside Bromberg, and said so at Nystedt: 'Things aren't as hot as they were at Jastrow are they, *Untersturmführer*!' He laughed and was surprised that I too was there. I was also there when the war ended, and we set off on the march towards Germany. There were irregulars who were now even braver. I can still remember well *SS-Untersturmführer* Steinmaier's orders, given on the last day: 'Any enemy attack that affects the company will be bloodily repulsed!' Eventually we got through in one piece.

CHAPTER 20

The *Heimatschutz* of the Ethnic Germans in Hungary

To understand the circumstances better, it is necessary to go a long way back. The Batschka was at that time part of Yugoslavia. In Transylvania, there existed, even before 1940-41, civilian defence or guard units of the German ethnic group called *Deutsche Mannschaft* (abbreviated to DM). In these districts the ethnic group was more tightly organised than in Trianon Hungary, where there was no *Deutsche Mannschaft* until June 1943. But when in 1940 northern Transylvania, and in 1941 the Batschka, returned to Hungary, the self-defence organisation in these districts remained in existence. The Batschka DM played an important part in securing the ethnic group against the Serbian *soldateska* in the days when Yugoslavia was falling apart and the Hungarian *Honvéd* had not yet come in.

In Hungary, in 1943, the *Deutsche Mannschaft* was given a new lease of life by the *Volksbund* of the Germans. In June it was also introduced – but without the permission of the Hungarian Ministry of the Interior – in the old Trianon districts of Hungary. The leaders of the DM in November 1943 were Adalbert Feldinger in the Batschka, Viktor Lange in northern Transylvania, Samuel Moderer in western Hungary, Franz Obels in District Centre and Jakob Bieber in the Danube-Drau areas.

The DM was a loose organisation of the individual groups belonging to localities. These groups were being used exclusively within their respective communities. Every *Volksbund* official was obliged to become a member of the respective local unit. On Sundays unarmed military drill was carried out, which later was especially useful to those who joined the Waffen-SS. As early as 1943, demands were made especially by the Batschka District Leader, Sepp Spreitzer, for the DM to be armed, in view of the spreading Serbian-communist acts of sabotage.

After the occupation of Hungary by the German Wehrmacht, in March 1944, the DM was declared, by the OKW/Wehrmacht Command Staff, as a provincial auxiliary instrument of the German occupying forces. At the same time it was stipulated that as far as entitlement to supplies was concerned, members of the DM were to be regarded as German soldiers and to be treated as such. Although the DM was recognised by the responsible Wehrmacht service authorities as a provincial auxiliary instrument, it represented neither a police nor a military formation. As an organisation of the German *Volksgruppe* (ethnic group) in Hungary, it was under the command of the *Volksgruppenführer* (ethnic group leader). In 1944 the former District Leader Centre, Hugo Binder, became head of the DM at provincial level. On the other hand, the German *Volksgruppe*, together with its leadership, was in the charge of the SS *Hauptamt Volksdeutsche Mittelstelle* (*Volksdeutsche Mittelstelle*).

In spring 1944 the DM was partly armed by the Royal Hungarian *Honvéd*. In the Batschka it guarded the harvest and was also called upon for security tasks. In Transylvania and Ruthenia (Carpatho-Ukraine, Northern Hungary) the DM was deployed to track down and eliminate Soviet parachutists.

As the Red Army approached in August and September 1944 it became necessary to form an organised military armed force of self-protection for the *Volksgruppe*. Thus, the *Heimatschutz* of the German *Volksgruppe* in Hungary, was formed as an armed formation of the *Volksbund* of the Germans in Hungary, to reinforce the defensive forces. The *Heimatschutz* was thought of as a mobile armed force, centrally co-ordinated, organised in independent units of company strength, with a sphere of operation which was not limited to local areas. Its mission was to protect and defend the areas of German settlement within Hungary. All men between the ages of sixteen and sixty capable of military service were included in the conscription of the *Volksbund*. Thus, the *Heimatschutz* corresponded to the *Volkssturm* in the Reich. Conscription was carried out by the SS *Ersatz* Command, Hungary.

The *Heimatschutz* was organised in companies and armed with light infantry weapons, including *Panzerfäuste*, made available by the Wehrmacht. The companies were led and trained by 8 officers and 15 NCOs, who were detached from the Waffen-SS. The formations were organised on military lines, their members outwardly marked as combatants (if only by an armband). The individual companies and platoons operated in accordance with military orders. Thus the *Heimatschutz* possessed all the distinctive characteristics of a military unit. Its members, regarded whilst in action as soldiers within the scope of military law, were classified as combatants, as defined by international convention.

Provincial commandant of the *Heimatschutz* was the Senior SS and Police Commander Hungary, *SS-Gruppenführer* and General of Police Otto Winckelmann. In that capacity he was under the command of the Head of the *Volksdeutsche Mittelstelle*, *SS-Obergruppenführer* Werner Lorenz.

Obergruppenführer Lorenz, who personally stayed in the Batschka between 2 and 10 October, wanted to form the *Heimatschutz* to a total strength of 14,000-15,000 men. The idea of building this up into a 33rd SS Volunteer Grenadier Division may well have come up at this time. Whatever the case, this intention could not be realised, because almost all the male ethnic German population had already been recruited in the third SS recruitment drive in Hungary. Further problems arose with armament. There was a shortage of uniforms in many places, so that the men of the *Heimatschutz* for the most part carried out their duties in civilian clothes, which earned them the nickname 'Floppy Hat Division'.

The possibility cannot be ruled out that in November 1944 groups of the *Heimatschutz* were swept into the maelstrom of the defensive fighting in Transdanubia. They were organisationally under the command of, or incorporated within, the 31st SS Division. For individual members of the *Heimatschutz* this is verifiably the case.

The idea actually did come up, of a new division. The tactical number '33' also came up somehow. So the designation, 'Floppy Hat Division', led in post-war literature again and again to the supposition that a '33rd SS *Freiwillige* Grenadier Division' or 'Waffen-Cavalry-Division' really existed. Even Paul Hausser writes in his book *Soldaten wie andere auch*, "At the end of November the Soviets crossed the Danube to the north of the Drau estuary and thrust forward as far as Lake Balaton. In this process a Hungarian SS Division, the 33rd Division, newly-formed, is said to have been destroyed." Papa Hausser evidently means here the 31st SS *Freiwillige* Grenadier Division, but even at the back of his mind is the number 33.

In actual fact there was no lack of intention to form a 33rd SS Division out of the *Heimatschutz*. But this intention was never realised, so that the 33rd SS Division belongs to those divisions of the Waffen-SS that were never formed. (Under the number 33, the French SS Division 'Charlemagne' was formed).

The total strength of the *Heimatschutz* was about 5,000 men, a large part of them lads still too young for military service. The *Heimatschutz* played a part in the evacuation of the ethnic German population. They took over the protection of the refugee columns and were used for policing and public order duties.

Training of the young men for the *Heimatschutz* took place in a total of four training camps located in Futok, Villany, Nemetbóly and Nyergesuj-Falu. These were organised as military training camps. It should be stressed that the young lads, in most cases just twelve years old, were by no means lacking in enthusiasm. Indeed, they were the best élite from the youngest youth of the *Volksgruppe!*

In the course of the evacuation of the Batschka, the training camp in Futok, with over 100 young men, moved to Hidas in Swabian Turkey, with the personnel playing an active part in returning Batschka German children. The company arrived in Hidas on 15 October 1944, just as it became known that Reich Administrator Horthy was no longer prepared to continue to fight on the German side. Acting on a 'spot' decision, the lads of the *Heimatschutz* with their company commander, *SS-Untersturmführer* K. from Neusatz, occupied the local police station until the situation in Budapest calmed down.

As a consequence of the enemy advance in Transdanubia the training camps were moved back. At the beginning of December the units of the *Heimatschutz* were concentrated around Odenburg. The headquarters of the *Volksgruppe* leadership was also there, after it had been moved out of encircled Budapest. Fresh young men also continued to come to the *Heimatschutz*, mainly from the areas of German settlement that were still free. But old men (over fifty years of age) were also still coming. From the end of November the name "*Heimatschutz*" was also officially used. With time, armament improved and everyone was clad in field grey. Military training was carried out, directed by the detached SS officers and NCOs. In spring 1945, manoeuvres of the *Heimatschutz* also took place in Agendorf (Agfalva), at which the *Volksgruppenführer* Dr Franz Basch and the National Leader Ferenc Szálasi were present. Szálasi was very impressed by the troops and, after the parade, spoke in commendation of them. At the end of November, 120 young men were moved from Odenburg to Bogenriegel, nothing is known of their later whereabouts (probably employed as flak auxiliaries).

After the fall of Budapest, defensive positions were dug outside Odenburg, and the *Heimatschutz* were ordered to man them. However, at first this did not happen. Once again a German large-scale offensive was begun to beat the Soviets back across the Danube. Operation 'Frühlingserwachen' ('Spring Awakening') failed after some initial successes. While the attack was still going well, an advance command of the *Heimatschutz* was dispatched to follow up the attack. A public order service arrived in the German settlements that were to be liberated. This advance command was subsequently lost without trace.

As the Soviets were moving closer and closer in the second half of March (by 4 April 1945 practically the whole of Hungary was occupied by the enemy!), the *Heimatschutz* was once again supposed to be deployed in the defence of Odenburg. But Dr Basch succeeded in relieving it from being deployed and to move it to Austria. On the territory of the Hungarian state, only one instance is known of the *Heimatschutz* seeing action at the front. This was at Pusztasomorja, on the moorland to the north-east of the Neusiedler-See.

The greater part of the *Heimatschutz* moved to Waidhofen on the Ybbs (Lower Austria), where those not capable of frontline service, the older men and the sick were released and advised to go and look for their families as civilian refugees. Another section accompanied the *Volksgruppe* leadership to their new headquarters, Weyregg on the Attersee. Those sections of the *Heimatschutz* were dissolved on 3 May 1945. The certificates of discharge for the men were issued through the *Volksdeutsche Mittelstelle* head office.

The *Heimatschutz* companies capable of frontline service, however, were brought up in the Lower Austria area for deployment at the front. Thus a group of company strength at Mariazell was organised for action by a special unit. A unit of some 40 men was said to have been wiped out by the Soviets at the Kalter Wand. The remnants were taken prisoner.

The other companies ready for action were assigned in Gutenstein to *Kampfgruppe* Keitel of the 37th SS Cavalry Division 'Lützow', and took part in the defensive fighting in the mountain positions. Their last position was Hill 1056. Finally they were given the task, as rearguard, of making the road impassable for vehicles, to prevent the Soviets following up quickly. During the final days there were repeated individual counter-attacks with the soldiers of the 1st SS *Panzer* Division 'Leibstandarte Adolf Hitler', in which the Hungarian German lads acted with great bravery and some were decorated with the Iron Cross 2nd Class. After the surrender they set off westwards to escape the Soviets. Thus ends the history of the *Heimatschutz* of the German *Volksgruppe* in Hungary, whose every last young man voluntarily marched out with loyal dedication to defend their homeland and their people.

Officer List of the 31st SS Volunteer Grenadier Division

Errors excepted, since even contemporary sources are contradictory, so that the regimental posts and their holders, which were also subject to many changes, can no longer be precisely established.

Note: 00 represents a day or a month that is not known more precisely. A date in square brackets does not indicate the unknown date when the post was taken up or relinquished, but is simply a date when the individual concerned appeared in the Division.

Divisional Staff

Div. CO (24.09.44-09.05.45): *Ofhr.* (*Brif.* from 01.04.45) Gustav Lombard
Ia (Operations) (01.10.44-09.05.45): *Stubaf.* Otto Reuter
Ib (Supplies) (01.10.44-05.11.44): *Ostuf.* Ernst-Friedrich Fritscher
  (05.11.44-00.00.45): *Ostuf.* Anton Büntgen
  (01.03.45)-00.04.45: *Ostuf.* Johann Lehner
Ic (Intelligence) (01.11.44-00.05.45): *Ostuf.* Gerhard Kraushaar
Arms & Equipment (00.00.00-09.05.45): *Hstuf.* Neubert
Radio Technical Station (00.00.00-00.01.45): *Ostuf.* Sebastian
  Vital
IIa (Adjutant) (00.07.44-00.00.45): *Ostuf.* (later *Hstuf.*) Georg Kuhnert
  (00.02.45-09.05.45): *Hstuf.* Marzel Reichel
IIb (Orderly officer) (00.00.44-00.10.44): *Ostuf.* Robert Meyer
  (00.10.44-00.12.44): *Ustuf.* Friedrich Kox
Escort Officer (00.02.45-09.05.45): *Ustuf.* Hans-Joachim Raehmel
IVa (Intendant) (00.10.44-00.01.45): *Ostubaf.* Karl von Türck
  (00.01.45-00.03.45): *Stubaf.* Dr Gustav Gewecke
  (00.03.45-00.01.45): *Hstuf.* Rolf Werner
  (00.04.45-00.05.45): *Stubaf.* Bruno Witte
IVb (Div. Medical Officer) (01.10.44-09.05.45): *Stubaf.* (From 30.01.45
  Ostubaf.) Dr Karl Matz
IVd (Div. Vet) (01.10.44-09.05.45): *Ustuf.* Dr med. vet.Besselberg
1Ve (Div. Chemist) (01.10.44-09.05.45): *Ostuf.* Franz Geiger
CO, Div. HQ (00.00.45-00.05.45): *Stubaf.* Wiegand
  (? 01.10.44-09.05.45): *Ostuf.* Eduard Franz Bakos
CO, Div. Radio Station (00.00.00-00.05.45):*Ustuf.* Lambert Randenrath

SS Vol. Gren. Rgt 78

Rgt. CO (01.10.44-00.00.45): *Stubaf.* Robert Schneider

(01.03.45-00.05.45): *Ostubaf.* Hermann Frimmersdorf
I Btn CO (00.00.44-00.10.44): *Stubaf.* Karl Praekke
   (00.10.44-00.12.44): *Stubaf.* Kurt Pachur
II Btn CO (00.10.44-00.01.45): *Hstuf.* Theodor Clausen
   (00.01.45-09.05.45): *Hstuf.* Emil Maitre
III Btn CO (00.01.45-00.00.45): *Hstuf.* Theodor Clausen
14th (Pz.Jg.) Company CO (01.10.44-27.11.44): *Ostuf.* Franz Stibach
CO 4/II (00.00.44-00.03.45): *Ustuf.* Heinrich Gores

SS Vol. Gren. Rgt 79

Rgt. CO (01.10.44-09.05.45): *Stubaf.* (from 30.1.45 *Ostubaf.*) Sepp Syr
   (in Rgt. HQ) (01.10.44-09.05.45): *Ostuf.* Michael Ambrosi
I Btn CO (01.10.44-00.12.44): *Stubaf.* Heinrich Albrecht
   (00.12.44-00.02.45): *Stubaf.* Kurt Pachur
   (00.02.45-00.00.45): *Hstuf.* Robert Gloning
II Btn CO (01.10.44-00.02.45): *Hstuf.* (from 30.01.45 *Stubaf.*) Ewald
Schuhmacher
   (00.02.45-00.05.45): *Stubaf.* Heinrich Albrecht
   Adjutant (00.01.45-09.05.45): *Ustuf.* Hundertmark
   Orderly officer (00.01.45-09.05.45): *Ustuf.* Bender
   Paymaster (00.01.45-09.05.45): *Ostuf.* Becksen
III Btn CO (01.10.44-00.00.45): *Stubaf.* Egon Zill (unconfirmed)
   (00.00.45-00.00.45): *Hstuf.* Werner Zimmermann or according to other
   sources *Hstuf.* Georg Petrus
CO 4/I (01.10.44-26.11.44): *Ustuf.* Fritz Holderer
CO ?/I (01.10.44-25.11.44): *Ustuf.* Alfred Berger
3/I (00.00.44-00.03.45): *Ustuf.* Karl-Heinz Consilius
HQ Coy. ? (01.10.44-00.00.45): *Ustuf.* August Arnold
Platoon commander in 4/I (01.10.44-00.12.44): *Hscha.* Hans Zick
Officers whose position is unknown: *Ustuf.* Pradl, *Ustuf.* Schwenk

SS Vol. Gren. Rgt. 80. (old formation, October-December 1944)

Rgt. CO (01.10.44-25.11.44): *Stubaf.* Friedrich Karl Scanzony von Lichtenfels
   (25.11.44-00.00.00): *Ostubaf.* Walter Domes
I Btn CO? (00.00.44-25.11.44): *Ostubaf.* Walter Domes

SS Vol. Gren. Rgt. 80 (new formation, previously Pol. Rgt. 'Brixen')

Rgt CO (12.10.44-00.00.45): *Oberstlt.d.Schupo* Ernst Korn
   ([00.03.45]-00.00.45): *Stubaf.* Rudolf Schon
   Adjutant (00.00.45-00.00.45): *Ostuf.* Erich Moller
I Btn CO (00.00.45-00.00.45): *Stubaf.* Helmuth Gantz
14th Coy. CO (00.00.00-00.00.45): *Ustuf.* Gerhard Hiecke

SS Vol. Art. Rgt. 31

Rgt. CO (00.00.44-00.09.44): *Stubaf.* Karl-Friedrich Dehnen
    (00.09.44-00.01.45): *Ostubaf.* Hans Zeysing
    (00.01.45-09.05.45): *Staf.* Hans-Kurt Kaestner
    Adjutant (00.00.45-09.05.45): *Ustuf.* Hans Michael Buehl
    Signals officer [00.02.45]: *Ostuf.* Karl Wehland
I Abt. CO (01.10.44-09.05.45): *Hstuf.* Josef Mailhammer
    3./A.R. (00.00.00-00.04.45): *Ustuf.* Fritz Meise
    4./A.R. (00.00.00-09.05.45): *Ustuf.* Heinz Schwarz
II Abt. (CO 00.10.44-00.01.45): *Stubaf.* Karl-Friedrich Dehnen
    (00.01.45-00.05.45): *Stubaf.* Johannes Neugebauer
    Abt. Doctor (00.00.44-00.05.45): *Hstuf.* Dr Franz Gettmann
III Abt. CO (05.01.45-09.05.45): *Hstuf.* Hans Dotterweich
    Battery COs (00.00.00-00.05.45): *Ustuf.* Klughart, *Ustuf.* Meindel
    Abt. Doctor (00.10.44-00.05.45): Dr Weber
IV Abt. CO (00.01.45-09.05.45): *Hstuf.* Günther Maasz
Officers whose position is unknown: [00.11.44]: *Ostuf.* Hans Dorando, Ustuf.
    Reiner Klotz, *Hstuf.* Eisse deVries
    [00.12.44]: *Ustuf.* Tiberius Herrling, *Hstuf.* Konrad Ipsen, *Ustuf.* Arnold
    Limbach, *Ostuf.* Otto Schonert, *Ustuf.* Karl Schweizer
    [00.01.45]: *Ostuf.* Arnold Seliger, *Ustuf.* Karl Uwelius, *Ustuf.* Wolfgang
    Viertel, *Ustuf.* Bruno Wessely
    [00.02.45]: *Ustuf.* Rudolf Hempel, *Ustuf.* Rolf Kluvetasch, *Ustuf.* Hans-
    Joachim Koch, *Ustuf.* Herbert Preuss, *Ustuf.* Hans-Heinz Proetel, *Ustuf.*
    Friedrich Rasch, *Ustuf.* Karl Werler, *Ustuf.* Karl-Heinz Wilhelm
    [00.03.45]: *Ustuf.* Herbert Engelbrecher, *Ustuf.* Alfons Kosseg, *Ustuf.*
    Franz Linde, *Ustuf.* Hans Schwarz, *Ustuf.* Rudolf Sell
    [00.04.45]: *Ustuf.* Günther Haedecke, *Ustuf.* Hans-Georg Kleisch, *Ostuf.*
    Josef Landrock, *Ostuf.* Hans-Joachim Lindow, *Ustuf.* Helmuth
    Weitermann, *Hstuf.* Günther Woltersdorf

SS Vol. Fusilier Btn. 31 (old formation, October-December 1944)

Btn CO (01.10.44-00.01.45): *Hstuf.* (from 9.11.44 *Stubaf.*) Ludwig Zeitz

SS Vol. Fusilier Btn. 31 (new formation, ormer Hungarian Btn 'Szálasi')

Btn CO (00.02.45-30.04.45): *Ustuf.* Zvonimir Bernwald

SS Vol. Pioneer Btn 31

Btn CO (01.10.44-09.05.45): *Stubaf.* Hermann Otto
    Adjutant (01.10.44-00.04.45): *Hscha.* Hoffmeister
    (00.04.45-09.05.45): *Ustuf.* Heinz Hummel
    Btn Doctor (01.10.44-09.05.45): *Hstuf.* Dr Albrecht Hermann
    Officer z.b.V. (00.04.45-09.05.45): *Ostuf.* Hans Bahr

1st Coy. CO (01.10.44-09.05.45): *Ostuf.* Gerhard Hillmann
  I Platoon (01.10.44-00.04.45): *Ustuf.* Heinz Hummel
  (00.04.45-09.05.45): *Hscha.* Hoffmeister
  II Platoon (01.10.44-00.01.45): *Ustuf.* Bernd Pabel
  (00.01.45-09.05.45): *Ustuf.* Max Stubenrauch
  III Platoon (01.10.44-00.04.45): *Oscha.* Werner Rauner
2nd Coy. CO (01.10.44-00.04.45): *Ostuf.* Hans Bahr
  (00.04.45-09.05.45): *Ustuf.* Kurt Schmidt
  I Platoon (01.10.44-00.04.45): *Ustuf.* Kurt Schmidt
  II Platoon (01.10.44-09.05.45): *Ustuf.* Kiebauch
  III Platoon (01.10.44-09.05.45): *Ustuf.* Jahn
3rd Coy. CO (01.10.44-09.05.45): *Ostuf.* Werner Schroder

SS Volunteer *Panzerjäger* Abt.31

Abt. CO (01.10.44-09.05.45): *Stubaf.* Richard Landwehr
  Adjutant (01.10.44-09.05.45): *Ustuf.* Heinz Sebastian
1st Pz.Jg. Coy. (00.00.44-00.04.45): *Ostuf.* Günther Gottwald

SS Vol. *Nachrichten* Abt. 31

Abt. CO (01.10.44-00.12.44): *Hstuf.* Albert Reimann
  (00.12.44-09.05.45): *Hstuf.* Alois Kindshofer
  Adjutant (00.00.45-09.05.45): *Ostuf.* Henschel
  Abt. Doctor (01.10.44-09.05.45): *Oju.* Dr Peter Reidl
  Radio Technical Station (01.10.44-09.05.45): *Ustuf.* Karl Stecker
Tel. Coy. CO (01.10.44-09.05.45): *Ostuf.* Karl Heinz Dremcker
  Officer z.b.V. (01.10.44-09.05.45): *Ustuf.* Jürgen Joost
  I Platoon (01.10.44-09.05.45): *Ustuf.* Siegfried Koller
  II Platoon (00.00.44-09.05.45): *Ustuf.* Georg Bantelmann
  III Platoon (01.10.44-09.05.45): *Ustuf.* Hans Villier
Radio Coy. CO (01.10.44-09.05.45): *Ostuf.* Ottfried Schwalbe
  Platoon commanders (01.10.44-09.05.45): *Ustuf.* Kurt Meitzel
  (01.10.44-09.05.45): *Ustuf.* Waldemar Graf
Light *Nachrichten* Column (00.10.44-09.05.45): *Oscha.* Hugo Krallmann
Officers whose position is unknown: (00.00.44-09.05.45): *Ustuf.* Günther Voss,
  Ustuf. Otto Eichhorn, *Ustuf.* Hans Reich, *Ustuf.* Werner Fleischhauer,
  Ustuf. Wladi Sopko
  (00.04.45-09.05.45): *Ustuf.* Gerd Lingner

SS Vol. *Nachschub* Abt. 31 (until 16.01.45)

Abt. CO (01.10.44-00.01.45): *Hstuf.* Wilhelm Morisse
Supply Column (mot.) (01.10.44-00.01.45): *Ostuf.* Rudolf Herzog
Supply Column (horse-drawn) ?
SS Vol. *Nachschub* Coy. (01.10.44-00.12.44): ? *Hstuf.* Alois Kindshofer

SS *Verwaltungstrupp* Abt.31 (until 16.01.45)

Abt. CO ?
Bakery Coy. ?
Butchery Coy. ?
Admin. Coy. ?
SS Field Post Office (31 01.10.44-00.04.45): *Hstuf.* Heinrich Planer

SS Vol. Motor Vehicle Workshop Coy. 31

?

SS Supply Rgt.31 (from 16.1.45)

Rgt CO (00.01.45-09.05.45): *Hstuf.* (from 30.01.45 *Stubaf.*) Wilhelm Morisse
Motor Vehicle Coy. (00.01.45-00.00.45): *Ostuf.* Rudolf Herzog
Supply Column (horse-drawn) ?
Nachschub Platoon ?
Munitions Coy. ?

SS Medical Abt. 31 (until 16.1.45)

Abt. CO (01.10.44-00.01.45): *Stubaf.* Dr Karl Matz
1st Medical Coy. (01.10.44-00.01.45): *Hstuf.* Dr Siegfried Klaus Bock
2nd Medical Coy. (01.10.44-00.01.45): *Hstuf.* Dr Erich Scherer
Surgeon none
Intern (01.10.44-00.00.45): *Ustuf.* Krummel

SS Medical Coy. 31 (from 16.1.45)

Coy. CO (00.01.45-09.05.45). *Stubaf.* Dr Otto Röhrs
I Platoon (00.01.45-09.05.45): *Hstuf.* Dr Berger
II Platoon (00.01.45-09.05.45). *Hstuf.* Dr Erich Scherer
Surgeon (00.01.45-09.05.45): *Hstuf.* Dr Erich Königsdorfer

SS Motor Ambulance Platoon

CO (01.10.44-09.05.45): *Ostuf.* Hans Keller

SS Vol. Veterinary Coy. 31

CO (01.10.44-00.05.45): *Ustuf.* Dr. Peter Pertschy
Position unknown: (00.00.45) : *Ustuf.* Fritz Bittner

Officers whose position within the Division is unknown

[00.10.44]: *Hstuf.* Paul Barton, *Ustuf.* Georg Mayr, *Ustuf.* Otto Diesterweg
[00.12.44]: *Ustuf.* Hans Schindler
(01.10.44-25.11.45): *Ustuf.* WoUgang Döhler (killed 25.11.44)
(01.10.44-09.05.45): *Ostuf.* Leo Patina, *Ustuf.* Walter Egon Börner
(00.10.44-00.05.45): *Hstuf.* Albert Geng, *Hstuf.* Heinrich Köwner

(00.00.44-00.02.45): *Ustuf.* Harry Owsianowsky

(00.00.44-00.05.45): *Ustuf.* Hans Pfeiffer, *Ustuf.* Elias Hermann Demtschück, *Hstuf.* Helmuth Bricks

[00.01.45]: *Ostuf.* Herbert Burmeister, *Ustuf.* Wilhelm Diehl, *Ustuf.* Gottfried Herrfurth, *Ustuf.* Rudolf Kaupa, *Hstuf.* Erik von Major, *Ostuf.* Stefan Neleauser, *Ustuf.* Wilhelm Steinke, *Hstuf.* Dr. Emil Tickert

[00.02.45] : *Ustuf.* Hans-Joachim Ritz, *Ostuf.* Heinz Rössler

[00.03.45] : *Ostuf.* Karl Heckmann, *Ostuf.* Werner Scholz

(00.01.45-00.05.45): *Ustuf.* Wilhelm Lucken

(00.01.45-00.05.45): *Stubaf.* Dr. Wolfgang Richter (probably Rgt. Doctor)

(00.03.45-00.05.45): *Ustuf.* Johann Prokopy

APPENDIX II

Explanation of Geographical Names and Gazeteer

The Banat is the region whose boundaries are marked in the west by the Theiss and the Danube, in the south by the Danube, in the north approximately by the Maros (Mieresch) River, and in the east by the mountains (Banater Bergland). Through the Trianon Peace Treaty, the western part of the Banat (with Grossberetschek) had to be ceded by Hungary to Serbia, the eastern part (with Temeschwar) to Rumania, while only a small tip of the Banat in the north remained part of Hungary.

Syrmia is the region between the Danube and the Save in Croatia.

The Batschka is the region between the Danube and the lower course of the Theiss, the boundaries of which run in the north roughly along the line Baja–Szeged; by and large it corresponds with the Hungarian Komitat Bács-Bodrog. In the northern and southern Batschka, also called Upper and Lower Batschka, it is geographically divided by the Franzen Canal (Ferenc-csatorna), but politically divided by the frontier of the Treaty of Trianon 1920 which left 20% of the Batschka with Hungary, but assigned 80% to the Kingdom of the Serbs, Croats and Slovenes. Between 1941 and 1945 the southern part also reverted again to Hungary.

Swabian Turkey is the area of German settlement roughly between the Danube, the Drau, Lake Balaton and the Sió Canal in the Hungarian Komitaten of Baranya (German Braunau, administrative centre: Fünfkirchen/Pécs), Tolna (German Tolnau, administrative centre: Szekszárd) and Somogy (German Schmodei, administrative centre: Kaposvár).

Transdanubia is the name of the large western region of Hungary whose boundaries are marked in the north and east by the Danube, in the west by the Hungarian border or the Alpine foothills, and in the south by the Drau; in German literature it is mostly simply designated as 'Westungarn' (western Hungary), which is not quite accurate; in Hungarian 'Dunántúl' ('beyond the Danube').

Batschka

German	Serbo-Croat	Hungarian
Alt-Betsche	Stari Becej	óbecse
Altker	Pasicevo/Zmajevo	ókér
Altschowe	Stara Save	ósóvé
Bajmok	Bajmok	Bajmak
Batsch	Bac	Bács
Batsch-Monoschtor	Backi Monostor	Monostorszeg
Batsch-Neudorf	Backo Novo Selo	Bácsújlak

Batsch-Sentiwan	Prigrevica Sveti Ivan	Bácsyentiván
Bereg	Backi Breg	Béreg
Brestowatz	Brestovac	Szilberek
Bukin	Bukin/Mladenov	Bökény
Bulkes	Buljkes/Maglic	Bulkeszi
Deronje	Deronje	Dernye
Despot-St Iwan	Despot-Sveti-Ivan	úrszentiván
Doroßlo	Doroslovo	Doroszló
Feketitsch	Feketic	Bácsfeketehegy
Filipowa	Filipovo	Szentfülöp
Futok	Futok	Futak
Gajdobra	Gajdobra	Szépliget
Gakowa	Gakovo	Gádor
Hodschag	Odzaci	Hódság
Jarek	Jarak	Tiszaistvánfalva
Josefsdorf/Schabalj	Zabalj	Zsablya
Karawukowa	Karavukuvo	Bácsordas
Katsch	Kac	Káty
Kernei	Krnjaja/K1jajicevo	Kerény
Kleinker Mali	Ker/Dobro Polje	Kiskér
Kolut	Kolut	Küllöd
Kruschiwl	Krusevlje	Körtes
Kula	Kula	Kúla
Kulpin	Kulpin	Kölpény
Kutzura	Kucura	Kucora
Legin	Ridjica	Regöce
Maria-Theresiopel	Subotica	Szabadka
Miletitsch Srpski	Miletic	Rácmilitics
Morawitz Stara	Moravica	Bácskossuthfalva
Neusatz	Novi Sad	újvidék
Neuschowe	Nova Save	újsóvé
Obrowatz	Obrovac	Boróc
Palanka	Palanka	Palánka
Parabutsch	Parabuc/Ratkovo	Paripás
Patschir	Pacir	Pacsér
Schajkasch-St Iwan	Sajkas-Sv Ivan	Sajkássyentiván
Sekitsch	Sekic/Lovcenac	Szeghegy
Siwatz	Sivac	Szivác
Sombor	Sombor	Zombor
Sonta	Sonta	Szond
Stanischitsch	Stanicic	Örszállás
Teletschka	Telecka	Bácsgyulafalva
Topola	Topola	Topolya
Torschau	Torza/Savino Selo	Torsza
Towarisch	Tovarisevo	Bácstóváros
Tscheb	Cib/Celarevo	Dunacséb
Tscherwenka	Crvenka	Cservenka

Tschonopel	Conoplja	Csonoplya
Waldneudorf	Budisava	Tiszakálmanfalva
Wekerledorf	Nova Gajdobra	Wekerlefalva
Weprowatz	Verpovac/Krusic	Vepröd
Werbaß (Alt, Neu)	Vrbas	Verbász
Wikitsch	Vikic	Bácsbokod
-	Glozan	Dunagálos
-	Srbobran	Szenttamás

Danube-Drau-Dreieck

Hungarian (German)	Croatian
Albertfalu (Albertsdorf)	Grabovac
Bán	Popovac
Baranyavár	Branjin Vrh
Bellye	Bilje
Bolmány	Bolman
Csuza	Suza
Dályok	Dubosevica
Darázs	Draz
Daróc	Vardarac
Föherceglak	Knezovo
Hercegszölös	Knezevi Vinogradi
Izsép	Topolje
Kácsfalu (Katschfeld)	Jagodnjak
Karancs	Karanac
Keskend	Kozarac
Kisfalud	Branjina
Kisköszeg	Batina
Laskó	Brestovac
Laschkafeld	Ceminac
Löcs	Luc
Pélmonostor	Beli Manastir
Sepse	Kotlina
Szentiván	Majska Medja
Szentistván	Petlovac
Vörösmart	Zmajevac

Additional

Agram	Zágráb/Zagreb
Donau	Duna
Drau	Dráva
Groß-Betschkerek	Nagybecskerek/Beckerek, Petrograd
Eisenburg	Vasvár
Erlau	Eger
Esseg	Eszék/Osijek
Fünfkirchen	Pécs

Gran	Esztergom
Großwardein	Nagyvárad/Oradea
Güns	Köszeg
Hermannstadt	Nagyszeben/Sibiu
Klausenburg	Kolozsvár/Cluj
Kronstadt	Brassó/Brasov
Mieresch	Maros
Ödenburg	Sopron
Pantschowa	Pancsova/Pancevo
Plattensee	Balaton
Preßburg	Pozsony/Bratislava
Raab	Györ
Steinamanger	Szombathely
St Gotthard	Szentgotthárd
St Martinsberg	Pannonhalma
Stuhlweißenburg	Székesfehérvár
Temeschwar/Temeschburg	Temesvár/Timisoara
Theiß	Tisza
Waitzen	Vác
Werschetz	Versec/Vrsec
Weißkirchen	Fehértemplom/Bela Crkva
Wieselburg	Mosonmagyaróvár

Glossary

Abteilung / Abt.	Battalion / department / section, dependent upon context
Aufklärungs Abteilung	Reconnaissance battalion
Ausbildungs	Training
Ausbildings-und-Ersatz / Ausb.u.E.	Training and Replacement
Bannführer	Middle-ranking Party official responsible for an administrative area equivalent to a district
Chef	Commander
Fahnenjunker	Officer cadet
Fallschirmjäger	Paratroop
Fallschirmpanzerdivision	Parachute panzer division
Feldpost	Field post, i.e. German forces' postal service
Feldwebel	Sergeant
Festung	Fortress, or more usually referring to a 'fortified place'
Freiwillige	Volunteer
Führer-Begleit	Führer Escort
Gau	Nazi administrative district
Gauleiter	High-ranking Nazi official responsible for a *Gau*
Gebirgsartillerie	Mountain artillery
Gebirgsdivision	Mountain division
Gebirgskorps	Mountain corps
General der Artillerie	General of artillery
Generalfeldmarschall	Field Marshall
General der Infanterie	General of infantry
Generalleutnant	Lieutenant-General
Generalmajor	Major-General
Generaloberst	General
General der Panzertruppen	General of armoured troops
Hauptmann	Captain
Heimatschutz	Home Defence Force
Honvéd	Hungarian army
	Ia First General Staff Officer (operations)
	Ib Second General Staff Officer (supply and administration)
	Ic Third General Staff Officer (intelligence)
Jagdpanzer	Tank hunter
Kampfgruppe	Battle group
K.u.K.	Imperial and Royal [Army], the old Austrian army of the Habsburg Empire
Junkerschule	Officer school
Kompanie	Company

Kreis	Administrative region, approximately equivalent to a county in size
Leutnant	Lieutenant
Nachrichten	Signals
Nachschub	Rations, e.g. Rations Company
Oberleutnant	First lieutenant / senior lieutenant
Oberst	Colonel
Oberstleutnant	Lieutenant-colonel
Oberwachtmeister	Sergeant-major (in artillery, flak, cavalry, transport, mounted signals)
OKH	Army High Command
OKW	Armed Forces High Command
1. Ordonnanzoffizier	Assistant to Ia
Panzer Abteilung	Tank battalion
Panzerjäger Abteilung	Tank hunter battalion
Panzerkorps	Tank corps
Panzerzerstörer	Tank destroyer
Polizei	Police
Regimentsadjutant	Regimental adjutant
Rittmeister	Captain (in cavalry and transport units)
schwere Panzer Abteilung	Heavy tank battalion
SS-Artillerie-Schule	SS Artillery School
SS-Brigadeführer	SS Major-General
SS-Führungshauptamt	SS Main Operations Office
SS-Gruppenführer	SS Lieutenant-General
SS-Hauptsturmführer / SS-Hstuf.	SS Captain
SS-Mann	SS Enlisted Man
SS-Oberführer	SS Brigadier
SS-Obergruppenführer / SS-Obergruf.	SS General
SS-Oberscharführer	SS Senior Sergeant
SS-Obersturmbannführer / SS-Ostubaf.	SS Lieutenant-Colonel
SS-Obersturmführer / SS-Ostuf.	SS Lieutenant
SS-Rottenführer	SS Senior Lance-Corporal
SS-Stabsscharführer	SS Staff Sergeant
SS-Standartenführer/ SS-Staf.	SS Colonel
SS-Sturmbannführer / SS-Stubaf.	SS Major
SS-Sturmscharführer	SS Staff Sergeant
SS-Untersturmführer / SS-Ustuf.	SS Second Lieutenant
StuG	See Sturmgeschütz
Sturmgeschütz	Assault gun
Sturmgeschütz Abteilung	Assault gun battalion
Sturmgeschütz Brigade	Assault gun brigade
Verwaltungstruppen	Administrative troops
Volksbund	lit. 'People's League', but referring in this case to a an ethnic group's governing body
Volksdeutsche Mittelstelle	Ethnic German Central Office

Volksgruppe	Ethnic group, sometimes also used to refer to the officially-recognised administrative apparatus of an ethnic group
Volksgruppenführer	Officially-recognised leader of an ethnic group, e.g. of the Serbian Banat
Volksdeutsche	Ethnic German
Volksgrenadier	People's grenadier
Volkssturm	German equivalent of the Home Guard
Wachtmeister	Sergeant (in artillery, flak, cavalry, transport, mounted signals)
Waffenschule	Weapons school
z.b.V.	For special purposes
Zug	Platoon
Zugführer	Platoon commander

Bibliography

Unpublished sources:

Sammlung Wolfgang Vopersal, Bundesarchiv Militärarchiv, Freiburg (Zeichen N 756/198).

Kriegstagebücher, Anlagen, OB Südost, Heeresgruppe Süd, Bundesarchiv Militärarchiv, Freiburg (Aktenzeichen RH 19 XI/14, XI/24, XI/26, V/41, V/53, V/66, V/57).

Many additional documents in the possession of the Bundesarchiv, Koblenz; Deutschen Dienststelle (WASt), Berlin; Berlin Document Center; Südtiroler Kriegsopfer- und Frontkämpferverband.

Reports, memoirs, documents of various types in the possession of former members of the Division or their widows, as well as people from Germany, Hungary and Slovakia.

'Begräbnisprotokoll', from Babarc, *Frau* Theresie Lászlo.

Lombard, Gustav 'Wie Gustav Lombard in sowjetische Kriegsgefangenschaft geriet und sie erlebt hat', Bundesarchiv Militärarchiv, Freiburg (Aktenzeichen MSg 1/2867).

Various documents via Hans Holzträger.

Oberläuter, Erwin 'Die Flucht vor der Gewalt', Regensburg, 1978.

'Vermisstenbildlisten' from the German Red Cross.

Spaeter, H. 'Nachträge zur Geschichte der Division 'Brandenburg'. Stellenbesetzungsliste', in the possession of Dr F.J.M. Nooij, Holland.

Published sources:

Ahlfen, Hans von *Der Kampf um Schlesien 1944/45* (Stuttgart: Motorbuch Verlag, 1991)

Becker, Rolf O. *Die Flucht. Niederschlesien 1945* (Landshut: Aufstieg Verlag, 1990)

Borus, Dr J. *Somogy megye múltjából* (Kaposvár: Levéltári Évkönyv 1, 1970)

Dálnoki, Veress Lajos vitéz *Magyarország honvédelme a második világháború elõtt és alatt 1920-1945* (München, 1973)

Der Freiwillige, various articles

Dienstalterliste der Waffen-SS, Stand 1.10.1944, mit Nachträgen bis zum 30.1.1945

Franz, Hermann *Gebirgsjäger der Polizei* (Bad Nauheim: Podzun Verlag, 1963)

Frießner, Hans *Verratene Schlachten* (Hamburg: Holsten Verlag, n.d.)

Füzes, Dr Miklós *Modern rabszolgaság. Magyar állampolgárok a Szovjetúnió munkatáboraiban 1945-1949* (Budapest, 1990)

Gosztonyi, Péter *Endkampf an der Donau 1944/45* (Wien/München: Molden Taschenbuch Verlag, 1978)

Gunter, Georg Letzter Lorbeer. *Geschichte der Kämpfe in Oberschlesien Januar-Mai 1945* (Dülmen: Oberschlesischer Heimatverlag, n.d.)

Hausser, Paul *Soldaten wie andere auch* (Osnabrück: Munin Verlag, 1966)

Hausser, Paul *Waffen-SS im Einsatz* (Pr. Oldendorf: Verlag Schütz, 1953)

Hnilicka, K. *Das Ende auf dem Balkan 1944/45* (N.p., n.d.)

Holzträger, Hans 'Das Regiment 'Siebenbürgen' im Kampf um die Heimat im Herbst 1944' in *Der Freiwillige*, July/August 1992

Husemann, Friedrich *Die guten Glaubens waren. Geschichte der 4. SS-Polizei-Pz.Gren.Div. Bd 2, 1943-45* (Osnabrück: Munin Verlag, 1988)

Imhoff, Kurt *Nachträge zur Pionierchronik der Waffen-SS. Pioniereinheiten der 31. und 23. SS-Divisionen* (Dresden: PiKa, 1988)

Janko, Dr Sepp *Weg und Ende der deutschen Volksgruppe im Jugoslawien* (Graz: Leopold Stocker Verlag, 1982)

Kern, E. *Die letzte Schlacht. Ungarn 1944-45* (Wels: Verlag Welsermühl, 1960)

Kern, E. *Generalfeldmarschall Ferdinand Schörner. Ein deutsches Soldatenschicksal* (Pr. Oldendorf: Verlag K.W. Schütz, 1976)

Klietmann, Dr K.-G. *Die Waffen-SS, eine Dokumentation* (Osnabrück: Verlag 'Der Freiwillige', 1965)

Krätschmer, Ernst Günther *Die Ritterkreuzträger der Waffen-SS* (Pr. Oldendorf: Verlag K.W. Schütz, 1982)

Kumm, Otto Vorwärts, *Prinz Eugen! Geschichte der 7. SS-Freiw.Gebirgs-Div. 'Prinz Eugen'* (Osnabrück: Munin Verlag, 1978)

Lepre, George *Divisionschronik der 13. SS-Division 'Handschar'* (Parsippany, New Jersey, 1993)

Lombard, Gustav 'Jahresringe. Erinnerungen an die sowjetische Kriegsgefangenschaft' in *Deutschen Soldatenjahrbuch*

Mehner, Kurt *Die Waffen-SS und Polizei* (Norderstedt: K.D. Patzwall, 1995)

Munoz, Antonio *Forgotten Legions. Obscure Combat Formations of the Waffen-SS* (Boulder, Colorado: Paladin Press, n.d.)

Neidhardt, Hans *Mit Tanne und Eichenlaub. Kriegschronik der 100. Jäger Division* (Graz/Stuttgart: Leopold Stocker Verlag, 1981)

Niehoff & von Ahlfen *So kämpfte Breslau* (Stuttgart: Motorbuch Verlag, 1978)

Nowarra, Heinz *Naheaufklärer 1910-1945. Die Augen des Heeres* (Stuttgart: Motorbuch Verlag, 1981)

Paul, Wolfgang *Der Endkampf um Deutschland* (München: W.-Heye Verlag, 1978)

Payer, A. von G. *Armati Hungarorum* (München: Körösi Csoma Sándor Historische Gesellschaft e.V., 1985)

Preradovich, Nikolaus von *Die Generale der Waffen-SS* (Vowinckel Verlag, 1985)

Sajti, Enikö A. *Délvidék 1941-44. A magyar kormányok délszláv politikája* (Budapest: Kossuth kiadó, 1987)

Scharochin, M. & V. 'Petrusin Forsirowanije Dunaja wojskami 57-j armii i sachwat operatiwnwo plazdarma w rajone Batinü' in *Vojenno Istoritschiskij Zhurnal*, 1961/2

Schimack, A. *Die 44. Infanterie-Division. Das Tagebuch der Hoch- und Deutschmeister* (Wien: Verlag Austria Press, 1969)

Schramm, P. *Kriegstagebuch des OKW 1944-1945* (N.p., n.d.)

Spaeter, Helmuth *Die Geschichte des Panzer-korps 'Großdeutschland'* (Eching, 1991)

Spielberger, W.J. et al *Leichte Jagdpanzer* (Stuttgart: Motorbuch Verlag, 1992)
Steiner, Felix *Die Armee der Geächteten* (Osnabrück: Munin Verlag, n.d.)
Szebeni, Ilona *Haza fogunk menni. Kényszermunkán a Szovjetúnióban 1945-1949* (Debrecen, 1993)
Tessin, G. *Verbände und Truppen der deutschen Wehrmacht und Waffen-SS im Zweiten Weltkrieg 1939-1945* (Osnabrück: Biblio Verlag, 1977)
Tieke, W. & F. Rebstock *...im letzten Aufgebot 1944-45. Die Geschichte der 18. SS-Freiw.Pz.Gren.Div. 'Horst Wessel'* (Regensburg, 1994/95, 2 vols)
Tilkovszky, Dr Lóránt *Ez volt a Volksbund* (Budapest: Kossuth kiadó, 1976)
Tilkovszky, Dr Lóránt *SS-toborzás Magyarországon* (Budapest: Kossuth kiadó, 1976)
Veress, Csaba D. *A Dunántúl hadi krónikája 1944-45* (Budapest: Zrinyi kiadó, 1984)
Vetter, Dr Roland & Dr Hans Keiper *Unser Tscherwenka. Der Weg einer Batschkadeutschen Großgemeinde in zwei Jahrhunderten* (Heimatausschuß Tscherwenka, 1983)
Vincx, J. & V. Schotanius *Nederlandse vrijwilligers in Europese krijgsdienst 1940-1945 Deel 3* (Antwerp: Etnika, n.d.)
Weißbuch der Deutschen aus Jugoslawien. Ortsberichte 1944-1948 (München: Donauschwäbische Kulturstiftung, 1991)
Yerger, Mark C. 'Command Roster of the 31. SS-Division, February-March 1945' in *Siegrunen* #39
Zilm, Franz Rudolf *Die Geschichte des I deutschen Kavallerie-Korps im Zweiten Weltkrieg* (Rheinbach, 1992)

Index

Index of places

259

Index of people

Index of military units

Stackpole Military History Series

Real battles. Real soldiers. Real stories.

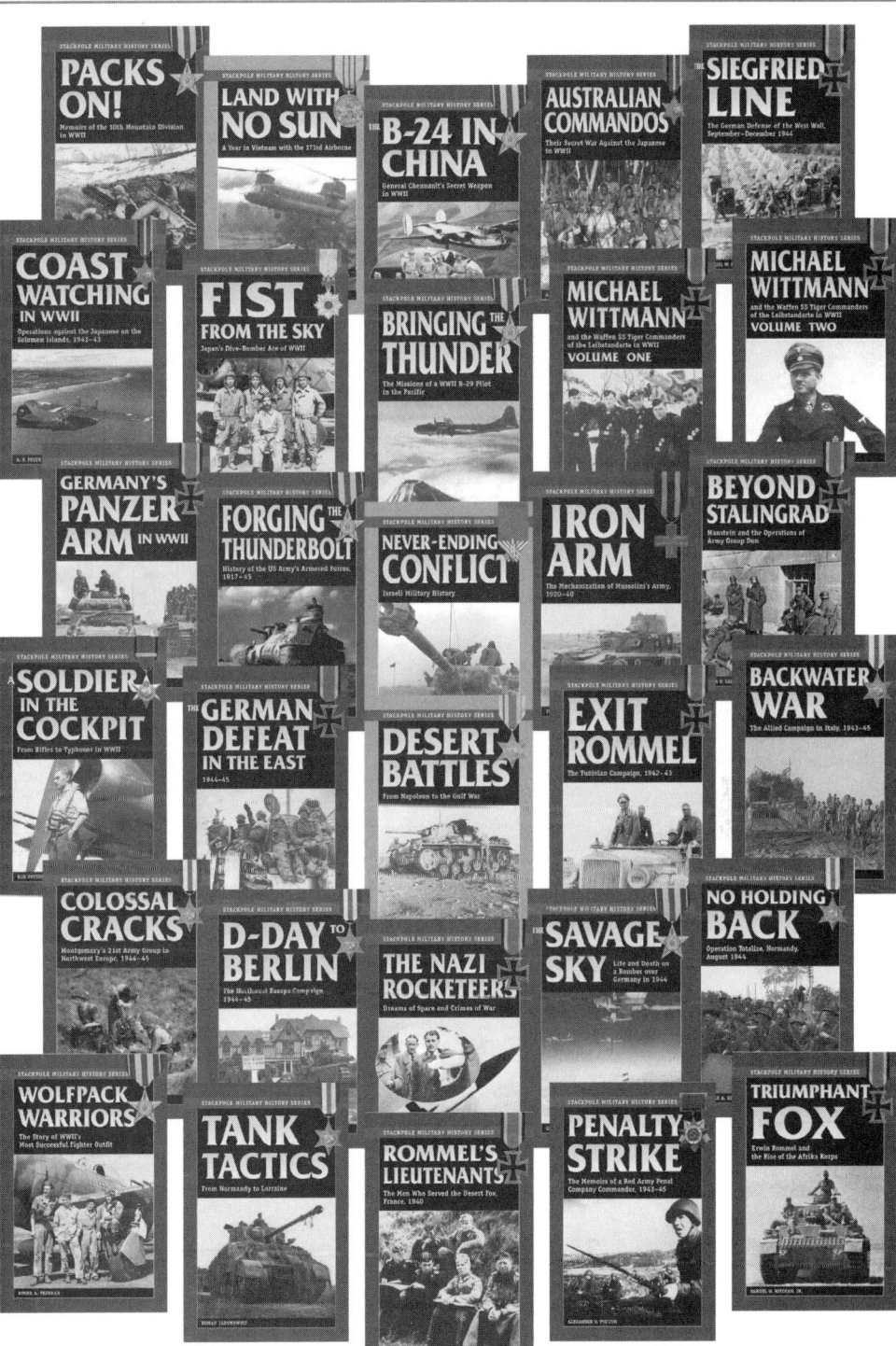

Stackpole Military History Series

Real battles. Real soldiers. Real stories.

Stackpole Military History Series

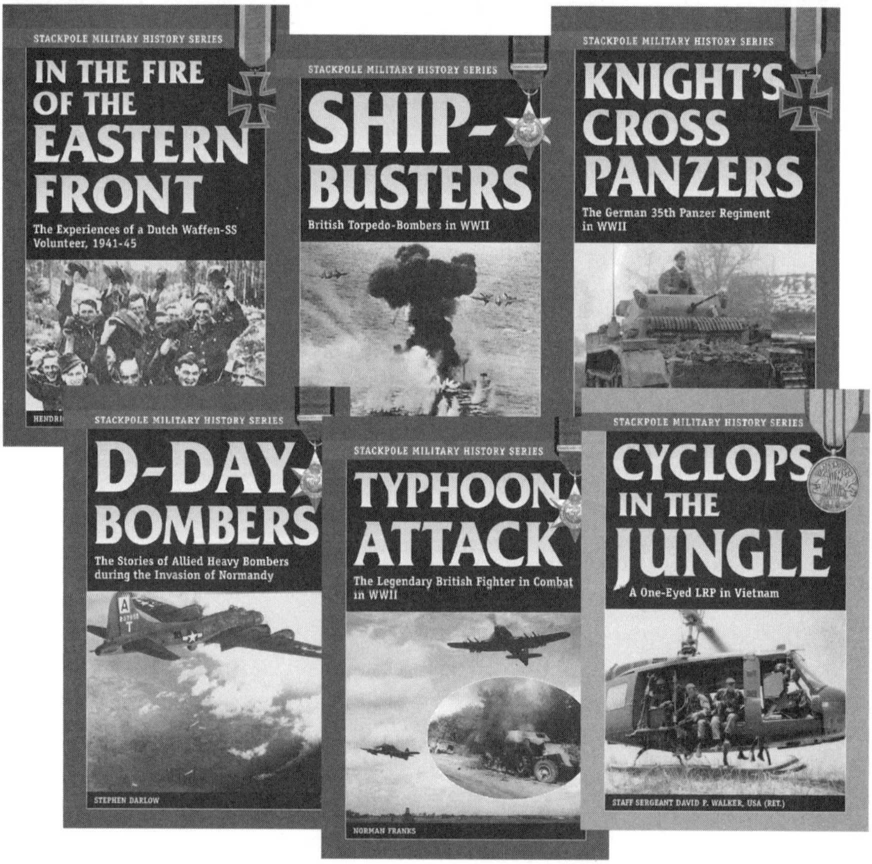

Stackpole Military History Series

TWILIGHT OF THE GODS
A SWEDISH VOLUNTEER IN THE
11TH SS PANZERGRENADIER DIVISION "NORDLAND"
ON THE EASTERN FRONT
Edited by Thorolf Hillblad

This is the exciting true story of Erik Wallin, a Swedish soldier
who volunteered for the Waffen-SS during World War II.
Wallin served in the Panzer Reconnaissance Battalion of the
11th SS Panzergrenadier Division "Nordland," a unit
composed largely of men from Denmark, Norway, and Sweden.
Sent to the Eastern Front, the 11th SS fought in the Courland
Pocket in late 1944 and then battled the Red Army along the
Oder River and in Berlin, where the Soviets destroyed the
division. Few memoirs of non-Germans in the Waffen-SS exist,
and *Twilight of the Gods* ranks among the very best.

$18.95 • Paperback • 6 x 9 • 160 pages • 16 b/w photos, 1 map

WWW.STACKPOLEBOOKS.COM
1-800-732-3669

Stackpole Military History Series

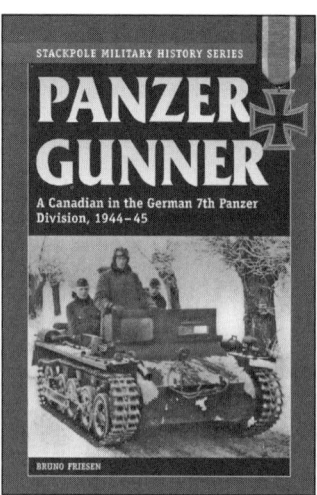

PANZER GUNNER
A CANADIAN IN THE GERMAN
7TH PANZER DIVISION, 1944–45
Bruno Friesen

Six months before World War II erupted in 1939, young Bruno Friesen was sent to Germany by his father, a German-speaking Mennonite who came to Canada from Ukraine and believed the Third Reich offered a better life than Canada. Friesen was drafted into the Wehrmacht three years later and ended up in the 7th Panzer Division. Serving as a gunner in a Panzer IV tank and then a Jagdpanzer IV tank hunter, Friesen fought the Soviets in Romania in the spring of 1944, Lithuania that summer, and West Prussia in early 1945.

$18.95 • Paperback • 6 x 9 • 240 pages • 56 b/w photos, 4 maps

WWW.STACKPOLEBOOKS.COM
1-800-732-3669

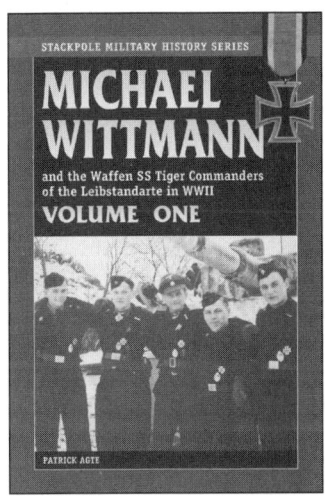

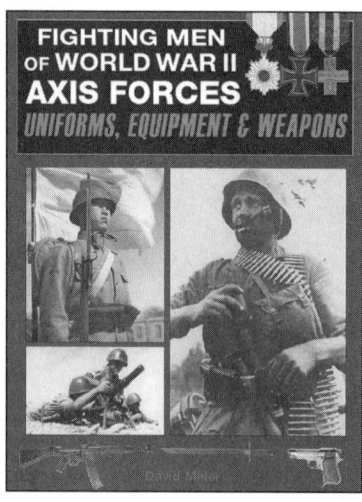 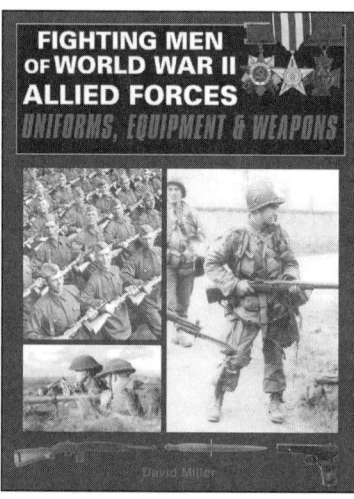